Essentials of

Everything you need to know to administer, score, and interpret the major psychological tests.

I'd like to order the following *Essentials of Psychological Assessment:*

- ❑ WAIS®-IV Assessment (w/CD-ROM) / 978-0-471-73846-6 • $48.95
- ❑ WJ III™ Cognitive Abilities Assessment, Second Edition / 978-0-470-56664-0 • $38.95
- ❑ Cross-Battery Assessment, Second Edition (w/CD-ROM) / 978-0-471-75771-9 • $48.95
- ❑ Nonverbal Assessment / 978-0-471-38318-5 • $38.95
- ❑ PAI® Assessment / 978-0-471-08463-1 • $38.95
- ❑ CAS Assessment / 978-0-471-29015-5 • $38.95
- ❑ MMPI®-2 Assessment, Second Edition / 978-0-470-92323-8 • $38.95
- ❑ Myers-Briggs Type Indicator® Assessment, Second Edition / 978-0-470-34390-6 • $38.95
- ❑ Rorschach® Assessment / 978-0-471-33146-9 • $38.95
- ❑ Millon™ Inventories Assessment, Third Edition / 978-0-470-16862-2 • $38.95
- ❑ TAT and Other Storytelling Assessments, Second Edition / 978-0-470-28192-5 • $38.95
- ❑ MMPI-A™ Assessment / 978-0-471-39815-8 • $38.95
- ❑ NEPSY®-II Assessment / 978-0-470-43691-2 • $38.95
- ❑ Neuropsychological Assessment, Second Edition / 978-0-470-43747-6 • $38.95
- ❑ WJ III™ Tests of Achievement Assessment / 978-0-471-33059-2 • $38.95
- ❑ Evidence-Based Academic Interventions / 978-0-470-20632-4 • $38.95
- ❑ WRAML2 and TOMAL-2 Assessment / 978-0-470-17911-6 • $38.95
- ❑ WMS®-IV Assessment / 978-0-470-62196-7 • $38.95
- ❑ Behavioral Assessment / 978-0-471-35367-6 • $38.95
- ❑ Forensic Psychological Assessment, Second Edition / 978-0-470-55168-4 • $38.95
- ❑ Bayley Scales of Infant Development II Assessment / 978-0-471-32651-9 • $38.95
- ❑ Career Interest Assessment / 978-0-471-35365-2 • $38.95
- ❑ WPPSI™-III Assessment / 978-0-471-28895-4 • $38.95
- ❑ 16PF® Assessment / 978-0-471-23424-1 • $38.95
- ❑ Assessment Report Writing / 978-0-471-39487-7 • $38.95
- ❑ Stanford-Binet Intelligence Scales (SB5) Assessment / 978-0-471-22404-4 • $38.95
- ❑ WISC®-IV Assessment, Second Edition (w/CD-ROM) / 978-0-470-18915-3 • $48.95
- ❑ KABC-II Assessment / 978-0-471-66733-9 • $38.95
- ❑ WIAT®-III and KTEA-II Assessment (w/CD-ROM) / 978-0-470-55169-1 • $48.95
- ❑ Processing Assessment / 978-0-471-71925-0 • $38.95
- ❑ School Neuropsychological Assessment / 978-0-471-78372-5 • $38.95
- ❑ Cognitive Assessment with KAIT & Other Kaufman Measures / 978-0-471-38317-8 • $38.95
- ❑ Assessment with Brief Intelligence Tests / 978-0-471-26412-5 • $38.95
- ❑ Creativity Assessment / 978-0-470-13742-0 • $38.95
- ❑ WNV™ Assessment / 978-0-470-28467-4 • $38.95
- ❑ DAS-II® Assessment (w/CD-ROM) / 978-0-470-22520-2 • $48.95
- ❑ Executive Function Assessment (w/CD-ROM) / 978-0-470-42202-1 • $48.95
- ❑ Conners Behavior Assessments™ / 978-0-470-34633-4 • $38.95
- ❑ Temperament Assessment / 978-0-470-44447-4 • $38.95
- ❑ Response to Intervention / 978-0-470-56663-3 • $38.95
- ❑ Specific Learning Disability Identification / 978-0-470-58760-7 • $38.95
- ❑ IDEA for Assessment Professionals (w/CD-ROM) / 978-0-470-87392-2 • $48.95
- ❑ Dyslexia Assessment and Intervention / 978-0-470-92760-1 • $38.95
- ❑ Autism Spectrum Disorders Evaluation and Assessment / 978-0-470-62194-3 • $38.95

Please complete the order form on the back.
To order by phone, call toll free 1-877-762-2974
To order online: www.wiley.com/essentials
To order by mail: refer to order form on next page

Essentials

of **Psychological Assessment** Series

ORDER FORM

Please send this order form with your payment (credit card or check) to:
John Wiley & Sons, Attn: J. Knott, 111 River Street, Hoboken, NJ 07030-5774

QUANTITY	TITLE	ISBN	PRICE

Shipping Charges:	Surface	2-Day	1-Day
First item	$5.00	$10.50	$17.50
Each additional item	$3.00	$3.00	$4.00

For orders greater than 15 items,
please contact Customer Care at 1-877-762-2974.

ORDER AMOUNT _____

SHIPPING CHARGES _____

SALES TAX _____

TOTAL ENCLOSED _____

NAME_____

AFFILIATION_____

ADDRESS_____

CITY/STATE/ZIP _____

TELEPHONE _____

EMAIL_____

❑ Please add me to your e-mailing list

PAYMENT METHOD:

❑ Check/Money Order   ❑ Visa   ❑ Mastercard   ❑ AmEx

Card Number _____ Exp. Date _____

Cardholder Name *(Please print)* _____

Signature _____

Make checks payable to **John Wiley & Sons.** Credit card orders invalid if not signed.
All orders subject to credit approval. • Prices subject to change.

To order by phone, call toll free 1-877-762-2974
To order online: www.wiley.com/essentials

Essentials of Dyslexia Assessment and Intervention

Essentials of Psychological Assessment Series
Series Editors, Alan S. Kaufman and Nadeen L. Kaufman

Essentials of 16 PF® Assessment
by Heather E.-P. Cattell and James M. Schuerger

Essentials of Assessment Report Writing
by Elizabeth O. Lichtenberger, Nancy Mather, Nadeen L. Kaufman, and Alan S. Kaufman

Essentials of Assessment with Brief Intelligence Tests
by Susan R. Homack and Cecil R. Reynolds

Essentials of Bayley Scales of Infant Development–II Assessment
by Maureen M. Black and Kathleen Matula

Essentials of Behavioral Assessment
by Michael C. Ramsay, Cecil R. Reynolds, and R. W. Kamphaus

Essentials of Career Interest Assessment
by Jeffrey P. Prince and Lisa J. Heiser

Essentials of CAS Assessment
by Jack A. Naglieri

Essentials of Cognitive Assessment with KAIT and Other Kaufman Measures
by Elizabeth O. Lichtenberger, Debra Broadbooks, and Alan S. Kaufman

Essentials of Conners Behavior Assessments™
by Elizabeth P. Sparrow

Essentials of Creativity Assessment
by James C. Kaufman, Jonathan A. Plucker, and John Baer

Essentials of Cross-Battery Assessment, Second Edition
by Dawn P. Flanagan, Samuel O. Ortiz, and Vincent C. Alfonso

Essentials of DAS-II® Assessment
by Ron Dumont, John O. Willis, and Colin D. Elliot

Essentials of Dyslexia Assessment and Intervention
by Nancy Mather and Barbara J. Wendling

Essentials of Evidence-Based Academic Interventions
by Barbara J. Wendling and Nancy Mather

Essentials of Forensic Psychological Assessment, Second Edition
by Marc J. Ackerman

Essentials of IDEA for Assessment Professionals
by Guy McBride, Ron Dumont, and John O. Willis

Essentials of Individual Achievement Assessment
by Douglas K. Smith

Essentials of KABC-II Assessment
by Alan S. Kaufman, Elizabeth O. Lichtenberger, Elaine Fletcher-Janzen, and Nadeen L. Kaufman

Essentials of Millon™ Inventories Assessment, Third Edition
by Stephen Strack

Essentials of MMPI-A™ Assessment
by Robert P. Archer and Radhika Krishnamurthy

Essentials of MMPI-2® Assessment, Second Edition
by David S. Nichols

Essentials of Myers-Briggs Type Indicator® Assessment, Second Edition
by Naomi Quenk

Essentials of NEPSY®-II Assessment
by Sally L. Kemp and Marit Korkman

Essentials of Neuropsychological Assessment, Second Edition
by Nancy Hebben and William Milberg

Essentials of Nonverbal Assessment
by Steve McCallum, Bruce Bracken, and John Wasserman

Essentials of PAI® Assessment
by Leslie C. Morey

Essentials of Processing Assessment
by Milton J. Dehn

Essentials of Response to Intervention
by Amanda M. VanDerHeyden and Matthew K. Burns

Essentials of Rorschach® Assessment
by Tara Rose, Nancy Kaser-Boyd, and Michael P. Maloney

Essentials of School Neuropsychological Assessment
by Daniel C. Miller

Essentials of Specific Learning Disability Identification
by Dawn Flanagan and Vincent C. Alfonso

Essentials of Stanford-Binet Intelligence Scales (SB5) Assessment
by Gale H. Roid and R. Andrew Barram

Essentials of TAT and Other Storytelling Assessments, Second Edition
by Hedwig Teglasi

Essentials of Temperament Assessment
by Diana Joyce

Essentials of WAIS®-IV Assessment
by Elizabeth O. Lichtenberger and Alan S. Kaufman

Essentials of WIAT®-III and KTEA-II Assessment
by Elizabeth O. Lichtenberger and Kristina C. Breaux

Essentials of WISC®-IV Assessment, Second Edition
by Dawn P. Flanagan and Alan S. Kaufman

Essentials of WJ III™ Cognitive Abilities Assessment, Second Edition
by Fredrick A. Schrank, Daniel C. Miller, Barbara J. Wendling, and Richard W. Woodcock

Essentials of WJ III™ Tests of Achievement Assessment
by Nancy Mather, Barbara J. Wendling, and Richard W. Woodcock

Essentials of WMS®-IV Assessment
by Lisa Whipple Drozdick, James A. Holdnack, and Robin C. Hilsabeck

Essentials of WNV™ Assessment
by Kimberly A. Brunnert, Jack A. Naglieri, and Steven T. Hardy-Braz

Essentials of WPPSI™-III Assessment
by Elizabeth O. Lichtenberger and Alan S. Kaufman

Essentials of WRAML2 and TOMAL-2 Assessment
by Wayne Adams and Cecil R. Reynolds

Essentials

of Dyslexia Assessment and Intervention

Nancy Mather
Barbara J. Wendling

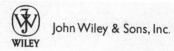
John Wiley & Sons, Inc.

Published by John Wiley & Sons, Inc., Hoboken, New Jersey.

Published simultaneously in Canada.

This publication is designed to provide accurate and authoritative information in regard to the subject matter covered. It is sold with the understanding that the publisher is not engaged in rendering professional services. If legal, accounting, medical, psychological or any other expert assistance is required, the services of a competent professional person should be sought.

Designations used by companies to distinguish their products are often claimed as trademarks. In all instances where John Wiley & Sons, Inc. is aware of a claim, the product names appear in initial capital or all capital letters. Readers, however, should contact the appropriate companies for more complete information regarding trademarks and registration.

For general information on our other products and services please contact our Customer Care Department within the U.S. at (800) 762-2974, outside the United States at (317) 572-3993 or fax (317) 572-4002.

Wiley also publishes its books in a variety of electronic formats. Some content that appears in print may not be available in electronic books. For more information about Wiley products, visit our website at www.wiley.com.

Library of Congress Cataloging-in-Publication Data:

Mather, Nancy.
    Essentials of dyslexia assessment and intervention / Nancy Mather and Barbara J. Wendling.
      p. ; cm. — (Essentials of psychological assessment series)
    Includes bibliographical references and index.
    ISBN 978-0-470-92760-1 (pbk)
    ISBN 978-1-118-15265-2 (ebk)
    ISBN 978-1-118-15266-9 (ebk)
    ISBN 978-1-118-15264-5 (ebk)
    1. Dyslexia. I. Wendling, Barbara J. II. Title. III. Series: Essentials of psychological assessment series.
    [DNLM: 1. Dyslexia. WL 340.6]
    RC394.W6M38   2012
    616.85'53—dc23
                                                  2011019563

10 9 8 7 6 5 4 3 2

I dedicate this book to my wonderful nieces and nephew: Kristen, Nancy,
Charlie, Joanna, and Emily. You are the best!!!
—Aunt Nancy

In loving memory of my father and in honor of my mother.
Thank you for giving me life!
—Barbara

There are many poor readers among very bright children, who,
because they are poor readers, are considered less keen than
their class-mates. This book should really be dedicated to the
thousands of bright children thus misjudged.

—Stanger & Donohue, 1937, p. 43

CONTENTS

SERIES PREFACE

In the *Essentials of Psychological Assessment* series, we have attempted to provide the reader with books that will deliver key practical information in the most efficient and accessible style. The series features instruments in a variety of domains, such as cognition, personality, education, and neuropsychology. For the experienced clinician, books in the series will offer a concise yet thorough way to master utilization of the continuously evolving supply of new and revised instruments, as well as a convenient method for keeping up to date on the tried-and-true measures. The novice will find here a prioritized assembly of all the information and techniques that must be at one's fingertips to begin the complicated process of individual psychological diagnosis.

Wherever feasible, visual shortcuts to highlight key points are utilized alongside systematic, step-by-step guidelines. Chapters are focused and succinct. Topics are targeted for an easy understanding of the essentials of administration, scoring, interpretation, and clinical application. Theory and research are continually woven into the fabric of each book, but always to enhance clinical inference, never to sidetrack or overwhelm. We have long been advocates of "intelligent" testing—the notion that a profile of test scores is meaningless unless it is brought to life by the clinical observations and astute detective work of knowledgeable examiners. Test profiles must be used to make a difference in the child's or adult's life, or why bother to test? We want this series to help our readers become the best intelligent testers they can be.

Essentials of Dyslexia: Assessment and Intervention is designed for assessment professionals, educators, and parents who are interested in understanding, assessing, and helping individuals who have dyslexia. This new *Essentials* book meets the demands of current educational reforms. Instead of focusing on the use and interpretation of assessment instruments, the focus is squarely upon the most common type of learning disability: dyslexia. In order to diagnose a disability, one must first understand the nature of the disability. The authors of *Essentials of Dyslexia: Assessment and Intervention,* world-renowned intervention experts Nancy Mather and Barbara Wendling have created a readable resource that makes current research accessible to a variety of audiences. A glossary is included to assist readers who may be unfamiliar with some of the terms.

Each chapter focuses on a different aspect of dyslexia, beginning with helping the reader to understand what dyslexia really is. Subsequent chapters deal with the history of the disorder; research related to the brain, genetics, and environment; assessment of the cognitive and linguistic correlates of dyslexia; assessment and instruction of reading and spelling skills; technology applications; and dyslexia in other languages. In addition to all of the instructional strategies contained within the chapters, a detailed appendix includes summaries of evidence-based commercial programs for the treatment of dyslexia. This book demonstrates how targeted assessments resulting in an accurate diagnosis can lead to the most appropriate interventions for the many students who struggle to learn to read and spell.

Alan S. Kaufman, PhD, and Nadeen L. Kaufman, EdD, Series Editors
Yale University School of Medicine

ACKNOWLEDGMENTS

We are deeply grateful to Drs. Bennett and Sally Shaywitz for their willingness to contribute to a chapter in this book. In addition, Dr. Bennett Shaywitz provided us with a helpful critique of the genetics chapter. Martha Youman was an essential contributor to our preparation of this book: writing one chapter, contributing to another, reviewing others, and creating several figures. We would also like to thank Drs. Kathleen Puckett and Blanche O'Bannon for their timely chapter on technology. Throughout the preparation of this book, Dr. Robert Colligan provided us with many current research articles related to dyslexia for which we were very appreciative. We also want to thank Ron Hockman, C. Wilson Anderson, Jr., and Stephanie Bieberly for their contributions of informal assessment measures. We sincerely appreciate the willingness of all contributors to write descriptions of evidence-based interventions for the Appendix. We are indebted to Marquita Flemming, Senior Editor, and Sherry Wasserman, Senior Editorial Assistant from John Wiley & Sons, Inc. for their support and guidance during the development and production of this book. Leigh Camp, Production Editor, guided us skillfully through the final stages of preparation. Finally, we express our deepest gratitude to Drs. Alan and Nadeen Kaufman for their leadership and vision that led to the creation of the *Essentials* series and for their interest in and support of this project.

Chapter One

UNDERSTANDING DYSLEXIA

In the first half of this century the story of dyslexia has been one of decline and fall; in the second half it has culminated in a spectacular rise. From being a rather dubious term, dyslexia has blossomed into a glamorous topic; and rightly so, for with a prevalence of around 5% the condition is remarkably common.

—Frith, 1999, p. 192

WHAT IS DYSLEXIA?

Steven, a second-grade student, knows only four letters of the alphabet. His teachers have tried to help him memorize letters and their sounds, but he always seems to forget what he has learned the next day. Lately, he has started to say that he is dumb and that's the reason he can't learn to read and spell.

Maria is in middle school. She is often confused by letters that have similar sounds, such as spelling *every* as *efry*. These subtle sound confusions are also apparent in her speech when she pronounces certain multisyllabic words, saying "puh-si-fic" when she means to say "specific." She sometimes confuses words that have similar sounds. Even though she has a good vocabulary, she may say "that book really memorized me" when she really meant "mesmerized." At times, she avoids saying certain words because she is unsure about their pronunciation.

Jeff is a junior in high school. He recently took the SATs and only finished half of each section. He said he knew how to do the rest of the questions, but he didn't have enough time to attempt them. He wonders why his peers seem to always have plenty of time when reading takes him so long.

Mr. Brogan has just attended his fifth-grade son's Individualized Education Program (IEP) meeting at the local elementary school. His son, Matthew, is having great difficulty learning to read and spell. Even though he has an adapted spelling list, Matthew still forgets how to spell the words when the weekly spelling test is given. He spells words just the way they sound, not the way they look, such as spelling *they* as *thay*. When Mr. Brogan hears Matthew's fifth-grade teacher, the special education teacher, and the school psychologist describing his son's severe reading and spelling difficulties, he immediately thinks: "That was just like me."

What do these four people who struggle with certain aspects of literacy have in common? They all have dyslexia. Although this seems to be an accurate label to explain difficulty in learning to read and spell, confusion exists regarding what having dyslexia actually means.

WHAT DYSLEXIA IS AND IS NOT

What is dyslexia? This simple question is asked every day by both parents and teachers as they struggle to understand why a child is not learning to read with ease. It is a question asked by Matthew who wonders why reading and spelling are so difficult. It is also a question asked by older students like Jeff as they attempt to determine why reading is so effortful and why they read so much more slowly than their peers. Although Mr. Brogan was well aware that he had always struggled with reading, when he hears the description of Matthew's difficulties and that the school team thinks that Matthew has dyslexia, he realizes that he too has dyslexia that was never diagnosed. He now understands the reasons why he never reads for pleasure and why the stack of books that others have suggested he read sits undisturbed by his bedside.

Over the last century, researchers who are concerned with the diagnosis and treatment of dyslexia have attempted to answer the following three questions (Tunmer & Greaney, 2010, p. 229):

1. What is it?
2. What causes it?
3. What can be done about it?

The goal of this book is to attempt to answer these three questions in a straightforward way so that dyslexia can be easily understood by educational professionals and parents alike, as well as by individuals who have dyslexia. Although we do not yet have conclusive answers to the questions above, fortunately, over the last century, researchers, medical professionals, and practitioners have learned a lot about dyslexia, as well as how this disorder affects reading and spelling development.

The word *dyslexia* comes from the Greek words δυσ- dys- ("impaired") and lexis ("word"). Although numerous definitions exist, dyslexia can be most simply defined as a neurobiological disorder that causes a marked impairment in the development of basic reading and spelling skills. More specifically, dyslexia is manifested in

DON'T FORGET
....

Dyslexia is a neurobiological disorder that affects the development of both decoding (written word pronunciation) and encoding (spelling).

deficiencies in word-level reading skills; it affects decoding (pronouncing printed words) and encoding (spelling words; Vellutino & Fletcher, 2007). Thus, dyslexia is a complex cognitive disorder of neurobiological origin that affects the development of literacy (Shastry, 2007; Vellutino & Fletcher, 2007).

Both parents and professionals are often confused regarding the difference between a specific learning disability (SLD) and dyslexia. They often wonder if a student is diagnosed with an SLD in reading, does this mean that he has dyslexia? The answer to this question is: Maybe. Essentially, SLD is a broader category that encompasses several different types of disorders, including dyslexia, the most common and carefully studied type of SLD (Shastry, 2007). In addition, the terms *dyslexia, specific developmental dyslexia, specific reading disability*, and *reading disability* are often used interchangeably to describe this neurodevelopmental disorder (DeFries, Singer, Foch, & Lewitter, 1978; Vellutino & Fletcher, 2007).

In some school districts, school psychologists and special and general educators do not use the word *dyslexia* when describing students with severe reading disabilities. In fact, the term *dyslexia* has fallen in and out of popularity from the early 1930s (Rooney, 1995). Many states do not use the word *dyslexia* in their state regulations, whereas a few, such as Texas, have specific laws that must be adhered to regarding both assessment and service delivery to school children with dyslexia. As of 2011, 12 states have specific statewide dyslexia laws: California, Colorado, Hawaii, Kentucky, Louisiana, Mississippi, New Jersey, New Mexico, Ohio, Texas, Virginia, and Washington. Four additional states have dyslexia laws working through the legislative process: Arkansas, Kansas, Oklahoma, and Wisconsin. Although South Dakota does not have a dyslexia law at this time, it has developed a statewide dyslexia handbook.

In the coming years, we are likely to see the term "dyslexia" being used more often. A reason that it may become more commonplace is that the proposed text revisions for the *Diagnostic and Statistical Manual of Mental Disorders, Fifth Edition* (DSM-5), the guidelines of the American Psychiatric Association that are widely used by psychologists and mental health professionals, have suggested that the

$\equiv$ *Rapid Reference 1.1*

. . . .

DSM-5 Rationales for Proposed Recommendation to Change *Reading Disorder* to *Dyslexia*

The name change would:

- be consistent with international use.
- provide better alignment with the requirements for SLD identification under the reauthorization of the Individuals with Disabilities Improvement Act of 2004 (IDEA 2004) that no longer require the documentation of a discrepancy between intellectual ability and achievement. (The proposed revision would not require a discrepancy between measurements of intellectual ability and academic performance, which was required for Reading Disorder in DSM-IV.)
- focus on the accuracy and fluency of reading, and not on disorders in reading comprehension. (Problems in reading comprehension alone would be viewed as stemming from oral language comprehension problems, and would not meet the criteria for dyslexia.)

term *reading disorder* should be replaced by *dyslexia*. Rapid Reference 1.1 reviews the major rationales for this suggested change in terminology.

SUBTYPES OF READING PROBLEMS AND DYSLEXIA

Not all types of reading problems are considered to be dyslexia. Gough and Tunmer (1986) developed a model that they called the simple view of reading (SVR). This model has two major components: decoding (reading words) (D) and oral language or listening comprehension (LC), which results in this simple equation: Reading Comprehension (RC) = D × LC. This equation suggests that reading performance is influenced by both word recognition skill (D) and listening comprehension or the ability to understand what is being read orally (LC). Aaron, Joshi, and Quatroche (2008) have modified the formula slightly to RC = WR × LC, where RC is reading comprehension, WR = word recognition, and LC = Listening Comprehension. The only difference in this modification is that word recognition (WR) replaces decoding (D).

The SVR model then predicts that three different types of poor readers exist: (1) those who can understand the text when it is read aloud, but have trouble reading the words (dyslexia); (2) those who can read words accurately but do not comprehend what they read (poor comprehenders); and (3) those who have trouble with both (mixed reading disability). Readers with mixed reading disability often have oral language impairments or limited access to linguistic and experiential opportunities during their preschool years (Tunmer & Greaney, 2010). Although many poor readers have poor comprehension or a mixed disability that requires interventions directed toward improving both oral language and reading, the focus of the book is on readers with dyslexia who have listening comprehension and verbal abilities that are often higher than their word reading and spelling skills.

Throughout the century, varying subtypes of dyslexia have been described. In the 1930s, Orton described both word blindness (trouble remembering word images) and word deafness (trouble with word sounds; Orton, 1937). Currently, the most common subtypes of dyslexia identified by research include phonological, surface, and deep. Other terms used to describe dyslexia subtypes include auditory (dysphonetic) or visual (dyseidetic; Boder, 1971; Johnson & Myklebust, 1967), that are similar to phonological and surface dyslexia, respectively.

In the 1970s, the theory of a dual route model of reading was proposed. This theory specified that two interactive, yet distinctive pathways exist: a direct, lexical route for automatic recognition of high-frequency words and an indirect, sublexical phonological decoding route for pronunciation of unfamiliar words (Coltheart, 1978, 2007). A weakness in either pathway could affect the development of reading skills and result in two different subtypes of dyslexia: phonological dyslexia (i.e., difficulty with nonword reading) and surface dyslexia (i.e., difficulty with irregular word reading; Castles & Coltheart, 1993; Coltheart, 2007). An individual with phonological dyslexia experiences trouble with phonological awareness tasks and applying phonics, whereas an individual with surface dyslexia is able to read phonically regular nonwords but experiences greater difficulty with exception words or words with an irregular element that do not have regular, predictable grapheme–phoneme correspondences (e.g., once). The two critical indicators of surface dyslexia are the (1) regularization of the spellings of words with irregular elements (e.g., they as *thay*) and (2) poorer performance reading irregular words than phonically regular words. Although a difference between nonword reading and irregular word reading and spelling is insufficient to identify different subtypes, these differences in performance may be indicative of different etiologies of dyslexia.

Impairments in nonword reading can range from mild to a complete

DON'T FORGET

A difference between the ability to read and spell nonwords and the ability to read and spell irregular words may have clinical significance and be indicative of different subtypes of dyslexia.

inability to read nonwords. Deep dyslexia is a term that has been used to describe a severe impairment in nonword reading. Deep dyslexia is accompanied by other types of word reading errors, including: semantic errors (e.g., gate is read as fence), visual errors (e.g., house is read as horse), and derivational errors (e.g., mountain is read as mountainous; Coltheart, Patterson, & Marshall, 1980). Deep dyslexia is often described as an acquired reading disorder due to stroke or other brain injury. These individuals seem unable to use letter-sound relationships to decode words. They have difficulty reading function words (e.g., as, the, so), infrequent words, and nonwords, and make semantic substitutions and morphological errors (Rastle, Tyler, & Marslen-Wilson, 2006). Individuals with phonological dyslexia often exhibit symptoms of deep dyslexia, leading some researchers to state that both types of dyslexia are simply different points on a continuum of severity (Crisp, Howard, & Lambon Ralph, 2011; Crisp & Lambon Ralph, 2006; Freidman, 1996).

DON'T FORGET

Dyslexia is not a primary problem in reading comprehension, but rather a problem in reading and spelling words.

CHARACTERISTICS OF DYSLEXIA

As with SLD, in order to understand dyslexia, a key aspect is explaining what it is not (Tunmer & Greaney, 2010). Although the clinical features of dyslexia can overlap with other disorders, such as attention deficit hyperactivity disorder (ADHD) and specific language impairment (SLI), dyslexia is a distinct disorder that has specific characteristics. With dyslexia, the primary problem is with written language, not spoken language (Pennington, Peterson, & McGrath, 2009). Not all individuals with dyslexia, however, will have all the symptoms and characteristics. Rapid Reference 1.2 provides a list of conditions that may coexist but would not be considered to be defining features of dyslexia.

Rapid Reference 1.3 provides an overview of the most common characteristics of dyslexia. Some of these characteristics are most likely to be present in young children (e.g., trouble rhyming words), whereas others are more apparent in secondary students and adults (e.g., a slow reading rate or poor spelling). The earliest warning signs of dyslexia are sometimes noted in the child's spoken language, although sometimes oral language development is perfectly normal. As the individual ages, warning signs are noted in the slowness of reading and spelling development. In addition, students with deficient word reading skills often avoid reading, and as a result, they spend less time practicing reading (Tunmer & Greaney, 2010).

≡ *Rapid Reference 1.2*

....

What Dyslexia Is Not

A pervasive oral language impairment.
A primary problem in attention or behavior.
A primary problem in reading comprehension or written expression.
Low motivation or limited effort.
Poor vision or hearing.
Primary emotional or behavioral problems.
Autism.
Childhood schizophrenia.
Limited intelligence.
Related to ethnic background or family income.
A result of poor teaching or limited educational opportunity.

≡ *Rapid Reference 1.3*

....

What Dyslexia Is: Symptoms and Characteristics

Difficulty learning to rhyme words.
Difficulty learning the letter names and letter sounds of the alphabet.
Confusions of letters and words with similar visual appearance (e.g., *b* and *d* and *was* and *saw*).
Confusions of letters with similar sounds (e.g., /f/ and /v/).*
Reversals and transpositions of letters and words that persist past the age of 7 (e.g., *p* and *q*, and *on* and *no*).
Trouble arranging letters in the correct order when spelling.
Difficulty retaining the visual representation of irregular words for reading and spelling (e.g., *once*).
Spelling the same word in different ways on the same page (e.g., *wuns, wunce,* for *once*).
Spelling words the way they sound rather than the way they look (e.g., *sed* for *said*).
Difficulty pronouncing some multisyllabic words correctly (e.g., *multiblication*).
Slow word perception that affects reading rate and fluency.

*Note when a letter is enclosed between two forward slashes / / it refers to the letter sound, not the letter name.

In addition to these characteristics, many individuals with dyslexia have strengths in areas that are not affected by the disorder (e.g., math, science), and their oral language and listening comprehension abilities are often higher than their reading and spelling skills. The individual with dyslexia typically has adequate achievement in areas where reading skills are not of primary importance (Betts, 1936). One central concept of dyslexia is that it is unexpected in relationship to the person's other abilities. Thus, dyslexia is often associated with underachievement in reading, rather than low reading achievement per se. One would expect that the person would be reading at a higher level when considering her other abilities. Although this concept of unexpected underachievement has been the central defining feature of dyslexia (Tunmer & Greaney, 2010), Tønnessen (1997) points out that it is really our lack of knowledge that makes the underachievement "unexpected" because we have not gained enough insight into the causes of dyslexia. In other words, if we had a better understanding of the underlying causes of dyslexia, an individual's difficulties with reading and spelling would be expected.

CAUTION

Individuals with dyslexia may show any combination of characteristics shown in Rapid Reference 1.3; however, most individuals will not exhibit all of these characteristics.

Research has indicated that intelligence does not predict reading for individuals with dyslexia even though it is a reasonable predictor for individuals without reading impairments (Ferrer, Shaywitz, Holahan, Marchione, & Shaywitz, 2010). This is because many individuals with dyslexia have average or even superior intellectual abilities. Individuals with any level of intelligence may have dyslexia. Thus, an intellectually gifted law student may have dyslexia that results in a compromised reading rate, as may an individual with a mild intellectual disability who struggles to learn to read even basic sight words. Because dyslexia is a neurobiological disorder, it can occur in an individual with any level of intelligence or in combination with other disabilities, such as vision and hearing impairments or attention deficit hyperactivity disorder. Although some definitions have suggested that dyslexia only occurs in individuals with average or above intelligence, this assertion is not true. No one ever claims that articulation or motor problems can only occur in children with average or above intelligence because it is understood that most disabilities occur across the full range of intellectual functioning. However, for children with severe intellectual disabilities, learning to read may be secondary to developing life skills, such as communication, self care, and community living skills, as these adaptive abilities are central to the individual obtaining independence and self sufficiency.

Some children with dyslexia are identified in first grade, whereas other individuals are not diagnosed until they enter college, or even when entering an advanced graduate degree program. This is particularly true of students who have advanced verbal abilities. It is not unusual to find a medical student who could navigate through high school and college with only mild difficulty, but then becomes overwhelmed and not able to manage the heavy reading demands of medical school (Voeller, 2004). Some individuals with dyslexia are never identified at all, and as adults they attempt to negotiate their lives so that little reading and writing are involved.

Some students do not receive any early intervention, and their difficulties with reading and writing continue into their secondary years. Figure 1.1 presents a writing sample from David, a ninth-grade student, along with a translation that attempts to preserve the intent of his message as he accidentally omitted several words when writing the sample. His assignment was straightforward. During the first week of school, David's English teacher had asked the students to write something about themselves that they would like her to know. David wrote the following paragraph regarding the impact of having a disability that has affected his spelling development. Although he knows that he is not "stupid," he is reluctant to tell his girlfriend about his disability.

PREVALENCE OF DYSLEXIA

Estimates of the prevalence of dyslexia vary and are influenced by how dyslexia is defined and identified. Earlier in the century, Betts (1936) estimated that between 8% and 15% of children have varying degrees of reading disability, with about 4% of the school population being diagnosed as *word blind*, an earlier term that was used to describe dyslexia. More recent estimates suggest that 5% to 8% of the school-age population is the most accurate estimate of individuals who

CAUTION

Although early intervention is critical for individuals with dyslexia, it is important to keep in mind that intervention can be effective at any age.

have dyslexia (e.g., DeFries et al., 1978; Muter & Snowling, 2009; Sireteanu, Goertz, Bachert, & Wandert, 2005). Some estimates, however, are higher, ranging from 5% to 20% of the school-age population having dyslexia and up to 40% of the entire U.S. population experiencing some type of reading difficulty (Shaywitz, 2003; S. E. Shaywitz & Shaywitz, 2001). In addition, nearly 80% of children who are in special education diagnosed with learning disabilities are

Figure 1.1 David's Note to His Ninth-Grade Teacher

Translation: Like me, I have a disability. I've had it since third grade. I'm often quitting because of my disability. For example, I know how hard it is. I can't spell right. I've been trying for all my life. I know I'm afraid to write a note to my girl friend. She doesn't know that I have it but I don't know how to tell her because I don't know how she is going to act. I don't know why I am telling you but I know that I'm not stupid.

there because of reading problems. As with any disorder, the symptoms can range from mild to severe, and the impact of the disorder is influenced by the environment and appropriate early intervention and treatment.

DEFINITIONS OF DYSLEXIA

Even though researchers have been studying dyslexia for over one hundred years, there is still not a strong consensus regarding a clear, useful definition (Tønnessen, 1997). Although numerous professional organizations around the

≣ *Rapid Reference 1.4*

IDA Definition of Dyslexia

Dyslexia is a specific learning disability that is neurological in origin. It is characterized by difficulties with accurate and/or fluent word recognition and by poor spelling and decoding abilities. These difficulties typically result from a deficit in the phonological component of language that is often unexpected in relation to other cognitive abilities and the provision of effective classroom instruction. Secondary consequences may include problems in reading comprehension and reduced reading experience that can impede growth of vocabulary and background knowledge. (Adopted by the IDA Board, November 2002. This definition is also used by the National Institutes of Child Health and Human Development [NICHD; 2002].)

world have attempted to develop a definition of dyslexia, no universally accepted definition exists. Recently, the International Dyslexia Association (IDA; formerly called the Orton Dyslexia Society) Research Committee, a group composed of investigators and representatives from advocacy groups, and the National Institute of Child Health and Human Development (NICHD) proposed a revised definition of *dyslexia*. Rapid Reference 1.4 presents this definition.

More recently, the Professional Standards and Practices Committee of the International Dyslexia Association (IDA) has provided a set of standards to guide the preparation, certification, and professional development of reading teachers. Rapid Reference 1.5 presents the explanation provided of dyslexia within these practice standards.

≣ *Rapid Reference 1.5*

Explanation of Dyslexia in the IDA 2010 Professional Standards

Dyslexia is a language-based disorder of learning to read and write originating from a core or basic problem with phonological processing intrinsic to the individual. Its primary symptoms are inaccurate and/or slow printed word recognition and poor spelling—problems that in turn affect reading fluency and comprehension and written expression. Other types of reading disabilities include specific difficulties with reading comprehension and/or speed of processing (reading fluency). These problems may exist in relative isolation or may overlap extensively in individuals with reading difficulties (Moats et al., 2010, p. 3).

Rapid Reference 1.6 provides several examples of other definitions of dyslexia from around the world. Although the emphasis is on phonological processing in the IDA definition and explanation, other cognitive abilities are mentioned as well in other definitions (e.g., British and Ireland Dyslexia Associations). Some of the terminology (e.g., phonological awareness, rapid automatized naming) may not be familiar to all readers at this point, but these terms are explained and discussed in more detail in later chapters and are also listed in the Glossary of this book.

≡ Rapid Reference 1.6

Examples of Dyslexia Definitions

National Institute of Neurological Disorders and Stroke
Dyslexia is a brain-based type of learning disability that specifically impairs a person's ability to read. These individuals typically read at levels significantly lower than expected despite having normal intelligence. Although the disorder varies from person to person, common characteristics among people with dyslexia are difficulty with spelling, phonological processing (the manipulation of sounds), and/or rapid visual-verbal responding. In adults, dyslexia usually occurs after a brain injury or in the context of dementia. It can also be inherited in some families, and recent studies have identified a number of genes that may predispose an individual to developing dyslexia.

British Dyslexia Association
Dyslexia is a specific learning difficulty that mainly affects the development of literacy and language related skills. It is likely to be present at birth and to be lifelong in its effects. It is characterised by difficulties with phonological processing, rapid naming, working memory, processing speed, and the automatic development of skills that may not match up to an individual's other cognitive abilities.

Dyslexia Association of Ireland
Dyslexia is manifested in a continuum of specific learning difficulties related to the acquisition of basic skills in reading, spelling and/or writing, such difficulties being unexplained in relation to an individual's other abilities and educational experiences. Dyslexia can be described at the neurological, cognitive, and behavioural levels. It is typically characterised by inefficient information processing, including difficulties in phonological processing, working memory, rapid naming and automaticity of basic skills. Difficulties in organisation, sequencing, and motor skills may also be present.

Spanish Federation of Dyslexia

Dyslexia is a difficulty in distinguishing and memorizing letters or groups of letters, the order and rhythm of letter order to form words, and poor structure of phrases, which affects both reading and writing.

Dyslexia Association of Singapore

Dyslexia is a neurologically based specific learning difficulty that is characterised by difficulties in one or more of reading, spelling and writing. Accompanying weaknesses may be identified in areas of language acquisition, phonological processing, working memory, and sequencing. Some factors that are associated with, but do not cause, dyslexia are poor motivation, impaired attention, and academic frustration. The extent to which dyslexia is apparent in a particular language is affected by the quantity and quality of exposure to that language and other languages. Dyslexics are likely to have greater difficulty with languages that have more complicated orthographic, phonological, and/or grammatical systems.

Hong Kong Dyslexia Association

Dyslexia is a specific learning difficulty related to mastering and using written language. Dyslexic learners typically have difficulties in reading, writing, and spelling. Dyslexia may be caused by a combination of phonological, visual and auditory processing deficits. It is often unexpected when compared with a child's general ability and is not due to lack of intelligence or lack of opportunity to learn.

Health Council of the Netherlands, Working Definition

Dyslexia is present when the automatization of word identification (reading) and/ or word spelling does not develop or does so very incompletely or with great difficulty. The term *automatization* refers to the establishment of an automatic process. A process of this kind is characterized by a high level of speed and accuracy. It is carried out unconsciously, makes minimal demands on attention, and is difficult to suppress, ignore, or influence. The working definition used means that dyslexia is characterized in practice by a severe retardation in reading and spelling that is persistent and resists the usual teaching methods and remedial efforts. Upon examination, it will be accompanied by very slow and/or inaccurate and easily disturbed word identification and/or word spelling.

Kuwait Dyslexia Association

Dyslexia is a learning disability that manifests primarily as a difficulty with written language, particularly with reading and spelling. It is separate and distinct from reading difficulties resulting from other causes, such as a non-neurological deficiency with vision or hearing, or from poor or inadequate reading instruction.

Many of these definitions contain similar components. All of these definitions describe dyslexia as a learning disability or neurological disorder that affects the development of reading skill. Most attempt to describe the two key symptoms of dyslexia: (1) poor reading and spelling ability that is unexpected in relationship to other abilities, and (2) a lack of automaticity and ease with reading and spelling words. Although problems in comprehension may result from the poor decoding, dyslexia is not primarily a problem in reading comprehension. Several of the definitions attempt to specify the causes or correlates of dyslexia, such as poor phonological awareness or slow rapid naming, whereas others describe the limited response to treatment as a symptom.

MISCONCEPTIONS ABOUT DYSLEXIA

It is likely that the variations in definitions of dyslexia, as well as the use and misuse of the term, contribute to existing misconceptions. One common misconception is that people with dyslexia cannot read at all. As with most disorders, dyslexia occurs on a continuum, and the severity level is a matter of degree—from mild to severe. Most individuals with dyslexia can learn to read, but typically continue to have impairments in rate and fluency, as well as relatively poor spelling. It is critically important that educators, parents, and the individuals with dyslexia be aware of the common misconceptions about dyslexia so that they can understand the true nature of the disorder. Several of these misconceptions are presented in Rapid Reference 1.7 accompanied by a factual counterpoint.

CONCLUSION

Although a universal definition of dyslexia has yet to be developed, researchers and scientists from around the world have reached an increasing consensus regarding the characteristics and symptoms of this disorder, as well as how dyslexia affects reading and spelling development. Despite the fact that dyslexia is a lifelong condition and certain accommodations may always be needed in educational and vocational settings, the prognosis is good for individuals who receive intensive, systematic interventions.

Unless a parent or teacher has personally experienced the pain and academic stress caused by dyslexia, it is hard to understand the impact of this disorder on self-esteem and school and vocational performance (Voeller, 2004). It is critical that both parents and educational professionals understand the plight of the child with dyslexia. Over a century ago, Hinshelwood (1902) observed: "It is evident that it is a matter of the highest importance to recognise as early as

≝ *Rapid Reference 1.7*

....

Common Misconceptions About Dyslexia
- People with dyslexia cannot read.
  - Most do learn to read at some level, although their rate is often slow.
- Individuals with high intellectual ability cannot have dyslexia.
  - Intelligence does not predict dyslexia: Many highly intelligent people have dyslexia.
- Dyslexia is seeing things backwards.
  - Dyslexia is much more complex than seeing letters and numbers backwards.
- Dyslexia is a rare disorder.
  - Approximately 5% to 8% of the population has mild to severe dyslexia.
- Dyslexia cannot be diagnosed until at least third grade.
  - At-risk symptoms for dyslexia may be identified in individuals as young as five years of age.
- Children will outgrow dyslexia.
  - Dyslexia is a lifelong disorder, but intervention can reduce the impact.
- More boys than girls have dyslexia.
  - Present estimates indicate that the prevalence rate for boys is only slightly higher than for girls.
- All struggling readers have dyslexia.
  - Many other reasons than dyslexia may cause reading problems such as low intellectual ability, poor oral language, attentional problems, poor instruction, and lack of opportunity.
- Young children who reverse letters (e.g., *b* for *d*) have dyslexia.
  - Beginning writers often reverse letters but most will master these letter-sound correspondences with practice. In addition, while letter reversals are often associated with dyslexia, not all individuals with dyslexia will reverse letters.
- The type of instruction employed can cause dyslexia.
  - While the quality of instruction makes a difference in how readily a child learns to read, the use of a certain reading approach does not cause dyslexia. Dyslexia is a neurobiological disorder that is not caused by ineffective instruction.

possible the true nature of this defect, when it is met with in a child. It may prevent much waste of valuable time and may save the child from suffering and cruel treatment. . . . The sooner the true nature of the defect is recognised, the better are the chances of the child's improvement" (p. 10).

The purpose of this book is to increase understanding of dyslexia, both the causes and treatments. In the following chapters, the historic influences, the role of the brain and genetics, the relationship of dyslexia to other disorders, the cognitive, linguistic, and academic factors that are part of an assessment for dyslexia, descriptions of the most efficacious treatment approaches including advances in technology, dyslexia in English Language Learners, and dyslexia in the schools, will be explained.

🖉 TEST YOURSELF 🖉

1. The terms *dyslexia* and *specific reading disability* are used to describe a neurodevelopmental disorder that *primarily* affects the development of
   a. decoding (word reading).
   b. reading comprehension.
   c. encoding (spelling).
   d. written expression.
   e. all of the above.
   f. both a and c.

2. Although many definitions of dyslexia have been proposed, a universally accepted definition does not exist. True or False?

3. The focus of the most recent definition of dyslexia by IDA (2002) indicates that dyslexia is characterized primarily by
   a. poor attention.
   b. poor phonological awareness.
   c. slow rapid automatized naming.
   d. all of the above.

4. The concept of unexpected underachievement suggests that the person's
   a. academic areas are all high or low.
   b. other abilities are lower than predicted by the individual's reading.
   c. other abilities are often higher than the individual's reading skills.
   d. reading skills are lower than expected for the individual's age or grade.

5. Some individuals are not diagnosed with dyslexia until reading demands become unmanageable. True or False?

6. Individuals with dyslexia can have any level of intelligence. True or False?

7. **Gough and Tunmer's (1986) simple view of reading suggests that reading comprehension (RC) is the product of**
    a. decoding×linguistic or listening comprehension (D×LC).
    b. decoding×reading comprehension (D×RC).
    c. phonological awareness×decoding (PA×D).
    d. listening comprehension×reading comprehension (LC×RC).

8. **The effects of dyslexia can be reduced by**
    a. time—children will outgrow it.
    b. proper instruction.
    c. nothing—it cannot be cured.
    d. early identification.
    e. both b and d.

9. **Although prevalence ranges vary, about what percent of the school-age population is estimated to have dyslexia?**
    a. Less than 1%
    b. More than 25%
    c. Between 5% and 8%
    d. Over 40%

10. **All individuals who struggle with reading have dyslexia. True or False?**

Answers: 1. f; 2. True; 3. b; 4. c; 5. True; 6. True; 7. a; 8. e; 9. c; 10. False

Chapter Two

A BRIEF HISTORY OF DYSLEXIA

Every child would read if it were in his power to do so.
—Betts, 1936, p. 5

As noted by Betts in 1936, all children want to learn to read; for some, however, learning to read is a daunting task that requires years of carefully crafted interventions. Physicians and educators have attempted to understand for well over a century why reading is so difficult for some individuals, and most importantly, what can be done to resolve these difficulties. Dyslexia is often described as the most common learning disability. In fact, reading is the primary problem for approximately 80% of the individuals identified as having learning disabilities (U.S. Department of Education, 2006). Although some people think that learning disability is a new category, the conceptual foundations of learning disability are nearly as longstanding as many of the other disability categories, and the roots can be traced back to at least the early 1800s (Hallahan & Mercer, 2002; Wiederholt, 1974). In fact, the systematic investigation of learning disabilities began around 1800 with Gall's examination of adults who had lost the capacity to speak (Hammill, 1993). Interestingly, many of the conclusions that were drawn in the late 1800s regarding the existence and persistence of this disorder are still pertinent today.

Initially, dyslexia was considered to be one of the aphasias, which included losses to some aspects of language including reading and writing. It was first referred to as *word blindness*, a label selected to describe individuals who were not physically blind, but seemed to have limited ability to recall the visual images of words necessary for reading and spelling. The individual could actually see the letters and words, but could not pronounce the words or interpret their meanings when reading. Over the next few decades of the 1920s and 1930s, the term *word blindness* would be replaced by *dyslexia, developmental dyslexia,* or *specific reading disability*. In this chapter we begin with a brief review of the earliest descriptions of dyslexia, and then we highlight the particular contributions of a few of the early pioneers, including Drs. James Hinshelwood, Grace Fernald, Samuel Orton, Norman Geschwind, Albert Galaburda, Marion Monroe, Samuel Kirk, Helmer Myklebust, and Doris Johnson. Figure 2.1 presents a timeline of these contributions.

EARLY CASE STUDIES AND INVESTIGATIONS BY PHYSICIANS

The first case studies of individuals who had lost the power to read—usually because of a stroke or brain injury—were adults. These patients were described by physicians from the United Kingdom, Germany, and the United States who attempted to identify the characteristics, etiology, and methods that would be most effective for treating these reading disorders (Anderson & Meier-Hedde, 2001). Word blindness was described as being either *acquired* or *congenital*. Acquired word blindness resulted from trauma after the person had already learned to read, whereas congenital word blindness was present before the person had learned to read (Pickle, 1998).

EXAMPLES OF THE EARLIEST REPORTS

In 1872, Sir William Broadbent described the cortical damage present in an autopsy of an individual who had speech disturbances and reading disabili-ties. Five years later, Kussmaul, a German neurologist, described an adult patient with severe reading disabilities and noted that ". . . a complete text blindness may exist although the power of sight, the intellect, and the powers of speech are intact" (1877a, p. 595). Thus, the term *word blindness* was first applied

DON'T FORGET

Acquired word blindness resulted from some type of trauma to the brain, whereas congenital word blindness was present from birth.

to individuals with aphasia who had lost the ability to read (Kussmaul, 1877b). By emphasizing the specificity of the reading disability, Kussmaul gave birth to the idea of dyslexia or specific reading disability (Hallahan & Mercer, 2002). Kussmaul (1877c) also introduced the term *word deafness* to describe individuals whose hearing was perfect, but who had trouble under-standing words that were heard. Kussmaul (1877c) believed that some of the cases that had been recorded as aphasia could be more aptly described as *word blindness* or *word deafness* as the patients were still able to express their thoughts in speaking or writing (p. 770).

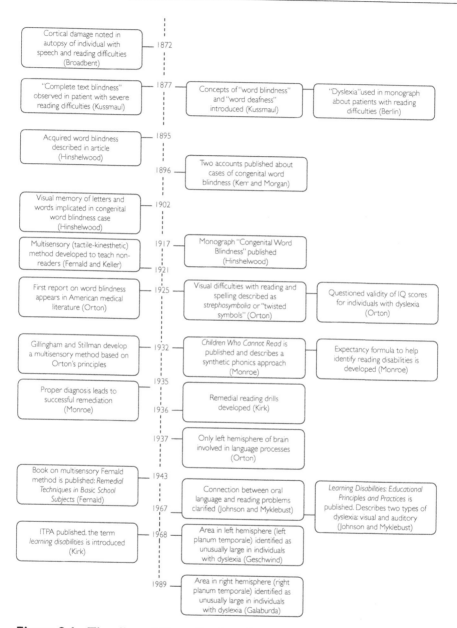

Figure 2.1   Timeline of Contributions by Highlighted Early Pioneers

Although some online sources, such as *Wikipedia*, note that dyslexia was first described by Oswald Berkhan in 1885, it appears that the first physician to actually write using the term *dyslexia*, was Rudolph Berlin, a German ophthalmologist, who used the word to describe reading problems that were a result of cerebral disease (Richardson, 1992; Wagner, 1973). Berlin described several of his patients who had difficulty reading printed words and complained of headaches when reading. In 1884, Berlin wrote a monograph on dyslexia that described this condition as belonging to a group of aphasias and being related to Kussmaul's word blindness, although not as severe. In postmortem dissections of six cases, Berlin found anatomical lesions in the left hemisphere (Wagner, 1973). Although the term *dyslexia* had been introduced, the term *word blindness* was used more frequently during this time period.

In 1896, two more accounts of congenital word blindness were published. James Kerr, a health officer, wrote the first account in which he described a boy of average intelligence who suffered from word blindness despite being able to spell the separate letters (cited in Critchley, 1964). Pringle Morgan (1896) wrote the second article that described the characteristics of an intelligent 14-year-old boy with "congenital word blindness" who excelled in arithmetic but could not read. Morgan provided the following description:

> His greatest difficulty has been—and is now—his inability to learn to read. This inability is so remarkable, and so pronounced, that I have no doubt it is due to some congenital defect . . . The following is the result of an examination I made a short time since. He knows all his letters and can write them and read them. In writing from dictation, he comes to grief over any but the simplest words. For instance, I dictated the following sentence: "Now, you watch me while I spin it." He wrote, "Now you word me wale I spin it" and again, "Carefully winding the string round the peg" was written "culfuly winder the sturng rond the pag." In writing his own name, he made a mistake, putting "Precy" for "Percy," and he did not notice the mistake until his attention was called to it more than once . . . I then asked him to read me a sentence out of an easy child's book without spelling the words. The result was curious. He did not read a single word correctly, with the exception of "and," "the," "of," "that," etc.; the other words seemed to be quite unknown to him, and he could not even make an attempt to pronounce them . . . He seems to have no power of preserving and storing up the visual impression produced by words—hence the

words, though seen, have no significance for him. His visual memory for words is defective or absent, which is equivalent to saying that he is what Kussmaul has termed "word blind." I may add that the boy is bright and of average intelligence in conversation . . . his eyesight is good. The schoolmaster who has taught him for some years says that he would be the smartest lad in the school if the instruction were entirely oral. (1896, p. 94)

Both Pringle Morgan and James Hinshelwood extended the work on acquired word-blindness in adults to congenital word-blindness in children (Hallahan & Mercer, 2002).

DR. JAMES HINSHELWOOD

In 1895, James Hinshelwood, an ophthalmologist and surgeon at the Glasgow Eye Infirmary, wrote an article that described acquired word blindness. In 1902, he provided a detailed description of a case of congenital word-blindness where the reading problem was attributed to a defect in the visual memory of letters and words. He described a 10-year-old boy with adequate visual acuity who could not learn words by sight but instead spelled out words letter by letter. Hinshelwood observed that since this boy had trouble learning to read by sight alone, he would benefit from a multisensory teaching method. Hinshelwood further noted that the diagnosis of word blindness is easy to make because the features of the disorder are distinct and easily understood. Over a century later, Shaywitz (2003) concurred that the diagnosis of dyslexia is as precise and accurate as any known medical condition.

In 1917, Hinshelwood reviewed the articles that were written by Kerr and Morgan in his seminal monograph entitled *Congenital Word-Blindness*. Within this monograph, Hinshelwood attempted to clarify a distinction between word blindness and more generalized developmental delays by summarizing:

When I see it stated that congenital word-blindness may be combined with any amount of other mental defects from mere dullness to low-grade mental defects, imbecility, or idiocy, I can understand how confusion has arisen from the loose application of the term congenital word-blindness to all conditions in which there is defective development of the visual memory center, quite independently of any consideration as to whether it is a strict local defect or only a symptom of a general cerebral degeneration. It is a great injustice to the children affected with the pure type of congenital word-blindness, a strict local affection [*sic*], to be placed in the same category as others suffering from generalized cerebral defects, as the former can be successfully dealt with, while the latter are practically irremediable. (1917, pp. 93–94)

Because Hinshelwood believed that word blindness was caused by a defect in the part of the brain that stored the visual images of words, he speculated that the cause of the problem could be found in the angular and supramarginal gyri of the left or dominant side of the brain, specifically the left angular gyrus. Hinshelwood believed that the deficit was confined to the visual memory center in an otherwise normal and healthy brain (Hinshelwood, 1917). Hinshelwood also attempted to develop specific procedures for teaching children with word blindness. He believed that ". . . the child must have personal instruction and be taught alone" (p. 99). Rapid Reference 2.1 provides a summary of Hinshelwood's major conclusions, many of which are still relevant today. Although Hinshelwood noted that many of his cases were highly intelligent, with the advent of intelligence tests, Samuel Orton was able to provide a certain degree of objectivity to support this notion (Hallahan & Mercer, 2002).

DR. SAMUEL ORTON

Dr. Samuel Orton, a psychiatrist and neuropathologist, is credited with the first report on word blindness that appeared in the American medical literature.

≡ *Rapid Reference 2.1*

Hinshelwood's Conclusions Regarding Word Blindness
Particular areas of the brain are involved.
The children often have average or above intelligence and good memory in other respects.
The problem with reading is localized, not generalized to all areas of performance.
The children do not learn to read with the same ease as other children.
The children require individualized instruction.
The earlier the problem is identified, the better so as not to waste valuable time.
The children must be taught by special methods to help them overcome their difficulties.
The sense of touch helps children retain the visual impressions of letters and words.
Persistent and persevering attempts will help children improve their reading.

Orton agreed with Hinshelwood that word blindness: (a) was not related to mental retardation, (b) ranged from mild to severe, and (c) was caused by differences within the brain. Orton surmised that the left hemisphere was the only side of the brain that was involved in language processes and

DON'T FORGET

Orton was the first to suggest that word blindness may be due to brain differences rather than brain damage.

described the right side of the brain ". . . as either useless or unused" (S. T. Orton, 1937, p. 13). Orton also questioned the validity of intelligence test scores for children with word blindness. Because these tests often measured aspects of the disability, Orton (1925) surmised that ". . . it seems probable that psychometric tests as ordinarily employed give an entirely erroneous and unfair estimate of the intellectual capacity of these children" (p. 582).

One specific characteristic that Orton observed in the children he studied was the poor recall of both the orientation and sequencing or ordering of the letters when reading and spelling. To describe this phenomenon, Orton coined the term *strephosymbolia*, which means "twisted symbols" (J. Orton, 1966; S. T. Orton, 1925, 1937). Orton hypothesized that the reversal errors that were common in children with reading disabilities could be attributed to a lack of cerebral dominance in the left hemisphere. Essentially, he speculated that the images recorded in the dominant left hemisphere of the brain (e.g., *on*) were stored as mirror images in the nondominant right hemisphere (e.g., *no*). For individuals with dominant left hemispheres, this mirror image would be suppressed, but for children with mixed dominance, the image would not be suppressed and would, therefore, contribute to the reversals of letters and transpositions of words (e.g., *was* for *saw*). Although the theory regarding mixed cerebral dominance as Orton described it is unsupported today, some evidence suggests that children with dyslexia do in fact activate some right hemisphere portions of the brain to compensate for deficiencies in the left hemisphere. Specifically, as children with dyslexia learn to read, they fail to make good sound-symbol associations in the left hemisphere of the brain; therefore, they rely on memorization of words, a function that takes place in the right hemisphere (S. E. Shaywitz & B. A. Shaywitz, 2008). Regardless of the inaccuracy of his theory, Orton had an enduring impact on the development and use of remedial interventions through his observation that multisensory phonics instruction is essential.

Orton (1925) addressed the type of remedial instruction that would be most beneficial for these children, stating: ". . . the logical training for these children would be that of extremely thorough repetitive drill on the fundamentals of phonic association with letter forms, both visually presented and produced in writing, until the correct associations were built up and the permanent elision of the reversed images and reversals in direction were assured. The flash method would seem from this point of view not only to be inadequate to correct early mistakes in orientation, but also to put these children under an unnecessary and unjust handicap, at least until they had acquired the fundamentals in readily available form. The child has no opportunity to puzzle out whether a symbol means *p* or *q* by the flash method, and many such errors might well be perpetuated" (p. 614).

Orton also developed an educational approach for teaching children with reading disabilities. Between 1932 and 1936, he directed the Language Research Project of the Neurological Institute of New York. One of his associates was Anna Gillingham, a psychologist, who with the assistance of Bessie Stillman, an educator, organized Orton's principles into a remedial, multisensory approach to alphabetic phonics that was designed to teach the English language structure, including phonemes, morphemes, and spelling rules.

DON'T FORGET

Orton (1925) indicated that a sight word (or look-say) approach to reading would not be beneficial for children with dyslexia. Instead, these children required a multisensory, structured phonics approach.

This became known as the Orton-Gillingham approach when June Orton in 1966 used this term in a book chapter. Today, the Orton-Gillingham approach is the basis for many of the current remedial reading approaches, including the Wilson Reading System. Orton was one of the first pioneers to recognize the importance of sound blending to the application of phonics. He observed: "It is this process of synthesizing the word as a spoken unit from its component sounds that often makes much more difficulty for the strephosymbolic child than do the static reversals and letter confusions" (S. T. Orton, 1937, p. 162). Orton also believed that tracing could help build up the associations between letters and sounds and eliminate the tendency of children to reverse and transpose letter sequences when reading and spelling. Thus, the alphabetic methodology that Orton and Gillingham developed is referred to as multisensory in nature, a visual-auditory-kinesthetic-tactile (VAKT) approach, as many senses are employed when teaching the structure of written English. Emphasis is placed on how a letter looks, sounds, and feels (J. Orton, 1966). Within this approach, the teacher provides training in both reading and spelling. The teacher shows a letter, the child produces the sound, the teacher says the sound, and the child names and writes the letter. Rapid Reference 2.2 summarizes the major principles underlying the Orton-Gillingham methodology. Rapid

≋ Rapid Reference 2.2

Major Principles Underlying the Orton-Gillingham Approach
Is adapted to meet individual needs.
Provides carefully structured and sequenced instruction in both reading and spelling.
Focuses on establishing connections between sounds and letters, and how to blend the sounds together into a whole word.
Provides instruction in how to organize individual letters and sounds into larger units.
Emphasizes use of multisensory procedures.

Reference 2.3 summarizes the step-by-step progression that is recommended in the Orton-Gillingham technique. Nearly a century later, the need for this type of intensive, systematic approach continues to be noted (Duff & Clarke, 2010; National Reading Panel, 2000). The importance of Orton's many contributions to the understanding and treatment of dyslexia was recognized by the establishment of the Orton Dyslexia Society in 1949, which became known as the International Dyslexia Association as of 1997.

DRS. NORMAN GESCHWIND AND ALBERT GALABURDA

Although many pioneers in the field of dyslexia had suggested an anatomical basis for reading disorders, Geschwind (1962) began an extensive study of brain anatomy to pinpoint the specific parts of the brain that caused these difficulties. In 1968, along with his research team, Geschwind was finally able to demonstrate conclusively that an area of the left planum temporale, a triangular area in the left hemisphere responsible for auditory processing, was unusually larger in individuals with dyslexia (Geschwind & Levitsky, 1968). His findings supported the brain lateralization hypothesis proposed by Orton, but further localized brain abnormalities to major areas associated with reading. Thus, unlike Orton, who proposed that dyslexia occurred as a result of interference of the right hemisphere in reading tasks, Geschwind suggested that

DON'T FORGET

During initial studies of brain anatomy in individuals with dyslexia, neurologists found abnormalities in the left planum temporale, a specific area in the left hemisphere responsible for auditory processing.

≡ *Rapid Reference 2.3*

The Orton-Gillingham Technique (J. Orton, 1966)

1. The child is shown a letter and repeats its name after the teacher.

2. The teacher demonstrates how to form the letter, and the child traces over the model. The child then copies the word, and then writes the word from memory.

3. Each phonic unit is presented on individual cards with consonant letters on white cards and vowel letters on salmon-colored cards. The sound is introduced with a key word. The student repeats the key word before he provides the sound.

4. The letter sounds are taught in groups as rapidly as they can be learned. The first letters introduced with their corresponding sounds are a (short sound as in cat), b, f, h, j, k, m, p, and t.

5. After the names and sounds are learned, blending is introduced. A consonant, vowel, and consonant are presented, and the student provides the sounds rapidly until she can produce the whole word.

6. The teacher then pronounces a word slowly and separates the sounds. The teacher then asks the child to repeat the word, name the letters, write the word while naming each letter, and then read back the word.

7. Once mastery is assured, additional letters and corresponding sounds are introduced. The manual provides the following sequence of letter introduction: g (as in get), o, initial r and l, n, th (as in this), u, ch, e, s, sh, d, w, wh, y, v, and z.

8. Consonant blends are introduced and then the following letters and blends with their corresponding sounds are presented: qu, x, y, ph, and s (as /z/).

9. The long sounds of all vowels are introduced and the vowel consonant –e spelling pattern (e.g., a_e, safe).

10. The student reads material with a controlled vocabulary (decodable text) to practice this alphabetic approach to words.

dyslexia occurred because a specific area of the left hemisphere needed for reading was abnormal.

In the 1980s, Galaburda continued the investigation of Geschwind's original hypothesis related to planum temporale abnormalities that caused distortions in reading. However, his investigations, unlike Geschwind's, revealed right planum temporale abnormalities that resulted in a more symmetric pattern of the left and right hemispheres of individuals with dyslexia (Galaburda, 1989). Today, neurologists continue to search for anatomical markers for dyslexia that follow Geschwind's and Galaburda's original hypotheses (e.g., Leonard & Eckert, 2008; Rumsey et al., 1997). In particular, studies by Leonard and Eckert (2008) propose three profiles that are possible in individuals with and without dyslexia. Specifically, an asymmetrical brain with a leftward planar asymmetry is considered normal and is expected to result in accurate and efficient reading and writing. In other words, in normal brains the left hemisphere is larger than the right hemisphere. On the other hand, individuals with exaggerated leftward planar asymmetry (larger than normal) are likely to show decreased phonological decoding abilities. Finally, children with relative structural symmetry, resulting from enlarged right planum temporale, demonstrate multiple language deficits. Figure 2.2 provides a visual representation of the possible profiles resulting from symmetry and asymmetry. Geschwind and Galaburda began the neurological investigation of dyslexia, but today technology provides more insight into the neurological markers of dyslexia. For more information on the brain and dyslexia refer to Chapter 3.

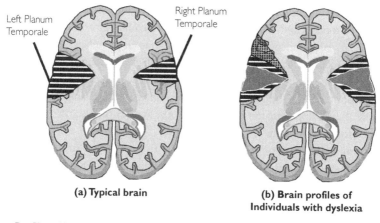

(a) Typical brain

(b) Brain profiles of Individuals with dyslexia

Profiles of individuals with dyslexia (b)

▬▬▬ Asymmetrical profile based on enlarged left planum temporale

▨▨ Symmetrical profile based on enlarged right planum temporale

▦▦ Exaggerated leftward asymmetry profile from enlarged left planum temporale

Figure 2.2   Differences in Plana Temporale

This figure illustrates the theory derived from Geschwind and Galaburda's planum temporale abnormalities. Three possible planum temporale profiles are possible. Leftward asymmetry is expected and considered to be the norm (left). Symmetry is seen in some individuals with dyslexia (gray), which is expected to result in multiple language deficiencies. Exaggerated leftward asymmetry (dotted) is found in other individuals with dyslexia and often results in deficiencies in phonological awareness.

PSYCHOLOGISTS AND EDUCATORS EXPLORING DIAGNOSIS AND TREATMENT

Although medical doctors were the first to identify and address dyslexia, various psychologists and educators also made significant contributions to our understanding of dyslexia in the 1920s through the 1960s. Many of these psychologists were somehow connected to or influenced by Orton's work.

DR. MARION MONROE

> **DON'T FORGET**
> ....
> Synthetic phonics approaches start with single sounds and letters that are then blended into whole words.

Dr. Marion Monroe, a research psychologist who served as Orton's associate in Iowa, continued development of his diagnostic procedures and remedial interventions for children with dyslexia. In her classic book, *Children Who Cannot Read* (Monroe, 1932), she described a synthetic phonics approach where the teacher provides instruction in consonants and vowels and then shows the child how to blend the sounds together to pronounce words. Synthetic phonic approaches start with single sounds and letters and show the child how to blend the sounds together to pronounce simple words (blending), and to break the words apart (segmentation) to spell those words. In the 1930s, Monroe described (a) the characteristics of poor readers, (b) the appropriate remedial methods, and (c) the use of an expectancy formula for predicting the level of reading skill.

Characteristics of poor readers. Similar to the findings of Orton, Monroe and Backus (1937) noted that children with poor reading tended to show the following characteristics: (a) excessive reversals, (b) line and word skipping, (c) slow reading rate, (d) errors on words with similar spelling configurations (e.g., *bread* and *beard*), and (e) complaints of eyestrain when reading. Orton (1937) and Monroe and Backus also described another group of children with *word deafness*. Although children with this condition had adequate hearing, they had difficulties recalling the auditory patterns of spoken words and lacked proper discrimination of speech sounds.

Monroe and Backus noted that these children exhibited some of the following characteristics when reading: (a) errors in vowel and consonant sounds, (b) additions and omissions of sounds, (c) confusion of words that sound alike, and (d) poor understanding of oral directions. Monroe drew attention to the importance of analyzing a child's reading errors, prior to developing an instructional plan. Rapid Reference 2.4 provides a list of the types of oral reading errors she described (1932, 1935).

≡ *Rapid Reference 2.4*

Types of Oral Reading Errors Described by Monroe
Faulty vowels (e.g., *bag* as *big*).
Faulty consonants (e.g., *sent* as *send*).
Reversals of letters (e.g., *b* and *d*) or the sequence of letters (e.g., *was* and *saw*).
Addition of sounds (e.g., *tack* read as *track*).
Omission of sounds (e.g., *blind* read as *bind*).
Substitutions of words (e.g., *house* read as *home*).
Repetitions of words and phrases.
Addition of words.
Omission of words.
Aided words (supplied by another).

Remedial methods. Monroe (1932) also observed that the methods used for children with reading disabilities, differ from those that are used with the majority of children. She noted: "The problem of remedial instruction in reading is to find a possible method of learning for those children who have not been able to learn by methods adapted to the group. The methods found helpful for reading-defect cases may not be necessary or advisable in ordinary instruction" (p. 113). In addition, the remedial work was modified to meet the needs of each individual. In applying remedial techniques, Monroe and Backus (1937) observed: ". . . each child received careful individual diagnostic study and each remedial teacher attempted first to understand the child and then to adapt instruction to his needs" (p. 112).

Monroe also noted that the careful selection of books and reading materials was an important part of the remedial program; the selected materials should be at each child's level of reading achievement, not at his or her grade level. Monroe and Backus (1937) observed that reading disabilities were often ". . . aggravated by inappropriate reading material" (p. 29). Classroom teachers often had reading books for only one grade level so that the teacher could not adjust the difficulty level to address individual needs.

CAUTION

Unfortunately many children with dyslexia today are still being given books to read that are far beyond their reading achievement levels. Developing readers must be provided with appropriate books matched to their present levels of reading skill.

Monroe (1935) found that with proper diagnosis, the remedial work was usually highly successful. The foundation of this remedial success includes ". . . careful observation of the pupil, with thorough diagnostic analysis, careful tabulation and study of his errors, and ingenuity in applying specific treatment" (p. 228). The teacher was then to design exercises to correct the specific difficulties and errors (Monroe & Backus, 1937). The remedial work should continue until the child's reading was in line with her other capacities. Not all children, however, made adequate progress. Although the remedial work was effective in 95% of the cases, Monroe and Backus (1937) found that: "The remedial work was unsuccessful in about 4 or 5 percent of the cases, in that this percentage of cases did not show improved scores on the retests" (p. 151). These children with the most severe reading disabilities would require increased individualized services from a highly trained reading specialist.

Rapid Reference 2.5 summarizes Monroe's findings regarding the rate of student progress under remedial instruction.

DON'T FORGET

Case studies from history remind us that children with the most severe reading disabilities will require intensive and extensive remedial work to learn to read.

DON'T FORGET

As noted by Monroe, the reading methods used for remedial instruction are not necessary for the majority of children who learn to read with ease.

≡ Rapid Reference 2.5

Monroe's Findings Regarding the Factors Affecting the Rate of Student Progress Under Remedial Instruction

    The child's level of intelligence.
    How early the problem was identified.
    Number of hours spent in training.
    Number of months during which training was continued.
    The severity of the reading disability.
    The extent of personality and behavior difficulties.
    The closeness of supervision of the remedial techniques.
    The experience of the teacher in providing remedial instruction.

The use of an expectancy formula. Monroe (1932) can also be credited with the first attempts to create an expectancy formula to help identify a reading disability. The purpose of this type of discrepancy was to predict a person's "aptitude" or potential for reading, based upon his other characteristics. In order to determine a reading disability, as well as the severity, Monroe created an expectancy formula to see if a child's reading achievement was in harmony with his other achievements. To determine the expectation of the reading level, three factors were con-

> **DON'T FORGET**
> ....
> Under the provisions of the Individuals with Disabilities Education Improvement Act (IDEA, 2004), a discrepancy between IQ and achievement is not a requirement for diagnosing children with a reading disability.

sidered: chronological age, mental age (based on the Stanford-Binet intelligence test), and level of arithmetic computation. A person's intact abilities were used to predict the present level of reading skill. Essentially, this type of formula was an attempt to operationalize the concept of *unexpected underachievement*. This type of discrepancy formula is still in use today. Until IDEA (2004), to be eligible for specific learning disabilities (SLD) services, students had to show a discrepancy between their intelligence test score (predicted achievement) and their reading achievement score (actual achievement). Although a discrepancy is no longer required under IDEA 2004, districts may still use some type of discrepancy formula for eligibility decisions.

Level of intelligence. Monroe (1932) also recognized that individuals with any level of intelligence, including those with superior intelligence, could struggle to learn to read. Monroe noted: "It seems that we are measuring a discrepancy between reading and other accomplishments which may occur in either direction at any intellectual level" (p. 17) and that "the reading defects may occur at any intellectual level from very superior to very inferior, as measured by intelligence tests" (p. 6). She was particularly fascinated by the cases of intellectually gifted

> **DON'T FORGET**
> ....
> The conceptual origins of the ability-achievement discrepancy for SLD identification can be traced back to Monroe (1932).

children who struggled to learn to read, noting: "The children of superior mental capacity who fail to learn to read are, of course, spectacular examples of specific reading difficulty since they have such obvious abilities in other fields"

≡ *Rapid Reference 2.6*

....

Major Conclusions from Monroe (1932, 1935) and Monroe and Backus (1937)
Different factors affect performance in different children.
Profiles on tests can be used to show patterns of strength and weakness.
Poor sound blending is often a cause of reading disability.
Reading errors should be analyzed to understand instructional needs.
Children require intensive remedial training.
The training should continue until reading is in harmony with the child's other
capacities and achievement.
Books and reading materials should be adapted to the child's level of reading
achievement.
Methods must be modified to meet the needs of each individual.
Problems arise in behavior and personality but disappear as reading improves.
Children of all levels of intelligence can struggle to learn to read.

(p. 23). She provided the following description of a bright child struggling to learn to read:

Betty represents a case of reading retardation in a very bright little girl. She was completing the second year in school without having been able to learn to read. When examined she was seven years and four months of age, with a mental age of ten years, I.Q. 135. Arithmetic measured high second grade. Reading and spelling measured very low first grade. . . . She had a most engaging manner and had learned many ways of diverting attention from the fact that she could not read. When the reading tests were presented she pushed them aside and said, "Let's don't do any reading. I know some arithmetic games that are lots of fun. Please teach me some third-grade arithmetic problems." When finally persuaded to attempt the tests she showed considerable emotional tension, clearing her voice, saying "ah" several times before attempting each word, and flushing over her obvious errors. (p. 10)

Rapid Reference 2.6 provides a summary of Monroe's major conclusions.

DR. GRACE FERNALD

Similar to Orton and Monroe, Grace Fernald developed a multisensory technique called the Fernald Method which she summarized in her book *Remedial Techniques in Basic School Subjects* (1943). In the 1920s, Fernald, who had a hearing impairment, worked with Helen Keller, who was both blind and deaf, to promote the use of tactile-kinesthetic methodologies for teaching word recognition skills to nonreaders (Fernald & Keller, 1921). Unlike the Orton-Gillingham approach, Fernald de-emphasized phonics and instead, emphasized a whole-word approach to word learning (Hallahan & Mercer, 2002). Fernald stressed the importance of providing children with meaningful reading and writing activities, so the methodology is used first with writing stories, and then as skill improves, reading stories. She observed: "The child is much more interested in writing and reading fairly difficult material that is on the level of his understanding than simpler material which is below his mental age level" (1943, p. 44).

The Fernald method has been used effectively to teach struggling readers of all ages. Because the method involves tracing, it can actually help children increase their abilities to pay attention to the details in words and visualize the sequence of letters within words. This method consists of four stages through which a student progresses as skill increases. Before starting, the teacher explains to the student that she will be taught a new way to learn words that has been successful with other learners. Rapid Reference 2.7 provides an overview of the four stages of this method.

DR. SAMUEL A. KIRK

From early in his career, Dr. Samuel Kirk was fascinated by the enigma of children with specific reading disabilities. Kirk (1974) recognized that: "Disabilities in reading, writing, and spelling have been of interest to neurologists, ophthalmologists, psychologists, and educators since and before the beginning of this century" (p. 1). As part of his early training, he worked as a resident instructor at the Institute for Juvenile Research under the tutelage of Dr. Marion Monroe.

DON'T FORGET

The central reason for diagnosing dyslexia should be to plan remediation.

Kirk (1984) explained how Monroe's book, *Children Who Cannot Read,* was his bible for a while, and how her system of diagnosing reading errors and profiling abilities and disabilities continued to influence his work in later years. While looking through the files at the institute, Kirk noted that one of the young boys had been diagnosed as *word blind*, a term he had never heard before. After studying the writings of Hinshelwood, Monroe, and Fernald, Kirk arranged to tutor the boy. After seven months, the boy was reading at third-grade level and was returned to public school (Kirk, 1976, pp. 242–243). Kirk stressed that the diagnosis of children was for the purpose of remediation, not for classification or categorization. In this regard, Kirk and Johnson (1951) stated: "The purpose of any diagnosis, or the

≣ Rapid Reference 2.7

Four Stages of the Fernald Method

First stage. In the first stage, the student selects a word that she cannot read but would like to learn. The teacher and student discuss the meaning of the word using the following steps:

1. *Write the word.* The teacher sits beside the student and asks the student to watch and listen while the teacher (1) says the word, (2) uses a crayon to write the word in large print in manuscript or cursive (depending on which writing style the child uses) on an index card, and (3) says the word again while running a finger underneath the word.

2. *Model word tracing.* The teacher says, "Watch what I do and listen to what I say." The teacher then (1) says the word; (2) traces the word using one or two fingers, saying each part of the word while tracing it; and (3) says the word again while running a finger underneath the word. The student then practices tracing the word using these steps.

3. *Practice tracing.* The student continues tracing the word until she can write the word from memory. The student says each part of the word while tracing it.

4. *Write from memory.* The student attempts to write the word from memory. When the student feels ready, the teacher removes the model and asks the student to write the word from memory. The student says the word while writing. If at any point the student makes an error, the teacher stops the student immediately, covers the error, and models the tracing procedure again before proceeding.

5. *The word is filed.* After the student writes the word correctly three times without the model, the student files the word in a word bank alphabetically to practice on a later date.

Second stage. By the second stage, the student no longer needs to trace words and can learn a word by looking at the word after the teacher writes it, saying the word, and then writing it.

Third stage. By the third stage, the student is able to learn new words directly from printed words without having them written. When reading with the student, the teacher tells her any unknown words. After reading, the student reviews and writes the unknown words.

Fourth stage. By the fourth stage, the student begins to notice similarities between unknown and known words and can recognize many new words without being told what they are.

determination of etiology, is to assist in structuring the most adequate rehabilitation procedures" (p. 109).

As were the other early pioneers, Kirk was concerned about finding the most efficacious ways to instruct children who were struggling to learn to read. His master's thesis (1933) compared two methods for teaching reading, the look-say approach and the Fernald kinesthetic approach. In his analysis, Kirk found that retention for word learning was improved when tracing was added to the teaching procedure. In fact, he found that writing letters, words, and sentences from memory

DON'T FORGET

Tracing letters and words and writing them from memory can reduce reversal errors and help with word retention.

was an aid in the removal of reversal errors. With Thorleif Hegge, Kirk went on to develop the Hegge, Kirk, and Kirk Remedial Reading Drills (1936), which evolved from his study of children with reading disabilities, as well as influences from the earlier works of Orton, Monroe, and Fernald. Rapid Reference 2.8 summarizes the major instructional strategies that were incorporated into these drills. Today, these original drills have been revised and are still in use with individuals with dyslexia (S. A. Kirk, W. D. Kirk, Minskoff, Mather, & Roberts, 2007; Roberts & Mather, 2007).

Kirk was also interested in developing an assessment instrument that would document strengths and weaknesses within an individual, or what is referred to as *intraindividual variations*. In order to identify specific disabilities, Kirk and colleagues developed the *Illinois Test of Psycholinguistic Abilities* (ITPA; S. A. Kirk,

DON'T FORGET

Individuals with dyslexia often have marked intraindividual variations, strengths and weaknesses, and sometimes an ability-achievement discrepancy with their basic reading and spelling skills being lower than their other abilities or overall ability.

≡ *Rapid Reference 2.8*

Instructional Strategies Used in the Hegge, Kirk, and Kirk Remedial Drills

- One response to one symbol.
- Minimal change (only initial or final consonant changes in the first and second sections).
- Lessons progress from easy to hard.
- Frequent repetition and review.
- Verbal mediation (see and say).
- Multisensory learning (see, say, and trace).

McCarthy, & W. D. Kirk, 1968). The ITPA was historically important for two reasons: (1) it measured intraindividual differences, and (2) it articulated the principle of using assessment to guide instruction. Although Monroe (1932) had described both of these ideas previously, they gained widespread popularity with the use of the ITPA (Hallahan & Mercer, 2002). Kirk is also credited for being the first to use the term *learning disabilities* to describe children with disorders in language, speech, and reading (Hallahan & Mercer, 2002; S. A. Kirk, 1963). In defining SLD, Kirk noted the relevance of both intraindividual variations, as well as an ability-achievement discrepancy. In an interview Kirk explained: "I like to define a learning disability as a psychological or neurological impediment to development of adequate perceptual or communicative behavior, which first is manifested in discrepancies among specific behaviors or between overall performance and academic achievement. . . ."(Arena, 1978, p. 617).

DRS. DORIS JOHNSON AND HELMER MYKLEBUST

Drs. Doris Johnson and Helmer Myklebust helped to clarify the relationships between oral language and reading problems, as well as the symptoms and subtypes of dyslexia. They noted that difficulty learning spoken language interferes with learning to read (Johnson & Myklebust, 1967) and that learning disabilities, such as dyslexia, result from altered processes, not from a generalized incapacity to learn (p. 8). Essentially, there is "a deficit in learning in the presence of basic integrity" (p. 25). They emphasized the importance of careful diagnostic study in planning intervention programs for children and stated: "The single most important factor in planning for a child with a learning disability is an intensive diagnostic study" (p. 50). Although Myklebust's original work was in the area of deafness, he found that many of the children who were referred to his clinic had normal hearing acuity, but trouble in understanding what they heard (Hallahan & Mercer, 2002). Myklebust (1954) stated: "It is apparent that there is a need to view the problem of auditory disorders in children as one requiring differential diagnosis" (p. 8). In 1967, Johnson and Myklebust wrote a book entitled: *Learning Disabilities: Educational Principles and Practices*. Within this book, they described two types of dyslexia: visual and auditory. Rapid Reference 2.9 summarizes the major characteristics of these two types of dyslexia.

In regard to treatment, individuals with visual dyslexia need to be taught a systematic approach to attacking words. As with the Orton-Gillingham approach, reading instruction begins with single letters that can be blended

≡ Rapid Reference 2.9

Characteristics of Visual and Auditory Dyslexia

Visual Dyslexia
- Confuses letters and words with similar appearance.
- Difficulty developing a sight vocabulary.
- Slow rate of word perception.
- Reversals (e.g., *b* for *d*), inversions (e.g., *u* for *n*), and transpositions (e.g., *was* for *saw*) in reading and writing.
- Difficulty retaining visual sequences and reproducing a visual sequence of letters from memory.

Auditory Dyslexia
- Difficulty hearing the differences among speech sounds.
- Trouble remembering the sounds of letters.
- Difficulty discriminating short vowel sounds.
- Difficulty with blending and segmentation.
- May be able to read silently better than orally.

into words. The teacher selects two or three consonants that are different in appearance and sound (e.g., m, t, s) and a short vowel, and then teaches the child to blend these sounds into meaningful units (Johnson & Myklebust, 1967).

Individuals with auditory dyslexia often respond best to a whole word approach during the initial stages of reading acquisition. Once they have developed a basic sight vocabulary, these children do, however, require specific training with substantial practice in how to blend together letter sounds. They first should learn to develop syllables into words, and then how to combine individual sounds into words (Myklebust & Johnson, 1962).

Johnson and Myklebust (1967) also discussed the importance of clinical teaching when working with individual children with learning disabilities as ". . . these children

DON'T FORGET

To read, a child must be able to distinguish similarities and differences in sounds, perceive sounds within words, synthesize sounds into words, and divide them into syllables (Johnson & Myklebust, 1967, p. 173).

≡ *Rapid Reference 2.10*
....

Principles of Clinical Teaching
The teacher is aware of the student's strengths and weaknesses.
Through direct observation of the child, approaches are adjusted to adapt to his particular strengths and weaknesses.
Instruction focuses on increasing both strengths and weaknesses.
Different methodologies are applied with different children.
The intent of remediation is to modify behavior and increase learning.
All facets of behavior are addressed (e.g., emotional adjustment).

present a challenge diagnostically and educationally" and "it is incumbent upon the community of specialists involved to meet this challenge" (p. 25). They describe the clinical teaching approach as ". . . broad, inclusive, and dynamic" (p. 65). The teacher must meet the child at several levels. They noted that: "A ten-year-old may be functioning at his age level in comprehension of the spoken word but at the six-year-old level in reading. Without an understanding of these discrepancies, it is impossible to plan an adequate educational program" (p. 53). Thus, clinical teaching requires the teacher to be fully aware of the child's strengths and weaknesses prior to beginning an intervention program. Rapid Reference 2.10 summarizes the main principles of clinical instruction.

CONCLUSION

This chapter provided a brief summary of the history of dyslexia, as well as descriptions of the contributions made by a few of the early pioneers. Many other psychologists and educators have made significant contributions to our understanding of dyslexia, including Alfred Strauss, Laura Lehtinen, Newell Kephart, Marianne Frostig, William Cruickshank, June Orton, Raymond Barsch, Margaret Rawson, Roger Saunders, Renee Herman, and Romalda Spalding; and in the present, we have many leading experts, such as Marcia Henry, Louisa Moats, Sally and Bennett Shaywitz, and Barbara Wilson, who continue to expand and refine our knowledge. Much of what we know about dyslexia today was discovered and discussed throughout the last century. Rapid References 2.11 and 2.12 provide a summary of relevant insights from history regarding the characteristics of dyslexia, as well as insights regarding both assessment and intervention. The emergence of neuroimaging technology, such as fMRI, PET, and SPECT,

≡ *Rapid Reference 2.11*

Insights from History Regarding the Characteristics of Dyslexia
Dyslexia runs in families.
Certain parts of the brain appear to be involved.
Difficulties are apparent with word reading and spelling.
Confusions are noted with speech sounds.
Reversals of letters and transpositions of letters may be apparent.
Reading is slow and laborious.
Adults with dyslexia often have a slow reading rate and poor spelling.
Dyslexia does not affect all domains of functioning; strengths are often present.
Difficulty learning to read has a profound effect on self-esteem.
Problems in behavior and motivation decrease as reading skill improves.
Affective factors must be considered in the treatment plan.

≡ *Rapid Reference 2.12*

Insights from History Regarding Assessment and Intervention
Comprehensive evaluations are needed to diagnose dyslexia.
Specific problems exist in cognitive, linguistic, or perceptual processes that affect reading and spelling development.
Intraindividual variations are often present with oral language and mathematical abilities being more advanced than reading and writing skill.
Attempts have been made to quantify the concept of *unexpected reading failure* through the use of various discrepancy procedures.
Dyslexia can affect an individual of any level of intelligence.
The problem is lifelong, but interventions are effective.
Early intervention is critical.
One-to-one or small group instruction is essential.
Multisensory instruction can help improve visual memory of letter forms and words.
Structured, explicit, systematic phonics programs are often needed for mastery of sound-symbol relationships.
The teacher must receive adequate training and supervision in these methodologies.

has advanced the study of dyslexia, allowing the brain to be viewed while the individual performs reading tasks (see Chapter 3). Much was known about the causes and treatments for dyslexia over a century ago and research and technology continue to enhance that knowledge.

🐟 TEST YOURSELF 🐟

1. Physicians provided many of the earliest reports of individuals with dyslexia or word blindness who had lost the ability to read because of injury or stroke. True or False?

2. The terms *word blindness* and *word deafness* were used in the past to describe the observed characteristics of individuals with dyslexia. True or False?

3. Orton believed that a sight-word approach would be particularly helpful for children with word blindness. True or False?

4. Orton felt that intelligence tests provided an unfair estimate of the intellectual capacity of children with word blindness. True or False?

5. The Orton-Gillingham approach
   a. proceeds in a step-by-step progression.
   b. is multisensory.
   c. teaches reading and spelling words together.
   d. can be adapted to meet individual needs.
   e. all of the above.

6. Both the Orton-Gillingham (O-G) and Fernald methodologies are multisensory in nature, but only O-G provides direct, systematic phonics instruction. True or False?

7. Monroe found that all children made adequate progress when provided with remedial reading programs. True or False?

8. A person of superior intelligence cannot have dyslexia. True or False?

9. Monroe's reading index was a discrepancy procedure designed to compare a child's actual reading level to the expected reading level (based on chronological age, mental age, and arithmetic performance). True or False?

10. The concept of intraindividual variations, such as measured on the ITPA, refers to the strengths and weaknesses among one's abilities. True or False?

Answers: 1. True; 2. True; 3. False; 4. True; 5. e; 6. True; 7. False; 8. False; 9. True; 10. True

Chapter Three

THE BRAIN AND DYSLEXIA

Nancy Mather, Barbara Wendling, Martha Youman, Sally Shaywitz, and Bennett Shaywitz

Most of us have spent some time wondering how our brain works. Brain scientists spend their entire lives pondering it, looking for a way to begin asking the question, How does the brain generate mind? The brain, after all, is so complex an organ and can be approached from so many different directions using so many different techniques and experimental animals that studying it is a little like entering a blizzard, the Casbah, a dense forest. It's easy enough to find a way in—an interesting phenomenon to study—but also very easy to get lost.

—Allport, 1986, pp. 17–18

Dyslexia is neurobiological in origin, meaning that problems are located within the brain (Hudson, High, & Al Otaiba, 2007). This chapter first reviews the 19th-century history relating brain abnormalities to disturbances in language function and then introduces basic brain anatomy. We then review the neural systems relating to reading and dyslexia, focusing on those studies using functional brain imaging, particularly functional magnetic resonance imaging (fMRI).

HISTORICAL STUDIES RELATING BRAIN FUNCTION TO LANGUAGE DIFFICULTIES

Knowledge of the neural systems for reading emerged from 19th-century reports of individuals who suffered damage to regions in the left hemisphere of the brain involved in language. One region, involving the area related to expressive language located in the left inferior frontal gyrus, was described in 1861 by Paul Broca in an individual with expressive aphasia; that is, the man

43

could understand language but had difficulty producing it. Twenty years later, in 1881, the German neurologist, Carl Wernicke, described a different type of aphasia, receptive aphasia. The patients could speak fluently, but had difficulty understanding what they heard. In addition, they essentially spoke gibberish, which made it difficult to understand their language. For these patients damage was present in the left temporoparietal region, an area that is now referred to as Wernicke's area (Sousa, 2005). A decade later, the French neurologist Jules Dejerine, described individuals in their 60s who had suddenly lost their ability to read usually because of a stroke, a condition that was referred to as "acquired alexia" (Dejerine, 1891, 1892). Reports of children with developmental dyslexia (in that era termed "congenital word blindness") first appeared at the end of the 19th century (Morgan, 1896). Throughout the early years of the 20th century many more cases continued to be described by British and American physicians, especially the British ophthalmologist James Hinshelwood. For example, in 1902, Hinshelwood provided a detailed description of two cases of children with congenital word-blindness. He linked the reading problem to a defect in the visual memory of letters and words, and attributed the problem to brain dysfunction. Others, including Samuel Orton (1925), also posited that dyslexia was caused by physiological deficits in the brain. With the development of noninvasive brain imaging, particularly functional brain imaging, dyslexia has been shown unequivocally to be related to dysfunction within the neural systems of brain. A more detailed examination of the early history of dyslexia can be found in S. Shaywitz (2003) as well as Chapter 2 of this book.

THE STRUCTURE OF THE BRAIN AND THE NEURAL SYSTEMS FOR READING

Some readers of this book may be well-versed in brain research, while others may be novices. While it is not necessary to become an expert regarding the brain, basic knowledge of the brain and its functions is helpful for understanding dyslexia. Therefore, this section begins with an overview of the basics. Figure 3.1 illustrates the left hemisphere of the brain and identifies two areas (Broca's and Wernicke's) that have been associated with language and reading. Rapid Reference 3.1 summarizes the main functions of the major components and features of the brain. After the overview, the remainder of the chapter focuses on the neurobiological findings detailing differences between typical readers and those with dyslexia.

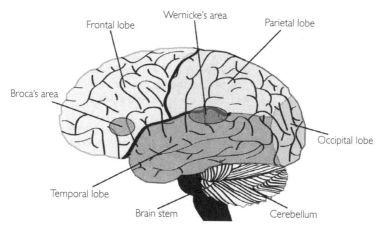

Figure 3.1   Left Hemisphere of Brain

This figure shows a picture of the left hemisphere of the brain with the four cerebral lobes, as well as Broca's and Wernicke's areas, two areas associated with language and reading. *Source:* Reprinted from S. Shaywitz (2003) with permission.

≡ *Rapid Reference 3.1*

Functions of the Major Areas of the Brain

Cerebral Hemispheres: The largest portion of the brain, a bilateral structure comprising the frontal, parietal, temporal, and occipital lobes.

Gyrus: A ridge or smooth area on the cerebral cortex surrounded by one or more depressions (sulci).

Sulcus: A furrow or depression in the cerebral cortex. Large sulci are called fissures and separate the lobes of the brain.

Cerebral White Matter (CWM): Comprised of the axons of neurons and connecting neurons within the brain and from brain to brain stem and spinal cord.

Frontal Lobe: The most anterior (front part) of the cerebral hemisphere involved in executive functions such as planning, organizing, problem solving, selective attention, and also personality. The most anterior portion of this lobe is called the prefrontal cortex. Most purposeful behaviors are initiated in this area. The posterior (back) portion of this lobe consists of the premotor and motor areas, called the motor cortex. The frontal lobes are well-connected to the limbic system, a complex series of neurons related to emotions.

Parietal Lobe: The parietal lobes are located posterior to the frontal lobe at the top of the brain and contain the primary sensory cortex. These lobes receive data from the skin via the thalamus (a series of neurons deep within the cerebral cortex) that process touch and sensation information such as heat, cold,

(continued)

and pain, as well as the position of the body in space. This sensory processing communicates with the primary motor area, which lies in the frontal lobes.

Temporal Lobe: Located inferiorly (below) the frontal and parietal lobes, its functions include hearing, speech perception, and some types of memory. It contains the primary auditory cortex and the hippocampi, which are important for memory functions. The right lobe is mainly involved in visual memory. The left lobe is mainly involved in verbal memory.

Occipital Lobe: Located in the back of the brain, this area processes visual information and is referred to as the visual cortex. Nerve impulses from the retina travel via the thalamus to the occipital lobes. The visual cortex has more nerve cells (neurons) than all of the other areas of the brain combined.

Corpus Callosum: Composed of white matter that connects the right and left hemispheres facilitating information transfer and processing.

Cerebellum: The portion of the brain (located at the back) that helps coordinate movement (balance and muscle coordination). Some researchers believe that this area is important for the automatization of skills.

Brain stem: The lower extension of the brain that connects to the spinal cord and is sometimes referred to as the reptilian brain. The brain stem is responsible for the basic neurological functions necessary for survival (breathing, digestion, heart rate, blood pressure) and for arousal (being awake and alert).

THE STRUCTURE OF THE BRAIN

The brain has three main components: the cerebral cortex, the cerebellum, and the brain stem. The cerebral cortex comprises four lobes: frontal, parietal, temporal, and occipital. Most of the specialized language processing system is found within the left cerebral hemisphere of the brain within specific regions of the frontal, temporal, parietal, and occipital lobes. The cerebellum, located at the back of the brain, controls posture, balance, and coordination. The brain stem, which connects the brain to the spinal cord, controls essential survival functions, such as breathing and heartbeat.

Gross anatomical features of the brain include the ridges (gyri) and furrows or grooves (sulci). The fine structure of the brain includes the neurons (the gray matter) and supporting glial cells. The neuron is comprised of the cell body and usually several protrusions from the cell body that receive impulses from other neurons (dendrites) and another protrusion that sends impulses to other neurons (the axon). An intricate pattern of connections allows for the coordination of the complex cognitive, emotional, and motor functions of the brain. These connections occur via white matter pathways that connect the diverse portions of the cerebral cortex and cerebellum with one another and motor and sensory neurons within the brain stem and spinal cord. The white matter consists of myelinated nerve fibers formed by the axons that project from the nerve cell. The myelin is primarily a white fatty substance, hence "white matter," that insulates the nerve fibers and conducts impulses between different areas of gray matter. One very large white matter structure, the corpus callosum, facilitates movement of information between the right and left cerebral hemispheres. Neurons also connect with one another via chemicals termed neurotransmitters (e.g., the catecholamines, dopamine, and norepinephrine; and the indoleamine, serotonin).

NEURAL SYSTEMS FOR READING

As noted above, our understanding of the neural systems for reading emerged more than a century ago, with descriptions of adults who, usually due to a stroke, suddenly lost their ability to read, a condition termed acquired alexia. These postmortem studies, pioneered by Dejerine as early as 1891, suggested that a portion of the left posterior brain region (which includes the angular gyrus and supramarginal gyrus in the inferior parietal lobule and the posterior aspect

DON'T FORGET
....
Most language-related processing takes place within specific regions of the left hemisphere of the brain.

of the superior temporal gyrus) is critical for reading (Dejerine, 1891). Another left posterior brain region, one more ventral in the occipitotemporal area, was also described by Dejerine (1892) as critical for reading. Within the last two decades, the development of functional brain imaging, particularly functional magnetic resonance imaging (fMRI), has provided the most consistent and replicable data on the location of the neural systems for reading and how they differ in readers with dyslexia. FMRI is noninvasive and safe, and can be used repeatedly: properties that make it ideal for studying people, especially children. The signal used to construct fMRI images derives from the determination of the blood-oxygen-level dependent (BOLD) response; the increase in BOLD signal in regions that are activated by a stimulus or task results from the combined effects of increases in the tissue blood flow, volume, and oxygenation. During cognitive tasks the changes are typically in the order of 1% to 5%. To date, fMRI in individuals with dyslexia can be carried out reliably only at a group level. The technology for determining brain activation at an individual subject level remains a work in progress. Rapid Reference 3.2 provides examples of the types of reading-related tasks that children and adults have been asked to do during fMRI studies.

Reflecting the language basis for reading and dyslexia, three neural systems critical for reading are localized in the left hemisphere (see Figure 3.2): two left

≡ Rapid Reference 3.2

Types of Reading-Related Tasks Used During fMRI
Letter identification: are *N* and *M* the same letter?
Single letter rhyming: do /b/ and /d/ rhyme?
Nonword rhyming: do *jupe* and *doop* rhyme?
Homophone or rhyming judgment: do *steak* and *rake* rhyme?
Real word identification: is *feak* a real word?
Vocabulary: are *apple* and *pear* in the same semantic category?
Sentence verification: You can sit on a chair. (True or False?)

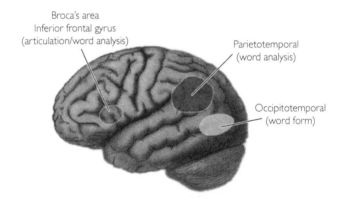

Figure 3.2   The Neural Systems for Reading

This figure illustrates three neural systems for reading on the surface of the left hemisphere: an anterior system in the region of the inferior frontal gyrus (Broca's area) believed to serve articulation and word analysis; and two posterior systems, one in the parietotemporal region believed to serve word analysis, and a second in the occipitotemporal region (termed the word-form area) believed to serve for the rapid, automatic, fluent identification of words.

Source: Reprinted from S. Shaywitz (2003) with permission.

hemisphere posterior systems, one around the parietotemporal region and another in the left occipitotemporal region, and an anterior system around the inferior frontal gyrus (Broca's area; Brambati et al., 2006; Helenius, Tarkiainen, Cornelissen, Hansen, & Salmelin, 1999; Kronbichler et al., 2006; Nakamura et al., 2006; Paulesu et al., 2001; B. Shaywitz et al., 2002; S. Shaywitz et al., 2003; S. Shaywitz et al., 1998).

Many brain imaging studies in children and adults with developmental dyslexia (see below) have documented the importance of the left parietotemporal system in reading, properties involving word analysis, operating on individual units of words (e.g., phonemes). The parietotemporal system encompasses portions of the supramarginal gyrus in the inferior parietal lobule, portions of the posterior aspect of the superior temporal gyrus, and in some studies, may even encompass portions of the angular gyrus in the parietal lobe. The second posterior reading system is localized in the left occipitotemporal area, which Cohen and Dehaene have termed the visual word-form area (VWFA; Cohen et al., 2000; Dehaene, Cohen, Sigman, & Vinckier, 2005; Vinckier et al., 2007). Just how the VWFA functions to integrate phonology (sounds) and orthography (print) is as yet unknown, though some have suggested that visual familiarity, phonological processing, and semantic processing all make significant but different contributions to activation of the VWFA (Cohen, Jobert, Le Bihan, & Dehaene, 2004; Henry et al., 2005; Johnson & Rayner, 2007; Xue, Chen, Jin, & Dong, 2006). Still another reading related neural circuit involves an anterior system in the left inferior frontal gyrus (Broca's area), a system that has long been associated with articulation and also serves an important function in word analysis (Fiez & Peterson, 1998; Frackowiak et al., 2004).

> ## CAUTION
> In individuals with dyslexia, fMRI can be carried out reliably only at a group level. The determination of brain activation at an individual subject level is not possible at the current time.

The reading systems of children and adults with dyslexia. Converging evidence from many laboratories around the world has demonstrated what has been termed a neural signature for dyslexia; that is, inefficient functioning of left posterior reading systems during reading real words and pseudowords, and often what has been considered as compensatory overactivation in other parts of the reading system. The evidence from functional brain imaging has, for the first time, made visible what previously was a hidden disability (S. Shaywitz, 2003).

> ## DON'T FORGET
> Dyslexia is a real disability, made visible by functional brain imaging technology.

For example, fMRI was used to study 144 boys and girls, some with dyslexia and some without dyslexia, as they read pseudowords and real words (B. Shaywitz et al., 2002). The results indicated significantly greater activation during phonologic analysis in typical readers than in readers with dyslexia in the posterior reading systems. These data converge with reports from many investigators using functional brain imaging in dyslexia that show a failure of left hemisphere posterior brain systems to function properly during reading. (See reviews in Richlan, Kronbichler, & Wimmer, 2009; S. Shaywitz & B. Shaywitz, 2005). Recent studies report similar findings in German (Kronbichler et al., 2006) and Italian (Brambati et al., 2006). Rapid Reference 3.3 summarizes the findings related to the neural signature of dyslexia.

Development of reading systems in dyslexia. While converging evidence points to three important neural systems for reading, few studies have examined age-related changes in these systems in typical readers or in children with dyslexia. FMRI was used to study age-related changes in reading in a cross-sectional study of 232 boys and girls, some with dyslexia and some without reading impairments, as they read pseudowords (B. Shaywitz et al., 2007). Findings indicated that the neural systems for reading that develop with age in typical readers differ from those that develop in readers with dyslexia (see Figure 3.3). Specifically, a system for reading that develops with age in readers with dyslexia involves a more *posterior and medial system*, in contrast to a more *anterior and lateral system* within the left occipitotemporal area in typical readers.

Interestingly, this difference in activation patterns between the two groups of readers parallels reported brain activation differences observed during reading of two Japanese writing systems: Kana and Kanji. Left anterior lateral occipitotemporal activation, similar to that seen in typical readers, occurred during reading Kana (Nakamura, Dehaene, Jobert, Le Bihan, & Kouider, 2005). Kana script employs symbols that are linked to the sound or phonologic element (comparable to English and other alphabetic scripts). In Kana and in alphabetic scripts, children initially learn to read words by learning how letters and sounds are linked, and then, over time, these linkages are integrated and permanently instantiated as a word form.

≡ Rapid Reference 3.3

....

Neural Signature of Dyslexia
   Disruption of posterior reading systems in the left hemisphere while reading
      real or nonsense words.
   Overactivation in other areas of the reading system.
   Involvement of parietotemporal system that includes the primary auditory
      cortex and Wernicke's area.
   Involvement of the occipitotemporal system that includes VWFA.
   Involvement of the posterior left frontal lobe that includes Broca's area.

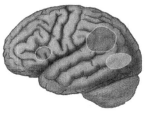 

Nonimpaired   Dyslexic

Figure 3.3 Neural Signature for Dyslexia: Disruption of Posterior Reading Systems
This schematic view depicts the left hemisphere brain systems in both nonimpaired readers (left) and readers with dyslexia (right). In readers with dyslexia, the anterior system is slightly overactivated compared with systems of nonimpaired readers; in contrast, the two posterior systems are underactivated. This pattern of underactivation in left posterior reading systems is referred to as the neural signature for dyslexia.
Source: Reprinted from S. Shaywitz (2003) with permission.

In contrast, posterior medial occipitotemporal activation, comparable to that observed in readers with dyslexia, was noted during reading of Kanji script (Nakamura et al., 2005). Consideration of the mechanisms used for reading Kanji compared to Kana provides insights into potentially different mechanisms that develop with age in readers with dyslexia contrasted to typical readers. Kanji script uses ideographs where each character must be memorized, suggesting that the left posterior medial occipitotemporal system functions as a memory-based system. It is reasonable to suppose that as children with dyslexia mature this posterior medial system supports memorization rather than the progressive sound-symbol linkages observed in typical readers. There is evidence that readers with dyslexia are not able to make good use of sound-symbol linkages as they mature and instead, come to rely on memorized words. For example, phonological deficits continue to characterize struggling readers even as they enter adolescence and adulthood (e.g., Bruck, 1992; S. Shaywitz et al., 1999). Poor adult readers read words by memorization so that they are able to read familiar words but have difficulty reading unfamiliar words (S. Shaywitz et al., 2003).

Thus, these results support and now extend previous findings to indicate that the system responsible for the integration of letters and sounds, the left anterior lateral occipitotemporal system, is the neural circuit that develops with age in typical readers. Conversely, readers with dyslexia, who struggle to read new or unfamiliar words, come to rely on an alternate system, the left posterior medial occipitotemporal system that functions via memory networks.

DON'T FORGET

Extensive research demonstrates that individuals with dyslexia rely on memorization of words rather than phonetic decoding and, therefore, are often unable to decode unfamiliar words.

Although readers with dyslexia exhibit an inefficiency of functioning in the left occipitotemporal word-form area, they appear to develop ancillary systems involving areas around the inferior frontal gyrus in both hemispheres as well as the right hemisphere homologue of the left occipitotemporal word-form area (B. Shaywitz et al., 2002). While these ancillary systems allow readers with dyslexia to read accurately, their reading continues to be nonfluent; that is, slow and effortful.

A summary of the neurological characteristics of individuals with dyslexia is presented in Rapid Reference 3.4.

STATISTICAL ISSUES IN FUNCTIONAL BRAIN IMAGING

As functional brain imaging matures, investigators are becoming increasingly aware of potential concerns in the analysis of functional images. This awareness

≡ *Rapid Reference 3.4*

Neurological Characteristics of Individuals with Dyslexia
The brains of individuals with dyslexia show different and less efficient patterns of processing when reading:

- Less activation of posterior reading systems in left hemisphere.
- Less temporoparietal activation.
- Less occipitoparietal activation.
- More activation left frontal, right frontal, and right occipitotemporal systems.
- Age-related differences noted between nonimpaired readers and those with dyslexia, especially in the VWFA.
- Readers with dyslexia tend to rely on memorization of words.
- Differences persist into adulthood, affecting development of reading fluency and spelling.

has focused primarily on two issues: multiple testing and nonindependence errors in the analysis of correlation data. The issues and terms discussed in this section may be familiar to some readers but not to others. To aid the readers with less background in this topic, Rapid Reference 3.5 provides a simplified explanation of the key statistical issues. The issues involving multiple testing arise because of the very large numbers of data points that emanate from an fMRI study. For example, it has been estimated that relatively simple image production involves 40,000 to 500,000 data points. By necessity,

DON'T FORGET

The neural systems used for reading differ for typical readers and readers with dyslexia.

Individuals with dyslexia use a more posterior and medial system. Furthermore, as they mature, they may use right hemisphere systems to compensate for their inability to make sound-print associations.

≡ *Rapid Reference 3.5*

Simplified Explanation of Key Issues

Multiple testing: The more comparisons you make within a sample, the more likely it is that you will find a difference or relationship of note. The danger is that the finding may not generalize to an independent sample and you may have false positives and false negatives.

False positive (Type I error): A Type I error is an incorrect conclusion that a finding is significant even though it is not. This is analogous to a pregnancy test being positive even though the woman is not pregnant, or a court finding someone guilty who is actually innocent, or a diagnosis indicating that someone has a specific disability who actually does not.

False negative (Type II error): An incorrect conclusion that a finding is not significant even though it really is. This is analogous to a pregnancy test being negative even though the woman is really pregnant, or a court finding someone innocent who was indeed guilty, or a diagnosis indicating that someone does not have a disability who actually does have it.

Nonindependence error: This type of error involves using the same data to look for and then calculate results that may lead to a bias in the results, and incorrect conclusions. There must be independence between selection and analysis. A sample that is not representative of the whole population is a simplistic example of selection bias, the most common type of a nonindependence error. If researchers generalize to an entire population based on conclusions from a nonrepresentative sample, errors will occur.

analysis of such a large volume of data involves multiple comparisons and the resulting well-known concern about false positives. A false positive, or Type I error, is an incorrect conclusion that a finding is significant when, in fact, it is not. Efforts to control for false positives by using traditional Bonferroni correction is not effective because in a data matrix of 500,000 by 500,000 data points, the calculated alpha level might be, for example, 1×10^{-8}—an overly cautious alpha level that is likely to produce Type II errors. A Type II error, or a false negative, is an incorrect conclusion that a finding is not significant when in fact, it really is. In an effort to remediate this statistical conundrum, multiple comparison methods have been designed to control the rate of false positives. Such methods include control for family-wise errors (FEW; Nichols & Hayasaka, 2003) and those that control for false discovery rate (FDR; Genovese, Lazar, & Nichols, 2002). The efficacy of these methods is yet to be fully determined and remains a subject of intense discussion.

More recently, investigators have become aware of still another statistical issue, the problem of nonindependence errors, particularly in studies designed to correlate brain imaging to social-emotional factors (Vul, Harris, Winkielman, & Pashler, 2009). Some statisticians consider nonindependence errors a special case of selection bias (Lazar, 2009). This problem arises when an investigator performs a whole-brain analysis for a particular correlation, selecting those data points where there is a significant correlation between brain activation and, for example, a particular behavior such as depression. These selected data points are then used in secondary analyses to obtain an aggregated final measure of correlation of the brain activation and behavior. The problem, as noted in the paper by Vul and associates, is that the process of preselecting only those points where there is significant correlation and then using these preselected data points in the final analysis will inflate the level of significance. The remedy for nonindependence errors is to avoid double dipping, and to use one set of data for the preselection and a totally different data set for the secondary, aggregated analysis.

CAUTION

Findings from fMRI studies may be subject to both Type I and Type II errors as well as selection bias due to statistical issues in the methodologies used to design the study and analyze the data.

Issues of multiple testing and nonindependence errors have not only been a problem in brain imaging but also arise in other important areas touching on behavioral issues, for example, genetic studies (Benjamini, 2008; Efron, 2008). In fact, genetic studies often have had to be retracted because the studies could not be replicated. It is important that end-users of functional brain imaging be aware of these issues and watch for new developments related to these two significant statistical issues.

BRAIN STRUCTURE ABNORMALITIES IMPLICATED IN DYSLEXIA

In addition to the findings from fMRI studies, a variety of studies have examined structural brain changes in individuals with dyslexia. The earliest of these studies examined postmortem brains from individuals with a history of dyslexia who had died tragically from motorcycle accidents (Galaburda, 1989). More recent studies use quantitative, often automated, MRI techniques as well as techniques that track structural changes in cerebral white matter using diffusion tensor imaging (DTI). For completeness, these studies are referenced, but the reader is cautioned that, in contrast to the results from fMRI studies, the findings from these structural and DTI studies are more variable, often inconsistent, and difficult to interpret. With the use of MRI and DTI technology, some of the structural differences documented in individuals with dyslexia include (a) unusual symmetry (same size on left and right hemispheres) and asymmetry (different size) of structures in the cerebrum (Leonard & Eckert, 2008); (b) irregularities in the corpus callosum of children and adults with dyslexia (Sun, Lee, & Kirby, 2010); (c) white and gray matter abnormalities (El-Baz, Casanova, Gimel'farb, Mott, & Switala, 2008; Eliez et al., 2000); and (d) volume differences and smaller volumes in the cerebral lobes and the cerebellum (Eckert et al., 2003; Zadina et al., 2006).

> **DON'T FORGET**
> ....
> MRI and DTI are imaging techniques that show the inactive brain, allowing researchers to make comparisons between typical and abnormal structures. MRI scans show the different structures of the brain. DTI scans highlight the neural fibers that connect the lobes of the brain with each other.

More recent studies have demonstrated a widespread network of neural systems involved in dyslexia. For example, structural magnetic resonance imaging (MRI) and novel surface-based image analysis techniques were used to measure cortical thickness, sulcal depth and cortical folding complexity across the entire medial and lateral surface of the brain in groups of readers with dyslexia and readers with no reading impairments. Findings indicated differences between these groups in parietotemporal-occipital cortices bilaterally, as well as right inferior frontal gyrus, and anterior cingulate regions in the left hemisphere, and right dorsal and ventral frontal regions (Tosun et al., 2009).

In another recent report, DTI was used to examine correlations between white matter structure, as measured by the diffusion parameter fractional anisotropy (FA), and reading ability in a large sample of individuals with dyslexia compared to typical adolescents and young adults. Findings indicated many brain areas with significant correlations between FA, a DTI measure of white matter microstructure and reading, including the left temporal-parietal area that has emerged consistently as a region related to reading ability. However, in addition, in this large sample size study using DTI, more widespread correlations were observed than found in other studies, suggesting that an extensive bihemispheric network of brain regions is involved in reading processes (Lebel et al., 2010).

> ## CAUTION
>
> Although brain images that use MRI and DTI technology provide evidence of structural differences in some individuals with dyslexia, these studies are variable, inconsistent, and difficult to interpret.

IMPLICATIONS OF BRAIN IMAGING STUDIES

A growing body of evidence from around the world clearly indicates that dyslexia is real. These findings are universal, having been demonstrated not only in readers of English, but also in readers of Italian, French, and German (e.g., Brambati et al., 2006; Kronbichler et al., 2006; Paulesu et al., 2001) and with similar findings in readers of logographic languages, such as Chinese, where the visual symbols most commonly represent morphemes and syllables rather than phonemes (Perfetti, 2011). In addition, the disruption of the neural systems for reading is found in both younger and older readers, providing strong evidence for the persistence of reading difficulties, particularly the lack of fluency that results in slow reading throughout life.

> ## CAUTION
>
> Readers with dyslexia do not read quickly and, consequently, are at a distinct disadvantage compared to typical peers when taking high-stakes, timed standardized tests. It is important to ensure that a sufficient amount of extended time is provided on all high-stakes tests. "A dyslexic needs extra time the same way a diabetic requires insulin" (Shaywitz, 2003, p. 322).

Inefficient functioning in the VWFA also has important practical implications regarding the provision of accommodations for individuals with dyslexia. For the first time, fMRI has provided neurobiological evidence

Neural Basis for Extended Time

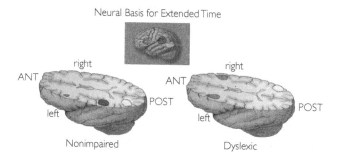

right   right

ANT   ANT

POST   POST

left   left

Nonimpaired   Dyslexic

Figure 3.4   Neural Basis for the Requirement for Extended Time for Students with Dyslexia on High-Stakes Testing

This image shows a cutaway view of the brain so that both left and right hemispheres are visible. Nonimpaired readers (left panel) activate three left hemisphere neural systems for reading: an anterior system and two posterior systems. Readers with dyslexia (right panel) have a disruption in the left hemisphere posterior neural systems for reading but compensate (partially) by developing anterior systems in left and right hemispheres and the posterior homologue of the visual word-form area in the right hemisphere. However, the critical VWFA remains underactivated.

Source: Reprinted from S. Shaywitz (2003) with permission.

demonstrating that readers with dyslexia require the accommodation of extra time on high-stakes standardized tests. The nonfluent reading observed in both children and adults with dyslexia provides the neurobiological evidence for the biologic necessity for the accommodation of additional time on high-stakes tests. Figure 3.4 illustrates the neural basis for the justification of the accommodation of extra time, a necessity for individuals with dyslexia. A further implication is that past high school or the early years of postsecondary schooling, if the initial diagnosis of dyslexia was accurate, there should be no need for further assessment to reconfirm the diagnosis or to provide a rationale for the need for accommodations.

CONCLUSION

The brain imaging studies reviewed in this chapter provide the neurobiological evidence that clarifies our current understanding of the nature of dyslexia. Dyslexia is real, and actual brain differences do exist. Understanding how brain structures and functions contribute to the classroom challenges that children face will ultimately inform more tailored interventions for these children (Katzir & Pare-Blagoev, 2006).

 **TEST YOURSELF**

1. **Historically, which term was used to describe developmental dyslexia?**
   a. Acquired dyslexia
   b. Congenital word blindness
   c. Acquired alexia
   d. Broca's aphasia

2. **The main function of cerebral white matter is to**
   a. separate lobes within the cerebral cortex.
   b. generate responses to environmental conditions.
   c. connect portions of the cerebral cortex, cerebellum, brain stem, and spinal cord.
   d. process language-related information.

3. **The visual word-form area (VWFA) is located in the**
   a. angular gyrus in the parietal lobe.
   b. occipitotemporal area.
   c. temporal lobe.
   d. anterior system in the inferior frontal gyrus.

4. **The corpus callosum is a white matter structure that connects**
   a. the cerebral cortex and the cerebellum.
   b. the frontal lobe with the occipital lobe.
   c. the left and right cerebral hemispheres.
   d. the brain stem with the cerebrum.

5. **Studies in children with dyslexia using fMRI show a failure of right hemisphere posterior brain systems to function properly during reading. True or False?**

6. **Most language-related tasks are processed in the**
   a. cerebellum.
   b. brain stem.
   c. right hemisphere.
   d. left hemisphere.

7. **The visual cortex is located in the**
   a. frontal lobe.
   b. parietal lobe.
   c. temporal lobe.
   d. occipital lobe.

8. **The primary auditory cortex is located in the**
   a. frontal lobe.
   b. parietal lobe.
   c. temporal lobe.
   d. occipital lobe.

9. **Expressive aphasia may result from damage to**
   a. Broca's area.
   b. Wernicke's area.
   c. Gerner's area.
   c. the cerebellum.

10. **Readers with dyslexia tend to rely on the memorization of words. True or False?**

11. **Readers with dyslexia use the same neural systems as nonimpaired readers, but they are less fluent. True or False?**

12. **The folds in the cerebral cortex create the appearance of smooth areas or ridges and furrows in the brain. The smooth areas or ridges are _____ and the furrows or grooves are _____.**

13. **Brain structure differences persist into adulthood, affecting development of reading fluency, and spelling. True or False?**

14. **FMRI has been useful in determining which particular regions of brain are used in performing a task, because fMRI measures**
   a. the electrical stimulation in the brain.
   b. the amount of blood in the brain.
   c. the blood-oxygenation-level dependent response.
   d. all of the above.
   e. none of the above.

15. **Little variability exists between brain structures in individuals with dyslexia. Brain imaging techniques can be used without additional testing to diagnose dyslexia. True or False?**

Answers: 1. b; 2. c; 3 b; 4. c; 5. False; 6. d; 7. d; 8. c; 9. a; 10. True; 11. False; 12. gyri, sulci; 13. True; 14. c; 15. False

Chapter Four

GENETICS AND THE ENVIRONMENT

The route through childhood is shaped by many forces, and it differs for each of us. Our biological inheritance, the temperament with which we are born, the care we receive, our family relationships, the place where we grow up, the schools we attend, the culture in which we participate, and the historical period in which we live—all these affect the paths we take through childhood and condition the remainder of our lives.

—Wozniak, 1991

One of the oldest debates in developmental psychology is nature versus nurture: the role of genes (nature) and the environment (nurture) in determining a child's development (Hulme & Snowling, 2009). One reason for studying genetic influences is to attempt to tease apart the effects of nature versus nurture. Clearly, both play a significant role in dyslexia and an individual's reading development. Development is based on three main classes of influences: genes (G), environments (E), and the interactions between the two (G × E; Hulme & Snowling, 2009). Multiple genetic and environmental risk factors are involved (Pennington, 2009).

GENETICS

Children inherit their genetic information from their parents. Some children are born with genes that give them an increased risk of developing dyslexia (Hulme & Snowling, 2009). Scientists have known for many years that genes have a substantial influence on the development of both reading and spelling skills and that dyslexia runs in families (Bishop & Snowling, 2004; Grigorenko, 2004; Hallgren, 1950; Muter & Snowling, 2009; Pennington & Olson, 2007). Early studies and case reports provided strong evidence to support the familial transmission of dyslexia (e.g., Bakwin, 1973; DeFries, Singer, Foch, & Lewitter, 1978; Hallgren, 1950).

People are born with dyslexia; dyslexia is not acquired. If reading problems develop during an individual's lifetime due to specific brain damage, the disorder is referred to as acquired alexia, not dyslexia. Thus, children from families where a close relative has dyslexia are predisposed to having reading difficulties (Muter & Snowling, 2009). Between 30% and 50% of children with a parent who has dyslexia will develop the disorder (Pennington & Lefly, 2001; van Bergen et al., 2011). If one child in the family has dyslexia, about half of his sisters and brothers are also likely to have dyslexia (Shaywitz, 2003, p. 99). Sometimes, a parent does not recognize that she has dyslexia until one of her children has been diagnosed. In addition, parents may not know whether or not relatives have dyslexia, but they are usually able to accurately report on the reading and spelling difficulties of family members (Pennington, 2009). Thus, a formal educational evaluation for dyslexia should begin with exploration of a family history of reading difficulty (Uhry & Clark, 2005).

DON'T FORGET

Family history can help predict risk for dyslexia so that early, intensive environmental interventions can be prescribed to reduce the risk of reading failure (Olson, 2006).

CAUTION

When a child has poor reading and is referred for a reading evaluation, it is important to attempt to determine whether a family history of such problems exists. If it does, informing parents of the genetic influences of dyslexia alerts them to the possible at-risk status of other children in their family (Muter & Snowling, 2009).

GENES AND CHROMOSOMES

The field of molecular genetics is concerned with the study of how hereditary information is passed from one generation to the next, as well as which specific genes may contribute to the development of disorders. Although the human genome is not fully understood, this genome contains all of the biological information that would be needed to build a living person. Biological information is encoded on these genes in deoxyribonucleic acid (DNA), which is often referred to as the building block of the human body. The human genome is currently estimated to contain between 20,000 and 25,000 genes that are then expressed in human DNA. Genes instruct each cell type, such as brain cells or liver cells, when to make sets of proteins. Genes are the hereditary units located on chromosomes, which are the threadlike structures located in the nucleus of each cell. Each chromosome has proteins and a single molecule of DNA containing many genes. Chromosomes are arranged in pairs within the nucleus of the cells. Humans have 23 pairs of chromosomes, and they determine everything from the color of your eyes to your gender. For example, pair 23 determines the sex of a child. If the child inherits two Xs, she will be a girl. If the child inherits one X and one Y chromosome, he will be a boy. The mother always contributes an X chromosome and the father may contribute either an X or a Y chromosome, so the gender of the child is determined by the father. Half of the chromosomes come from the mother, and half come from the father, which is why children inherit traits from each parent.

Each chromosome is divided into two arms that are based on the center where the strands cross over (see Figure 4.1). The use of letters and numbers provides the location of a gene on a specific chromosome, much like the number on a street address. The number represents the number of the chromosome, the letter "p" is used to represent the short arm of the chromosome, and the letter "q" represents the long arm.

Because genes play a central role in brain development, researchers during the last decade have attempted to identify the specific genes that are relevant to the transmission of dyslexia. Since reading is a cultural invention, genes that are designed specifically for reading do not exist, and there is no one gene that causes dyslexia. Instead, there are only genetic influences on the development of reading proficiency (Pennington & Olson, 2007). Because dyslexia is familial and heritable, researchers had initially hoped that dyslexia would be explained by just one or only a few genes, but unfortunately, the results have been

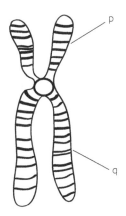

Figure 4.1 Example of a Human Chromosome

disappointing (Meaburn, Harlaar, Craig, Schalkwyk, & Plomin, 2008; Thomson & Raskind, 2003). As of yet, the functions of specific genes and the exact roles these genes play in dyslexia are not completely understood, and the research findings are complex. What is known, however, is that multiple genes of small effect as well as environmental factors contribute to the development of dyslexia (Grigorenko, 2005; Pennington, Peterson, & McGrath, 2009). When multiple genes are involved, it is difficult to pinpoint the role of any one gene because the effect of that one gene is too small to be distinguishable. The genes work in concert with one another, in addition to environmental influences, creating the phenotype (dyslexia). This is analogous to trying to determine a constellation by viewing a single star. The star's effect is too small to see the bigger picture. The constellation is created by the combination of many stars, just as many genes contribute to dyslexia.

In addition, depending on the type of reading skill being evaluated (real word reading, nonword reading, or irregular word reading), different genes appear to be involved (Berninger, Nielsen, Abbott, Wijsman, & Raskind, 2008). The results from molecular genetic studies have implicated genes on five different chromosomal regions: 1p, 2p, 6p, 15q, and 18p, with more modest evidence identifying genes on the following regions: 6q, 3p, 11p, and Xq (Williams & O'Donovan, 2006). Dyslexia is therefore associated with genes on more than one chromosome but to date, the region on 6p has shown to be the most significant and the best replicated link (Hulme & Snowling, 2009; Olson, 2006; Pennington & Olson, 2007). Although findings have been replicated across several studies, no single locus has been confirmed by all of the studies (Grigorenko, 2005; Raskind, 2001) and in fact, a recent genome-wide association study concluded, "The finding of more general significance is that no associations greater than 0.5% were detected even though the sample of 4000 provided 99% power to detect them" (Meaburn et al., 2008, p. 736).

Several studies have investigated a number of isolated families with a high incidence of severe dyslexia, but it has been difficult to generalize the genetic mechanisms that are involved in these rare cases to the general population (Grigorenko, 2009). Parents with dyslexia who have children with dyslexia tend to be more severely impaired on word-reading and rapid automatized naming skills than parents with dyslexia who have children without dyslexia (van Bergen et al., 2011). Results from a longitudinal study suggest that the literacy difficulties of children with a family risk of dyslexia are longstanding with no evidence of catching-up in these skills between 8 and 13 years (Snowling, Muter, & Carroll, 2007). These results, however, have not been replicated in other studies and must be viewed with caution. The genetic influences of dyslexia appear to be most pronounced in cases that involve relatively severe phonological impairments that are out of line with the person's other cognitive and linguistic abilities (Bishop & Snowling, 2004). Overall, findings suggest that the heritability of dyslexia is higher in individuals who have poor ability to repeat nonsense words (Bishop, Adams, & Norbury, 2004). Research findings also suggest the heritability of orthographic coding, the ability to distinguish between written real words and pseudoword homonyms (Thomson & Raskind, 2003).

The concept of heritability is complex. Wang (2011) provides a clear explanation:

> Many behavioral genetic studies are designed to estimate the relative contributions of genetics versus environmental factors on various outcomes or diagnoses. The numerical parameter that is used to quantify genetic influences is known as heritability, which has a numerical range of 0 to 1.00 and is symbolized as h2. For example, studies of Attention-Deficit/Hyperactivity Disorder (AD/HD) estimate its heritability to be between 0.60 and 0.90, while studies of intelligence quotient (IQ) estimate its heritability from 0.50 to 0.85, with values tending higher with increasing age (that is, genetic factors have a larger influence in older ages). It should be understood that heritability is an abstract mathematical parameter that is not known to have a tangible reality. That is, if the heritability of reading disability is 0.75, it does not imply that 75% of all cases of dyslexia have an exclusively genetic etiology, or that the child of a person with dyslexia has a 75% chance of having dyslexia, or any such implication. Heritability merely describes the proportion of the statistical variance in a trait that was attributable to genetics in a particular research study. (pp. 13–14)

CAUTION

Findings from longitudinal studies indicate the longstanding literacy problems of individuals with dyslexia, but they do not suggest that individuals cannot make progress in literacy skills.

DON'T FORGET

No single gene is responsible for the transmission of dyslexia in families. Instead, many genes of small effect appear to increase the risk involved.

TWIN STUDIES

Much of the research regarding the heritability of dyslexia has been based on the findings from twin studies. Twin studies provide a means of teasing apart the genetic and environmental influences underlying the etiology of dyslexia (Bishop, 2009). Identical twins derive from the same egg and sperm (monozygotic; MZ) so they share all genes, whereas fraternal twins come from two different eggs and sperm (dizygotic; DZ) so they share, on average, half of their genes. Twins also share the same environment at home, share the same parents, and usually attend the same schools. These commonalities of genetics and environment make twins the ideal population for studying individual differences.

In a study several decades ago, Bakwin (1973) examined the reading performance of 676 pairs of same sex twins. Of the MZ twins, 84% had a history of reading disabilities, whereas among the DZ twins, only 29% had reading disabilities. This type of finding provides evidence of the genetic influence because the reading performance of MZ twins who share all genes is more similar than the performance of the DZ twins who only share half of their genes (Olson, 2006). The fact that there was not 100% similarity among the MZ twins regarding their reading disability provides evidence that nongenetic factors are also involved in the development of dyslexia.

The Colorado Longitudinal Twin Study of Reading Disability (LTSRD), which began in 1982, is the first study in which the twins were selected for having a history of reading difficulties. Similar to results obtained from previous longitudinal studies, Wadsworth, DeFries, Olson, and Willcutt (2007) found that the 10-year-old twins with reading difficulties still had significant reading problems on follow-up assessments 5 to 6 years later, indicating that the same genetic influences are involved in reading performance at both time points. Other research has suggested that the same cognitive abilities that contribute to dyslexia (e.g., phonological awareness, orthographic coding, and short-term verbal memory skills) are equally important for the development of advanced reading ability (Boada et al., 2002). Rapid Reference 4.1 summarizes several findings from LTSRD twin studies across several decades (Olson, 2006).

CAUTION

Although much progress has been made in discovering the genes that are most related to dyslexia, additional research is needed. In addition, genes do not operate in isolation, and their expression is affected by a range of environmental influences.

≡ *Rapid Reference 4.1*

Sample Findings from the Longitudinal Twin Study of Reading Disability

Early studies indicated genetic influence on reading disability.

Deficits in orthographic coding have shown the most significant genetic influence.

Deficits in phoneme awareness, phonological decoding, and orthographic decoding are partially influenced by the same genes.

The relationship between phoneme awareness and phonological decoding is stronger than the relationship between phoneme awareness and orthographic coding.

The genetic influences on reading measures are stable across the school age years.

The genetic influence is more pronounced in poor readers with higher intelligence test scores than those with lower intelligence scores.

The same cognitive variables that influence dyslexia also support advanced reading skill.

Another major longitudinal study of over 13,000 twins is the Twins Early Development Study (TEDS), which began in England and Wales from 1994 to 1996. The focus of TEDS is broader than the Colorado twin study, as a major goal is to investigate the genetic and environmental origins of the most common childhood problems, not just reading and attentional problems. As with findings from LTSRD, results from TEDS studies have indicated that both reading and writing abilities are predicted by both genetics and shared environmental factors (Oliver & Plomin, 2007).

CAUTION

Even though dyslexia is highly heritable, specific genes can only account for a very small amount of the variability in reading ability (Meaburn et al., 2008). Environmental factors play an important role.

GENDER DIFFERENCES

Throughout the past century, scientists have attempted to determine whether boys are more likely to have dyslexia than girls. Hinshelwood (1917) claimed that boys had a higher incidence of word blindness than girls. Although the ratio of males to females in both research-based and referral samples of children with dyslexia varies depending on the type of methodology employed, studies typically report a slightly greater number of males than females with reading problems, with an increased number of males in more severely impaired samples (Hawke, Olson, Willcutt, Wadsworth, & DeFries, 2009). However, there is little to no evidence to suggest that the reading difficulties experienced by boys and girls result from a differential genetic etiology (Hawke, Wadsworth, & DeFries, 2006). Some possible reasons for the increased number of boys identified with dyslexia follow.

Hawke et al. analyzed reading and spelling assessment data from 1,133 twin pairs in which at least one member had a history of reading difficulties. They concluded that greater variability existed among the scores of the males than of the females and that this variability can account for the increased prevalence of males, particularly in more impaired samples. Because their performance is more extreme (lower and higher than females), more males would be selected when cutoff scores, such as two standard deviations below the mean on standard scores on reading tests, are used to select the sample.

Similar differences appear to also exist in writing skill. Berninger et al. (2008) found in examining both children and adults with dyslexia that males were more impaired in handwriting, spelling, and composing than were females. Although boys performed similarly to the girls on the reading measures, men were more impaired than women in accuracy and rate of reading passages orally, as well as orthographic skills.

Another factor that affects gender ratios in reading disorders is that identification often depends on school procedures (Shaywitz, 2003, p. 31). In school settings, boys with dyslexia are more likely to be referred for testing than are girls. This may be the case because boys usually exhibit more externalizing (acting out) disorders, whereas girls have lower rates of comorbid disorders, and when they do, they are more likely to have internalizing disorders, such as anxiety and depression (Pennington et al., 2009). Furthermore, dyslexia research often uses subjects that have been classified by schools as having learning disabilities, therefore creating a biased sample overrepresented by boys. Studies that employ selection criteria independent from school classification often yield comparable numbers of reading disabilities between boys and girls (Shaywitz, 2003, p. 32).

CAUTION

More males are often identified as having reading disorders; however, it is believed that both males and females are similarly affected by dyslexia.

COMORBIDITY

A central characteristic of complex behavioral disorders like dyslexia is that it tends to co-occur with other complex disorders in the population more often than would be expected by chance (Caron & Rutter, 1991; Pennington & Olson, 2007). The term that is used to refer to this overlap of disorders is *comorbidity*. This means that two disorders can coexist, but they differ and do not cause each other. Approximately 60% of children with reading disability also meet the diagnostic criteria for another disorder, making it the rule rather than an exception (Ebejer et al., 2010; Willcutt & Pennington, 2000). Understanding comorbidity is important because practitioners need to understand which condition to treat first, as well as understanding the differences between students with comorbid disorders and those who have a specific disorder in isolation (Willcutt et al., 2007).

The most common disorders that co-occur with dyslexia and can also contribute to reading problems include attention deficit hyperactivity disorder (ADHD), speech sound disorder (SSD), and specific language impairment (SLI). ADHD involves difficulty focusing or sustaining attention; SSD involves problems in the articulation of sounds and the accuracy of sound production and appears to be independent of other language disorders; and SLI involves more generalized atypical oral language development. While there is some overlap, differences do exist among these disorders. As examples, a deficit in phonological processing is closely associated with dyslexia but not with SLI when it occurs in the absence of dyslexia (Catts, Adlof, Hogan, & Ellis-Weismer, 2005). Similarly, nonword repetition, also a measure of short-term phonological memory, is impaired in individuals with both a language and reading impairment, but not in individuals with a language impairment alone. Nonword repetition is particularly impaired in individuals with reading decoding problems. Thus, poor performance on nonword repetition tasks appears to be a marker for a language impairment that co-occurs with dyslexia (Baird, Slonims, Simonoff, & Dworzynski, 2011; Catts et al., 2005). Although these are all distinct disorders, and the genetic influences are not identical, language and reading impairments are often closely related clinical conditions (Rice, Smith, & Gayan, 2009). In addition, individuals with dyslexia can also have problems in behavior, motor coordination, and mathematics.

DON'T FORGET

....

Comorbidity means that two different disorders can be present within an individual.

Although each of these three disorders has distinct characteristics, individuals with one or more of these disorders can exhibit low performance on the same types of cognitive and linguistic tasks. For example, performance on tasks involving short-term memory (e.g., repeating a string of digits), as well as the ability to repeat nonsense words orally (say, "preambinatory"), can be problematic for individuals with ADHD, SSD, and SLI (Grigorenko, 2009). Thus, a child with dyslexia and another child with SLI may both have difficulty repeating a string of digits or orally presented nonsense words. One possible explanation for this comorbidity is that numerous components and combinations of genes appear to be deficient in more than one disorder so that a shared genetic etiology exists (Grigorenko, 2009).

The most common comorbid condition with dyslexia appears to be ADHD. Estimates suggest that 15% to 40% of children with dyslexia are also diagnosed with ADHD, and 25% to 40% of children with ADHD are also diagnosed with dyslexia (Semrud-Clikeman et al., 1992; Willcutt & Pennington, 2000). Although these disorders differ, both dyslexia and ADHD share both cognitive and genetic risk factors; in fact, the 6p locus appears to contribute to dyslexia, ADHD, and SSD (Pennington & Olson, 2007). ADHD is even more heritable than dyslexia with an average heritability of .73, which suggests that nearly three-fourths of the symptoms characterizing this neurodevelopmental condition can be accounted for by genetics, with only one-fourth attributed to environmental factors. Essentially, this means that the shared environment of twins will have little effect on the development of this disorder and that any differences in behavior result from nonshared environmental influences in the school or home (Willcutt, Pennington, Chhabildas, Olson, & Hulslander, 2005).

Using a large population-based birth cohort, Yoshimasu et al. (2010) found that the risk for reading disability was much higher for children with ADHD than for those without ADHD and that among the children with ADHD, the risk was similar for both boys and girls. Among children without ADHD, however, the boys were more at risk for reading disability than girls. One further study that has addressed comorbid conditions is the International Longitudinal Twin Study (ILTS) that includes twin pairs from Australia, Norway, Sweden, and the United States (Ebejer et al., 2010). The purpose of this study is to identify genetic and environmental influences on the development of early literacy,

CAUTION

Because of the high comorbidity between dyslexia and ADHD, clinicians should assess all children with ADHD for the presence of a comorbid reading disability (Yoshimasu et al., 2010).

language, and behavior. As with earlier research, Ebejer and colleagues found that inattention and hyperactivity-impulsivity were partially independent and that the strongest relationship was between reading and inattention. Thus, inattention appears to undermine reading development as children progress through school.

Clearly, the attempt to identify specific genes implicated in dyslexia and other developmental disorders is complex and further research is needed. Rapid Reference 4.2 summarizes several important points that have been learned from research. In the future, there may be a gene-based diagnostic test that could identify dyslexia prior to school entry so that specialized interventions could be started at a younger age. Although some progress has been made in understanding the contribution of specific genes to dyslexia, at present the search results for candidate genes are inconclusive and more complex than ever imagined. In addition, the genetic foundation of dyslexia may not be formed by isolated genes, but rather by a combination of genes and the pathways that they regulate (Grigorenko, 2009).

ENVIRONMENT

Even though some aspects of reading development are under genetic influences, the environment to which children are exposed also plays a key role in reading outcomes. Clearly, learning and behavior can be modified by the environment. The genotype of dyslexia would be the inherited characteristics,

---

≡ Rapid Reference 4.2

....

Summary of Research on Genetics and Dyslexia
  Dyslexia has a genetic basis.
  Slightly more males than females are identified as having dyslexia (on average about 1.5:1), but males have a higher referral rate (Pennington, 2009).
  The heritability is higher in individuals with severe phonological impairments.
  Gender ratio estimates vary depending on the methodology employed.
  Multiple genes on various chromosomes are implicated.
  High comorbidity exists between dyslexia and ADHD, SSD, and SSI.
  Dyslexia may also co-occur with problems in language, motor skills, and mathematics.
  The genetic influences may vary by age, gender, or language.
  Further research is needed to clarify exactly how specific genes contribute to dyslexia.
  Environmental factors can also influences outcomes.

whereas the phenotype, the characteristics of the person, would be determined by the interaction between the expression of genes and the environmental factors in both the home and the school. Environment can increase or decrease the potential of the genetic factors. Thus, learning is affected by the complex relationships among individual characteristics, as well as by family- and school-based influences (Goldstein & Brooks, 2007). Although neither the home nor school environment cause dyslexia, both can have an impact on a child's reading development. Because most research involves biological family units, it is difficult to separate genetic influences from environmental influences (Hart & Petrill, 2009).

HOME ENVIRONMENT

Essentially, the two main ways that home environment affects reading performance is parental involvement and commitment to their child's reading performance, as well as the alignment of the home and school culture. In addition, strong verbal abilities and intelligence are also protective, or compensatory, factors. Parents are often the first to observe their child's difficulties with early literacy skills. They may note that their child does not seem to retain the letter names, want to look at the print during reading time, or recognize her own name after numerous exposures. The child may also have mild articulation difficulties that result in faulty pronunciations of words. Rapid Reference 4.3 presents several early warning signs that parents may note.

Early reading experiences are also important for language and vocabulary growth. Clearly, an impoverished linguistic environment will affect a child's reading development. Rapid Reference 4.4 lists several factors in the home environment discussed by Aaron, Joshi, and Quatroche (2008) that could negatively affect reading achievement. As they note, these influences do not mean that children in poor circumstances are destined to fail at reading, or that children from wealthy families are guaranteed to succeed. Instruction can have a positive

≡ Rapid Reference 4.3

Early Warning Signs of Dyslexia
  Mild speech or articulation problems.
  Trouble rhyming words.
  Trouble recalling the letter names.
  Not interested in looking at print.

≡ Rapid Reference 4.4

Factors in the Home Environment That Affect Reading Achievement
The number and quality of books in the home.
The number of pages read daily.
The number of school absences.
The number of hours spent watching television.
The educational level and income of the parents.

impact on reading achievement, irrespective of the child's initial reading ability (Foorman et al., 2006). Research has found that the shared environmental influences (i.e., home, parents, school) are dominant for print knowledge during the preschool years; however, by the end of first grade, genetic influences may account for 65% to 80% of the variation in a child's response to instruction (Samuelsson et al., 2008).

If parents are concerned about their child's reading, it is of critical importance that they pursue a good comprehensive evaluation for their child. The evaluation should explain the reading difficulties and propose appropriate interventions that result in specific, intensive instruction in reading and writing from a skilled, knowledgeable reading teacher. Ideally, the evaluation and instruction would be provided at school. Often, however, the instruction provided in schools lacks intensity, and an outside tutor is needed. Fortunately, some schools have highly trained reading teachers with specific training in systematic interventions for dyslexia.

SCHOOL ENVIRONMENT

Although some children learn to read prior to school entry, many children begin to learn to read in kindergarten and first grade. Several factors influence how effective the school environment can be in addressing the needs of students with dyslexia. Of foremost importance is the student's relationship with his teachers. Ideally, student-teacher and teacher-parent relationships should be supportive and cooperative. Classroom teachers have the primary responsibility for creating a nurturing environment where all students feel respected, valued, and supported academically, emotionally, and socially (Mather & Goldstein, 2008). Although all children can benefit from a positive classroom environment, an excellent classroom teacher and a supportive classroom environment are critical for children with dyslexia. Because children with dyslexia often have

low self-esteem related to the slowness of their reading and writing development, a teacher must be particularly sensitive and ensure that situations are
avoided that would be embarrassing to the child, such as asking the child to read
aloud in front of the class or to change papers with another student for grading
purposes.

Children with dyslexia require appropriate instruction. Results from intervention studies suggest that the nature of the program is less important than its com-
prehensiveness and intensity (Fletcher,
Lyon, Fuchs, & Barnes, 2007). For
example, Torgesen, Alexander and colleagues (2001) found the same positive
outcomes for two different reading
programs that both provided intensive,
systematic one-to-one instruction.
Effective instructional elements include
small group instruction with high
response rates, the provision of immediate feedback, and the sequential mastery
of topics, all elements of good teaching (National Joint Committee on Learning
Disabilities, 2005). Children with dyslexia must also spend time reading. Rapid
Reference 4.5 lists several factors in the school environment that can affect reading improvement and achievement. For detailed information about appropriate
reading and spelling instruction for individuals with dyslexia, see Chapters 7–9 as
well as the interventions described in the Appendix.

DON'T FORGET

Effective intervention includes
small group instruction, sequential
presentation of content, and
provision of immediate feedback.

≡ *Rapid Reference 4.5*

Factors in the School Environment That Affect Reading Achievement
The provision of early intervention in preschool and kindergarten to at-risk
students.
The amount and type of training of the general education and special educa-
tion teachers.
The size of the class or classes.
The opportunities for reading practice.
The implementation of a structured, intensive reading methodology.
The amount of individualized or small group instruction.
The availability of appropriate reading materials.
The availability of technology.
The acceptance of individual differences.

CONCLUSION

For now, what is known is that multiple genetic and environmental risk factors can contribute to dyslexia (S. Shaywitz & B. Shaywitz, in press). Genetics appears to play an ongoing role in reading whereas the influences of environment impact early reading more. As we learn more about the roles of genes and the environment, we will be better able to design appropriate early intervention plans for young children with dyslexia. One benefit of recognizing that dyslexia is often inherited is that it may be helpful in the early identification of children at-risk for dyslexia so that intervention occurs during the optimal developmental period for learning to read. When early instruction is provided in school, the children learn the fundamentals of reading, thus reducing the influence of environmental differences that existed in preschool settings (Hart & Petrill, 2009).

Fortunately, our knowledge from genetic research is developing rapidly and more will be known in the coming years. However, currently and for the foreseeable future, genetic diagnosis is more of a promise than a reality. Reading is complex, and it involves various genetic and environmental influences. There is no one single reading gene or reading environment. The interaction of genes and specific environments is what affects reading development.

🖋 TEST YOURSELF 🖋

1. A specific gene has been identified that is responsible for the transmission of dyslexia. True or False?

2. Typically, slightly more males are diagnosed with dyslexia than females, and the referral rates for males are greater than females. True or False?

3. Comorbidity means that a person can have two different disorders at the same time. True or False?

4. The human genome
   a. is fully understood.
   b. contains 2,000–5,000 genes.
   c. contains all the biological information necessary to build a human being.
   d. is comprised of an X chromosome and a Y chromosome.

5. The roles of the specific genes that can contribute to dyslexia are not fully understood. True or False?

(continued)

6. **High comorbidity exists between dyslexia and**
   a. Specific Language Impairment.
   b. Speech Sound Disorder.
   c. Attention-Deficit/Hyperactivity Disorder.
   d. all of the above.

7. **Approximately, ____% of children with dyslexia are also diagnosed with ADHD.**
   a. 5–8
   b. 15–40
   c. 40–50
   d. more than 50

8. **Understanding the role that genetic and environmental factors play in dyslexia is important**
   a. for the diagnosis of dyslexia.
   b. because it facilitates early identification of children at-risk for dyslexia.
   c. because environment is more important than genetics.
   d. so that people will think dyslexia is a real disorder.

9. **The home environment appears to exert greatest influence on an individual's reading development**
   a. throughout the person's life.
   b. during the elementary school years.
   c. primarily in the preschool years.
   d. it does not influence reading.

10. **Reading problems are most closely related to problems with**
   a. impulsivity.
   b. hyperactivity.
   c. inattention.
   d. sleep deprivation.

Answers: 1. False; 2. True; 3. True; 4. c; 5. True; 6. d; 7. b; 8. b; 9. c; 10. c

Chapter Five

ASSESSMENT OF THE COGNITIVE AND LINGUISTIC CORRELATES OF DYSLEXIA

> Everything that can be counted does not necessarily count; everything that counts cannot necessarily be counted.
>
> —Einstein

Much of the research on dyslexia has centered on the cognitive and linguistic processes that contribute to and underlie dyslexia. To date, researchers have identified several specific cognitive and linguistic abilities that when deficient, may affect one's ability to learn to read and spell. These various processes are often assessed as part of a comprehensive evaluation for dyslexia. Essentially, the goal of a diagnostic evaluation is to determine what process or processes are not working properly and how they are affecting and slowing reading and spelling development (Hulme & Snowling, 2009).

A vast body of evidence exists regarding the role of phonological awareness and phonemic awareness in the development of reading skills. Research has also documented the influence of rapid automatized naming (RAN), processing speed, orthographic coding, morphological awareness, memory span, and working memory. In fact, new research documents that orthographic and morphological awareness are as critical as phonological awareness to the development of literacy (Berninger & May, 2011). Although oral language supports the development of reading skill and provides the basis for reading comprehension, poor oral language by itself, is not considered to be a primary factor or correlate that affects the development of basic reading skills and spelling. (Some individuals with dyslexia do, however, have comorbid language disorders.) Thus, a multiple deficit approach is important when studying and diagnosing a complex disorder such as dyslexia (McGrath et al., 2011).

This chapter explores the various correlates of dyslexia. A correlate is not the same as a cause, but rather it is an underlying ability that is associated with dyslexia. Although several correlates and predictors of dyslexia have been identified, most is known about the role of phonological awareness. In fact, poor phonological awareness has been described as the single best predictor of risk for early reading failure (Uhry, 2005).

PHONOLOGICAL AWARENESS

Phonological awareness refers to the ability to perceive and manipulate the sounds that make up the words in a person's language. For most children, the development of phonological awareness occurs automatically as part of language learning (Goswami, 2010). For a few children, however, awareness of language sounds does not come naturally or easily. When these children enter school, they do not understand the relationships between spoken and written words and their sounds and letters. In fact, many children with reading difficulties show problems in phonological awareness before they learn to read (Hulme & Snowling, 2009). Impaired phonological awareness is often described as the key deficit, early marker, proximal cause, or predominant core cognitive correlate of dyslexia (Catts, Adlof, Hogan, & Weismer, 2005; Fletcher, Lyon, Fuchs, & Barnes, 2007; Shaywitz, 2003; Snowling, 2000; Uhry, 2005).

As noted, in the discussion of definitions (Chapter 1), the most recent IDA definition of dyslexia indicates that phonological processing is the core problem responsible for difficulties in word recognition and identification, as well as acquisition of the alphabetic principle (Lyon, S. Shaywitz, & B. Shaywitz, 2003). Thus, poor phonological awareness makes it difficult for individuals with dyslexia to understand how speech sounds map to print for decoding and spelling words. Individuals with dyslexia are believed to have poorly specified phonological representations that make it difficult for them to acquire phonological awareness, alphabetic mapping, and letter-sound decoding (Vellutino & Fletcher, 2007). Put more simply, many individuals with dyslexia have trouble translating letter strings into their corresponding sound sequences (Pennington, 2009).

Understanding phonological awareness. As students learn to read and spell an alphabetic language like English, a critical first step is becoming aware that speech can be divided or segmented into a series of discrete sounds. This ability is often described as *phonological awareness*, a broad term that encompasses the ability to recognize that words are composed of discrete speech sounds and to perceive and manipulate language sounds. Phonological awareness is part of the larger unit of auditory perception, but it is only involved with the sounds that correspond to speech (Miller, Sanchez, & Hynd, 2003). This umbrella term includes the abilities to rhyme words, segment or break words into syllables, and be able to isolate and count the number of phonemes (Aaron, Joshi, & Quatroche, 2008).

A narrow aspect of phonological awareness is phonemic awareness. In phonemic awareness, the level of analysis is the phoneme, a single speech sound. Individual speech sounds are presented in slashes. For example, the word *sheep* is composed of three phonemes, /sh/ /ee/ and /p/. In writing, phonemes are represented by a single letter or a group of letters referred to as graphemes. The English alphabet has 26 letters that represent 42–44 dif-

> ## DON'T FORGET
> When a letter is enclosed in forward slashes / /, say the speech sound, not the letter name.

ferent phonemes or speech sounds. Of all the phonological awareness abilities, phonemic awareness is most important for early reading and spelling (Uhry, 2005). The ability to manipulate phonemes, as opposed to syllables, is most highly related to reading skill (Pennington, 2009).

Phonological awareness contributes to the accurate acquisition of word reading and spelling skills in three ways. It helps children (1) understand the alphabetic principle or how spoken words are represented in print; (2) recognize the ways that letters represent sounds in words, reinforcing knowledge of letter-sound correspondences; and (3) determine a word when it is only partially sounded out (Torgesen & Mathes, 2000). The alphabetic principle refers to the understanding that letters represent sounds that are ordered in a sequence in both spoken and written words (Uhry, 2005).

Beginning readers face two main challenges in acquiring the alphabetic principle (Torgesen & Mathes, 2000). First, when words are spoken, the phonemes overlap with one another, a process referred to as coarticulation. This overlapping of sounds permits the rapid communication of speech, rather than a sound-by-sound pronunciation (Fletcher et al., 2007). Thus, in fluent speech, one hears the word "dog" as one sound, rather than hearing three distinct sounds /d/ /o/ /g/. This process is automatic and quite unconscious (Liberman & Shankweiler, 1991).

> ## CAUTION
> Phonological awareness is not the same as phonics. *Phonological awareness* is the ability to hear the distinct sounds that make up words; this ability often develops before children learn to read. *Phonics* refers to an instructional method that facilitates reading and spelling development by teaching the relationships between sounds and letters and how to represent sounds in writing.

The second challenge is that in English there is not always a regular one-to-one correspondence between the phonemes (speech sounds) and the graphemes (written letters). The number of sounds in a word is not necessarily the same as the number of letters. For example, the word "shut" has four letters but three sounds: /sh/ /u/ /t/ whereas the word "box" has three letters but four sounds: /b/ /o/ /k/ and /s/. When children are first learning to spell, they listen carefully to words and attempt to record each of the sounds that they hear. For this reason, it makes perfect sense when a young child spells the word "box" as "boks."

DON'T FORGET

Phonological awareness is an oral language skill that provides the basis for learning phonics, or how letters are used to represent speech sounds for reading and spelling.

Symptoms of poor phonological awareness. Individuals with dyslexia exhibit a variety of symptoms that can indicate problems with phonology and the production and mastery of speech sounds. These difficulties can affect development in speech, word reading, and spelling. In many cases, however, speech develops normally, but word reading and spelling do not. Throughout their school careers, readers with dyslexia often have trouble reading phonically regular nonsense words that conform to English spelling patterns, a problem that has been associated with a deficit in phonemic awareness (NRP, 2000; Rack, Snowling, & Olson, 1992; Uhry & Clark, 2005). Rapid Reference 5.1 describes the different symptoms of poor phonological awareness that can affect speech, word reading, and spelling. Interestingly, research indicates that not all children with phonological deficits display problems in word reading, suggesting that other factors in addition to phonological awareness, such as motivation and interest, may affect the development of reading and spelling performance; thus, poor phonological awareness indicates a high risk for dyslexia, but dyslexia is not inevitable (Catts & Adlof, 2011).

Level of analysis. English words can be divided into four main levels of analysis: words, syllables, onsets and rimes, and phonemes. Figure 5.1 illustrates the word *alphabet* divided into syllables, onsets and rimes, and phonemes. In the English language, syllables are formed by a single vowel or vowels with varying combinations of consonants. The *onset* refers to the initial part of the syllable (i.e., one or

CAUTION

"Longitudinal research has shown that phonological awareness is *necessary but not sufficient* for becoming a good reader."
(Torgesen & Mathes, 2000, p. 5)

≡ *Rapid Reference 5.1*

Symptoms of Poor Phonological Awareness: Problems in Speech, Reading, and Spelling

- Articulation errors (e.g., *boo* for *blue, wooster* for *rooster*).
- Mispronunciations of multisyllabic words (e.g., *aminal* for *animal*).
- Trouble remembering sound-symbol relationships (e.g., the sound /bl/ is made with the letters b and l).
- Overreliance on whole-word and context cues when reading.
- Trouble pronouncing and spelling phonically regular nonsense words.
- Difficulty applying phonics to pronounce unfamiliar words.
- Slow reading rate.
- Difficulty sequencing sounds in words when spelling.
- Confusions between similar-sounding sounds (e.g., vowels, voiced and unvoiced consonant pairs).
- Tendency to rely on the visual appearance of words when spelling rather than on the phoneme-grapheme relationships.

more consonants) that precedes the vowel in a monosyllabic word, and the rime is the ending unit. Every syllable in English has a rime but not necessarily an onset. For example, in the two-syllable word "open," the first syllable "o" is considered to be a rime without an onset. The second syllable "-pen" contains the onset "p-" and the rime "-en." Anthony and Francis (2005) described the following two overlapping patterns of development: (1) children increase their sensitivity to the smaller parts of words as they grow older; and (2) they can first detect and manipulate syllables in words, then onsets and rimes, and finally phonemes.

> **DON'T FORGET**
>
> An *onset* includes the consonants before the vowel, whereas the *rime* is the ending unit that begins with a vowel. Every syllable in English has a rime, but not necessarily an onset. The *rime* is the part of the word that rhymes.

Production of phonemes. The ability to produce the sounds for different phonemes also follows a developmental course. Children can pronounce phonemes such as /m/ and /n/ by age 3, whereas phonemes such as /r/ and /z/ can take several more years to master; as a general principle, sounds that are produced in the front of the mouth (e.g., /m/) are acquired earlier than those that are produced in the back of the mouth (e.g., /r/; Aaron et al., 2008).

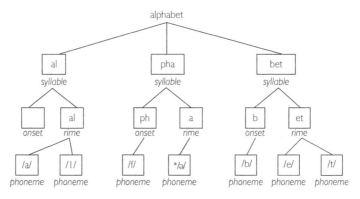

Figure 5.1   Levels of Analysis for the Word *Alphabet*
This figure depicts the levels of analysis for the word *alphabet*. This word is first divided into three syllables, *al, pha,* and *bet*. Syllables can then be divided into onsets and rimes. The syllable *al* does not have an onset because it lacks an initial consonant. Onsets and rimes can then be divided into phonemes. Note that the grapheme *ph* is made up of two letters (a digraph) that together form the one sound /f/. The schwa sound is an unstressed vowel sound in an unaccented syllable that sounds like the u in the word "ugh."
* The upside down e (phonetic symbol) is used to represent the schwa sound made by the vowel a in this syllable.

In addition, English has eight pairs of voiced and unvoiced consonants that are produced in the same manner and the same place in the mouth. The only difference in the manner of production of these phonemes is that one uses the vocal cords (voiced), whereas the other does not (unvoiced). If you say the words *big* and *pig* with your hand on your throat, you can feel that the production of the /b/ sound involves the vocal cords, whereas the production of the /p/ sound does not. Both children and adults with poor phonological awareness often confuse these sounds both in speaking and in spelling. For example, a student may pronounce the word "multiplication," as "multiblication," or "potato" as "butado." Rapid Reference 5.2 lists these pairs and provides an example of child-friendly terminology introduced as part of The Lindamood Phoneme Sequencing Program for Reading, Spelling, and Speech (LiPS; Lindamood & Lindamood, 1998, 2011). In the program, the unvoiced sounds are referred to as quiet sounds, whereas the voiced sounds are described as noisy. Notice that the /th/ sound can be unvoiced as in the word "thin," or voiced as in the word "then."

CAUTION

Early ear infections can contribute to articulation difficulties and interfere with mastery of phonemes.

≡ *Rapid Reference 5.2*

The Eight Voiced and Unvoiced Consonant Pairs

Unvoiced	Voiced	Terminology (Lindamood & Lindamood, 1998)
/p/ (pig)	/b/ (big)	Lip poppers
/t/ (time)	/d/ (dime)	Tip tappers
/k/ (kite)	/g/ (gate)	Scrapers
/f/ (fan)	/v/ (van)	Lip coolers
/th/ (thin)	/th/ (then)	Tongue coolers
/s/ (sew)	/z/ (zoo)	Skinny air sounds
/sh/ (sure)	/zh/ (measure)	Fat air sounds
/ch/ (chair)	/j/ (juice)	Fat pushed sounds

Reading teachers need to be able to identify children who struggle with the perception and production of phonemes, as well as to determine exactly which phonemes are the most troublesome for the child (Aaron et al., 2008).

ASSESSMENT OF PHONOLOGICAL AWARENESS

Individuals with dyslexia tend to perform poorly on all types of phonological tasks, but often do not have difficulty on other types of language tasks, such as measures of vocabulary or sentence comprehension (Fraser, Goswami, & Conti-Ramsden, 2010). The phonological deficit is domain-specific (i.e., affects development of reading but not other areas), and higher-order cognitive and linguistic abilities are often intact (S. E. Shaywitz & B. A. Shaywitz, 2003). As noted in Chapter 4, poor phonological awareness is closely associated with dyslexia, but not with specific language impairment when it occurs in the absence of dyslexia (Catts et al., 2005). Thus, an important part of a comprehensive assessment of dyslexia includes evaluation of performance on different types of phonological awareness tasks, as well as other oral language tasks to identify strengths. In order to assess phonological awareness, it is necessary to have some understanding of how and when these skills develop.

DON'T FORGET

Although some children have both a specific language impairment and dyslexia, these are distinct developmental disorders (Catts et al., 2005).

Development of phonological awareness. For most children, phonological awareness and knowledge of phoneme-grapheme correspondences develop naturally over the preschool and early elementary years, progressing from the skill of rhyming words to the ability to hear and manipulate the individual sounds within words. As general guidelines, many children in preschool and most students in kindergarten are able to rhyme words. The majority of first-grade students can count syllables, delete part of a compound word, and count and blend syllables (Smith, 1997). By the second grade, most children can perform all types of tasks involving phonemic manipulations, such as deleting a sound from the beginning, middle, or end of a word. Thus, when assessing children in preschool and kindergarten, it is necessary to ensure that they understand how to do the task; tasks involving phonemic substitution and manipulation are often too difficult for these children, and low scores may only

Rapid Reference 5.3

Development of Phonological Awareness

By Age 3 to 4:
  Produces rhymes spontaneously without knowing they rhyme (vocal play).

By Age 4 to 5:
  Can identify the number of syllables in a word by tapping or clapping.
  Can blend syllables into a whole word when presented with the syllables.
  Can delete a syllable from a word and state what remains.
  Can recognize that two words end the same or rhyme (rhyme identification).

By the End of Kindergarten:
  Can produce rhymes (rhyme production).
  Can identify the initial sounds in words.
  Can blend two phonemes.

By the End of First Grade:
  Given a group of words, can identify words that rhyme and those that do not.
  Can group words together or categorize words by rhyming characteristics.
  Can break apart and identify all of the sounds in words with four to five
    phonemes (segmentation).
  Can put together four or five phonemes to pronounce a word (blending).

By the End of Second Grade:
  Can perform all phonemic awareness and manipulation tasks: rhyming, blending, segmenting, deleting, substituting, and reversing phonemes.

indicate that the tasks were too hard (Aaron et al., 2008). Rapid Reference 5.3 provides an overview of the development of phonological awareness.

Standardized measures. A variety of instruments are available to assess various aspects of phonological awareness. The Comprehensive Test of Phonological Processing (CTOPP) also includes measures of phonological memory, such as nonword repetition. Asking a child to repeat a nonword or a polysyllabic word (e.g., administrator) is one of the simplest ways to assess phonological abilities as individuals with dyslexia often have

DON'T FORGET

Individuals with dyslexia often have trouble pronouncing long unfamiliar words and nonwords with accuracy.

deficits in their ability to repeat nonsense words and longer words with accuracy (Bishop, Adams, & Norbury, 2004; Hulme & Snowling, 2009). Individuals with dyslexia also have difficulty reading and spelling nonwords, which is discussed in Chapter 6. Rapid Reference 5.4 provides an overview of commonly used measures of phonological awareness.

☰ Rapid Reference 5.4

Commonly Used Standardized Measures of Phonological Awareness

Test Name	Age Range	Abilities	Publisher
Comprehensive Test of Phonological Processing (CTOPP)	5–0 to 24–0	Phonological awareness (elision, blending words, sound matching), phonological memory (memory for digits, nonword repetition), and rapid naming	PRO-ED
Kaufman Test of Educational Achievement (KTEA-II)	4–6 to 90+	Phonological awareness, associational fluency, naming facility	Pearson
Lindamood Auditory Conceptualization Test, 3rd ed. (LAC-3; 2004)	5–0 to 18–11	Isolated phoneme patterns, tracking phonemes, counting syllables, tracking syllables, tracking syllables and phonemes	PRO-ED

(continued)

Commonly Used Standardized Measures of Phonological Awareness

Test Name	Age Range	Abilities	Publisher
Phonemic-Awareness Skills Screening (PASS; 2000)	1 to 2 grades	Rhyming, sentence segmentation, blending, syllable segmentation, deletion, phoneme isolation, phoneme segmentation, and substitution	PRO-ED
Phonological Awareness Literacy Screening (PALS Pre-K; 2004)	3–0 to 5–0	Name writing, alphabet knowledge, and print and word awareness	University of Virginia
Pre-Reading Inventory of Phonological Awareness (PIPA; 2003)	4–0 to 6–11	Rhyme awareness, syllable segmentation, alliteration awareness, sound isolation, sound segmentation, and letter-sound knowledge.	Pearson
Test of Phonological Awareness, 2nd ed: PLUS (TOPA-2+; 2004)	5–0 to 8–0	Recognize phonemes in spoken words and the relationships between letters and phonemes	PRO-ED
Test of Phonological Awareness in Spanish (TPAS; 2004)	4–0 to 10–11	Initial sounds, final sounds, rhyming words, and deletion	PRO-ED
Test of Phonological Awareness Skills (TOPAS; 2003)	5–0 to 10–11	Rhyming, incomplete words, sound sequencing, and phoneme deletion	PRO-ED
Woodcock-Johnson III Tests of Cognitive Abilities	2–0 to 90+	Blending, auditory attention, incomplete words, auditory memory, phonemic awareness, rapid naming	Riverside Publishing

Informal measures. A teacher or parent can use informal procedures to explore a child's phonological awareness development. The adult may say familiar words and ask the child for words that rhyme, ask the child to indicate by clapping or tapping how many syllables or phonemes are in a word, or ask the child to name several words that start with a certain sound. Rapid Reference 5.5 illustrates questions to ask to informally evaluate a child's phonological awareness (Mather, Bos, Podhajski, Babur, & Rhein, 2000). The tasks are ordered by difficulty level. If a child has difficulty on one or more of the tasks, practice in these skills can be provided as part of the instructional program at home or school. Teachers have the opportunity to observe the child's classroom performance and identify children at-risk for reading failure. For example, limited ability to pair sounds with letters in attempted spellings is a good indicator of at-risk status (Uhry, 2005).

≡ Rapid Reference 5.5
....

Informal Assessment of Phonological Awareness

1. Word Discrimination
   I'm going to say two words, and I want you to tell me whether they are the same or different. For example, if I say "star, star," you would say "same." If I say "horse, rock" you would say "different." Now you try one: dog-tree. Additional words: sheep-sheep, bird-couch, hill-hall

2. Rhyme Recognition
   I am going to say three words, and I want you to tell me the two words that end the same or rhyme. If I say: What rhymes with cat . . . hat or sun? You would say hat because cat and hat end the same or rhyme. Now you do one. What rhymes with fun: hat or run? Additional words: bed—red or blue; meat—milk or seat; house—horse or mouse?

3. Rhyme Production
   I'm going to say two words that rhyme. Tree rhymes with see, and dog rhymes with log. Now you do one. Tell me a word that rhymes with tree? Additional words: hop, tan, back

4. Syllable Blending
   I am going to say the parts of a word and then say the parts together fast. (Pause about 1/2 second between parts.) If I say cup . . . cake fast, it would be cupcake. Sun . . . shine would be sunshine. Now you do one. What is base . . . ball? Additional words: play-ground, book-end, sun-set, down-town

(continued)

5. Syllable Segmentation

   Compound Words

   I'm going to use these blocks (chips) to break a word into parts. Cupcake has two parts. Push forward one block for each part as you say it. Then point to each block and say: This block is cup and this one is cake. Push the blocks back into a group. Now you do one. Use the blocks to tell and show me the two parts of football.

   Additional words: meat-ball, rain-drop, bill-board

   Syllables

   The word doctor has two parts. Push forward one block as you say each part. This first block is /doc/, and this next one is /tor/. Now you do one. Use the blocks to tell and show me the word paper.

   Additional words: win-dow, can-dle, tur-tle

6. Syllable Deletion

   Compound Words

   I'm going to say a word and leave off one part. If I say toothbrush . . . but don't say tooth, it would be brush. Now you do one. Say the word gold-fish. (Pause for a response.) Now say the word goldfish but don't say fish.

   Additional words: pan-cake, star-fish, hair-cut

   Syllables

   The word pencil has two parts. The first part is /pen/ and the second part is /cil/. If I say pencil . . . but don't say /cil/, it would be pen. Now you do one. Say the word candle. Now say the word candle but don't say /dle/.

   Additional words: funny, elbow, garden

7. Phoneme Recognition

   I'm going to say a word and then ask you to tell me another word that starts with the same sound. If I say what starts like the word "bat," you could say boy or bike or boat because all of the words start with the /b/ sound. Tell me a word that starts like the word "cat."

   Additional words: man, girl, toy

8. Phoneme Blending

   Now I'm going to say the sounds of a word slowly and then say the word. Pronounce each phoneme as it sounds in the word and pause about one second between the sounds. Listen: /s/. . ./ō/. . ./p/ is soap. Now you do one. What is . . ./b/. . ./ē/?

   Additional words: me, take, find, sport

9. Phoneme Segmentation

   I'm going to use the blocks (chips) to show you all of the sounds in a word. The word time would be /t/ /i/ /m/. Push a block forward as you say each sound. Now you do one. Show me the sounds in the word toe.

   Additional words: he, ten, slip, green

10. Phoneme Deletion

I'm going to say a word and leave off one sound. If I say seat but don't say /s/, it would be eat. If I say past but don't say /t/, it would be pass. Now you do one. Say sat but don't say /s/.

Additional words: tan without /t/; make without /k/; chart without /ch/

Note: This informal assessment was adapted from an assessment tool that was originally developed by N. Mather, B. Podhajski, N. Babur, and D. Rhein. The first version was entitled the *Screening of Early Reading Processes* and was published in Mather and Goldstein (2001). The phonological segmentation tasks were adapted from Sawyer's (1987) *Test of Awareness of Language Segments*. The most recent edition, the *Phonological Awareness Skills Screener* (PASS) was revised by N. Mather, J. Sammons, B. Podhajski, J. Kroese, and M. Varricchio.

RAPID AUTOMATIZED NAMING

Rapid automatized naming, or RAN, is the ability to rapidly name familiar objects or symbols. In RAN tasks children are presented with familiar objects, words, letters, or colors, and asked to name the objects they see as quickly as they can. Rapid naming has been connected to reading accuracy, reading speed, and reading comprehension. In kindergarten and first grade, early naming speed deficits are good predictors of students who will struggle with reading fluency later in school (Wolf, 2007). This may be due to the

CAUTION

Informal measures of phonological awareness and other cognitive skills should not be used to diagnose dyslexia but can be useful as screening tools for further evaluation.

fact that both naming speed and reading involve multiple perceptual, lexical, and motoric processes. Both RAN tasks and reading tasks require integrating visual-verbal information within an element of time or speed. The smooth integration of the contributions from visual (orthographic symbols), verbal (phonological labels and sounds), and attentional (conscious effort) systems is essential for reading (Neuhaus & Swank, 2002). Automaticity develops as the individual becomes more familiar with the phonological and orthographic properties of letters. Recent findings indicate that RAN is most highly related to speeded reading tasks and is a good predictor of irregular or exception word reading, but not nonword reading (Abu-Hamour, 2009).

In addition to phonological awareness, RAN has been identified as another core area associated with dyslexia. In fact, RAN and phonological awareness are identified as the two primary factors in the double-deficit theory of dyslexia (Wolf & Bowers, 1999). Individuals may have a problem in one or both of these areas that impact reading development. While phonological deficits may explain some of an individual's reading problem, deficits in temporal and perceptual processing may contribute as well.

Wolf and Bowers (1999) proposed three subtypes of reading impairment: (1) phonological deficit, intact naming speed; (2) naming speed deficit, intact phonological skills; and (3) double-deficit, impairments in both naming speed and phonological skills. Phonological deficits appear to have a stronger relationship to decoding accuracy, whereas naming deficits are more strongly related to reading fluency (Manis, Doi, & Badha, 2000). Those individuals with a double-deficit have more difficulty with reading (speed and accuracy) and are more difficult to remediate (Denckla & Cutting, 1999).

> ### DON'T FORGET
> ....
> Phonological awareness and RAN represent the two core deficits in the double-deficit theory of dyslexia.

Knowledge of the exact processes involved in RAN tasks is not only limited (Georgiou, Parrila, & Kirby, 2006), but also contradictory. Some researchers believe there is a phonological basis for naming speed deficits (Clarke, Hulme, & Snowling, 2005), others support a visual connection (Stein & Walsh, 1997), whereas others support a general processing speed (Kail, Hall, & Caskey, 1999) or a working memory deficit (Ramus & Szenkovits, 2008).

> ### CAUTION
> ....
> Researchers do not agree about the underlying processes involved in naming speed deficits. More research is necessary to clarify the specific processes involved in RAN tasks.

ASSESSMENT OF RAN

When evaluating individuals for dyslexia, it is important to include one or more measures of RAN as these tasks can help differentiate children with dyslexia from children with other forms of learning disabilities (Denckla & Rudel, 1976; O'Malley, Francis, Foorman, Fletcher, & Swank, 2002). Furthermore, the naming speed deficits associated with dyslexia persist into adolescence and adulthood (Denckla & Rudel, 1976; Korhonen, 1995; Vukovic, Wilson, & Nash, 2004) making RAN an important correlate of dyslexia in older individuals. In addition, because RAN tasks do not require any reading, they may be administered prior to the individual receiving any reading instruction, making RAN tasks an easy way to identify young children who are at-risk for reading difficulties. Further, studies in other languages with shallow orthographies (more consistent matches between sounds and letters) have found that slow naming speed, rather than poor phonological awareness, is the main cognitive correlate of dyslexia (Brizzolara et al., 2006; de Jong & Van der Leij, 2003; Wimmer & Mayringer, 2002). Chapter 11 provides a more detailed description of the relationship between RAN performance and dyslexia in other languages.

Standardized measures. As part of an evaluation for dyslexia, it is important to assess RAN because many researchers believe that RAN makes a unique contribution to the prediction of reading that extends beyond the role of phonological awareness (e.g., Bowers, 1993; McBride-Chang & Manis, 1996; Powell, Stainthorp, Stuart, Garwood, & Quinlan, 2007; Savage, Pillay, & Melidona, 2007; Wolf, Bowers, & Biddle, 2000). Rapid Reference 5.6 lists several of the standardized tools available that include measures of RAN or RAN-like tasks. Some of the standardized tests shown in Rapid Reference 5.4 include measures of phonological awareness and RAN and, therefore, are repeated here.

Informal measures. The nature of RAN tasks makes it easy to adapt them for informal use. For example, once a child knows the names of several colors, a rapid color-naming task can be prepared; or if the child knows the names of letters, a rapid letter-naming task can be created. These informal tasks can be timed, and performance can be compared to other classmates. Parents and teachers alike can observe if a child is struggling with naming known objects or colors in the course of a normal activity. Further, teachers may notice a child lags behind other classmates in learning the names of letters and being able to name them on demand. Rapid Reference 5.7 presents examples of several informal rapid naming tasks.

PROCESSING SPEED

Whereas much of the dyslexia research has focused on RAN as a correlate of reading, individuals with dyslexia can also demonstrate other speed-related deficits. Processing speed tasks are always timed and are clerical in nature. They involve tests such as circling the matching pictures, digits, or letters in a row or identifying if symbols are alike or different. Processing speed tasks may measure speed of input or perception, speed of output, or speed of integrating perceptual, cognitive, and output processes. In other words, a variety of processes are involved. Individuals may have difficulty in one or more aspect of processing speed. Automaticity of word recognition and reading rate appear to be impacted by an individual's cognitive processing speed.

≡ Rapid Reference 5.6

Standardized Measures of Rapid Automatized Naming

Test Name	Age Range	Abilities	Publisher
Comprehensive Test of Phonological Processing (CTOPP)	5–0 to 24–0	Phonological awareness, phonological memory, and rapid naming	PRO-ED
Dyslexia Early Screening Test, 2nd ed.	4–6 to 6–5	Phonological awareness, rapid naming	Pearson
Kaufman Test of Educational Achievement (KTEA-II)	4–6 to 90+	Phonological awareness, associational fluency, naming facility	Pearson
Process Assessment of the Learner: Test Battery for Reading and Writing	Grades K–6	Phonological awareness, rapid naming, orthographic awareness	Pearson
Rapid Automatized Naming and Rapid Alternating Stimulus Tests (RAN/RAS)	5–0 to 18–11	Naming tasks: letters, colors, numbers, or objects Alternating tasks: letters and numbers; letters, numbers, and colors	PRO-ED
Woodcock-Johnson III Tests of Cognitive Abilities	2–0 to 90+	Rapid naming of simple pictures	Riverside Publishing

Cognitive speediness, or mental quickness, has been considered an important aspect of intelligence for many years (Nettelbeck, 1994; Vernon, 1983). Kail (1991) observed: "In the face of limited processing resources, the speed of processing is critical because it determines in part how rapidly limited resources can be reallocated to other cognitive tasks" (p. 152). For example, how quickly a reader can recognize or decode a word impacts comprehension. If the reader's cognitive resources are focused on decoding a word, there will be limited resources available for comprehension.

Evidence of processing speed deficits has been noted on both linguistic and nonlinguistic tasks for individuals with reading disabilities (Shanahan

≡ Rapid Reference 5.7

Informal Measures of RAN

Color Naming
Using four to five colors known by the child, present either a series of blocks or a color chart using those known colors arranged in random order. Repeat the series of random colors so there is a total of 50 items. Ask the child to name the colors as quickly as he can. The time it takes to complete the task can be recorded and compared to the performance of other children in the classroom.

Object Naming
Using 5–10 objects, or pictures of objects, known by the child, present a series of these objects arranged in random order. Repeat the series of random objects so there is a total of 50. Ask the child to name the objects as quickly as she can. The time it takes to complete the task can be recorded and compared to the performance of other classmates.

Letter Naming
Using 10–20 letters known by the child, present a series of these letters arranged in random order. Repeat the series of random letters so there is a total of 50. Ask the child to name the letters as quickly as he can. The time it takes to complete the task can be recorded and then compared to the performance of grade peers.

et al., 2006). Some students may process linguistic information slowly, whereas others process symbolic information slowly (more common in dyslexia). Kail and Hall (1994) found that a general deficit in processing speed explained the observed link between RAN and reading. Other researchers have found that the brains of individuals with dyslexia process information more slowly than individuals without reading problems, including both visual processing speed (e.g., Demb, Boynton, & Heeger, 1998) and auditory processing speed (e.g., Tallal et al., 1996). Still other researchers, using diffusion tensor imaging, have found that the brain's white matter in the temporal-parietal area is organized differently in good and poor readers (Klingberg et al., 2000). This area of the brain is thought to be where visual and auditory information is integrated and then sent forward in the brain for additional processing. Differences in processing speed have been documented in infant studies. For example, 80% of infants that later develop dyslexia show a delayed brain response to speech sounds (Molfese, Molfese, & Modglin, 2001). Gender differences have also been noted on different types of processing speed tests. In a review of large-scale studies exploring gender differences in processing speed, Roivainen (2011) found no differences in general intelligence, but that females were faster on processing speed tasks involving letters and numbers as well as RAN tasks, whereas males were faster on tests involving reaction time and finger tapping. Females also outperformed males in reading and writing skills.

Because processing speed underlies performance in many areas and is not specific to one area or disability, it is sometimes referred to as a domain-general deficit rather than a deficit specific to just one type of disability. For example, disturbances of processing speed characterize both dyslexia and ADHD (Eden & Vaidya, 2008; McGrath et al., 2011), although children with dyslexia demonstrate greater deficits than children with ADHD (Shanahan et al., 2006). In fact, symbolic processing speed appears to be the shared cognitive deficit that explains their comorbidity (McGrath et al., 2011).

DON'T FORGET

Slow processing speed is a common characteristic in individuals with different disabilities. Sometimes referred to as a domain-general deficit, processing speed deficits are not specific to dyslexia, but individuals with dyslexia do appear to have slower speeds of processing than people with other types of disabilities.

ASSESSMENT OF PROCESSING SPEED

Due to the comprehensive nature of processing speed, many different types of tests and tasks provide insights into an individual's speed of processing. In addition to the RAN tests and tasks, measures of visual perceptual speed, auditory speed, speed of lexical access, reaction time, and even motor speed may be helpful. All processing speed tasks require individuals to rapidly scan or identify stimuli, make quick associations and accurate decisions, and then move quickly to the next item (Shanahan et al., 2006).

Standardized measures. Although the concept is broader than just visual perceptual speed, processing speed is typically measured on standardized tests through visual, clerical tasks that involve the rapid scanning of symbols, such as circling the matching digits in a row of six digits as quickly as possible. Rapid Reference 5.8 lists examples of standardized tests that include measures of processing speed.

Informal measures of processing speed. A simple way to evaluate an individual's processing speed is to

DON'T FORGET

Students with slow processing speed are often the last ones to complete tests and may require extra time.

☰ Rapid Reference 5.8

Standardized Measures of Processing Speed

Test Name	Age Range	Abilities	Publisher
Differential Ability Scales, 2nd ed.	2–6 to 17–11	Speed of information processing	Pearson
Wechsler Intelligence Scale for Children, 4th ed.	6 to 16	Processing speed (rate of test taking, perceptual speed)	Pearson
Woodcock-Johnson III Tests of Cognitive Abilities	2–0 to 90+	Processing speed (perceptual speed, speed of lexical access)	Riverside Publishing

create a visual scanning task and give the person two minutes to do the task. For example, using three-digit numbers, write them randomly in rows on a page. Ask the individual to circle the numbers that end in a specific digit (e.g., 3) as quickly as she can. After two minutes, record the number of correctly circled items. Another informal approach would be to create a page of upper- and lowercase letters arranged randomly in rows. Give the individual one minute to quickly circle all of a specified letter (e.g., lowercase b).

ORTHOGRAPHIC CODING

Printed word recognition involves two major component skills: phonological coding (using knowledge of letter-sound correspondences to read words), and orthographic coding (using letter and word patterns to aid in pronunciation); dyslexia is characterized by deficits in both types of coding (Pennington, 2009). Phonology enables the initial formation of lexical representations, but orthography provides more detailed representations that are the gateway to highly skilled reading (Perfetti, 2011). Essentially, orthography is the writing system of a language that includes letters, words, numbers, and punctuation marks. Orthographic awareness is awareness of how print works and how it looks—the visual representation of language (the letters and letter patterns that are used to represent the words in print). In addition to letters and words, orthography also includes numerals and punctuation marks.

Some languages have a close match between the sounds, or phonemes, and the letters, or graphemes, used to represent those sounds. Spanish, for example, is transparent at the phoneme-grapheme level and is described as having a shallow or transparent orthography. In contrast, English has many irregularities at the phoneme-grapheme level and, therefore, is considered to have a deep or opaque orthography because the system is far more complex than just mapping sounds to print. English spellings involve representations of sound, as well as word meaning. As noted in Chapter 11, languages such as English that have deep orthographies make decoding and encoding more difficult to master. Recognizing a printed word occurs at several different levels: recognition of individual letters, letter patterns, and morphemes, including root words (Adams, 1990). A skilled reader uses this knowledge to recognize words quickly and efficiently, as well as to decode unfamiliar words. If a reader is only able to recognize individual letters, word reading will be slow and inefficient. Whereas readers with dyslexia do not demonstrate greater difficulty than readers without dyslexia in recognizing letters presented in isolation (Hawelka & Wimmer, 2005), they do demonstrate greater difficulty in discriminating letters when they are presented in groups, such as words (Pernet, Valdois, Celsis, & Demonet, 2006). The presence of other visual stimuli appears to impair the ability to focus on the target stimulus.

One problem in visual recognition of orthographic units and words is a visual phenomenon referred to as crowding, which is reliably correlated with reading speed (Levi, Song, & Pelli, 2007) and consistently discriminates between readers with and without dyslexia. In essence, visual crowding means seeing less when more is presented. For example, identifying a familiar face in a large group of people or finding a specific item in drawer filled with many items may be difficult due to visual crowding, or visual overload. To recognize a word, the individual must not only detect the letters, but integrate them into a whole word. When a word is presented in a sentence, the additional visual stimuli to the left and right of the target word (in the periphery) interfere with the perception of that word. Features of the nearby words get mixed up with the target word's features. Research indicates that individuals with dyslexia demonstrate more difficulty in suppressing peripheral vision while reading than do nonimpaired readers (Geiger & Lettvin, 1987; Lorusso et al., 2004). The word analysis skills of individuals with dyslexia are slowed because of greater visual crowding effects that limit the rapid perception of letter strings and as a result, cause the reader to make numerous fixations (Martelli, De Filippo, Spinelli, & Zoccolotti, 2009). This may explain why some readers with dyslexia have difficulty with the visual demands of reading, and their eyes may even tear up when reading.

Orthography is particularly important for the accurate and quick recognition of irregular or exception words. Rapid Reference 5.9 identifies symptoms of individuals with poor orthographic awareness and knowledge. Because orthography also includes the numbers of a language, readers with poor orthography can also experience problems in mathematics. Although orthographic processing is a visual task, the visual processing tasks on many current cognitive tests are not synonymous with orthographic processing (Berninger, 1990). Most of the visual

DON'T FORGET

Orthographic awareness is knowledge of the writing system and the visual aspects of reading and spelling—letters, letter patterns, and words, whereas phonological awareness is knowledge of the speech sounds.

processing tasks on cognitive tests use shapes, designs, or pictures. Tasks that do not use letters or words do not tap orthographic processing ability. Rapid processing of symbols, such as letters or numbers, is more frequently measured by processing speed tasks, especially those measuring perceptual speed, making the task more similar to the orthographic processing demands of reading. Because of the nature of orthographic awareness, it can be measured by tasks

Rapid Reference 5.9

Symptoms of Individuals with Poor Orthographic Awareness

- Difficulty learning how to form symbols.
- Confusion of symbols similar in appearance (e.g., b for d, n for u).
- Trouble with near- and far-point copying tasks.
- Tendency to reverse or transpose letters or numbers.
- Trouble remembering how words look.
- Trouble reading exception or irregular words.
- Trouble with accurate and rapid word recognition; slow reading speed.
- Tendency to use different spellings for the same word.
- Tendency to omit word endings.
- Overreliance on the phonological rather than visual features of words.
- Trouble learning and retaining basic math facts.
- Difficulty counting in a sequence (e.g., counting by 2).
- Trouble with multistep math problems.

presenting written stimuli or through tasks requiring the reading and spelling of irregular words. A more detailed description of the different types of spelling tests used to measure orthography and morphology (the units of meaning in a language) is discussed in Chapter 6. Both orthographic and morphological awareness and knowledge are critical for the development of accurate word reading and spelling. As Perfetti (2011) explained:

> What develops along with phonology is orthography, and in skilled reading, orthographic representations take on an increased role. Finally, word meanings and their associated morphological constituents are important in ways that go beyond phonology. Reading is above all dependent on word knowledge, including the spoken forms, written forms, meanings, and morphosyntactic structures of words. Although we have learned that acquiring this lexical knowledge depends significantly on a skilled phonological component, we have more to learn about the fuller story of word knowledge and skilled reading." (p. 167)

MEMORY

Both memory span and working memory may also affect reading development. Memory span involves the ability to listen to information and then repeat it verbatim in a short time period, usually seconds. Common memory span tests ask individuals to repeat back a string of digits, words, or sentences that increase in length. One theoretical interpretation as to why poor readers have lower memory spans than average or good readers is that they articulate words more slowly because of inefficiency in accessing phonological information (Hulme & Snowling, 2009). In addition to poor memory span, the ability to make associations between verbal and visual information (verbal paired-associate learning) can also be difficult for individuals with dyslexia. In examining a large sample of normally developing children, Hulme, Goetz, Gooch, Adams, and Snowling (2007) found that phoneme awareness and paired-associate learning were independent predictors of variations in reading skill. Thus, other factors, beside phoneme awareness, contribute to the prediction of reading skill.

Working memory involves the capacity to hold information in immediate awareness while manipulating or transforming that information in some way. A common working memory test is to ask an individual to listen to a sequence of digits and then to say the digits back in sequence but in a reversed order. A widely accepted model of working memory identifies three major components: a central executive, a phonological loop, and a visuospatial sketchpad (e.g., Baddeley, 2003; Baddeley & Hitch, 1974). The central executive manages and coordinates the other two systems, which have been referred to as slave systems. The phonological loop, which processes verbal speech input, and the visuospatial sketchpad, which is devoted to visual input, hold information for very short, specific periods of time (Savage, Lavers, & Pillay, 2007).

Currently, the research on working memory's role in reading raises more questions than it provides answers. Many differing views exist. Some researchers view working memory as a domain-general deficit, affecting all areas of academic performance, not just reading (e.g., Swanson & Sachse-Lee, 2001). Others believe that phonological deficits, common in individuals with dyslexia, impair performance of the phonological loop in working memory, thus creating a bottleneck in processing (e.g., Gathercole, Willi, Baddeley, & Emslie, 1994). Still others suggest that working memory is more relevant to reading comprehension than to decoding (e.g., Oakhill, Cain, &

> # DON'T FORGET
> Memory span refers to the ability to remember information in the order it was given (e.g., remembering a series of numbers). Working memory also requires remembering information, but it involves manipulating or transforming the information in some way (e.g., hearing numbers forward but repeating them in reverse order).

Bryant, 2003). In addition, working memory deficits may be more related to other disorders. It appears that individuals with co-occurring problems, such as ADHD and dyslexia, frequently have a more general working memory deficit, whereas those with only dyslexia are more likely to have a phonological deficit (Savage, Lavers, et al., 2007). Savage and colleagues concluded: "Further work is required to specify the nature of WM problems in samples of poor readers, as distinct from other co-occurring problems such as ADHD" (p. 185).

ASSESSMENT OF WORKING MEMORY

A variety of tests and tasks are available to measure working memory. It is important to consider the nature of the task to determine which component or components of working memory may be tapped. For example, is the test a complex verbal working memory task, or is it a visual working memory task? As it relates to dyslexia, it appears that verbal working memory tasks and phonological working memory tasks, such as reversing the sounds in a word, cause the most difficulty (Hulme & Snowling, 2009). Rapid Reference 5.10 illustrates several standardized tests of working memory. Rapid Reference 5.11 suggests some informal methods for evaluating working memory.

≡ Rapid Reference 5.10

Standardized Measures of Memory Span and Working Memory

Test Name	Age Range	Abilities	Publisher
Differential Ability Scales, 2nd ed.	2–6 to 17–11	Working memory, short-term memory	Pearson
Stanford Binet, 5th ed.	2 to 85+	Working memory, visual working memory, verbal working memory	Riverside Publishing
Test of Memory and Learning, 2nd ed.	5 to 59–11	Verbal and nonverbal memory	PRO-ED
Wechsler Adult Intelligence Scale, 4th ed.	16 to 90	Working memory	Pearson
Wechsler Intelligence Scale for Children, 4th ed.	6 to 16–11	Working memory	Pearson
Wide Range Assessment of Memory and Learning, 2nd ed.	5 to 90	Working memory (verbal and visual)	PAR, Inc.
Woodcock-Johnson III Tests of Cognitive Abilities	2–0 to 90+	Working memory, auditory memory span, short-term memory, associative memory	Riverside Publishing
Working Memory Test Battery for Children	5 to 15	Central executive, phonological loop, and visuospatial sketchpad, working memory	Pearson

≡ Rapid Reference 5.11

Informal Measures of Memory Span and Working Memory

Span Tasks

Create a set of items that increase in number, or span. Present the items verbally to the individual who then must repeat them in sequence. For example, using digits create sets of three items for each span to be presented. That is, create

(continued)

three items with 2 digits each, three items with 3 digits each, three items with 4 digits each, and so on. Present items until the individual misses all three items at a level. You can also use words, pictures, or objects.

Working Memory Tasks

To create a working memory task, an intervening activity or transformation must occur before the individual is asked to recall the information. For example, one commonly used format presents the items forward, and the individual must recall them in reverse order. Using the series created for the span tasks, present them and ask the individual to recall them in reverse order. Another type of task presents a series of sentences and then requires the individual to recall the last word in each sentence.

CONCLUSION

Reading is a complex task requiring a number of cognitive and linguistic abilities. A skilled reader not only has these abilities intact, but is able to integrate the various processes fluently. Research is revealing more about the cognitive and linguistic correlates of dyslexia, but much is still unresolved or unknown. We do know, however, that training in phonological awareness is necessary but insufficient for good reading (NRP, 2000; Torgesen & Mathes, 2000). Adequate word identification skill also requires mastery of more complex phonic skills, as well as automaticity with sight words. Thus, fluent reading and accurate spelling involve the other cognitive and linguistic correlates discussed in this chapter: RAN, processing speed, orthographic coding, and memory span and working memory.

The simple act of decoding a word is not so simple after all. It is like an orchestra playing a tune. Multiple instruments are involved that must work together smoothly and efficiently to create the music. One instrument out of tune or out of time can interrupt and spoil the melody. In reading a word, visual and auditory information must be quickly mapped and held in immediate awareness until the word can be decoded. Just as with music, one process out of tune or out of time with the other processes can disrupt the act of reading. When several processes are impaired, one can struggle to read even simple words.

To properly diagnose an individual with dyslexia, it is important to collect information on the array of abilities and processes that are believed to impact reading and spelling development. Ideally, ideas about cognitive causes should lead to ideas about remediation (Frith, 1999). The hope is that identification of the cognitive processing weaknesses in an individual can lead to an accurate diagnosis, as well as to the development of an effective treatment or educational plan.

 **TEST YOURSELF**

1. **An early correlate of dyslexia that is known as the best predictor of reading failure is**
   a. slow processing speed.
   b. working memory deficits.
   c. poor phonological awareness.
   d. low performance of RAN tasks.

2. **The best example of a phonological segmentation task would be:**
   a. Tell me a word that rhymes with *bat*.
   b. Tell me a word that begins with the same sound as *bat*.
   c. How many sounds do you hear in the word *bat*?
   d. What word is composed of these three sounds: /b/ /a/ /t/.
   e. All of the above are examples of segmentation tasks.

3. **If a child is asked to look at a word carefully and try to pronounce the word by saying each sound, this requires**
   a. blending.
   b. syntax.
   c. context.
   d. phoneme-grapheme knowledge.
   e. both a and d.

4. **A voiced consonant is made**
   a. using the vocal cords.
   b. without the use of vocal cords.
   c. made in the front of the mouth.
   d. made in the back of the mouth.
   e. both a and c.

5. **The double-deficit theory of dyslexia involves**
   a. phonemic awareness and orthographic awareness.
   b. working memory and RAN.
   c. RAN and phonemic awareness.
   d. orthographic awareness and RAN.

6. **The syllable _____ illustrates an example of both an onset and a rime.**
   a. trap
   b. at
   c. ate

    d. apt

    e. oh

7. It is important to assess RAN in an evaluation of dyslexia because

    a. RAN is the most important correlate of dyslexia.

    b. low performance on RAN tasks persists into adolescence and adulthood.

    c. RAN can be assessed before reading instruction begins.

    d. both b and c.

    e. none of the above.

8. Processing speed deficits are thought to be domain-general. True or False?

9. Individuals who are learning to read in English may have difficulties with orthographic coding because

    a. there are phoneme-grapheme (sound to print) irregularities.

    b. words in English are generally longer.

    c. English is a shallow orthography.

    d. words cannot be separated into syllables.

10. The study of meaningful word parts is called

    a. orthography.

    b. morphology.

    c. phonology.

    d. wordology.

11. Processing speed is an important correlate of

    a. dyslexia.

    b. speech-language impairment.

    c. ADHD.

    d. a and b.

    e. a and c.

12. Informal measures of the correlates of dyslexia should be used to

    a. diagnose individuals with dyslexia.

    b. make decisions about placement and accommodations.

    c. identify individuals at risk who may need a more comprehensive evaluation.

    d. all of the above.

13. A common conceptualization of working memory includes a central executive, an attention loop, and a visual-spatial buffer. True or False?

14. **It is possible to assess risk of reading failure and dyslexia before reading instruction begins by using measures of**

    a. working memory and processing speed.

    b. RAN and phonological awareness.

    c. oral language and phonics.

    d. orthographic coding and memory span.

15. **Currently, the correlates of dyslexia are best explained by a single-deficit model, rather than a multiple-deficit model. True or False?**

Answers: 1. c; 2. c; 3. e; 4. a; 5. c; 6. a; 7. d; 8. True; 9. a; 10. b; 11. e; 12. c; 13. False; 14. b; 15. False

Chapter Six

ASSESSMENT OF DECODING, ENCODING, AND READING FLUENCY

> After studying each case of reading disability, the examiner will find it helpful to list these five general causative areas, constitutional, intellectual, emotional, educational, and environmental, then itemize under each all the factors discovered which may help to explain the child's difficulties.
>
> —Monroe & Backus, 1937, p. 33

Prior to planning and implementing instruction for a student who has dyslexia, a teacher needs to understand how reading and spelling skills develop, as well as which aspects of reading and spelling are difficult. In addition to understanding the various phases of development, psychologists, diagnosticians, and special educators must also understand what facets of literacy should be included as part of a comprehensive evaluation for documenting dyslexia. Although dyslexia affects reading comprehension because the person has difficulty with word recognition, it is quite distinct from a reading comprehension impairment (Hulme & Snowling, 2009).

DEVELOPMENT OF DECODING, ENCODING, AND READING FLUENCY

Reading and spelling follow similar developmental trajectories, but spelling skill lags behind reading because it is more difficult. The reason spelling is harder is that it requires recall of the entire word, whereas reading only requires recognition. In the early stages of literacy, print awareness is first demonstrated when a child who

DON'T FORGET

The alphabetic principle is the fundamental understanding that phonemes can be converted into graphemes. This letter-sound knowledge provides the foundation for the development of effective word identification.

is not yet reading knows what an environmental sign says (e.g., stop), that reading goes from left to right, and that the marks on a paper represent spoken language and can be read. As literacy develops, a child learns the letter names and what sounds each of the letters and letter combinations make. This basic understanding that a speech sound (phoneme) can be converted into a letter or letter string (grapheme) is referred to as the alphabetic principle. This early insight regarding sound-symbol relationships is critical as a first stage in reading and spelling development. The alphabetic principle has two parts. The first part is awareness that words are composed of sounds that are represented by letters. The second part, referred to as phonological recoding, is the ability to use the relationships between the sounds and letters to decode or encode words.

Through increased exposures to print, the child increases knowledge of sound-symbol or phoneme-grapheme connections and learns what letter combination or letter strings can go together in English. Children learn which letter sequences are legal and which are illegal. For example, young children soon recognize that they can write the letters "ck" at the end of the word but not "kc" and that the letters "ck" can never start a word. This ability to picture and store accurate visual representations of both letters and words (orthography) then provides the foundation for automaticity and ease with reading and spelling.

Ehri (1998) explained that skilled readers can identify different words in at least five different ways by (1) blending together the sounds of letters into words, (2) pronouncing and blending common spelling patterns, (3) retrieving sight words from memory, (4) making analogies to other words already known by sight, and (5) using context clues to predict words. Although capable readers can use any of these strategies for word identification, skilled reading is based on retrieving sight words rapidly and easily from memory, because all of the other cueing systems require attention and disrupt the reading process (Ehri, 1998). Unfortunately, children with the most severe dyslexia have difficulty recognizing letter sequences as decoding units, as well as learning to read individual words by sight (Torgesen, Rashotte, & Alexander, 2001). These individuals experience disruption in both reading and spelling development.

EHRI'S PHASES OF SIGHT READING

To understand what happens to readers with dyslexia, one has to consider how skill in word reading and spelling typically develops. Although several theories exist with similar phases and stages, one well-known theory of reading and spelling development was developed by Ehri (1998, 2000). Because the stages of development are not qualitatively distinct, Ehri (2005) suggests that phase theory rather than stage theory provides a more accurate description of the course of sight word and spelling development. To attain skill in sight word reading, Ehri (1998, 2000) described the following four overlapping phases that underlie development: prealphabetic, partial alphabetic, full alphabetic, and consolidated alphabetic.

During the prealphabetic phase, readers recognize words by environmental cues or selected visual attributes that are not connected to grapheme-phoneme relationships. Prealphabetic readers recognize words in the everyday environment. For example, the child may read the word *Pepsi* by recognizing the appearance of the can or may recognize the word *McDonald's* by seeing the golden arches (Ehri, 2007). In the partial alphabetic phase, readers make connections between some of the letters and sounds in written words. Many older children with dyslexia would be identified as partial alphabetic phase readers (Ehri, 2005). Partial-phase readers do not store sight words in memory in sufficient letter detail to recognize how they are similar yet different from other words. Partial-phase readers would have difficulty recalling the similarities and differences between similar words, such as "every" and "very."

In the full alphabetic phase, readers have complete connections between the letters and their sounds, and they can pronounce unfamiliar phonically regular words. In the consolidated alphabetic phase, the reader has a store of letter patterns that occur across many words. These larger units consist of morphemes (e.g., -ed for past tense), syllables (e.g., -dle in candle), or onsets (initial consonants in a syllable, e.g., the st- in sting) and rimes (the ending part of the syllable that starts with a vowel, e.g., the -ing in sting). Recognizing chunks or consolidated word parts makes it easier to read and spell multisyllabic words (Ehri, 2000). At this phase of reading, the application of letter-sound knowledge is more automatic and less effortful (Hulme & Snowling, 2009). Rapid Reference 6.1 summarizes Ehri's four phases of reading development.

The hallmark of skilled reading is the ability to read words accurately and quickly, a process that happens automatically (Ehri, 2007). This process is referred to as automaticity, which is defined as ". . . recognizing the pronunciations and meanings of written words immediately upon seeing them without expending any attention or effort decoding the words" (p. 151).

DON'T FORGET

A reader must have full knowledge of the connections between the phonemes and the graphemes. This knowledge must be at an automatic level before readers can acquire a substantial sight vocabulary and fluent reading can occur. In other words, accuracy is a prerequisite for fluency.

≡ *Rapid Reference 6. 1*

Four Phases of Reading Development (Ehri, 1998, 2000)

Phase 1 Prealphabetic: May recognize words from the environment but not based on phoneme-grapheme relationships (e.g., saying "Stop" when looking at a STOP sign).

Phase 2 Partial Alphabetic: Connects some sounds and letters, particularly beginning and ending consonants and long vowel sounds, but the connections are insufficient to store accurate representations of words.

Phase 3 Full Alphabetic: Connects all of the sounds and letters and can read phonically regular real words and nonsense words.

Phase 4 Consolidated Alphabetic: Uses orthographic and morphological knowledge; has a store of letter patterns (e.g., -tion, -ing, -able) that are recognized automatically.

Ehri explains that in order to recognize sight words instantly or within one second, readers must first be fully alphabetic. Thus, children must know phoneme-grapheme relationships before they can acquire a substantial sight vocabulary. Rapid word recognition develops as phonic word recognition improves (Moats, 2010). Unfortunately, a core problem for children with dyslexia is their limited ability to read sight words, phrases, and sentences automatically, rapidly, and fluently (Chard, Vaughn, & Tyler, 2002). Many individuals with dyslexia appear to form only partial representations of words, making it difficult to acquire both decoding and spelling skill. Ehri (2007) explains: "Compared to typically developing readers, poor readers have greater difficulty decoding new words, they take longer to learn words by sight, they secure partial rather than full representations of sight words in memory . . . and they read familiar words more slowly and take longer to unitize them" (pp. 153–154). Because of these difficulties developing word recognition and automaticity, individuals with dyslexia often avoid any tasks that require sustained reading, and this lack of practice contributes further to lower reading ability (Wiznitzer & Scheffel, 2009).

STAGES AND PHASES OF SPELLING DEVELOPMENT

As with word reading, spelling skills also evolve. Typically children with dyslexia will find learning to spell even more difficult than learning to read (Hulme & Snowling, 2009). When spelling, the individual has no visual cues and must mentally segment the sounds in the word, retrieve the appropriate grapheme used to represent each sound, and then produce the word. Although individuals with spelling difficulties appear to progress through similar phases as their peers, their development is slower. At times, their difficulties appear indicative of arrest in one of the stages in spelling development (Moats, 1991). In addition to Ehri, others have developed similar theories regarding spelling development (e.g., Gentry, 1984; Henderson, 1990). For example, Henderson outlined five developmental stages: (1) scribbles and pictures (i.e., the preliterate stage), (2) letter-name representation (i.e., letters are used to represent sounds), (3) recognition of within-word patterns (i.e., orthographic and morphological patterns are observed), (4) syllable juncture (i.e., consonants are doubled and patterns present in syllables are observed), and (5) derivational constancy (i.e., roots and derivations are used). Although the stages or phases described vary somewhat in enumeration and description from Ehri, the simpler theoretical models typically include five stages: prephonetic, semiphonetic, phonetic, transitional, and conventional. These five stages of spelling development are illustrated in Figure 6.1.

Prephonetic or prephonemic. In the initial and earliest phases of learning to spell, a child combines a string of unrelated letters to communicate a message. When first writing, many children are not aware of the alphabetic principle and simply write the letters they know, often the ones in their first names. At this phase, the child knows little about the alphabetic system and recognizes words through memory of selected visual features (Ehri, 2005).

Semiphonetic or partial alphabetic. At the semiphonetic phase, letters are used to represent sounds, but only a few sounds in words are represented. Children recognize some of the letters and sounds in words, such as the first and last letter sounds in the word. In some instances, students may use the names of letters rather than the letter sounds (Adams, 1990). For example, the word *while* may be written as "yl." During this phase, although spellings may follow logical linguistic patterns, children know very few correct spellings. A student may know consonant sounds, long vowel sounds, and an occasional sight word.

Phonetic or full alphabetic. At the phonetic phase, children produce spellings that demonstrate phoneme-grapheme correspondence. When writing, they attempt to record all of the sounds within a word and present them in the correct sound sequence. At this phase, students may over-rely on the sounds of words as a strategy for spelling. Thus, the words are often accurate in terms of the representation of sounds, but may not have the correct orthographic patterns (e.g., the suffix –tion spelled as "shun").

Transitional or consolidated alphabetic. At the transitional phase, the writer demonstrates awareness of many of the conventions of English orthography.

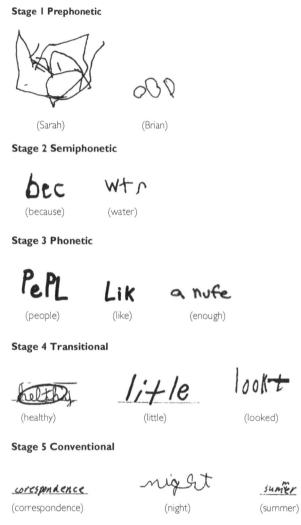

Figure 6.1   Five Stages of Spelling Development

For example, the student spells the ending of the past tense of a verb as -ed even when the ending sounds like a /t/, such as in the word trapped. Operating with chunks of words makes it easier for the student to both read and spell multisyllabic words (Ehri, 2000, 2005).

Conventional. At this phase, the writer possesses multiple strategies for determining standard spelling. Although not all words are spelled correctly, the writer regularly employs information from all sources, sounds (phonology), sight (orthography), and meaning (morphology) as an aid to English spelling.

A few of the theories of spelling development are more complex. For example, building on the work of Henderson and Beers (1980) and Henderson and Templeton (1986), Bear, Invernizzi, Templeton, and Johnston (2007) described five stages of spelling development. Within each of these five stages, the speller's knowledge about word features can be identified as early, middle, or late. Spellers advance through a sequential process of learning about the various word features through the following five stages: emergent, letter name, within word, syllables and affixes, and derivational relations. Emergent spellers (ages 2 to 5) are first acquiring the basic connections between sounds and letters. They progress from marks and scribbles to pretend writing where the letters have no relationship to the sounds. By the end of this stage, the child's spellings include only the most prominent sounds in the word.

Letter-name spellers (ages 5 to 8) solidify letter-sound knowledge by mastering consonants, short vowels, and most consonant blends and digraphs. In the beginning, they learn to segment the sounds within words and often use the name of the letter as a cue to represent the sound. In the within-word spelling stage (ages 7 to 10), writers learn how to spell preconsonantal nasals (e.g., the /m/ in jump), consonants blends and digraphs, most CVCe words (e.g., cave), some vowel teams, and some homophones (e.g., bear and bare). In the syllables-and-affixes stage (ages 9 to 14), writers begin to experiment with consonant doubling and the addition of suffixes and prefixes to spell multisyllabic words. In the early period, the writer still makes errors at places where the syllables and affixes meet and makes errors on unaccented second syllables (e.g., *mountin* for *mountain*). In the final stage, derivational relations (ages 10 to adulthood), writers increase their vocabulary by mastering the spellings of both Greek and Latin roots and use spelling rules correctly when adding affixes.

STRATEGY THEORY

The strategy theory depicts spelling development as being more continuous, suggesting that children incorporate a variety of spelling strategies from the very beginning of their acquisition of writing skills (Treiman, 1998). In addition, depending upon the complexity of a word, a child who is more advanced in spelling development may return to the use of an earlier strategy, such as spelling the word the way it sounds. Although they help depict spelling development, stage theories do not capture fully the complexities of the phonological, orthographic, and morphological representations that are related to spelling

(Treiman & Bourassa, 2000). Even though many children do incorporate varied aspects of linguistic knowledge in their initial spellings and reveal sensitivity to orthographic and morphological influences, the proposed stages and phases of development can help explain how reading and spelling abilities evolve, and how individuals with dyslexia often appear to get stuck or make extremely slow progress at a particular developmental stage. In addition, recognizing that spelling is a developmental process has instructional implications. That is, the instruction should be geared toward the individual's present level of spelling skill.

ASSESSMENT OF DECODING AND ENCODING

Several linguistic skills underlie the successful development of decoding and encoding. In addition to phonological awareness, which is discussed in Chapter 5, an evaluator should also explore the reader's orthographic and morphological awareness. An evaluator should also administer measures of word reading and spelling, as well as nonword or nonsense word reading and spelling to assess the reader's ability to use phonics.

ASSESSMENT OF ORTHOGRAPHIC AWARENESS

Orthography includes all of the symbols of a writing system, including numbers, punctuation, letters, and letter patterns. Individuals with dyslexia often have problems recalling letter patterns and letter strings, which then interferes with reading and spelling development. Imagine if you could not picture how a word appears in your mind's eye. You would then have to resort to relying on how the word sounds, rather than how the word looks. Thus, many individuals with dyslexia will spell words exactly the way they sound (e.g., thay, wus) rather than how they look.

Standardized measures. As a relatively new area of interest, the number of norm-referenced tests of orthographic awareness is limited, but growing (see Rapid Reference 6.2). Tests of spelling, especially those that employ both nonsense words and irregular words, are helpful for assessing orthographic awareness.

Informal measures. It is also possible to measure orthographic awareness informally. Both teachers and parents can observe how a child matches sounds with letters when writing. Rapid Reference 6.3 illustrates several ways to measure orthographic awareness informally.

MORPHOLOGY

Morphology deals with the study of words, their internal structures, and the meaningful units of words such as affixes (prefixes and suffixes), base words

Rapid Reference 6.2

Standardized Measures of Orthographic Awareness

Test Name	Age/Grade Range	Publisher
Diagnostic Assessments of Reading, Second Edition	K-3+	Riverside
Dynamic Indicators of Basic Early Literacy Skills, Sixth Edition (DIBELS-6)	PreK-3	University of Oregon
Illinois Test of Psycholinguistic Abilities-3 (ITPA-3)	5–0 to 12–11	PRO-ED
Process Assessment of the Learner II: Test Battery for Reading and Writing (PAL II)	K-6	Pearson
Star Early Literacy Computer-Adaptive Diagnostic Assessment	PreK-3	Renaissance Learning
Test of Irregular Word Reading (TIWRE)	3–0 to 94	PAR
Test of Orthographic Competence (TOC)	6–0 to 17–11	PRO-ED

Rapid Reference 6.3

Informal Measures of Orthographic Awareness

Writing Name
Ask the child to write her first and last names. If the child is young, ask for just the first name.

Writing the Alphabet
Ask the child to write the letters of the alphabet in order.

Recognizing Letters
Present written letters and ask the child to tell you the letter name. This can be done using lower- or upper-case letters. Make a page with letters that are similar in visual appearance (e.g., b and d, n and u, p and q). Ask the child to name the letters and count the number of errors that are made.

(continued)

Recognizing Words

Present a written sentence and ask the child to find a word, any word, and circle it. This illustrates if the child has the concept of a printed word. Extend the activity by asking the child to circle a specific word.

Word Pairs and Homophones

Present written word pairs representing the same word. One of the words in the pair should be spelled correctly and the other should be misspelled but represent the way the word sounds. For example, talk/tawk, blak/black, bote/boat, salmon/sammon, beleave/believe. Say the word aloud, and ask the child to identify which spelling of the word is correct. This can also be done using homophones (words that sound the same but have different meanings). Present written homophones and ask questions related to the word pairs. For example, write the words *meat* and *meet*. Ask the child, Which one can be eaten? Write the words *two* and *too*. Ask the child, "Which one is a number?" Write the words *see* and *sea*. Ask the child, "Which one has water?"

Embedded Words

Present written words embedded in a string of letters. For example, write "dmbluecst" or "xfthousewlm." Ask the child to find the word that is hidden in the letter string.

Read or Spell Irregular Words

Identify a list of age-appropriate words that contain an irregular element (e.g., they, said, once, ocean, yacht) and ask the student to read the words or dictate the words for the student to spell.

(can stand alone), and word roots (cannot stand alone). Knowledge of morphemes aids an individual in both decoding and encoding (e.g., Carlisle, 2004), especially when reading or writing multisyllabic words. In languages that have deep orthographies (many linguistic aspects affecting the connections at the sound-symbol level) like English, knowledge of these meaningful words and word parts is very helpful. Morphological knowledge includes how to inflect, or change the meaning of, a word following standard patterns of the language. Inflectional morphemes change the form of a word to give it a different meaning, but not the part of speech (e.g., verb tense—play and played, or singular-plural—girl-girls). These types of morphemes are described as grammatical morphemes. For example, adding an "s" to the end of a word is a standard pattern for forming a plural. "Here is one dog." "Now there are two_____" (dogs). Derivational morphemes often involve forming a new word from the same root (e.g., please, pleasure), which often result in a change in the part of speech. For example, by adding the suffix –ation to the word *create*, the word changes from a verb to the noun *creation*. Morphological knowledge enhances the individual's awareness of the spelling system as well as the meaningful parts of words, thereby aiding both decoding and vocabulary development. As individuals grow older, the importance of morphological awareness for predicting reading skill increases (Kuo & Anderson, 2006).

DON'T FORGET

Inflectional morphemes do not change the part of speech, whereas derivational morphemes often do.

ASSESSMENT OF MORPHOLOGY

Assessing an individual's morphological knowledge may require an evaluation in both receptive and expressive language modalities. Typically, speech-language professionals administer standardized measures of morphology (see Rapid Reference 6.4). Rapid Reference 6.5 presents a variety of informal methods for assessing morphology.

ASSESSMENT OF BASIC READING SKILLS AND SPELLING

Many standardized tests exist that are designed to measure various aspects of school achievement. Typically, in an evaluation for dyslexia an assessment that measures several facets of school achievement is administered. Not only do

≡ Rapid Reference 6.4

Standardized Measures of Morphological Knowledge

Tests	Age/Grade Range	Abilities Measured	Publisher
Clinical Evaluation of Language Fundamentals-4 (CELF-4)	5 to 21	morphology (receptive and expressive)	Pearson
Comprehensive Assessment of Spoken Language (CASL)	3 to 21	grammatical morphology (expressive)	Pearson
Test of Auditory Comprehension of Language-Revised (TACL-R)	3 to 11	grammatical morphology (receptive)	PRO-ED

≡ *Rapid Reference 6.5*

Informal Measures of Morphological Knowledge

Compound Words

Ask the individual to break the compound word into its parts and say what the parts mean. For example, use baseball (base-ball), chalkboard (chalk-board), or fireman (fire-man).

Affixes

Add an affix to a known word and have the individual describe the new meaning. For example, use skip and skipped, school and preschool, or do and undo.

Derivations

Provide words that have the same base word and ask the individual how the words are related. For example, ask the individual how ear, earring, eardrum, and earache are all related.

Pictures

Use pictures to illustrate grammatical morphemes, providing a receptive evaluation of knowledge. Ask the individual to point to the picture that illustrates the correct grammatical morpheme (e.g., "the boy is jumping over the fence" versus "the boy has jumped over the fence.")

these tests include measures of reading and spelling performance, but they also include other areas of functioning so that an evaluator can also document areas of strength, such as in oral language and/or mathematics. Rapid Reference 6.6 illustrates several widely used standardized assessments that provide measures of various aspects of word reading and spelling.

WORD READING AND WORD SPELLING

Both word reading and spelling accuracy and the breadth and depth of a sight vocabulary are included as part of a comprehensive evaluation for dyslexia. On standardized measures, evaluators typically assess an individual's reading and spelling accuracy by asking him to read or spell a list of unrelated words that are ordered by the level of difficulty. These lists typically

DON'T FORGET

Evaluation of word reading skills should include real words and nonsense words in both untimed and timed conditions.

≡ Rapid Reference 6.6

Commonly Used Individually Administered Achievement Tests

Tests	Age/Grade Range	Publisher
Diagnostic Achievement Battery, 3rd ed. (DAB-3)	6-0 to 14-11	PRO-ED
Kaufman Test of Educational Achievement, 2nd ed. (KTEA-2)	4-6 to 90+	Pearson
Peabody Individual Achievement Test-Revised/ Normative Update (PIAT-R)	5-0 to 22-11	Pearson
Process Assessment of the Learner: Diagnostics for Reading and Writing, 2nd ed. (PAL-II)	Grades K-6	Pearson
Wechsler Individual Achievement Test, 3rd ed. (WIAT-III)	4-0 to 19-11	Pearson
Wide Range Achievement Test, 4th ed. (WRAT-4)	5-0 to 94	Pearson
Woodcock Johnson III NU Tests of Achievement, 3rd ed. (WJ III ACH NU)	2-0 to 90+	Riverside Publishing
Young Children's Achievement Test (YCAT)	4-0 to 17-11	PRO-ED

contain all types of words including words with both regular and irregular elements. An evaluator should explore an individual's word recognition skill both reading lists of words, as well as reading text. Because of their well-developed language comprehension skills, some children with dyslexia have more difficulty reading single isolated words than they do reading text (Hulme & Snowling, 2009; Uhry & Clark, 2004). In addition, evaluation of word reading skills should include both accuracy and fluency with real and nonsense words in untimed and timed conditions (Christo, Davis, & Brock, 2009). Rapid Reference 6.7 illustrates some commonly used assessments that include measures of basic reading skills, as well as rate.

DON'T FORGET

Although individuals with dyslexia can recall the spelling of a word immediately after learning it, they tend to soon forget how to spell the word.

Rapid Reference 6.7

Commonly Used Standardized Measures of Reading

Test	Age Range	Publisher
Gray Oral Reading Tests, 4th ed. (GORT-4)	6–0 to 18–11	PRO-ED
Gray Silent Reading Tests (GSRT)	7–0 to 25–0	PRO-ED
Gray Diagnostic Reading Tests, 2nd ed. (GDRT-2)	6–0 to 13–11	PRO-ED
Nelson-Denny Reading Test	9–0 to 16–11	PRO-ED
Test of Irregular Word Reading Efficiency (TIWRE)	3–0 to 94	PAR
Test of Silent Reading Efficiency and Comprehension (TOSREC)	Grades 1–12	PRO-ED
Test of Silent Word Reading Fluency (TOSWRF)	6–6 to 17–11	PRO-ED
Test of Word Reading Efficiency (TOWRE)	6–0 to 24–0	PRO-ED
WJ III Diagnostic Reading Battery (WDRB)	2–0 to 80+	Riverside Publishing
Woodcock Reading Mastery Tests-Revised/Normative Update (WRMT-R/NU)	5–0 to 75+	Pearson

In assessing the spelling performance of individuals with dyslexia, it is important to go beyond an analysis of performance on classroom spelling tests. In comparison to individuals with typical spelling ability, individuals with dyslexia seem to be able to spell a word correctly immediately after learning the spelling, but then memory of the correct spelling fades rapidly (Schulte-Körne, Deimel, Bartling, & Remschmidt, 2004). Thus, an evaluator should also analyze a writer's spelling errors within daily writing samples. In addition, one single standardized spelling test will not provide enough information to understand the strengths and weaknesses of a student's spelling knowledge across various orthographic patterns, and a teacher will not be able to design appropriate interventions (Calhoun, Greenberg, & Hunter, 2010). Analysis of spelling errors from tests as well as writing samples will provide a teacher with insights into a student's linguistic knowledge that will be useful for instructional planning (Uhry & Clark, 2004).

In some cases, an evaluator will want to compare an individual's abilities to read and spell words with regular phoneme-grapheme correspondence (e.g., cab) to words that contain an irregular element (e.g., once). As noted earlier in the chapter, the recognition and spelling of words with irregular elements requires knowledge of orthography, the visual memory of common letter strings. The reader must both observe and recall letter patterns and letter strings; an ability

> **CAUTION**
>
> The results from only one spelling test will not provide enough information for error analysis to plan targeted instructional goals.

that has been referred to as graphemic parsing skills (Hulme & Snowling, 2009, p. 55). Put more simply, the reader is able to group together and recall common letter strings, such as "ght."

THE DUAL-ROUTE THEORY

The dual-route theory of reading and spelling suggests that two pathways are involved in learning words: a lexical procedure for reading real words and irregular words, and a nonlexical procedure that involves converting letters to phonemes in a serial order and aids in using phonics and reading nonwords (Coltheart, 1980; 2007). The knowledge of grapheme-phoneme correspondence rules, such as knowing that "ph" represents the speech sound /f/, is used by the nonlexical reading route.

Some poor readers have more difficulty reading irregular words than regular words, which has been referred to as developmental surface dyslexia. Other poor readers have trouble using phonics to pronounce nonwords but are able to read real words and irregular words, which has been called developmental phonological dyslexia. These different difficulties in learning to read relate to the lexical and nonlexical routes and provide further support for two different types of dyslexia, as well as the dual-route model of reading (Coltheart, 2007). In a study comparing typically achieving readers to students with poor reading skill, Abu Hamour (2010) found high correlations among all of the reading variables within the normally distributed data but insignificant correlations between irregular and nonword reading within the group of students with poor reading, providing further support to the dual-route theory. Among the 21 students with poor reading, 10 students presented problems in both nonword reading and irregular word reading; 9 students presented problems just in nonword reading; and 2 students presented problems only in irregular word reading. Thus, in typically developing readers a strong relationship exists among all reading skills, whereas with poor readers a disruption can exist in one or more aspect of reading performance.

The same type of pattern is apparent in spelling. Some people with dyslexia can spell nonwords and words with regular sound-symbol correspondence, but have trouble spelling irregular words. When words are spelled incorrectly, but the sounds are sequenced correctly, it indicates developing mastery of phonics, but difficulty accessing word representations (Christo et al., 2009). In other words, these individuals have poor lexical representations, but good knowledge of phoneme-grapheme correspondences; this problem with inadequate orthographic lexical representations cannot be explained by low intelligence, poor motivation, or limited learning opportunities (Romani, Olson, & Di Betta, 2007). The errors that these individuals tend to make when spelling are to regularize the irregular element of the word, capturing the sounds of the word, but not the unusual or atypical spelling pattern (e.g., spelling said as sed and they as thay). As with reading, poor spelling of irregular words is referred to as surface dysgraphia (because the problem has to do with writing), whereas difficulty with the conversion of phonemes into graphemes is called phonological dysgraphia (Romani et al., 2007). Individuals with this problem have difficulty spelling nonwords and produce spellings where the order of the sounds is incorrect. Poor spelling is an indicator of dyslexia across the lifespan. In fact, it is at times the only remaining indicator of dyslexia in adulthood (Romani et al., 2007).

DON'T FORGET

....

Poorly specified lexical representations in spelling are caused by an orthographic impairment that differs from difficulty sequencing sounds correctly (a phonological impairment).

NONWORD READING AND SPELLING

Another important component of an evaluation for dyslexia is to have an individual read and spell nonwords or pseudowords, which is a direct way to investigate the development of phonic skills. The reading of a nonword requires the reader to apply spelling-sound correspondences to translate a written word that is not stored in memory into speech (Berninger & Richards, 2010). Nonwords are words that are not real and have no meaning, but they do conform to English spelling patterns and rules (e.g., flib and litch). Children with the most severe problems in phonological awareness will have the most difficulty reading and spelling nonwords (Hulme & Snowling, 2009).

In order to spell both nonwords and real words, the person must be able to isolate the phonemes in spoken words and then assign a letter or letters to each sound (Lervåg & Hulme, 2010). The spelling of nonwords also involves knowledge of common orthographic spelling patterns and spelling rules, such as knowing to double the consonant in the nonword strubbing or that litch would most likely be spelled as -tch rather than as -ch because the /ch/ sound follows a short vowel.

In their clinical work evaluating individuals with dyslexia, Uhry and Clark (2004) observed that the standardized test results often follow this pattern: Intelligence and listening comprehension > reading comprehension > decoding words in text > decoding words in lists > nonsense word reading and spelling (p. 69). Thus, it is often not unusual for an individual with dyslexia to read words correctly within a passage that are missed when reading a list of words. Making comparisons among an individual's scores

DON'T FORGET

A comparison of an individual's scores across different types of reading tasks can lead to helpful insights regarding the most effective type of intervention for that individual.

across different types of word reading tasks often has instructional implications (Christo et al., 2009). If an individual struggles to read nonsense words, instruction should focus on phonics. If an individual can read nonsense words, but struggles reading irregular words, instruction should focus on orthographic patterns and sight word learning. If an individual is accurate in reading real words and nonsense words, but reads slowly, an intervention to increase fluency would be appropriate.

ASSESSMENT OF READING FLUENCY

A comprehensive evaluation for dyslexia must also include measures of reading fluency. Measures of reading fluency are often more sensitive than word reading measures in detecting reading problems (Meisinger, Bloom, & Hynd, 2010; Sofie & Riccio, 2002). An accurate assessment of fluency also involves consideration of the depth and breadth of a reader's sight vocabulary. In fact,

CAUTION

Accurate reading does not guarantee fluent reading. It is also important to assess an individual's rate of reading.

the extent of a child's sight vocabulary is the most important factor for explaining differences in reading fluency (Torgesen, Alexander, et al., 2001). Sometimes, fluency and rate of reading are not included as part of a reading evaluation. If fluency is not evaluated, readers who have learned to decode accurately but still lack fluency, a common characteristic of individuals with dyslexia, may be misunderstood, as well as misdiagnosed. Meisinger and colleagues (2010) found that children with reading disabilities were underidentified when fluency measures were not included as part of the evaluation. Both standardized and curriculum-based measurements (CBM) are used to assess fluency. In addition, CBM measures are frequently used to set progress monitoring goals.

Oral reading is used to assess reading fluency because it is more reliable than silent reading (Jenkins, Fuchs, van den Broek, Espin, & Deno, 2003), primarily because what the reader is reading can be heard. Also, in order to measure prosody (expression), the individual must read aloud. Sometimes observable differences exist between a person's speed between oral and silent reading, as rate of articulation must be considered during oral reading.

Traditionally, the speed of reading a list of words has been the primary means of measuring fluency in children with dyslexia. Recently, researchers have found that focusing solely on rate, such as only calculating the number of words read correctly per minute, ignores other important aspects of reading, such as accuracy and prosody (Valencia et al., 2010). This focus on rate leads to incorrect identification of those needing special services. The process overidentifies children who do not require special services and underidentifies those who do, especially children struggling with reading comprehension and English language learners (Valencia et al., 2010). In addition, the emphasis on rate encourages teachers to focus on building speed rather than increasing vocabulary and comprehension.

CAUTION

If rate is the only indicator measured for reading fluency, incorrect conclusions may be drawn regarding which individuals need reading support and what is the most appropriate type of instruction.

METHODS OF ASSESSING FLUENCY

An assessment of reading fluency must explore the various components that comprise fluency: accuracy, rate, and prosody. All aspects of reading fluency must be considered when determining a reader's instructional needs. Some of the most common methods used for assessing aspects of fluency include informal reading inventories, curriculum-based measurements of reading (R-CBM), and standardized measures of reading that include word lists, nonword lists, sentences, and passages. Qualitative information, such as observing the individual's reading performance and behaviors, as well as analyzing the errors made, is invaluable for diagnosis and instructional planning. Rapid Reference 6.8 lists several measures of reading fluency.

Accuracy. If a reader is given materials to read that are too difficult, she is likely to become frustrated (Betts, 1946). In order to match a reader's level of performance with appropriate books, informal reading inventories (IRIs) have been used for many years to determine both word reading accuracy, as well as

≡ Rapid Reference 6.8

Selected Measures of Reading Fluency

Test	Age/Grade Range	Areas Measured	Publisher
Dynamic Indicators of Beginning Early Literacy Skills, 6th ed. (DIBELS)	1–6	oral reading fluency	University of Oregon
Fluency Formula	K–8	oral reading fluency	Scholastic
Gray Oral Reading Tests, 4th ed. (GORT-4)	6–0 to 18–11	rate, accuracy, fluency, comprehension	PRO-ED
Qualitative Reading Inventory (QRI)	K–4	rate, accuracy, fluency, comprehension	Pearson
Reading Fluency Indicator	K–12	rate, accuracy, prosody, comprehension	Pearson
Test of Silent Reading Efficiency and Comprehension (TOSREC)	1–12	silent reading efficiency (rate & accuracy), comprehension	PRO-ED
Test of Silent Word Reading Fluency (TOSWRF)	6–6 to 17–11	accuracy and efficiency of recognizing printed words quickly	PRO-ED
Test of Word Reading Efficiency (TOWRE)	6–0 to 24–0	accuracy and speed of reading nonwords	PRO-ED

the level of comprehension. The percentage of words read correctly is used to calculate the accuracy level. When a reader's accuracy is below 90%, the text is considered to be too difficult. The concept of identifying an individual's independent level, instructional level, and frustration level is associated with IRIs. Typically, if the reader's accuracy level on a text is 99% or higher, the text is considered to be at the reader's independent level; 98–90% accuracy the instructional level; and less than 90% the frustration level (Betts, 1946). A simple way to judge if a book is too difficult for a child is referred to as the rule of thumb. The teacher counts out 100 words for the child to read and then starting with the little finger on one hand puts down a finger each time an error is made. If the rater reaches the thumb (five errors) before the child finishes the passage, it is likely that the text will be too difficult. One limitation of IRIs is the amount of time they take, especially when evaluating a struggling reader. In addition, they must be administered individually.

Rate. Rate is frequently assessed using R-CBM probes. This approach requires the individual to read a grade-level text orally for one minute. The teacher, using a copy of the same text, marks any errors made, and then calculates the total number of words read correctly. In educational settings that employ a Response-to-Intervention (RTI) model, R-CBMs are often used (Deno, 2003). A common benchmark for oral reading fluency is the number of words read correctly per minute (WRC) which is sometimes written as WCPM. Rapid Reference 6.9 illustrates the types of words that are considered to be read correctly, and the types that are considered to be errors. Although CBM measures are useful for monitoring progress, they are not sufficient for determining the existence of a disability or dyslexia; RTI is primarily a service delivery model, not a diagnostic model (Feifer, 2011).

CAUTION

Information obtained by RTI procedures can contribute to an understanding of the reading problem, as well as what interventions may be most effective, but this information alone is insufficient for making a diagnosis of dyslexia. Multiple sources of information are required including family history, standardized test results, prior interventions, classroom work samples, and teacher reports.

DON'T FORGET

If an individual makes an error and then self-corrects, it does not count as an error, but fluency and rate are affected by the self-corrections.

≡ Rapid Reference 6.9

Determining Correct and Incorrect Words

Words Read Correctly (WRC)
    Correctly pronounced words
    Repetitions
    Insertions
    Self-corrected words within 3 seconds
    Articulation/dialect differences

Words Counted as Errors
    Hesitations (longer than 3 seconds, examiner provides the word)
    Substitutions (e.g., reading house for home)
    Omissions (i.e., leaving out a word)
    Mispronunciations

To determine the number of errors, the instructor would record the total number of words read and then subtract the number of errors. This result is then recorded in a standard format of WRC/Errors. For example, after reading for one minute, Juan had read 140 words total. He made five errors, so $140 - 5 = 135$ words read correctly. This information, WRC and errors, would be recorded as 135/5.

Rapid Reference 6.10 illustrates common oral reading benchmarks. Note that oral reading fluency is not typically assessed during the first few months of first grade, which is why that column is blank. Also, within each grade and at each semester, there is an expected range of words correct per minute. The ranges reported in Rapid Reference 6.10 are WCPM at the 50th percentile to the 90th percentile. The rate, or automaticity, of individuals who are at or near these expected ranges is considered adequate. Others who are consistently above or below the expected range may be at risk for problems in reading fluency. It may seem odd that individuals above the expected range may be at risk. However, some individuals read very quickly but may have limited comprehension and expression. There is no value in reading quickly, if comprehension is limited. More comprehensive charts developed by Ron Hockman are presented in Table 6.1 (Grades 2–8) and Table 6.2 (K–1). These charts combine information from various sources and provide a summary of reading rates for commonly used R-CBM measures.

≡ Rapid Reference 6.10

Oral Reading Fluency Benchmarks (WCPM)

	Fall	Winter	Spring
Grade 1:	23–81	53–111	
Grade 2:	51–106	72–125	89–142
Grade 3:	71–128	92–146	107–162
Grade 4:	94–145	112–166	123–180
Grade 5:	110–166	127–182	139–194
Grade 6:	127–177	140–195	150–204
Grade 7:	128–180	136–192	150–202
Grade 8:	133–185	146–199	151–199

Ranges: WCPM at Percentile 50 to Percentile 90
Adapted from: Hasbrouck, J. E., & Tindal, G. (2006, April). Oral reading fluency norms: A valuable assessment tool for teachers. *Reading Teacher, 59,* 636–644.

Both accuracy and rate can be measured using the same R-CBM probe simply by adding in a calculation for accuracy (Rasinski, 2006). Using the one-minute reading probe, the teacher can determine the rate (WCPM) and then divide the WCPM by the total number of words read (words correct + errors) to obtain the accuracy level. For example, a beginning second-grade student read 85 words correctly out of a total of 100 words attempted. Her reading rate is 85 WCPM, which falls within the expected range for the Fall term of Grade 2 (see Rapid Reference 6.10). However, her accuracy level is only 85% (85 divided by 100 = .85 or 85%), which is below the frustration level (<90%). Instruction for this student should focus on building accuracy, rather than rate. Because a reading probe takes only one minute, it is possible to do more than one during each session. For example, three probes may be administered, and the median performance can then be used as the baseline to monitor progress.

DON'T FORGET

"CBM data alone cannot be used to diagnose a reading disability, even when gathered within an RTI service delivery model. A diagnosis of reading disability must be based on multiple data sources." (Feifer, 2011, p. 24)

Table 6.1 Curriculum-Based Measurement (CBM) Norms—Reading

	Grade	2nd **ORF	2nd *MAZE	3rd **ORF	3rd *MAZE	4th **ORF	4th *MAZE	5th **ORF	5th *MAZE	6th **ORF	6th *MAZE	7th **ORF	7th *MAZE	8th **ORF	8th *MAZE
Fall	Advanced	80	8	100	16	120	17	140	21	155	23	155	26	160	26
	Average-Goal	50	5	70	12	95	12	110	16	130	17	130	19	130	20
	Limited	25	3	50	7	70	8	85	10	100	11	105	14	105	15
Winter	Advanced	100	16	120	23	140	24	155	29	170	31	165	30	175	31
	Average-Goal	70	10	90	17	110	18	130	23	140	24	140	23	150	25
	Limited	45	6	65	10	85	12	100	16	110	18	110	17	115	18
Spring	Advanced	120	19	140	28	150	26	170	34	180	37	180	36	180	34
	Average-Goal	90	13	110	22	120	19	140	28	150	30	150	30	150	28
	Limited	65	9	80	15	100	13	110	21	120	23	120	23	125	22
	Target ROI	1.20	0.40	1.10	0.40	0.90	0.40	0.90	0.40	0.70	0.40	0.70	0.40	0.60	0.40
	Low ROI	0.60	0.20	0.55	0.20	0.45	0.20	0.45	0.20	0.35	0.20	0.35	0.20	0.30	0.20

	ORF Accuracy	MAZE Accuracy	ORF Accuracy	MAZE Accuracy	ORF Accuracy	MAZE Accuracy	ORF Accuracy	MAZE Accuracy	ORF Accuracy	MAZE Accuracy	ORF Accuracy	MAZE Accuracy	ORF Accuracy	MAZE Accuracy
Advanced Accuracy	99%		99%		99%		99%		99%		99%		99%	
Average-Goal	95%	80%	95%	80%	95%	80%	95%	80%	95%	80%	95%	80%	95%	80%
Limited	90%		90%		90%		90%		90%		90%		90%	

Source: Developed by Ron Hockman, Ed.S, School Psychologist. Used with permission.
All scores are number correct per minute, except Maze.
Scores between the Average-Goal score and the Limited score are considered at some risk or below average.
LSF = Letter Sound Fluency; LNF =Letter Naming Fluency; PSF = Phoneme Segmentation Fluency; NWF = Nonsense Word Fluency; WIF = Word Identification Fluency; ORF= Oral Reading Fluency; ROI = Rate of Improvement
* Maze scores are based on 3 minutes.
** ORF Scores are Words Correct per Minute.

127

Qualitative information is also helpful in pinpointing an individual's specific learning needs. One simple approach is to determine which of the following four characteristics best describes the person's reading: (1) fast and accurate, (2) fast and inaccurate, (3) slow and accurate, or (4) slow and inaccurate. If a

Table 6.2   Curriculum-Based Measurement (CBM) Norms—Early Literacy

		Kindergarten			
		LSF	LNF	PSF	NWF
Fall	Advanced	16	27	—	—
	Average-Goal	8	15	—	—
	Limited	3	6	—	—
Winter	Advanced	31	46	36	26
	Average-Goal	19	34	22	16
	Limited	9	20	8	7
Spring	Advanced	43	56	50	39
	Average-Goal	31	44	35	27
	Limited	20	31	15	16
	Target ROI	1.00	0.70	1.00	0.70
	Low ROI	0.50	0.35	0.50	0.35

		First Grade					
		LSF	LNF	PSF	NWF	WIF	**ORF
Fall	Advanced	36	53	50	36	25	30
	Average-Goal	26	41	35	25	17	10
	Limited	16	29	20	14	12	5
Winter	Advanced	48	63	50	58	52	50
	Average-Goal	38	52	35	50	39	25
	Limited	27	39	20	31	27	10

		LSF	LNF	PSF	NWF	WIF	**ORF
	Advanced	51	70	50	77	75	80
Spring	Average-Goal	40	58	35	54	62	50
	Limited	30	45	20	35	50	25
	Target ROI	1.00	NA	1.00	1.4	1.5	1.9
	Low ROI	0.50	NA	0.50	0.70	0.75	0.95

Source: Developed by Ron Hockman, Ed.S., School Psychologist. Used with permission.
The scores in Tables 6.1 and 6.2 have been amalgamated from the following sources:
Hasbrouck, J., & Tindal, G. A. (2006). Oral Reading Fluency norms: A valuable assessment tool for reading teachers. *Reading Teacher, 59,* 636–644.
Fuchs, L. S., & Fuchs, D. (2004). *Using CBM for progress monitoring.* Retrieved from http://www.studentprogress.org
DIBELS. (2010). *Benchmark goals.* Retrieved from https://dibels.uoregon.edu/
AIMSWEB. (2006). *R-CBM Norms.* Retrieved from http://aimsweb.com
Howell, K. W., & Nolet, V. (2000). *Curriculum-based evaluation: Teaching and decision making.* Belmont, CA: Wadsworth.
**ORF (Oral Reading Fluency) Scores are Words Correct per Minute.

person is fast and accurate, the focus of evaluation can be on prosody and comprehension to determine if all aspects of fluency are intact. If the person is fast and inaccurate, the evaluation would address word reading skill, and instruction would focus on building accuracy. If the person is slow and accurate, the evaluation would focus on fluency, and the instruction would focus on methods for building rate. If the person is a slow and inaccurate reader, the evaluation will focus on word reading skill, and instruction will involve both accuracy and rate building with accuracy as the first priority.

Prosody. It is more difficult to quantify and measure prosody than it is to measure accuracy or rate because the evaluation is more subjective in nature. In most cases, rubrics or rating scales are used to evaluate prosody. The rubric may provide four to six choices ranging from word-by-word reading in a monotone voice to expressive reading with good phrasing. Rapid Reference 6.11 illustrates a 4-point rubric adapted from Pinell and colleagues (1995). Using grade-level text, the individual reads aloud while the teacher or other rater listens. The individual can also be

> **DON'T FORGET**
>
> Evaluation of reading fluency includes measures of accuracy, rate, and prosody.

recorded while reading the text so that the rating can occur later. After the reading is completed, the teacher or rater consults the rubric and selects the rating that most closely matches the individual's reading. Accurate ratings can be established in less than one minute. Rapid Reference 6.12 provides a checklist adapted from Hudson, Lane, and Pullen (2005, p. 707) that provides a more detailed assessment of prosody.

≡ Rapid Reference 6.11

Sample Rubric for Rating Prosody
4: Reads with good use of phrasing and punctuation marks, has good expression, and an appropriate rate.
3: Reads with some expression and has a generally appropriate rate.
2: Generally reads in phrases but has limited expression and an inappropriate rate (too slow or fast).
1: Reads primarily word-by-word, lacks expression, and has an inappropriate rate (too slow or too fast).

Adapted from Pinell et al. (1995). *Listening to children read aloud: Oral fluency.* Washington, DC: U.S. Department of Education, National Center for Education Statistics. Retrieved from http://nces.ed.gov/pubs95/web/95762.asp

≡ Rapid Reference 6.12

Detailed Assessment of Prosody
1. Reader places stress and emphasis on appropriate words.
2. The reader's voice tone rises and falls at appropriate points in the text.
3. The reader observes punctuation marks in the text (e.g., voice tone rises near the end of a question and pauses with periods).
4. In narrative text with dialogue, the reader uses expression to convey characters' mental states, such as excitement, sadness, fear, or confidence.
5. The reader uses prepositional phrases, subject-verb divisions, and conjunctions to pause appropriately at phrase boundaries.

Adapted from Hudson, R. F., Lane, H. B., & Pullen, P. C. (2005). Reading fluency assessment and instruction: What, why, and how? *Reading Teacher, 58,* 702–714.

Readers with dyslexia often have a slow reading rate and trouble with prosody because much of their energy and effort is directed toward word identification. This difficulty identifying words with ease essentially becomes a bottleneck to comprehension. A similar phenomenon occurs with writing. Writers with dyslexia often have poor spelling, which then interferes with the ease of writing, as well as the selection of words to write. A child may wish to write "beautiful" but instead writes "good" because she knows how to spell this word. It is important to consider the impact of weaknesses in these underlying basic skills when evaluating an individual's reading comprehension or written expression. Otherwise, incorrect conclusions may be reached, and inappropriate instruction may be recommended.

CONCLUSION

A solid foundation in decoding and encoding skills is necessary to become a fluent reader. Without fluency, the reader struggles with comprehension. Individuals with dyslexia often lack the necessary foundation in these underlying basic skills. Even when they learn to decode and encode, they typically have compromised reading rates so they remain dysfluent readers, and their comprehension is impaired. Understanding the developmental phases of decoding and encoding can help a teacher or tutor identify where an individual is functioning, and as a result, plan more targeted assessment, and more appropriate instruction.

 **TEST YOURSELF**

1. **Reading and spelling follow similar trajectories, but spelling skill lags behind because**
   a. spelling requires more oral skills than reading.
   b. spelling requires recall of the entire word, whereas reading only requires recognition.
   c. spelling requires better visual skills than reading.
   d. the processes involved in spelling develop at an older age.

2. **The understanding that speech sounds can be converted into letter strings is referred to as**
   a. memory for literacy.
   b. phonemic awareness.
   c. spelling awareness.
   d. alphabetic principle.

3. **According to Ehri's phase theory, a reader who is at the partially alphabetic phase is able to**
   a. recognize all vowel sounds.
   b. recognize most consonants, long vowels, and a few sight words.
   c. recognize syllables and common morphemes.
   d. recognize all words that follow regular grapheme-phoneme correspondence.

4. **According to Ehri's phase theory, a reader who is at the alphabetic phase**
   a. has complete connections between phonemes and graphemes.
   b. is able to use common word parts as an aid to reading and spelling multisyllabic words.
   c. reads words quickly with ease.
   d. all of the above.
   e. none of the above.

5. **According to Ehri's theory of sight word development, as children enter the consolidated alphabetic phase, their application of letter-sound knowledge becomes less effortful. True or False?**

6. **One example of an informal measure of orthography is to ask the person to**
   a. read and spell real words.
   b. read and spell nonwords.
   c. read and spell irregular words.
   d. read and spell CVC words.

7. **Oftentimes, individuals with dyslexia cannot remember spelling rules and patterns, so they spell words**
   a. with all letters capitalized (e.g., THEY, WAS).
   b. using the wrong tense (e.g., sleep for slept).
   c. exactly as they sound (e.g., hape for happy, wuz for was).
   d. with fewer syllables.

8. **According to the dual route theory, a lexical procedure is needed for reading**
   a. real words.
   b. nonsense words.
   c. irregular words.
   d. all of the above.
   e. a and c.

9. In one minute, Martha read a total of 62 words and made 8 errors. What was her WRC?

10. CBM measures are part of most RTI models and are useful for monitoring progress, and sufficient for determining whether or not a student has dyslexia. True or False?

11. Instruction for readers who can read nonwords, but struggle reading irregular words should focus on
   a. phonology.
   b. fluency.
   c. orthography.
   d. morphology.

12. Measures of nonword or nonsense word reading can be most helpful in determining whether a reader
   a. reads quickly.
   b. can use phonics.
   c. comprehends text.
   d. reads slowly.

13. The independent level of word reading accuracy is often considered to be
   a. 99%.
   b. 94%.
   c. 92%.
   d. 90%.

14. A reader who reads word-by-word with limited expression may be described as having poor
   a. phonic skills.
   b. articulation.
   c. prosody.
   d. phonological awareness.

15. Individuals with dyslexia often direct their energy toward word identification; therefore their reading tends to be slow and lacks expression. True or False?

Answers: 1. b; 2. d; 3. b; 4. a; 5. True; 6. c; 7. c; 8. e; 9. WRC = 54/8; 10. False; 11.c; 12. b; 13. a; 14. c; 15. True

Chapter Seven

INSTRUCTION IN PHONOLOGICAL AWARENESS: EARLY READING/ SPELLING SKILLS

To learn to read is to light a fire; every syllable that is spelled out is a spark.

—Victor Hugo, *Les Misérables*

Because individuals with dyslexia tend to have poor phonemic awareness, direct instruction in phonological processing strategies is particularly beneficial (Uhry, 2005). A central finding from research on phonological awareness is that not only do phonological skills underlie early reading and spelling development, but they also can be taught (Soifer, 2005). Therefore, it is critical that children with dyslexia receive specific instruction in phonological awareness because this type of teaching makes a difference in beginning reading and spelling achievement (Berninger & Wolf, 2009). The relationship between phonological awareness and reading ability is reciprocal and bidirectional: As phonological awareness develops, reading improves and vice versa (Miller, Sanchez, & Hynd, 2003).

To be successful readers, children need to understand how sounds in speech relate to the printed words on a page (Uhry, 2005). This relationship between sounds and symbols, referred to as the alphabetic principle, can be taught to young children within the kindergarten and first-grade years, even if the children are lacking in phonological and grapheme-phoneme awareness. When students have trouble with these tasks, they need to spend time with activities that help them discover the relationships between sounds and letters. Although the beginning levels of instruction may not involve words or letters, instruction is most effective when phonological awareness training is combined with instruction in letter knowledge and word reading (Bishop & Snowling, 2004). As a general principle when teaching phonological awareness, students must move from easier tasks, such as rhyming, to more complex tasks, such as blending, segmenting, and manipulating phonemes (Anthony & Francis, 2005; Chard & Dickson, 1999). Rapid Reference 7.1 presents a summary of the recommendations of the National Reading Panel for teaching phonological awareness (NRP, 2000). Definitions of phonological awareness and phonemic awareness as well as their relationship to reading can be found in Chapter 5.

The two most important phonological awareness abilities for reading and spelling are blending (e.g., if I say these sounds, what word am I saying? /f/ /i/ /sh/) and segmentation (e.g., tell me the three sounds you hear in the word *fish*?; Ehri, 2006). Programs that provide instruction in blending and segmentation result in more improvement in reading than do those that place an emphasis on mastery of multiple skills (NRP, 2000). With both blending and segmentation, the instruction can begin with compound words (e.g., baseball), progress to syllables, onset-rimes, and then phonemes. In other words, the best sequence of instruction progresses from the largest units (whole words) to the smallest units (phonemes).

CAUTION

Direct training in phonological awareness skills may not always be the best use of instructional time for poor readers in the upper grades. Older poor readers appear to improve more from practice with accurate reading than from remediation of phonological awareness skills (Olson, 2011).

CAUTION

Too much time spent on phonological awareness activities may actually be counterproductive and the instructional time would be better spent on other activities, such as book reading and story writing.

DON'T FORGET

Instruction in phonological awareness is most effective when it is linked with instruction in phoneme-grapheme relationships.

BLENDING

Blending is necessary for applying phonics skills to pronounce unfamiliar words. Orton (1937) recognized that simply learning the sounds of the letters was of little use in and of itself unless the sounds could be put together into a spoken or printed word. He noted that it was critical to follow a step-by-step progression to ensure that the students could sequence and synthesize speech

≡ *Rapid Reference 7.1*

Summary of National Reading Panel Findings on Phonological Awareness
Many students benefit from phonological awareness training.
Individual children differ in the amount of training time needed.
Small group instruction is most effective.
Effective training time varies from 5 to 18 hours of total instructional time.
Ten minutes a few times weekly is often a sufficient amount of time to spend on a phonological awareness activity.
The most effective programs teach children how to segment phonemes in words with letters.
Phonological awareness training is more effective for improving the spelling of younger rather than older students with dyslexia.

≡ *Rapid Reference 7.2*

Teaching Blending
1. Begin with continuous speech sounds that can be sustained, such as /s/ and /m/.
2. Progress from words with two speech sounds to three, and then to four (e.g., me, tree, treat).
3. Gradually increase the length of the pause between the sounds from a one-fourth second pause to a half-second pause, to a full-second pause.
4. Demonstrate, model, and practice the process with written words that have regular phoneme-grapheme correspondence.

sounds. Blending instruction often begins with compound words and then progresses to syllables, onset-rimes, and then phonemes. When lettered tiles are added to the activity, the focus shifts to phonics instruction. Rapid Reference 7.2 describes a procedure for teaching sound blending.

SEGMENTATION

Segmentation is primarily important for encoding (spelling), which involves listening to the speech sounds and putting them in order. For spelling, the writer must apprehend the correct speech sound and then assign that sound to the correct grapheme. With dyslexia, the ability to segment written words into their underlying phonological elements is often impaired (S. E. Shaywitz & B. A.

Shaywitz, 2003). Segmentation can be particularly difficult for children because of coarticulation; consonant sounds are pronounced together with vowel sounds, making the middle sounds in words particularly hard for young children to hear (Uhry, 2005). Before being able to use the alphabetic principle, a reader must be able to segment all of the phonemes in a word, which is not usually accomplished until the age of 6 (Adams, 1990; Uhry, 2005). Research also suggests that the ability to segment phonemes helps children build their reading skills, particularly if they point to each word with their finger while reading (Uhry, 2005). Segmentation helps children recognize the word parts, including the syllables, onset-rimes, and phonemes. If a child cannot segment words, finger-point reading may not be beneficial to reading development. As with blending, instruction in segmentation often follows the sequence of compound words to syllables to onset-rimes to phonemes. With instruction in phonemes, activities often begin with consonant-vowel-consonant (CVC) words that end in common rimes (e.g., -at, -it, -ap). When lettered tiles are added to the activity, the focus shifts to decoding and beginning spelling instruction. Rapid Reference 7.3 provides guidance in teaching segmentation.

PHONEME-GRAPHEME RELATIONSHIPS

Connecting knowledge of sounds to the letters used to represent those sounds is an important goal of early literacy instruction. Thus, instruction in segmenting sounds is more effective when using letter tiles. This relationship must be taught explicitly, and children must have the opportunity to practice applying these skills in their reading and writing (NRP, 2000). Many of the methods and

Rapid Reference 7.3

Teaching Segmentation
1. Use manipulatives, such as tiles or blocks, to push apart the sounds.
2. Start with compound words with two parts (e.g., raincoat) and then progress to words with two, then three, syllables.
3. Break one-syllable words into onsets (consonants before the vowel) and rimes (the vowel and ending consonants; e.g., pl-ay).
4. At the phoneme level, progress from words with two speech sounds, to three, and then to four. Practice breaking apart the phonemes in words with regular phoneme-grapheme correspondence, where each speech sounds matches the most common grapheme for that spelling.

materials used to teach phoneme-grapheme relationships stem from the early work of Elkonin, a Russian psychologist, who studied the way young children mastered early reading skills. Elkonin used boxes drawn on paper to represent the sounds in a word, with each box representing a separate phoneme. Figure 7.1 provides an example of Elkonin boxes for the

DON'T FORGET

Blending and segmentation are two very important phonological awareness skills. Blending is the primary skill for decoding, and segmentation is the primary skill for encoding.

word "cat." Three boxes are drawn to represent the three phonemes in "cat." The teacher says the word slowly, articulating each sound clearly. The student places a chip or marker in each box as the individual sound is pronounced. Rapid Reference 7.4 summarizes the steps in an adaptation of the Elkonin procedure. An important benefit of using the Elkonin method is that the child is actively engaged in the task, making learning more effective.

Although the Elkonin procedure was not originally designed to teach spelling, it can be adapted for that purpose. After the individual can identify the sounds in a word, ask her to write the letter or letters used to represent that sound, reinforcing the phoneme-grapheme relationships. Alternatively, use letter tiles. As mentioned previously, phonological awareness instruction is

Figure 7.1 Elkonin Boxes for the Word "Cat"

≡ *Rapid Reference 7.4*

Steps in Adapted Elkonin Procedure

1. Begin with simple words that have a 1:1 correspondence between the number of sounds and the number of letters used to spell those sounds. For example, the word "cat" has three phonemes and is represented by three letters.

2. Using a picture that represents the simple word, draw the correct number of boxes below the picture (i.e., one box for each phoneme in the word).

3. Say the word slowly articulating each sound clearly. Ask the student to repeat the word. Then have the student push a color marker into each box as you say each sound. For example, as you say "/k/ . . . /a/ . . . /t/." the student should push one marker into the first box when you say /k/, a second marker into the middle box when you say /a/, and a third marker into the last box when you say /t/.

4. Ask the student to say the word slowly and push markers into the boxes as he says each sound.

5. Use color-coding to distinguish between vowels and consonants (e.g., use red chips for the vowels and yellow chips for the consonants).

6. Once a child can correctly segment three or four sounds, introduce letter tiles in place of the color chips.

7. Introduce additional phonic elements as the child progresses (e.g., blends, digraphs). These elements are represented in one box because they make one sound, further reinforcing the connection between sounds and letters.

enhanced when sounds are linked to graphemes. Figure 7.2 illustrates how Elkonin boxes may be adapted for spelling. Once the student has identified the phonemes in the word, then the teacher asks what letter is used to spell each sound. The student can use letter tiles or may write the letter that represents each sound in the corresponding box.

ORAL LANGUAGE

Oral language is both the foundation for learning and the primary means through which learning occurs. There is no doubt that language skills are critically important to learning to read or, for that matter, to learning any academic area. As noted in Chapter 1 of this book, however, dyslexia is primarily a problem with written language rather than spoken language (Pennington, Peterson, & McGrath, 2009), although individuals with dyslexia may have problems with

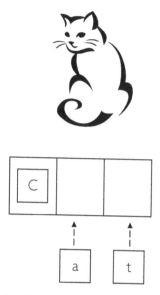

Figure 7.2   Using Elkonin Boxes for Beginning Spelling

word retrieval and pronouncing certain multisyllabic words. The problems of individuals who only have dyslexia are primarily evident in decoding and encoding rather than in language and reading comprehension. In fact, individuals with dyslexia often have language skills in the average range (Snowling, 2005). A typical child with dyslexia uses his good language skills to help compensate for weak phonics skills. Individuals with limits in oral language but intact phonological skills often learn to decode but have difficulty with comprehension, basically the opposite pattern of individuals with dyslexia. Of course, language development and language skills exist on a wide continuum and dyslexia can be present with or without other language problems (Snowling, 2011). Typical oral language development serves as a protective factor. Preschool children who have poor phonological awareness and delayed language are more likely to develop dyslexia than those with poor phonological awareness in the context of normal language development (Snowling, 2011). When language development is also delayed, the child will have difficulty with both decoding and reading comprehension. When oral language is an additional area of concern, instruction should include activities to promote vocabulary development and numerous opportunities to hear and interact with language in meaningful ways.

   Read aloud. An effective way to develop a child's phonemic awareness and language ability is to read aloud to the child (Adams, 1990). Exposing the child to the sounds and rhythm of language helps develop the prerequisite skills needed for learning to read. In addition, reading aloud provides opportunities to interact with the child, thus building and expanding language skills. Reading aloud to a child helps develop conceptual knowledge, background knowledge, and word knowledge. Without an adequate language base, learning to read is difficult. This applies to native English speakers with limits in oral language, as well as to English Language Learners.

Instruction for English language learners (ELLs). While the methods are the same when providing phonemic awareness and early phonics instruction to ELLs, there are some additional things to consider. Generally, if an ELL has learned to read in her native language (L1), learning to read in English will be easier. Similar cognitive and linguistic processes are involved in reading irrespective of the language. When literacy skills are well-established in L1, transfer of those skills to the second language (L2) is enhanced. However, if an ELL student is not literate in L1, it is necessary to build on what the student already knows. For example, if the child's first language is Spanish, instruction should use words that have sounds and graphemes common to both English and Spanish such as /f/, /d/, /t/, /n/, and the long vowels o and u. It is best to use familiar sounds and letters during instruction as unfamiliar phonemes and graphemes make learning more difficult. Start with what the student knows and help the student see the similarities between the two languages. This is true for vocabulary instruction as well. For example, nearly one-third of English words are cognates (i.e., words that have a similar look and meaning) in Spanish. Pointing out the connections between the English and Spanish words builds on what the student already knows and helps develop decoding, vocabulary, and comprehension skills.

DON'T FORGET

To facilitate learning for all students, including ELLs, connect new knowledge to prior knowledge.

EFFECTIVE COMMERCIAL PROGRAMS

A variety of commercial programs exist and can be used to help students develop phonological awareness and beginning letter-sound knowledge. Rapid Reference 7.5 lists programs that have a good research base or share the characteristics inherent in effective phonological awareness and beginning phoneme-grapheme instruction. (See the listed website to obtain additional information about each program.) In addition, several of these programs are described in more detail in the Appendix of this book (noted with an asterisk).

≡ Rapid Reference 7.5

Examples of Phonological Awareness and Phoneme-Grapheme Programs

Program	Website
Earobics (software)	www.earobics.com
*Fundations	www.wilsonlanguage.com
Hooked on Phonics Learn to Read	www.hookedonphonics.com
Ladders to Literacy	www.brookespublishing.com
*Lindamood Phoneme Sequencing Program (LiPS)	www.lindamoodbell.com
*Phonics and Spelling Through Phoneme-Grapheme Mapping	www.cambiumlearning.com
Phonemic Awareness in Young Children: A Classroom Curriculum	www.brookespublishing.com
*Phonic Reading Lessons: Skills and Practice	www.academictherapy.com
*Phono-Graphix	www.readamerica.com
Reading Readiness (Neuhaus Education Center)	www.neuhaus.org
*Read, Write, & Type	www.talkingfingers.com
*Road to the Code: A Phonological Awareness Program for Young Children	www.brookespublishing.com
Sound Partners	www.cambiumlearning.com
*S.P.I.R.E.	www.epsbooks.com

*A detailed description of the program is available in the Appendix of this book.

Rapid Reference 7.6 presents a summary of the basic principles followed by these programs (Adams, 1990; NRP, 2000; Uhry, 2005). The Institute for Education Sciences (IES) What Works Clearinghouse (http://ies.ed.gov/ncee/wwc/reports/) lists several additional commercial materials that show evidence of effectiveness for improving phonemic awareness including Early Intervention in Reading (www.earlyinterventioninreading.com), Stepping Stones to Literacy (www.steppingstonestoliteracy.com), and Ready, Set, Leap! (www.leapfrogschoolhouse.com), a preschool curriculum that uses a multisensory approach to teach early reading skills.

DON'T FORGET

Results from numerous research studies indicate that students with dyslexia benefit from direct, systematic instruction in phonological and phonemic awareness activities, as well as explicit teaching of phoneme-grapheme relationships.

CONCLUSION

For many developing readers, training in phonological awareness is necessary but insufficient for good reading (NRP, 2000; Torgesen & Mathes, 2000). Adequate word identification skill also requires mastery of more complex phonic skills, as well as automaticity with sight words. For students with dyslexia, however, training in phonological awareness when coupled with systematic instruction in letter-sound correspondences, is often critical and can help readers develop efficient word identification and improve spelling skills. Chapter 8 discusses instruction in word identification and spelling, and additional teaching procedures to help individuals with dyslexia move from phonological awareness to the knowledge and application of letter-sound associations.

≡ *Rapid Reference 7.6*

Principles of Effective Early Reading Instruction

1. Provide explicit, systematic instruction.
2. Use a sequence for instruction, such as described by Adams (1990):
   a. Rhyming
   b. Matching rhyme and alliteration
   c. Segmenting syllables
   d. Segmenting phonemes
   e. Manipulating phonemes
3. Teach letter names, and then use letters to represent sounds.
4. Teach regular spelling patterns first.
5. Gradually introduce more complex spelling patterns.
6. Integrate activities with reading and spelling.

🐾 TEST YOURSELF 🐾

1. **Phonological awareness training is most effective for improving reading and spelling in**
   a. students who have difficulty remembering how a word looks.
   b. younger students with dyslexia.

   c. ELLs.

   d. children with difficulties in reading comprehension.

2. Which consonant phoneme is a continuous sound?

   a. /b/

   b. /t/

   c. /g/

   d. /s/

   e. /p/

3. What is the most important phonological awareness ability for spelling?

   a. Segmentation

   b. Blending

   c. Rhyming

   d. Deletion

   e. None of the above

4. What is the most important phonological awareness ability for decoding?

   a. Segmentation

   b. Blending

   c. Rhyming

   d. Deletion

   e. None of the above

5. Instruction in phonological awareness is most effective when combined with phonics instruction. True or False?

6. Phonological awareness and phonemic awareness training primarily focus upon increasing understanding of speech sounds, as a basis for the development of phoneme-grapheme relationships. True or False?

7. Elkonin boxes are used to

   a. identify the configuration of a word.

   b. hold the classroom reading materials.

   c. help segment a word into its phonemes.

   d. none of the above.

8. How many Elkonin boxes are needed for the word *fox*?

   a. 1

   b. 2

   c. 3

   d. 4

9. **If a student's first language is Spanish and you are teaching English phonemes,**
   a. begin with phonemes that are common to both English and Spanish.
   b. begin with the vowels rather than consonants.
   c. begin with the phonemes for each letter in the English alphabet.
   d. begin with the phonemes for each letter in the Spanish alphabet.

10. **Good phonological awareness is the only requirement to become a skilled reader. True or False?**

Answers: 1.b; 2. d; 3. a; 4. b; 5. True; 6. True; 7. c; 8. d; 9. a; 10. False

Chapter Eight

INSTRUCTION IN BASIC READING AND SPELLING SKILLS

In all remedial work, the teacher should start first with the child and then find the appropriate method. Fit the method to the child, not the child to the method.

—Monroe, 1935, p. 227

Training in phonological awareness when coupled with systematic instruction in letter-sound correspondences is critical for helping individuals with dyslexia develop efficient word identification and spelling skills. For individuals with dyslexia, single-word reading is most affected because of weaknesses in phonological, orthographic, and morphological representations (Alexander & Slinger-Constant, 2004). Thus, the most effective methods are those that target the mastery of spelling-sound relationships and increase the reader's understanding of the links between the speech sounds and print (Hulme & Snowling, 2009). This chapter reviews the types of interventions that are most effective for helping individuals improve their basic reading and spelling skills. (An overview of instruction in phonological awareness and beginning word identification and spelling is found in Chapter 7.) In addition, teachers' understanding of language structure and processes is as important as the instructional methodologies they use to increase children's reading and spelling skills (Berninger & Fayol, 2008). For this reason, some basics regarding the structure of language are included in this chapter.

Unfortunately, many children with dyslexia struggle for several years before receiving optimal interventions (Raskind, 2001). The longer intervention is delayed, the greater impact upon the individual's motivation to read (Snowling & Hulme, 2011). Even when children with dyslexia do receive targeted treatments, their progress may still be slow. As discussed in earlier chapters of this book, individuals with the most severe reading impairments have basic cognitive deficits of biological origin that make it difficult for them to acquire basic reading skills even when they do receive adequate instruction (Vellutino & Fletcher, 2007). Children with dyslexia have to work extra hard and practice reading much longer than peers without dyslexia to approach average reading levels (Olson, 2011). Unfortunately, traditional special education instruction is often insufficient to close the reading gap between students with dyslexia and typical readers (Denton & Al Otaiba, 2011). These individuals require specialized instruction that is intensive, systematic, and delivered by a reading teacher who has training in the specific methodologies that are effective for students with dyslexia.

BASIC READING SKILLS

The terms *basic reading skills*, or *decoding*, refer to the ability to use the systematic correspondences between sounds and spellings to acquire a repertoire of words that can be recognized by sight (McCardle, Scarborough, & Catts, 2001). These skills allow readers to pronounce both familiar and unfamiliar words. Thus, decoding includes phonics, structural analysis, as well as instant recognition of sight words. Phonics is the reading method that is used to teach individuals how to pronounce words by identifying the sounds of the letters. Structural analysis involves breaking the words into parts or units, such as syllables, to make longer words easier to pronounce. Sight word recognition refers to the quick pronunciation of words without analysis of word structure.

Basic Phonics Terminology

Before undertaking phonics instruction, a reading teacher needs an understanding of language structure and how to present sounds and letters. Rapid Reference 8.1 reviews basic phonics terminology.

Phonics Approaches

Considerable evidence supports the conclusion that phonologically based interventions can improve the decoding accuracy of individuals with poor word reading skill (Snowling & Hulme, 2011). In fact, the last decade of research has provided further merit for the provision of explicit phonics instruction for both younger and older readers experiencing difficulty (Brady, 2011). The type of instruction will differ depending upon the age of the individual, as well as the present level of reading skill. Poor readers in grades K–2 almost always need a full program of instruction in basic decoding skills. According to Denton and Al Otaiba (2011), poor readers in grades 3 and above may need: "(a) a full

≡ *Rapid Reference 8.1*

....

Common Phonics Terminology

Affixes: prefixes (added as word beginnings) and suffixes (added as word endings).

Consonant: a speech sound in which the sound going through the vocal tract is obstructed by the lips, tongue, or teeth.

Consonant blend: two adjacent letters that maintain their own sounds.

Digraph: two adjacent consonant or vowel letters that make one new sound (e.g., ph, oa).

Diphthong: two adjacent vowel sounds that slide together when pronounced (ou, ow, oi, and oy).

Grapheme: a letter or letter string that represents a single speech sound (e.g., k or ck).

Irregular word: a word that contains an element that does not follow standard English pronunciations or spelling (e.g., the "ai" in *said*).

Morpheme: the smallest unit of meaning (e.g., affixes, root words).

Onset: the beginning consonant or consonants in a syllable.

Phoneme: the smallest unit of speech; a single speech sound.

Phoneme-grapheme correspondences: the connections between the speech sounds and the print.

Regular word: word that conforms to standard English spelling patterns.

Rime: the ending part of the syllable that begins with a vowel sound (e.g., -at).

R-controlled vowels: vowel sounds that are influenced by the /r/ sound (e.g., /ar/).

Voiced consonants: consonant sounds that use the vocal cords (e.g., /b/).

Vowel: a speech sound in which the sound goes through the vocal tract unobstructed.

Unvoiced consonant: a sound made without the vocal cords (e.g., /p/).

program of instruction in basic decoding and word recognition, (b) short-term concentrated word identification instruction focused primarily on multisyllable words and structural analysis, or (c) ongoing word study that provides only minimal support in basic word recognition but equips students for decoding and spelling complex words as well as using morphemic analysis to determine word meanings (i.e., using knowledge of meaningful word parts such as affixes and roots)" (p. 4).

Several different instructional approaches exist for teaching phonics including analogy, analytic, embedded, phonics through spelling, and synthetic. The first two approaches, analogy and analytic, rely on the student's previous knowledge and experience with print to deduce new learning. Analogy phonics instruction teaches unknown words by analogy to known words, often using word families. For example, using a rime the child knows such as -at in the word *cat,* unfamiliar words containing that rime are introduced. The child learns to read the new word *mat* or *flat* by analogy to *cat.* Analytic phonics approaches use a whole-to-part approach that teaches children to analyze letter–sound patterns once the word has been identified as a whole (Ehri, 2006). The letter-sound patterns are analyzed by comparing unknown words to known words. This approach starts with the whole word and teaches the child to break the word down into parts but avoids pronouncing sounds in isolation. Embedded phonics is an implicit approach that relies somewhat on incidental learning. Phonic skills are taught by embedding phonics instruction in text reading. This approach is not explicit or systematic and, therefore, is not generally recommended for individuals with dyslexia. The phonics through spelling approach teaches students to spell words phonetically. The student is taught to segment a word into phonemes, select the letters that spell those phonemes, and write the word. Synthetic phonics is the reverse of analytic, using a part-to-whole approach. The child learns to build the whole word from the individual parts through explicit instruction in converting letters to sounds and then blending to pronounce the word. Rapid Reference 8.2 summarizes these five different phonic instructional approaches. Put more simply, however, phonics approaches can be classified as going from part-to-whole (synthetic) or from whole-to-part (analytic).

Whichever phonics instructional approach is used, the instruction must be intensive and systematic to be effective for individuals with dyslexia. In general, systematic phonics instruction incorporates the following three principles: (1) letter-sound associations are taught directly, (2) a preplanned sequence of letter-sound associations is used, and (3) the associations are practiced in text as well as in isolation (Uhry & Clark, 2005).

Findings from the NRP report (2000) have indicated that students with severe dyslexia require a synthetic phonics approach. Two of the first developed synthetic phonics approaches that are still widely used are the Orton-Gillingham (Gillingham & Stillman, 1973; Orton, 1966), and the Slingerland approaches (Slingerland, 1981). These methods provide instruction aimed at strengthening visual and auditory associations through tracing. Although these approaches are highly effective for students with dyslexia, they require intensive teacher training. Several other easy-to-use synthetic phonics programs are described in the Appendix.

Many of the remedial phonics approaches are derived from or have been influenced by the Orton-Gillingham approach. Proponents of Orton-Gillingham

≣ *Rapid Reference 8.2*

Summary of Five Phonics Instructional Approaches

Analogy Phonics: Students learn unfamiliar words by analogy to known words. If the student knows the word *lip*, the rime –ip can be used to learn a new word such as *rip* or *trip* by blending the known rime with the new onset. Word families are often used with this approach.

Analytic Phonics: Uses a whole-to-part approach. The student uses a known word to analyze the letter-sound relations and then applies that to an unknown word. For example, if the student knows the word *house*, the *ou* letter-sound relation can be analyzed and applied to unfamiliar words such as *loud, mouse, cloud, proud*, or *pound*.

Embedded Phonics: An implicit approach that provides phonic skill instruction within text reading. Often used in conjunction with a whole language approach. Generally not recommended for students with dyslexia because it is not explicit or systematic.

Phonics Through Spelling: Teaches the student to segment a word into its phonemes and then select the letters that represent each phoneme to spell the word. This approach teaches the student to spell phonetically.

Synthetic Phonics: An explicit, part-to-whole approach that teaches the student the relationship between sounds and letters and then how to blend these sounds together to pronounce a word.

suggest that instruction must be individualized and presented in a cohesive sequence with a multisensory approach that provides sufficient practice and review; the development of phonological awareness and its application to phonic skills in the reading process is an essential goal of this type of instruction (Rooney, 1995). Rapid Reference 8.3 presents a systematic sequence for phonics instruction.

In a review of effective interventions for students who struggle with reading, Alexander and Slinger-Constant (2004) observed: ". . . that the younger the child, the more explicit the intervention must be; the older the child and the more severe the impairment, the more intensive the treatment, and the longer its duration must be. A systematic phonics approach results

DON'T FORGET

Although different approaches are effective for different people, most individuals with dyslexia require a highly structured phonics approach when initially learning to read to develop accuracy in word reading.

≡ *Rapid Reference 8.3*

A Systematic Sequence for Phonics Instruction
1. Sound blending
2. A few consonants and short a
3. Single consonants and short vowel sounds in a VC, CVC format
4. CVCe pattern
5. Consonant blends (e.g., sc, sl, sm)
6. Consonant digraphs (e.g., ch, sh, th)
7. Vowel digraphs (e.g., oa, ee, ay)
8. Diphthongs (ow, ou, oi, oy)
9. R-controlled vowels (e.g., ar, er, ir, ur)
10. Common prefixes (e.g., re-, un-, mis-, dis-, pre-, ex-, sub-)
11. Common suffixes (e.g., -s, -er, -ly, -ful, -ed, -est, -ing, -tion)
12. Silent letters (e.g., kn-, wr-, -mb)
13. Latin and Greek roots (e.g., tract, rupt, spect)
14. Systematic instruction in irregular words

CAUTION

Phonics programs help to develop decoding and encoding skills and accuracy, but they do not build fluency. Other methods must be employed to build fluency.

in robust results in word reading accuracy but is not effective in developing fluency in the older, more impaired reader" (p. 749). Thus, phonics approaches are designed to build both word reading skill and spelling accuracy, but not reading fluency. Examples of several systematic programs for phonics, structural analysis, and spelling instruction are presented in the Appendix of this book.

Decodable Text

Another important component of phonics instruction is to have the student practice sound-symbol relationships by reading decodable text. In this type of text, the vocabulary is controlled, and most of the selected words conform to regular phoneme-grapheme correspondences known by the student so that the words can be read through the application of phonics. Typically, high frequency words are introduced slowly and practiced in isolation and then reinforced within the stories. Many phonics programs come with sets of decodable books that reinforce and review the content of the lessons. The major purpose of using decodable text is so that readers can practice applying the phonics skills that they are learning in isolation, not to build vocabulary or reading comprehension. However, by reading decodable texts, students are assured of success, and their chances of increasing their reading fluency and comprehension in the future are increased (Smartt & Glaser, 2010). Phonics instruction is only one part of the reading program; it is important to ensure that children also listen to interesting, authentic stories that will promote vocabulary development and increase knowledge. Rapid Reference 8.4 provides examples of commercially available decodable texts.

CAUTION

The purpose of reading decodable text is to practice and reinforce phonics concepts. Children also need to listen to meaningful texts to increase both knowledge and vocabulary.

Structural Analysis

Structural analysis refers to the ability to analyze a word and break it down into its parts. Operating with chunks or word parts makes it easier to decode and encode multisyllabic words (Ehri, 2000). Once readers have mastered phoneme-grapheme connections, attention to word parts and syllable patterns can facilitate reading development.

Six syllable types. Several programs, including the Wilson Reading System, teach the students how to recognize and pronounce the six basic English syllable types (closed syllables; syllables with vowels and the silent e; open syllables; syllables ending in a consonant with -le; r-controlled syllables; and vowel team, digraph, and diphthong syllables). Overall, the closed syllable is the most common syllable. In the elementary grades, the most common syllables are the closed, open, and consonant -le syllables (Henry, 2010). Knowledge of the basic syllable types can help a struggling reader know how to pronounce the vowel sounds in words. Instruction in syllable types may also facilitate spelling, particularly mastery of words that end with a final silent e. Rapid Reference 8.5 provides a short description and examples of these six syllable types. A summary of generalizations regarding language structure grouped by syllable type appears in Rapid Reference 8.6.

≡ *Rapid Reference 8.4*

Examples of Decodable Texts

Bob Books—Offers decodable text for beginners or advanced beginners. Uses word families and compound words. Emergent readers begin with text that uses only the letters M, A, T, and S and then move toward long vowels (available at www.scholastic.com and most major bookstores).

Books to Remember—Provides a complete series of colorful decodable books. Readers begin with simple sentences and then move to short stories of decodable text (available at www.flyleafpublishing.com).

High Noon Books—Offers a large variety of decodable books including the "Sound Out Chapter Books Kit" and "Phonetic Fiction." These series can be used for adolescent and adult struggling readers (available at www.highnoonbooks.com).

J and J Readers—Provides a set of 36 decodable books for beginner, intermediate, and advanced students. Content advances to spark interest from young readers at the lower levels to older readers at higher levels (available at www.amazon.com or any major online bookstore).

Merrill Student Readers—Decodable texts that can be used to support any phonics program. Each book covers specific phonetic skills and provides high-frequency word practice (available at www.epsbooks.com).

Open Court Decodable Books—Multiple series separated by grade level offer decodable text (available at www.amazon.com or any major online bookstore; free resources are available at www.opencourtresources.com/teaching/OCRunits/decodable_books/decodables.html).

Phonics Practice Readers by Modern Curriculum Press—Offers three different series for variety of context. Each series includes practice on short vowels, long vowels, blends, and digraphs (available at www.amazon.com or any major online bookstore).

Power Readers and Supercharged Readers—Power Readers has 28 related decodable stories with recurring characters and activity pages aligned with the story and the phonics concept. The stories begin with simple, one-syllable short vowel words (sat) and gradually progress to simple, two-syllable words (rabbit, ringing). Supercharged Readers present more advanced skills in decodable chapter books (available at http://store.cambiumlearning.com).

Reading A-Z—Yearly membership includes access to 68 lessons with decodable text. Materials include instructions, printable resources, lesson plans, and teaching materials (available at www.readinga-z.com).

Reading Sparkers—Provides decodable text at four levels with assessment materials, computer-guided learning, games, and downloadable activities. Multiple options offer home and school editions as well as original printed materials sold individually (available at www.readingsparkers.com).

Wright Skills Decodable Books—The complete series offers comprehensive phonemic awareness, phonics, and word study resources for reading instruction (available at www.wrightskills.com).

≡ *Rapid Reference 8.5*

Six English Syllable Types

Closed syllable: at, mat (VC or CVC with short vowel sound).

Silent e: bike, shake (CVCe or CCVCe with a long vowel sound).

Open syllable: motion, go (long vowel sound and the syllable ends with a vowel mo-).

Consonant -le: candle, little.

R-controlled vowel: harm, turn, bird, fern, horn.

Vowel Team: boat, meat, out, coin, night.

≡ *Rapid Reference 8.6*

Summary of Language Structures Grouped by Syllable Type

I. Closed Syllable
   - When a vowel is **closed** or blocked in by one or more consonants, it is a closed syllable.
   - The vowel is short, such as in "dad, mom, it, black," and "hunt."
   - In upper-level phonics, the vowel can have the schwa sound of "uh" such as in "son, at-tach, as-sist, com-plete." The schwa sound is in the unaccented syllable.

Generalizations for Closed Syllables

Place a check mark in the I (Introduced) column when a generalization has been introduced. Place a + in the M (Mastered) column when the generalization has been mastered.

I   M

_____ _____ 1. A single vowel in the middle of a syllable is usually short (e.g., not, cat, picnic, cabin).

_____ _____ 2. Use "-ck" for /k/ at the end of a one-syllable word after one short vowel (e.g., back, deck, sick, cluck).

_____ _____ 3. Use "-tch" for /ch/ at the end of a one-syllable word after one short vowel (e.g., patch, etch, ditch). *Common exceptions: such, much, which, rich.*

_____ _____ 4. Use "-dge" on the end of a one-syllable word for /j/ after one short vowel (e.g., badge, edge, bridge).

(continued)

_____ _____ 5. In one-syllable words, double the final "f, l, s, z" after one short vowel (e.g., tell, mill, fluff, bluff, class, fizz, fuzz). (FLOSS rule)

_____ _____ 6. When a vowel comes before a double consonant, it is almost always short (e.g., dipper, supper, bonnet).

_____ _____ 7. Use "c" for the final /k/ sound when the word has two or more syllables (e.g., magic, terrific, Atlantic).

_____ _____ 8. When two consonants stand between two vowels, the syllable division usually occurs between the two consonants (e.g., nap/kin, ten/nis, but/ter).

_____ _____ 9. When three consonants stand between two vowels, the division occurs between a blend and the other consonants (e.g., mon/ster, pump/kin).

_____ _____ 10. When one consonant stands between two vowels, the consonant may belong to the first syllable (trav/el, reb/el), which is a closed syllable, or it may belong to the second syllable (be/long, re/bel), which is an open syllable.

_____ _____ 11. Doubling Rule: (1+1+1). In a one-syllable word, with one short vowel, ending in one consonant, double the final consonant before adding a suffix beginning with a vowel (to keep the vowel short) (-ing, -y, er) (e.g., sad, sadder, saddest).

Note: Do not double the final consonant when adding a suffix beginning with consonant (e.g., sadly, manly, sinful). Never double "v" and "x."

_____ _____ 12. Doubling Rule: (2+1+1). In a two or more syllable word, if the final syllable is accented, double the final consonant before adding a suffix beginning with a vowel (-ing, -er, -est) (e.g., omit, omitted, begin, beginning).

_____ _____ 13. Use "-est" for the suffix when comparing three or more things (e.g., tallest, youngest, nicest).

_____ _____ 14. Use "-ist" for people (nouns) who do things (e.g., artist, projectionist, activist).

II. Open Syllable
  • It is called the open syllable because the vowel is at the end of the syllable and says its name as in "hi, me, so, bi-."
  • In upper-level phonics, the open syllable can also be pronounced another way. When the vowel says its name, the accent is on that vowel.
  • When the vowel says "uh," the syllable is unaccented such as in "di/vorce."

Generalizations for Open Syllables

   I   M

_____ _____ 1. A vowel at the end of a syllable is usually long (e.g., hi, me, by, va/ca/tion, pre/tend, pi/lot, lo/cate).

_____ _____ 2. If a word ends in a consonant followed by a "y," change the final "-y" to "i" whenever adding suffixes (e.g., try, tried, rely, relied, reliable).

_____ _____ 3. Nouns ending in a vowel "-o" combination are made plural by adding "s" (e.g., radios, studios).

Note: Nouns ending in a consonant "-o" combination have no generalization, therefore, the dictionary must be used in each case (e.g., potato).

III. Silent "E" Syllable
  • It is often called the "magic e."
  • The "e" indicates that the preceding vowel is long (or says its name).
  • In beginning phonics, if the student counts back three letters beginning with the final "e" and lands on a vowel, then the vowel says its name (e.g., bake, like, compete).
        321 321   321
  • In upper level phonics, the silent e syllable may take on the sound of the schwa such as in "sur-face" or a semi-schwa-short sound such as "consider-ate." Either way, it is a silent e syllable.

Generalizatons for Silent "e" Syllables

   I   M

_____ _____ 1. Silent "e" on the end of a word usually makes the preceding vowel long (e.g., name, mule, Pete, compose, imitate).

_____ _____ 2. Usually drop the final "e" on words when you add a suffix beginning with a vowel (e.g., late, later, shine, shiner, fame, famous).

_____ _____ 3. Keep the final "e" when adding suffixes beginning with a consonant (e.g., shameless, movement).

_____ _____ 4. Use "-ize" as the suffix to add to whole words or to roots (e.g., modernize, authorize, criticize).

_____ _____ 5. "Cise" is a common Latin root and not really a suffix at all. The root "cise" means "to cut," that only makes sense when used with a prefix (e.g., incise, excise) or with a prefix and a suffix (e.g., incising, excised).

Unusual Silent e Generalizations

_____ _____ 6. No words in English end in "v." They end with "-ve" no matter whether the vowel is long or short (e.g., have, gave, drove, live). The silent "e" generalization is not consistent with "-ve" words.

_____ _____ 7. Never end a word with a single "z." Use "-ze" after a long vowel sound or a double vowel (e.g., freeze).

(continued)

IV. Vowel Team Syllable
- The most difficult of all of the syllable types is the vowel team syllable.
- There are 24 subtypes.
- Vowel teams can have one pronunciation, up to four pronunciations, or can have a unique pronunciation, and each combination has to be learned carefully (e.g., August, say, saw, shoulder, couple, avoid, meat, head, eight).

Generalizations for Vowel Team Syllables

I   M

_____ _____ 1. Use "i" before "e" except after "c" or when it says /a/ as in neighbor or weigh (e.g., priest, chief, receive, ceiling, vein, freight).

_____ _____ 2. "Ai" is most often followed by an "n" or "l" or "d" (e.g., rain, sail, aid).

_____ _____ 3. "Oa" is almost always used in one-syllable words (e.g., boar, roast, oat).

_____ _____ 4. "Ough," "augh," and "igh" are usually followed by a "t" (e.g., ought, caught, night).

_____ _____ 5. Use "se" at the end of a one-syllable word with a vowel pair instead of "s" so words are not confused as plural (e.g., grease, grouse, house).

_____ _____ 6. Nouns ending in a vowel "-y" combination (ay, oy, ey) are made plural by adding "s" (e.g., days, boys, donkeys).

Note: Nouns ending in a consonant "-y" combination (dy, ny) are made plural by changing the "y" to "i" and adding "es" (lady, ladies, pony, ponies).

_____ _____ 7. If the word ends in a vowel-"y" combination, just add the suffix (e.g., play, playing, played, player).

_____ _____ 8. Most nouns with a vowel pair ending in "f" form their plurals by adding "s" (e.g., roofs, chiefs).

V. Consonant-le Syllable
- Any time there is a consonant-le, the "e is not pronounced.
- They appear in words such as "terri-ble, cud-dle, Bi-ble, swiz-zle, and gig-gle, but NOT in nu-cle-us.

Generalizations for Consonant-le Syllables

I   M

_____ _____ 1. Most nouns ending in a consonant-le form their plurals by adding "s" (e.g., puzzles, ruffles, candles).

_____ _____ 2. Usually drop the final "e" when you add a suffix beginning with a vowel (e.g., cuddle, cuddling, sizzle, sizzling).

_____ _____ 3. Usually use the suffix "-able" when you are adding to a whole word and it means "able" (e.g., serviceable, workable, manageable).

_____ _____ 4. Usually use the suffix "-able" when the root word ends in a hard "c" or "g" (e.g., despicable).

_____ _____ 5. Use the suffix "-ible" when adding to a root word (e.g., visible, edible).

_____ _____ 6. Use the suffix "-ible" when the root word ends in a soft "c" or "g" (e.g., forcible, legible).

VI. R-Controlled Syllable
 * When a syllable has a single vowel followed by an "r," it is called an r-controlled syllable.
 * The letter "r" is so strong that it changes the vowel sound so that it is no longer short.

I   M

_____ _____ 1. Usually use "-er" as a suffix for one-syllable words when you mean a person who "does" (e.g., diner, jumper, hopper).

_____ _____ 2. Use "-or" for two or more syllable words when you mean a person or thing that "does" (e.g., professor, editor, incinerator). Tractor, doctor, and actor are common exceptions.

_____ _____ 3. Use "-ar" to form an adjective (e.g., singular, regular, popular) and "-ure" for all others (e.g., manure).

_____ _____ 4. Use "-er" for the suffix when comparing two things (e.g., taller, younger, nicer).

Plus Category
The Plus Category is for anything that does not fit into the other patterns.

Other Generalizations

I   M

_____ _____ 1. The letter "c" has the soft sound of /s/ when "e," "i," or "y" follows it (e.g., city, center, cyclone).

_____ _____ 2. The letter "g" has the soft sound of /j/ when "e," "i," or "y" follows it (e.g., gentle, ginger, gym).

_____ _____ 3. To keep the hard sound for (/g/) follow the "g" with a "u" when used before an "i" or "e" (e.g., guess, guide, guest).

_____ _____ 4. "Q" is always followed by a "u" and at least one other vowel (e.g., quit, quack).

(continued)

_____ _____ 5. Some common nouns have irregular plural forms (e.g., man, men; mouse, mice; tooth, teeth).

_____ _____ 6. Use "wr" as opposed to "r" for words that imply the meaning "twist" (e.g., wrench, wrestle, wrist, write, wrought, wrap, wrong, wreck, wry).

_____ _____ 7. Separate prefixes and suffixes as separate syllables (e.g., pre/vent/ing, trans/por/ta/tion).

Other Suffix Generalizations

I   M

_____ _____ 1. For most words, add "s" to make them plural (e.g., dogs, cars, figs).

_____ _____ 2. When a noun ends in "s," "x," "z," "ch," and "sh," add "-es" to make them plural (e.g., gases, taxes, buzzes, marches, brushes).

_____ _____ 3. Use "-ous" as the suffix when the word is an adjective (e.g., dangerous, marvelous).
Use "-us" as the suffix when the word is a noun (e.g., sinus, ruckus).

_____ _____ 4. For the suffix sound (n) that indicates a person, a nationality, or a religion, use "-an" (e.g., American, Lutheran).
For the suffix sound /eyun/ that indicates a person, a nationality, or a religion use "-ian" (e.g., Indian, Cambodian).
For the suffix saying the sound (n) usually use "-en" (e.g., ripen, redden, deaden).

_____ _____ 5. These suffixes mean people who do: -ist, -ee, -cian, -eer, -ier, -er, -ess (e.g., typist, employee, physician, engineer, brigadier, runner).
"-ess" means female (e.g., princess, countess).

Developed by C. Wilson Anderson, Jr. and modified by Stephanie Bieberly

In the Wilson Reading System, students use a simple syllable marking system to code each of the syllable types. Using a left-to-right movement, the reader draws a curved or straight line under each syllable and then identifies the type of syllable, codes the vowels with a long or short marking, puts a slash through the e if it is a silent e or consonant -le syllable, and draws a circle around the r-controlled vowels or vowel teams. Figure 8.1 illustrates this process.

Onset-rimes by syllable types. Instruction in onset-rimes can also be helpful for teaching students how to read and spell using word parts. The onset is

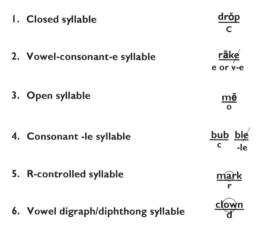

1. Closed syllable   drŏp / c

2. Vowel-consonant-e syllable   rāke̸ / e or v-e

3. Open syllable   mē / o

4. Consonant -le syllable   bub ble̸ / c -le

5. R-controlled syllable   mark / r

6. Vowel digraph/diphthong syllable   clown / d

Figure 8.1 Example of the Syllable and Vowel Marking System from Wilson Reading System

the beginning part of a syllable with includes one or more consonants (e.g., sh- in *ship* or c- in *cat*). The rime is the ending part of the syllable that begins with a vowel sound (e.g., -ip in *ship* or -at in *cat*). Every English syllable has a rime, but not necessarily an onset (e.g., on). These word parts can be combined to form multi-syllabic words (e.g., hotdog, clambake). Table 8.1 illustrates examples of common rimes arranged by different syllable types.

Glass-Analysis for Decoding Only. Glass-Analysis for Decoding Only is a technique for improving a student's ability to analyze common letter clusters in printed words to make them easier to decode. The method is designed to be used for one or two 15-minute sessions daily. The teacher presents individual words to the student on cards and asks the student to look at the whole word. The teacher does not cover up parts of the word. Rapid Reference 8.7 reviews the five steps of the method adapted from Glass (1973, 1976). When using this method, the instructor would only teach letter clusters that can be generalized to other words. Words can be selected from a student's reading or spelling materials.

High Frequency Words

High frequency words are the words that show up most frequently in reading materials. They are the most common words in the English language. Some of these words are regular and rule-governed in terms of spelling and pronunciation (e.g., and), whereas others contain an irregular element or elements

Table 8.1 Common Rimes by Syllable Type

Closed Syllables		CVCe Syllables	Vowel Teams Syllables	R-Controlled Syllables	Exception Patterns
-ab	-ill	-ake	-ain	-ar	-all
-ack	-im	-ale	-aw	-er	-ild
-ag	-in	-ame	-ay	-ir	-ind
-am	-ing	-ape	-ean	-or	-old
-amp	-ink	-ate	-eat	-ur	-ost
-an	-ip	-ice	-eed		
-ank	-ob	-ide	-een		
-ant	-ock	-ife	-eet		
-ap	-og	-ime	-eigh		
-ash	-op	-ine	-ew		
-at	-ot	-ite	-igh		
-ed	-uck	-ive	-ight		
-ell	-ug	-oke	-ough		
-ent	-um	-ope	-out		
-est	-ump	-ore	-ow		
-ick	-unk	-uke	-oy		
-ig					

(e.g., once). Reading requires the rapid mapping of letters onto phonological representations, followed by blending those representations into a whole word. Even if phonological abilities and phonics skills are intact, slow speed in mapping letters to the sounds can also impair reading performance, and result in poor retention of sight and irregular words. Methods that are multisensory and involve tracing seem most effective for teaching retention of high frequency and sight words. In addition, a teacher can color code or enlarge the irregular element in a word to highlight the atypical spelling pattern.

High frequency words are taught in tandem with a phonics approach (Brady, 2011). Table 8.2 contains lists of high frequency words that were compiled by Wilson Anderson based on a study of the major lists of commonly used words (e.g., Dolch, Fry). Group 1 contains the easiest, most frequent words, and Group 5 the most difficult. These words can be used for reading and/or spelling instruction.

≡ *Rapid Reference 8.7*

Steps in the Glass-Analysis Method

1. Identify the whole word. Present the word *carpenter* on an index card and say: "This word is *carpenter*." Review with the student which letters and letter clusters make which sounds.

2. Pronounce a sound in the word and ask the student to name the letter or letters that make that sound. Say: "In the word 'carpenter,' what letters make the 'car' sound? What letters make the 'ar' sound? What letters make the 'pen' sound? What letters make the 'ter' sound?"

3. Ask for the sound that certain letters or letter combinations make. Say: "What sound does E-R make? What sound does the T-E-R make?" Ask about each part of the word.

4. Take away letters (auditorily, not visually) and ask for the remaining sound. Say: "In the word 'carpenter,' if I took off the '/k/' sound, what would the word say?" Ask the same question omitting different word parts.

5. Identify the whole word.

They can be presented on flash cards or with tracing procedures, if needed for retention, such as described in the Fernald method. A teacher or parent can easily ascertain which words are known, and which need to be reviewed and practiced. Generally speaking, by the end of second grade, an individual should be able to read all of these words automatically with 100% mastery.

Fernald approach. The Fernald approach is a variation of the language experience approach where children write stories (Fernald, 1943). When the child comes to a word that she does not know how to spell, the teacher writes the word on a large card in manuscript or cursive. The child then traces the word with a finger, saying the word while tracing. The word is traced as many times as needed so that the whole word can be written without looking at the copy. This method can be particularly helpful for students with weaknesses in orthography that affect sight word learning and the spelling of irregular words. Betts (1946) observed that the Fernald approach that emphasizes visual, auditory, tactile, and kinesthetic modes, is most effective ". . . with children of normal and superior intelligence

DON'T FORGET

In using the Fernald approach, words are always written from memory and never copied.

Table 8.2 High Frequency Words

Group 1		Group 2			Group 3		Group 4		Group 5	
a	make	all	now	white	after	of	always	off	about	light
and	me	am	on	who	again	old	around	or	better	long
away	my	are	our	will	an	once	because	pull	bring	much
big	name	at	out	wish	any	open	been	read	carry	myself
blue	not	ate	please	with	as	over	before	right	clean	never
can	one	be	pretty	yes	ask	put	best	sing	cut	only
color	play	black	ran		by	round	both	sit	done	own
come	print	brown	ride		could	some	buy	sleep	draw	pick
down	red	but	saw		every	stop	call	tell	drink	seven
find	run	came	say		fly	take	cold	their	eight	shall
for	said	cat	she		from	thank	does	these	fall	show
funny	see	did	so		give	them	don't	those	far	six
go	the	do	soon		going	then	fast	upon	full	small
help	three	eat	that		has	think	first	us	got	start
here	to	four	there		had	walk	five	use	grow	ten
I	two	get	they		her	were	found	very	hold	today
in	up	good	this		him	when	gave	wash	hot	together
is	we	have	too		his	why	goes	which	hurt	try
it	where	he	under		how		green	work	if	warm
jump	yellow	into	want		just		its	would	keep	
little	you	like	was		know		made	write	kind	
look		must	well		let		many	your	laugh	
		new	went		live				about	
		no	what		may				better	

Source: Compiled from several lists of high frequency words by C. Wilson Anderson, M. A. T. Used with permission.

who have a short memory span for verbal material and who have difficulty in associative learning of the visual type" (p. 381). Rapid Reference 8.8 reviews the steps of a write-say method based upon the Fernald approach.

   Rapid word recognition chart. Although rapid word recognition develops as phonic word recognition improves (Moats, 2010), for children with severe reading difficulties interventions have been more successful in improving

≡ *Rapid Reference 8.8*

Write-Say Method Based on Fernald Approach
Select word and write it on a card.
Pronounce the word and have the student look at and say the word.
Have the student pronounce the word while tracing the word as many times as needed so the word can be written from memory.
Have the student write the word correctly three times and then file it alphabetically in a word bank.
Review the word periodically to ensure the student can read and spell the word with ease.

said	who	were	they	could	often
could	were	said	often	who	they
often	they	who	could	said	were
who	often	could	were	they	said
were	who	they	said	often	could

Figure 8.2 Example of a Rapid Word Recognition Chart Using Irregular Words

accuracy than rate (Torgesen, Rashotte, & Alexander, 2001). Thus, the most promising approaches to increasing sight word recognition focus on developing accuracy first and then building rate. Once the individual can accurately decode or recognize words, rate is increased by providing repeated practices viewing and naming those words quickly in multiple contexts. One example of a method for building rate of sight word recognition is a rapid word recognition chart (Carreker, 2005a). This method is an easy way to improve speed of recognition for words with an irregular element. The chart is similar to a rapid automatized naming (RAN) task. The teacher creates a matrix that contains five rows of six exception words (e.g., who, were, said), with each row containing the same six words in a different order (see Figure 8.2). After a brief review of the words and a warm-up where the teacher points randomly to 8 to 10 words on the chart, the student is timed for one minute while reading the words in the squares aloud. At the end of one minute, students can then count and graph the number of words they have read correctly. To finish up, the teacher can then point at random to any words that still require further practice.

SPELLING

For students with dyslexia, spelling creates even greater challenges than reading (Uhry & Clark, 2005). Although encoding (spelling) involves many of the same skills as reading, reading difficulties will improve over time with proper intervention, but spelling skills are more resistant to intervention (Shastry, 2007). Spelling is much more difficult than reading as one has to reproduce the entire word, not just recognize it; therefore, problems with spelling persist even after reading accuracy has developed (Snowling & Hulme, 2011). Teaching students with dyslexia how to spell is a long process that involves careful lesson planning (Carreker, 2005b). Although technology, such as spelling checkers, can help individuals with dyslexia, the person has to be able to produce a spelling that is close enough to be recognized by the computer program. In addition, when asked to select the correct spelling, an individual with dyslexia often has trouble distinguishing among words that are very similar in appearance (e.g., though, thought, through, thorough). As with decoding, it is important that the instruction be systematic and sequential. Several effective commercial spelling programs are described in the Appendix of this book. In addition, many phonics programs focus on both word reading and spelling. Research indicates that a reciprocal relationship exists between reading and spelling: accomplished readers use spelling patterns when they read, and conversely reading reinforces knowledge of spelling patterns (Adams & Bruck, 1995).

Instruction in Phonology, Orthography, and Morphology

Effective spelling instruction increases a student's understanding of the linguistic systems that underlie spelling, including phonology (how to order the speech sounds), orthography (how to recall common spelling patterns), and morphology (how to alter a word's meaning). Spelling instruction is enhanced when instruction is provided in all three systems, as well as the interrelationships (Berninger & Fayol, 2008).

To enhance phonological awareness, often the first goal of instruction, a teacher would provide activities such as Elkonin boxes, phoneme-grapheme mapping, and building words with tiles (see Chapter 7 for more information on these methods). To enhance orthographic awareness, the second goal of instruction, a teacher could focus instruction on common spelling patterns (e.g., -ight and -tion) that are impossible to sound out, but occur frequently in English spelling. Or, the focus could be on mastery of the spelling of a few words with irregular elements (e.g., once, ocean).

Instruction in morphology, the study of the smallest meaningful linguistic units (morphemes) occurs throughout spelling development. For example, a first-grade teacher will show children how to form plurals by adding the letter -s to words, or a more advanced lesson on when the plural form is spelled with -es. A teacher may help students understand when the final -e is dropped when adding a suffix (e.g., the dropping rule: When the base word ends in an e and a vowel suffix is being added, the final e is dropped: *hope* becomes *hoping*). A third-grade teacher may teach and have students practice the rule for doubling consonants when a suffix is being added (e.g., the doubling rule: The final consonant of a word is doubled when there is (a) one vowel in the last syllable, (b) one consonant after the vowel, (c) the last syllable is accented, and (d) a vowel suffix is added (e.g., *running, hopped* but not *jumping, raining*). However, the following seven letters in English rarely or never double: h, j, k, v, w, x, and y. In later grades, the teacher may help students understand the three different sounds made when the suffix -ed for past tense is added to a word (e.g., *rained, jumped, planted*). A more advanced lesson may focus on spelling of words with an irregular past tense spelling (e.g., *wept, said*). The key to knowing if the word has an irregular past tense spelling is whether or not the root word changes in pronunciation. If the root word changes in sound (e.g., *weep* becomes *wept; say* becomes *said*), the past tense spelling is irregular. If the pronunciation stays the same, (e.g., *rain* becomes *rained; jump* becomes *jumped*), the past tense is marked with an -ed, regardless of pronunciation. Understanding the rules that govern the English language helps students experience greater success with decoding and encoding words.

An example of instruction that teaches the interrelationships among phonological, orthographic, and morphological awareness would be to have children sort words using suffixes, such as plural pronounced as /s/ in *cats,* as /ez/ in *busses,* as /z/ in *bees,* or with no suffix as in *miss*

DON'T FORGET

Effective spelling instruction for individuals with dyslexia must help them make sense of the English writing system.

(Berninger & Fayol, 2008). For individuals with dyslexia, spelling instruction must help them make sense of the writing system of their language. Effective spelling instruction teaches students how to think about spelling, not just how to spell individual words (Carreker, 2005b).

Spelling Tests

Often, the main way spelling is assessed in schools is through the use of weekly spelling tests. Although this procedure may be appropriate for children who learn to spell easily, it is typically ineffective for students with dyslexia who require individualized, systematic spelling programs that build upon previous knowledge. Many times the words are too difficult for the student to spell, and he cannot even read the words with ease. In addition, the student may not even use the word in his writing. As a general rule, do not give children lists of words to memorize for a spelling test until they understand how the spelling system works (Ehri, 1998). Ehri indicated that children should be able to generate spellings that are phonetically complete and graphemically possible before they should be expected to memorize a list of words for a spelling test. She stated: "Learning the spellings of specific words by memorizing word lists should not begin until students understand how the conventional system works graphophonically. Once this point is reached, remembering the spellings of specific words will be much easier, so spelling instruction can shift to this learning activity" (1998, p. 34). Once students have mastered common patterns, they can turn to the mastery of irregular words.

Spelling flow list. In order to master irregular words, as an alternative to weekly testing, students can use a flow list, or a list that changes as the student learns to spell words. This is a different procedure from using a fixed spelling list, such as the kind that many teachers use for the weekly spelling test. The purpose of using a spelling flow list is to provide systematic instruction and review in order to promote mastery of spelling words. For this type of procedure, adapted from McCoy and Prehm (1987), the student selects words from his writing that are misspelled frequently, or the teacher may select the words from a high frequency word list, or a group of spelling patterns such as the -ight pattern. The selected words are then placed on the spelling flow list form. The student studies the words and the teacher tests her daily. The teacher marks each correctly spelled word with a C and each incorrectly spelled word with a check mark. When a word is spelled correctly 3 days in a row, it is crossed off the list, and a new word is added. All words that are spelled correctly for three days are filed alphabetically into a word bank. A week later, the teacher checks to make sure that the student still knows how to spell the words added to the bank. If a word is incorrect, the student adds the word back on her list. Figure 8.3 illustrates an example of a spelling flow list for a fourth-grade student with dyslexia who is having trouble mastering the spellings of irregular words.

Name: Jamie   Start date: 1/15

Word	M	T	W	TH	F	M	T	W	TH	F	M	T	W	TH	F
they	C	C	C					C							
said	C	√	√	C	C	C					√				
people	√	C	C	C					√						
would	√	C	√	C	C	C					√				
could	√	C	C	C				C					C		
should	√	C	C	C				C					C		
were				√	C	C	C					C			
any					C	√	√	C	C	C					√
people									√	C	C	√	√	C	
said											C	√	C	C	
would											C	C	C		
every											C	C	C		
busy													√	√	
because														√	
any														C	
friend														C	

C = Correct
√ = Incorrect

Figure 8.3   Example of a Spelling Flow List

Spelling Accommodations

Individuals with dyslexia will often need modifications and adjustments in the classroom spelling program. In most instances, the selected words on the classroom list are too difficult, and the instruction is unsystematic. In some cases, the spelling lists are merely a list of randomly selected words that may be appropriate for students at a certain grade level. It is not unusual for a student with dyslexia to miss nearly all the words on the spelling test, even though he has studied the words. Even if he does spell the words correctly on the spelling test, these same words are soon forgotten and misspelled in the following days. A spelling test from Ivan, an eighth-grade student, is presented in Figure 8.4. Notice he only spelled one word correctly. His teacher writes that Ivan should "study to take over." Ivan studied several hours for this test, but the words were too difficult for him. Hopefully Ivan's teacher will analyze his spelling errors and provide corrective feedback designed to help Ivan build his spelling skill. For example, Ivan needs to know that when spelling words in English the letter "s" does not follow an "x." The letter "x" is actually composed of two phonemes /k/ and /s/ so another /s/ sound is not needed. In addition, he needs a list of words that are selected with his skill level in mind. A careful analysis of a student's errors identifies the instructional needs of that student.

Figure 8.4   Ivan's Spelling Test

Spelling Instruction for Older Students

When working with older students who struggle with spelling, a crucial first step is to identify the cause of failure in order to provide the most effective interventions. Whereas some older students have difficulties with spelling because of weaknesses in phonological awareness, others may have adequate phonological awareness skills, but still have underdeveloped orthographic knowledge of conventional spelling patterns and rules. The most useful interventions will depend on the nature of the difficulties. Because most older students have spent a good deal of time writing, a good way to distinguish between weaknesses in phonological awareness versus limited knowledge of English orthography is to analyze the writer's spelling errors. Essentially, two broad types of spelling errors exist: phonetic spelling, which reflects poorly developed orthographic knowledge, and dysphonetic spelling, in which errors exist in the sound sequence of the word (Snowling, 2011). Phonetic spelling results from an over-reliance on phonology, whereas dysphonetic spelling often results from an under-reliance on phonology.

Weaknesses in phonology. Similar to emergent readers with dyslexia, some older readers with dyslexia experience difficulties with reading and writing because they have weaknesses in phonological awareness. These older students can often be identified by the use of immature spelling strategies and by unusual spellings that indicate confusions between sounds and limited awareness of the order of phonemes within words. Rapid Reference 8.9 adapted from Moats (2010) describes some common spelling errors that are seen in older students with poor phonological awareness. Rapid Reference 8.10 provides examples of several strategies that can be used to increase phonological awareness, as well as knowledge of phoneme-grapheme relationships.

Weaknesses in orthography. In contrast to students with weaknesses in phonology, others may struggle with reading and writing because they have underdeveloped knowledge of conventional spellings (e.g., students with limited exposure to text). For these students, intensive phonological awareness training would be of little use in spelling instruction because they often over-rely on phonology when spelling; that is they spell words the way they sound rather than the

DON'T FORGET

Individuals with dyslexia need to

- Understand how phonemes are represented with graphemes.
- Learn how to blend and segment phonemes to pronounce and spell words.
- Learn how to break words into smaller units, such as syllables, to make them easier to pronounce.
- Learn to recognize and spell common orthographic patterns (e.g., -tion).
- Learn how to read and spell words with irregular elements (e.g., ocean).
- Spend time engaged in meaningful reading and writing activities.

DON'T FORGET

A careful analysis of spelling errors is essential to providing the most appropriate instruction.

≡ *Rapid Reference 8.9*

Common Spelling Errors of Older Students with Weaknesses in Phonological Awareness

1. Omitting consonants within consonant blends (e.g., *mike* for *milk*, *paying* for *playing*).
2. Substituting vowels that are not close in sound (e.g., *dronk* for *drink*).
3. Confusing voiced and unvoiced consonant sounds due to difficulty differentiating the sounds (e.g., *efry* for *every*).
4. Omitting the schwa sound or syllables that contain the schwa sound (e.g., *compny* for *company*, *presdent* for *president*).
5. Confusing, deleting, or misplacing nasal (*n, m, ng*) and liquid sounds (*l, r*) (e.g., *sign* for *sing*, *clorel* for *color*, *amr* for *arm*).
6. Spelling a word that is far from the spelling of the original word (e.g., *pureck* for *park*).

≡ *Rapid Reference 8.10*

Spelling Strategies for Increasing Knowledge of Phonology and Phoneme-Grapheme Relationships

1. Provide explicit instruction and review of any sound-symbol confusions that are observed in spelling.
2. Provide practice ordering the sounds in words in the correct sequence.
3. Practice spelling words that conform to standard English spelling patterns.
4. Group words for instruction around patterns, such as onset-rimes or how to add affixes to root words.
5. Use a program like Phonics and Spelling Through Phoneme-Grapheme Mapping (see Appendix) to practice listening to and ordering sounds in the correct sequence.

way they look. Instead, appropriate interventions would focus on instruction in common spelling patterns and words with irregular elements. Rapid Reference 8.11 presents a list of common spelling mistakes that are often seen in students with good phonological awareness but underdeveloped knowledge of orthography (Moats, 2010). Rapid Reference 8.12 provides suggested interventions.

≡ Rapid Reference 8.11

Common Spelling Mistakes of Older Students with Weaknesses in Orthography

1. Using letter names to spell long vowels (e.g., *fel* for *feel*, *cam* for *came*, *criy* for *cry*).
2. Omitting nasals after vowels and/or before consonants (e.g., *jup* for *jump*, *pats* for *pants*).
3. Confusing short vowels with similar sounds (e.g., /i/ for /o/ as in *git* for *got*, /a/ for /e/ as in *bad* for *bed*).
4. Confusing sounds and deleting vowels in syllables that are controlled by the sound of the consonant (i.e., syllabic consonants; e.g., *lidl* for *little*, *pepl* for *people*, *bigr* for *bigger*, *opn* for *open*).
5. Making errors on inflectional endings (i.e., past tense, plurals; e.g., *wakt* for *walked*, *dawgz* for *dogs*, *litid* for *lighted*).
6. Spelling words the way they sound, not the way they look (e.g., *thay* for *they*, *sed* for *said*).
7. Omitting nasal sounds before stop consonants (e.g., *jup* for *jump*, *wet* for *went*).

≡ Rapid Reference 8.12

Spelling Strategies for Increasing Orthographic Awareness

1. Provide instruction in spelling patterns (e.g., teach common letter sequences in English, such as *ight*).
2. Teach English syllable patterns (e.g., closed CVC, r-controlled, etc.).
3. Teach common words with double letters in English (e.g., *tt*, *ff*, *ss*).
4. Teach spelling rules for adding prefixes and suffixes to root words.
5. Teach students to break words into syllables, write the spelling of each syllable, and then write the whole word from memory.
6. Have student keep a list of high frequency words that are often misspelled and review the correct spellings frequently.
7. Use multisensory techniques where the student says the word, traces the word several times, and then writes the word from memory.
8. Provide systematic review of high frequency words with irregular spellings (e.g., *once*, *said*) using a flow list procedure.

Effective Commercial Programs

Many of the programs mentioned in Chapters 7 and 8 are also effective for developing basic reading and spelling skills. In fact, a number of programs cover multiple areas of reading, oftentimes addressing all five areas of reading instruction: phonemic awareness, phonics, vocabulary, fluency, and comprehension. Rapid Reference 8.13 lists effective programs that are described in detail in the Appendix of this book. Rapid Reference 8.14 presents additional programs not previously mentioned that are helpful in developing an individual's basic reading and/or spelling skills. Several programs take advantage of the adaptability of software to target and customize instruction. For example, System 44 is a foundational reading and phonics program designed for struggling readers in grades 3–12; Lexia Reading uses web-enabled software to provide guided practice on foundational reading skills for grades Pre-K–12; and Accelerated Reader provides reading practice at appropriate reading levels for students in Pre-K–12 and even offers an option to connect from home for additional practice.

≡ Rapid Reference 8.13

Effective Programs for Basic Reading and/or Spelling Skills
   Barton Reading & Spelling System
   Herman Method
   Language! The Comprehensive Literacy Curriculum
   PAL Research-Based Reading & Writing Lessons
   Patterns for Success in Reading and Spelling
   REWARDS
   Road to Reading
   Sonday System
   Spelling by Patterns
   Spellography: A Student Roadmap to Better Spelling
   Wilson Just Words
   Wilson Reading System
   WORDS, 2nd Edition
   Wordy Qwerty: Foundations for Reading and Writing Fluency

(Detailed descriptions are provided in the Appendix of this book)

≡ Rapid Reference 8.14

Additional Programs for Developing Reading and Spelling Skills

Program	Website
Accelerated Reader	www.renlearn.com
Lexia Reading	www.lexialearning.com
Read 180	www.scholastic.com
SpellRead	www.spellread.com
Success for All	www.successforall.net
System 44	www.scholastic.com

CONCLUSION

Individuals with dyslexia require intensive interventions for word reading and spelling that teach the connections between the speech sounds and print in a systematic, explicit fashion. They require more reading instruction and more practice than their typically developing peers (Denton & Al Otaiba, 2011).

Fortunately, many structured programs exist that can be used to help students increase their word reading and spelling accuracy. Unfortunately, some schools do not implement these methodologies because of limited resources or a lack of teacher training. As a result, some students with dyslexia do not receive help in an appropriate or timely fashion. The longer an individual with dyslexia struggles without effective instruction, the greater the impact on her self-esteem and motivation to read or write. While working on basic skills, students must also engage in meaningful reading and writing activities so that they see the connections between skill development and the ultimate purpose of reading and writing: comprehension, learning, and enjoyment as well as the ability to communicate and express ideas.

DON'T FORGET

Instruction is most effective when: "...it is delivered within *structured, carefully sequenced, well-organized lessons* and when it includes *daily opportunities to read and respond to connected text* at an appropriate level of difficulty" (Denton & Al Otaiba, 2011, p. 7).

🖎 TEST YOURSELF 🖎

1. The word _____ contains a vowel digraph.
   a. toe
   b. bed
   c. fine
   d. phone
   e. toy
   f. both a and e

2. The word _____ contains a diphthong.
   a. oil
   b. pool
   c. boat
   d. feel
   e. none of the above

3. An effective method for teaching phoneme-grapheme relationships involves
   a. using text with pictures to illustrate meaning.
   b. applying grapheme-phoneme relationships in both reading and spelling.
   c. using letter tiles to blend and segment speech sounds.
   d. providing oral and written instructions.
   e. both b and c.

4. Decodable books contain many irregular words that must be recognized as sight words. True or False?

5. An important component of the Fernald approach is that words are written from memory, not copied from a model. True or False?

6. A closed syllable is:
   a. the most common syllable type.
   b. one in which the vowel sound is short.
   c. the vowel is followed by one or more consonant.
   d. all of the above.

7. In a consonant-vowel-consonant-e (CVCe) syllable, the vowel sound is _____.
   a. short
   b. unstressed
   c. long
   d. both b and c

8. **For individuals with dyslexia, the development of spelling accuracy often lags behind reading accuracy. True or False?**

9. **A spelling flow list**
   a. provides for daily testing of words.
   b. provides systematic review of words when errors are made.
   c. can be based upon words a student misspells.
   d. can be used to reinforce certain spelling patterns.
   e. all of the above.

10. **Two common, but distinct causes of poor spelling in older students include**
   a. inattention and lack of motivation.
   b. phonological awareness deficits and lack of knowledge of conventional spelling patterns (orthography).
   c. vocabulary deficiencies and difficulties in reading comprehension.
   d. none of the above.

Answers: 1. a; 2. a; 3. e; 4. False; 5. True; 6. d; 7. c; 8. True; 9. e; 10. b

Chapter Nine

INSTRUCTION IN READING FLUENCY

Students who do not develop reading fluency, regardless of how bright they are, are likely to remain poor readers throughout their lives.

—National Reading Panel, 2000

COMPONENTS OF READING FLUENCY

Reading is effortless for fluent readers because they are accurate, maintain a good rate of reading, and read with expression. The process they use to identify words is fast and nearly effortless or automatic. This concept of automaticity refers to the ability to recognize words rapidly with little attention required to the word's appearance. Although fluency has been defined in different ways, the various definitions focus on the ease of word reading. Rapid Reference 9.1 reviews several examples of definitions of reading fluency.

Thus, reading fluency is often defined as having three components: accuracy, rate, and prosody (Hudson, Lane, & Pullen, 2005; NRP, 2000). Accuracy is the ability to recognize or decode words correctly. To have automaticity with decoding, the individual must have a firm grasp of the alphabetic principle. In addition, the individual needs to have acquired a store of high frequency words, especially those that have irregular elements and cannot be decoded using phonics. Rate refers to

DON'T FORGET

Reading fluency is more than just the rate or speed of reading. The fluent reader is accurate, understands what is read, and reads with good expression.

speed of identification at the single word level as well as at the connected text level. A fluent reader must quickly recognize or decode the individual words on a page and must maintain speed while moving through the text. Expression, or prosody, describes the rhythms and intonations of language. Prosody interprets

≡ Rapid Reference 9.1

Sample Definitions of Reading Fluency

- "Fluency is the ability to read a text accurately and quickly. When fluent readers read silently, they recognize words automatically. They group words quickly in ways that help them gain meaning from what they read. Fluent readers read aloud effortlessly and with expression. Their reading sounds natural, as if they are speaking" (Armbruster, Lehr, & Osborn, 2001, p. 22).
- ". . . the ability to read connected text rapidly, smoothly, effortlessly, and automatically with little conscious attention to the mechanics of reading, such as decoding" (Meyer & Felton, 1999, p. 284).
- ". . . the ease or 'naturalness' of reading," including how a reader: (a) groups or phrases words as revealed through intonation, stress, and pauses; (b) adheres to the writer's syntax; and (c) expresses oneself in feeling, anticipation, and characterization during oral reading" (National Assessment of Educational Progress, 1995).
- Oral reading fluency is the combination of rate (i.e., how fast one reads) and accuracy (i.e., correct word identification). For oral reading, fluency may also involve expression or *prosody*, which means alternating pitch, tone and other vocal elements in response to punctuation (Bryant, Smith, & Bryant, 2008).

the cues in the text, such as responding to punctuation by raising or lowering your voice. Expression helps communicate the text meaning and can signal surprise, questioning, exclamation, as well as other meanings. Good prosody demonstrates comprehension because it signals that the reader understands the text. Struggling readers often read in a monotone manner, whereas fluent readers read with expression. Rapid Reference 9.2 provides a summary of the major components of reading fluency.

A good reader first learns to read accurately and is able to apply phonic skills and recognize numerous sight words. Accurate readers then develop appropriate rate or speed of reading. This automaticity with reading allows readers to adjust their speed of reading depending on the difficulty of the text. Finally, a reader with good accuracy and rate can focus on reading with expression by paying attention to punctuation marks and adjusting the voice to clarify and express the exact meaning of the text. Figure 9.1 illustrates the components of reading fluency and how they usually develop.

As noted by the arrow in Figure 9.1, as accuracy and rate improve, so does comprehension of text. In fact, the best predictor of reading comprehension

≣ Rapid Reference 9.2

Major Components of Reading Fluency

Accuracy
  Decodes unfamiliar words accurately.
  Uses context to help signal errors in word reading.
  Knows numerous words by sight.

Rate of Reading
  Recognizes most words at an automatic or near automatic level.
  Reads at a good speed or rate (words per minute).
  Maintains rate and knows when to adjust rate for more difficult material.

Expression or Prosody
  Attends to punctuation marks.
  Uses appropriate timing and phrasing.
  Reads with expression that helps communicate the meaning of the text.

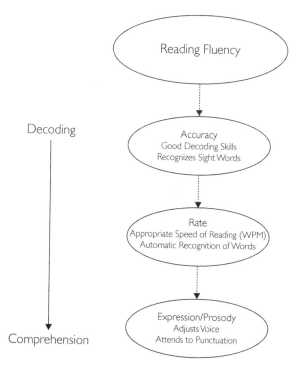

Figure 9.1   Components of Reading Fluency

is how fluently one reads (Chall, 1996; Chard, Vaughn, & Tyler, 2002; Fuchs, Fuchs, Hosp, & Jenkins, 2001; Laberge & Samuels, 1974; Stanovich, 1991). Reading fluency is a strong predictor of later reading achievement (Good, Simmons, & Kame'enui, 2001; Hintze & Silberglitt, 2005; Stage & Jacobsen, 2001). In addition, the National Reading Panel (NRP, 2000) identified reading fluency as one of the five critical areas of reading assessment and instruction. These findings led to the addition of reading fluency as one of the eight areas of classification for a learning disability in the Individuals with Disabilities Education Improvement Act of 2004 (IDEA, 2004).

Fluency is often described as the bridge between word identification and comprehension. This relationship between oral reading rate and comprehension is significant at the beginning stages of reading but also continues into middle school and high school. Individuals with dyslexia continue throughout the school years to read more slowly than typically developing readers (Uhry & Clark, 2005). Individuals with dyslexia

DON'T FORGET
....
Individuals with dyslexia often experience significant difficulty in developing fluent reading.

have underlying deficits in the automatic application of reading skills (Olson, 2011). This inability to read fluently is often described as one of the main symptoms of both adolescents and adults with dyslexia (Lyon, Shaywitz, & Shaywitz, 2003, p. 6). In fact, in languages other than English, poor fluency is the major characteristic that distinguishes between readers with and without dyslexia (Rodrigo & Jimenez, 1999; Tressoldi, Stella, & Faggella, 2001; Wimmer & Mayringer, 2002). For a more detailed explanation of reading fluency in different languages, see Chapter 11.

When reading, words may be sounded out, recognized by sight, or determined from the context (e.g., Ehri, 2002). The quickest, most efficient method is recognizing words by sight or from memory. Skilled readers pronounce words with little effort so that all of their attention is focused on the meaning of the text. Both sounding out words and guessing words from context require more time and, hence, reduce speed, accuracy, prosody, and even comprehension. Cognitive resources, including attention, are consumed with trying to pronounce a word.

Individuals can vary in the speed at which they read words. Decoding may occur phoneme-by-phoneme or by decoding larger orthographic units. Trouble with any of the processes involved, or lack of mastery of phoneme-grapheme connections, impacts speed of decoding. Even when a word is stored as a sight word, speed of word recognition varies. These differences in speed may be due to how much practice the individual has had with a word or individual differences in the rate of processing on cognitive tasks. The more practice an individual has with a word, the more easily the word is recognized (Levy, Abello, & Lysynchuk, 1997). Context also contributes to word recognition speed. Words are recognized more quickly in a meaningful context than in isolated words lists (Jenkins, Fuchs, van den Broek, Espin, & Deno, 2003; Stanovich, 1980), particularly for individuals with strong vocabulary knowledge (Torgesen & Hudson, 2005). For children with a more limited vocabulary, the context will not aid word recognition if the words are unknown. Finally, individual differences in reading speed may be due to personality or motivational traits or cultural influences. For example, some individuals may value accuracy over speed; some may be reflective, whereas others are more impulsive.

> **DON'T FORGET**
>
> The child's level of oral vocabulary knowledge impacts the ability to recognize and read words. Knowing the meaning helps the reader identify the word in print.

Typically, children become fluent readers during second and third grade and are able to use reading as a learning tool in fourth grade and beyond (Chall, 1996). Chall observed that children learn to read in grades 1 through 3 and then read to learn in grade 4 and higher. If an individual does not read fluently, then reading is laborious and the person tends to avoid reading, further exacerbating the problem (Rasinski, 2001).

> **DON'T FORGET**
>
> Children learn to read in grades 1–3, and then read to learn from grade 4 and higher.

READING FLUENCY INSTRUCTION

The purpose of fluency instruction is to increase automaticity with reading, thus making the act of reading easier so that a reader can devote all attention to comprehension. Although performance in reading fluency can be improved, dysfluent reading is unfortunately a highly stable characteristic that is difficult to remediate (Landerl & Wimmer, 2008; Torgesen, 2007). Even though struggling readers can close

> **DON'T FORGET**
>
> Although improvement is possible, it is difficult to remediate deficits in reading fluency.

the gap in decoding accuracy and comprehension, the gap in fluency typically remains for those with moderate and severe reading impairments (Torgesen, 2007). For those children with the most severe dyslexia, interventions have been more successful in improving the accuracy of word reading, rather than the rate (Torgesen, Alexander, et al., 2001). Fluency is more difficult to remediate (Hulme & Snowling, 2009).

Deciding Where to Begin Instruction

An individual must first be an accurate reader before instruction addresses building speed or rate. For beginning readers this means instruction should emphasize development of accurate word recognition and analysis skills (Pikulski & Chard, 2005). Once the reader has developed basic decoding accuracy, the emphasis shifts to reading and rereading a sentence to make it "sound like talking" (Stahl & Kuhn, 2002). With younger readers, fluency instruction can even begin with phrases that contain common words. Table 9.1 includes simple phrases that can be used to assess a child's ability to read basic sight words, or to practice reading common phrases.

Before beginning instruction for students in grade 2 or higher, it is important to determine the reader's accuracy level and reading rate. A simple guideline for determining the focus of instruction is to listen to the individual read an appropriate level passage aloud. If the reader makes more than one error for every ten words read, instruction should focus on building accuracy; if fewer errors are made, but the individual has a slow rate of reading, then instruction should focus on building speed (Simmons & Kame'enui, 1998). When focusing on increasing rate, an individual should have a 95%–98% accuracy level on the materials used,

Table 9.1 Sight Word Phrases for Assessment or Practice

Sets	Phrases in Set	Sets	Phrases in Set	Sets	Phrases in Set	Sets	Phrases in Set
Set 1	a big horse	Set 7	has found	Set 13	my brother	Set 19	too little
	a big house		has run away		my father		too soon
	a new book		has made		on the floor		up there
	a new hat		has come back		on the chair		up here
	a pretty home		he is		so much		
	a pretty picture		he was		so long		
			he would do		some bread		
			he would try		some cake		

Sets	Phrases in Set	Sets	Phrases in Set	Sets	Phrases in Set	Sets	Phrases in Set
Set 2	about it about him all night all day as he did as I said as I do as he said	Set 8	her father her mother his brother his sister	Set 14	the little dog the old man the funny rabbit the new coat the small boat the new doll	Set 20	was found was made we are we were went away went down
Set 3	at once at three at school at home by the house by the tree	Set 9	I am I was I will come I will go I may go I may get	Set 15	the little children the little chickens the red cow the little pig the small boy the old men	Set 21	will walk will go will buy will look will read will think
Set 4	can fly can live can play can run could eat could make	Set 10	if I must if you can if I may if you wish	Set 16	the funny man the black horse the red apple the white duck the black bird the white sheep	Set 22	when you come when I wish when I can when you know what I say what I want
Set 5	did not fall did not go down here down the street down the hill down there	Set 11	in the window in the water in the garden in the barn in the grass in the box	Set 17	the yellow ball the yellow cat then he came then he said they are they were	Set 23	with mother with us would like would want
Set 6	for them for him for the baby for the girl from the farm from the tree from home	Set 12	is coming is going it is it was must be must go	Set 18	to stop to go to the barn to the nest to the school to the farm to the house	Set 24	you are you were you will do you will like your sister your mother

Source: Reformatting of Edward Dolch's "The 95 Commonest Nouns and Basic Sight Vocabulary" by C. Wilson Anderson. Used with permission.

which is text at the low to high end of the instructional reading level. A brief review of methods for determining accuracy level and reading rate are described next. For more complete information on assessing reading fluency, see Chapter 6.

Determine accuracy level. A method for determining a reader's accuracy level is to calculate the percentage of correctly read words. Divide the number of correctly read words by the total number of words attempted. For example, if the individual reads 95 words correctly out of a total of 100 words, the accuracy rate is 95 percent (95 words read correctly divided by 100 words read = .95 or 95%). Once the individual's accuracy level is known, materials at the appropriate instructional level can be selected for building reading fluency.

Determine reading rate. Reading rate can be calculated by dividing the number of words read correctly by the total amount of reading time, or by counting the number of words read correctly in one minute. For example, time the individual reading a passage with 100 words. Count the number of words the individual read correctly and divide by the amount of time it took to read the passage. If the individual reads 90 words correctly out of the 100 in two minutes, the words correct per minute (WCPM) would be 45 (90/2 = 45). Alternatively, have the individual read a text for one minute. Count the total number of words read and subtract the number of errors to obtain the number of words correct per minute (WCPM). For example, if the individual read 100 words in one minute but made eight errors, the rate would be 92 WCPM.

> ## CAUTION
> ....
> A reader must have an adequate level of accuracy (95%–98%) on a text before instruction can focus on increasing speed of reading.

Effective Interventions

As noted in prior sections, the most effective instruction for individuals with dyslexia is explicit in nature, which means that nothing is left to chance. The teacher first provides a model or demonstration of the skill to be learned, followed by the learner practicing the skill under the close supervision of the teacher, who provides immediate corrective feedback as needed. After this guided practice phase is completed, and the teacher is reasonably sure that the student can do the task, then the learner practices the skill independently. This is sometimes referred to as the "I do, we do, you do" teaching sequence. In fact, the research findings related to effective instruction for reading fluency identify both explicit modeling of fluent reading and practice with corrective feedback as highly effective methods (Chard et al., 2002).

Explicit modeling. An example of fluent reading can be provided by the teacher, or other skilled reader, reading an appropriate passage aloud, or by using an audio recorded passage. After providing the model, the teacher goes through the passage again using a "think aloud" procedure to demonstrate to the students the process of reading fluently. For example, to assist with the development of prosody, the

> **DON'T FORGET**
>
> Explicit modeling of fluent reading is one of the most effective methods for improving reading fluency.

teacher may say, "When I see a question mark, I know my voice should go up at the end to indicate a question. When I see a comma, I pause, and when I see a period, I pause a bit longer." The teacher might also discuss how she combines words into meaningful phrases rather than reading word by word. She may demonstrate by sweeping her finger under phrases rather than pointing to each word individually. Explicit modeling demonstrates the end goal, in this case fluent reading, and explains the process of how to accomplish the goal. In this "I do" phase, the teacher provides the explicit instruction. Next, in the "we do" phase, the responsibility for performing the task begins to transfer to the student.

Repeated reading with corrective feedback. Reading a passage aloud several times with a tutor or skilled reader who provides immediate corrective feedback is another effective reading fluency intervention (Therrien & Kubina, 2006). Although various approaches to repeated readings exist, they typically share the following elements: (1) use a relatively short passage (50–200 words) at the reader's

> **DON'T FORGET**
>
> Immediate corrective feedback increases the effectiveness of the repeated reading intervention.

instructional reading level; (2) reader reads aloud while the instructor records time and errors; (3) reader practices the passage several times (aloud or silently); (4) reader reads aloud while the instructor records time and errors; (5) reader continues to reread passage until a predetermined goal is met; and (6) progress is recorded by entering words per minute and errors on first and final readings. Depending on the individual, it may be necessary to use a text at the reader's independent level, or a familiar instructional level text, to ensure that the reader can focus on increasing fluency. Rapid Reference 9.3 summarizes recommendations for improving student performance through repeated readings. The provision of immediate corrective feedback is an additional element that increases the effectiveness of repeated readings (Begeny, Daly, & Vallely, 2006; Nelson, Alber, & Gordy, 2004). One procedure, called phase-drill-error correction,

≡ *Rapid Reference 9.3*

Recommendations for Increasing Fluency through Repeated Readings
- Select interesting passages at the instructional level.
- Use decodable or independent level texts with struggling readers.
- Have students engage in multiple readings (three or four times).
- Students can read passages aloud to a more advanced reader.
- Trained tutors can provide students with additional practice.
- Provide corrective feedback on word errors.
- Teacher says correct word immediately.
- Student repeats correct word or phrase with the word.
- Establish a performance goal or criterion of the number of words per minute.
- Provide feedback on performance.
- How many words student read correctly during session.
- How current performance compares to last session.
- Provide short, frequent periods of fluency practice.
- Monitor progress using charts and graphs.
- Helps make instructional decisions (e.g., is the intervention working?).
- Helps student become aware of own performance and fosters independence.

requires the instructor to correct immediately any misread or skipped word and then ask the reader to repeat the phrase that contains the misread word. For maximum benefit, the repeated reading sessions should last 10–20 minutes and occur between three and five times a week (Therrien & Kubina, 2006).

Partner reading. In partner or paired reading, students read and reread a text with a partner. It is best to assign partners based on reading levels, pairing a student with higher-level reading skills with a student who has slightly lower-level reading skills. It is also possible to pair students with similar reading abilities. The text selected should be at the instructional level of the student with lower reading skills. To begin, the more advanced reader provides a model of fluent reading by reading the first paragraph while the other student follows along. Then the roles reverse and the less-skilled reader reads the same passage. Next, the partners discuss the paragraph by retelling what happened or identifying the main idea. The partners can ask each other questions such as "Who (or what) was the paragraph mainly about?" or "What was the most important thing that happened?" These steps are repeated until the passage is completed. Additionally, an error correction procedure can be incorporated. For example, if the reader makes an error (misreads, skips, or doesn't know a word), the partner points to the word and says "What is this word?" If the student reads the word correctly, the partner says "Yes, that word is _____. What word? (Pause for a response.) Please reread the sentence." If the student reads the word incorrectly, the partner tells the student what the word is, asks the student to repeat the word, and then to reread the sentence. The partner reading method can be taught to parents or siblings so that the struggling reader can get additional practice at home. This strategy is frequently used as part of the Peer-Assisted Learning Strategies (PALS), a classwide peer-tutoring program. Research related to PALS provides evidence of the effectiveness of partner reading (Fuchs, Fuchs, & Burish, 2000).

Readers' theater. The readers' theater uses scripts to engage students in practicing and rehearsing printed material to be performed before a group. A script can be selected or developed, and roles are assigned to the students. All students should have a copy of the script with their dialogue highlighted. It is best to begin with a small group and then expand the group size as students become more confident of their abilities. The students must practice repeatedly to develop their oral reading fluency. When performing the script in front of another group, the students read their assigned dialogue. They are not expected to memorize the script. This method is effective for older students struggling with reading fluency because it provides an opportunity for them to have a successful reading experience within a motivating context. Also, when rehearsing and performing for others, readers are motivated to practice enough times to deliver the lines fluently (Rasinski et al., 2005).

Tape-assisted/CD reading. When using this procedure, sometimes referred to as reading-while-listening or reading with a model, the student reads aloud along with a recording of a fluent reader. Some descriptions of tape-assisted reading indicate that the first time through, the reader follows along in the text while pointing to the words that are read, but does not read aloud. Most descriptions state that after the first silent reading, the student reads aloud in a quiet voice rather than just listening to the recording. Students need to be closely monitored during this procedure to ensure they are reading along. To build fluency, it may be helpful to have recordings at different levels of fluency, adjusting primarily the rate. Initial levels would be at a slower rate so that the reader can keep up with the recording. Then, as fluency builds, the rate can be increased. Prior to using the recording, help the student set a realistic fluency goal that identifies words per minute and maximum number of errors. These goals will vary and depend on each student's reading level. The student then practices reading the passage with the recording until the student feels she can read the passage independently. When the student is ready to try independent reading, the teacher times the reading for one minute and calculates the number of words read in that minute and the number of errors. Next, the teacher involves the student in charting progress and reviews any errors that were made.

Speed drills. High-frequency word lists (e.g., Dolch or Fry Instant Words), or graded word lists, provide good content for speed drills designed to help build automaticity of word recognition. The individual reads the words aloud for one minute and the teacher or tutor records the number of errors. High frequency words typically make up 50%–70% of all written material so it is important that the individual learns to recognize these words with ease.

Another type of speed drill focuses on building automaticity with specific letters, letter combinations, or word parts. Customized to meet the needs of the individual child, the drill worksheets are prepared using content on which the student has received instruction but lacks automaticity. For example, the speed drill may focus on reading words with short vowels, vowel digraphs, consonant digraphs, various syllable types, or common endings. The number of targets used in the drill depends on the individual and the skill to be practiced. Sometimes it may be only 5 or 6 different targets, and other times it may be 10–15 targets. In either case, each target is repeated randomly on the worksheet, 10 rows of six targets each, creating a number of opportunities to practice the target skill. Two copies of the worksheet are prepared: one for the student and one for the teacher.

Speed drills are introduced by reviewing with the student the purpose of the drill and the specific skill that will be practiced. Next, the student is asked to read as quickly as he can without making mistakes across each row from left to right. The teacher times the student for one minute and records on the copy any errors, hesitations, or self-corrections. Progress is charted by recording how many items the student read correctly. An initial goal is to read all 60 items in one minute with only one or two errors. Once the student achieves this goal, the number of total items can be increased, for example, 90–100 items on the worksheet.

Choral reading or neurological impress method. As mentioned previously, readers struggling with fluency benefit from hearing a model of fluent reading. Taking turns with the student while reading aloud allows the individual to practice phrasing and improve oral reading prosody, or expression. Echo reading (Heckelman, 1969; Morris & Slavin, 2002) is a simple method for taking turns with the student. The teacher reads a sentence aloud, and then the student reads it back.

The neurological impress method (Heckelman, 1969, 1986) is a method for choral reading. The teacher or another skilled reader uses a high-interest book or a content-area textbook from the classroom and sits next to the student so that both can see the text while reading. The student and the teacher read the text aloud together while the teacher points with the index finger to the words. The teacher reads at a slightly faster pace and encourages the student to try and keep up. When necessary, the teacher reminds the student to keep her eyes on the words. This activity can be completed in 10–15 minutes each day.

Monitor progress. Students are often motivated by graphing their progress. The graph or chart provides a visual representation of the student's performance, providing immediate feedback on performance in the current session and allowing comparisons to previous performances. Enhancing a student's awareness of his own learning is an important part of developing independence and responsibility. In addition, monitoring progress helps adjust goals and instruction so that the student can be successful. If the student is making limited progress, a more realistic goal may be needed. If progress is not being made, it suggests a change is needed in the instructional approach for that student. Curriculum-based measures of oral reading fluency are frequently used to monitor progress because they are quick and easy to administer. Rapid Reference 9.4 provides an estimate of realistic weekly progress monitoring goals for different grade levels.

Teachers should employ interventions that have evidence of effectiveness or include the effective components for improving fluency that are summarized in

≡ Rapid Reference 9.4

Example of Weekly Progress Monitoring Goals

Grade	Realistic Goals	Ambitious Goals
1	2.0 words per week	3.0 words per week
2	1.5 words per week	2.0 words per week
3	1.0 words per week	1.5 words per week
4	.55 words per week	1.1 words per week
5	.5 words per week	.8 words per week
6	.3 words per week	.65 words per week

Source: Adapted from Fuchs, Fuchs, Hamlett, Walz, & Germann (1993). Formative evaluation of academic progress: How much growth can we expect?, *School Psychology Review, 22,* 27–48.

≡ *Rapid Reference 9.5*

Summary of Effective Reading Fluency Interventions
- Explicit modeling of fluent reading
- Repeated readings (with corrective feedback is most effective)
- Partner reading
- Reader's theater
- Tape-assisted or CD reading (reading with a model)
- Speed drills
- Choral reading
- Neurological impress method

Rapid Reference 9.5. All of these interventions involve some form of progress monitoring, which in and of itself has proven to be effective in improving fluency.

Additional Instructional Methods

Various methods are available that have proven in practice to have beneficial effects for students. These methods, while lacking in research-based evidence of effectiveness, target specific skills and are helpful when teaching individuals who require remediation in those skill areas. Additionally, each method includes elements of effective instruction, such as demonstration and guided practice.

Phrase-cued reading technique. This technique helps overcome word-by-word reading. The teacher demonstrates how to group words together while reading sentences by drawing scoops under the phrases or by placing slashes between the phrases. The student is given a copy of the sentences and draws scoops under the words that go together. Next, the student practices reading the sentences using the phrasing that has been identified. For example, in the sentence "The man ran down the street," a scoop would be drawn under "The man ran" and another scoop under "down the street." The student reads the scooped words as a phrase with no pauses.

Alphabet prosody. This method helps the student understand how punctuation signals expression and removes the pressure to read words (Blevins, 2001; Carreker, 2005). Write the alphabet, or a portion of the alphabet, with punctuation marks interspersed. Use only the punctuation marks that the student knows. Begin by using commonly known punctuation such as periods, commas, question marks, and exclamation points. The exercise may look something like this: ABC. DEF? G! HIJ, KL.? MNO. PQR? ST! UVW, XYZ. The student reads the alphabet letters using the appropriate expression indicated by the punctuation mark. For example, the student reads ABC and then pauses to signal the period; reads DEF? raising his voice at the end of the sequence; exclaims the G!; pauses briefly after HIJ,; raises his voice at the end of KL.?; pauses after MNO. to signal a period or stop; raises his voice at the end of PQR? to signal a question; exclaims ST!; pauses briefly after UVW,; and states XYZ. Students can make up their own alphabet exercises, write them on cards, and trade with a classmate for practice.

Practice. To improve fluency, the individual must practice reading aloud and continue to hear examples of good, fluent reading. At home, parents, or older siblings, can provide practice by reading aloud to and with younger children. It is important for this practice to be oral reading rather than silent reading. The child must hear the model of fluent reading and then attempt to replicate that model. At school, the child should practice reading orally using one of the methods described previously, such as repeated reading or partner reading. Rereading text gives children the opportunity to read more words until they become automatic (Uhry & Clark, 2005). Unfortunately, independent silent reading has not proven to be an effective way to improve reading fluency (NRP, 2000). Programs such as "sustained silent reading" (SSR) or "drop everything and read" (DEAR) have benefits for fluent readers, but not for those who are struggling with fluency. A better use of time for a nonfluent reader would be guided or assisted oral reading practice with the teacher, other skilled reader, or recorded books. Additionally, round robin reading (RRR), where each reader takes a turn reading aloud, is ineffective for nonfluent readers to practice oral reading (Hasbrouck, 2006). Depending on the size of the group, each student may get very little chance to practice reading. In addition, the struggling reader may be embarrassed by his poor reading and would not provide a good model of fluent reading to the other students in the group. An alternative to round robin reading is cloze reading. The teacher reads the selection aloud, providing a good model of fluent reading, and then omits an important word. The students, as a group, must provide the missing word. While cloze reading does not provide the individual student with much opportunity to practice

CAUTION

Independent silent reading may not improve the fluency of a struggling reader. The struggling reader needs guided, oral reading practice with fluent models.

oral reading, it does provide a means to engage the student in a text while listening to a model of fluent reading.

Practice adjusting reading rate. Because reading is so effortful, many individuals with dyslexia have not learned how to adjust their reading rates and attempt to read information in an encyclopedia at the same pace that they read a comic book or novel. To learn to monitor reading speed, encourage students to adjust their rate depending on the purposes of reading. Students can practice skimming through a chapter to get a general sense of the information and then moving through the chapter more slowly to study for the weekly test. The teacher can model for the students how to change rate of reading for different types of materials.

Carver (1990) used the analogy of adjusting one's reading speed to the shifting of gears in a car. Another analogy could be shifting the gears on a bicycle. First and second gears are the slowest, most powerful gears. First gear is used to memorize materials. Second gear is used to learn material. Third gear is the typical reading rate. The fourth gear, skimming, and the fifth gear, scanning, are the fastest but least powerful gears. These gears are useful when one is trying to locate a specific piece of information or trying to get the general sense of a passage without reading every word.

Fluent readers are able to monitor their reading pace and shift gears depending on the goals. If one is trying to memorize material for a test, the reading pace is slow and reflective, characterized by stopping and reviewing the material. If one is reading a novel for pleasure, the pace is steady and fluent. If one is searching for information in a catalog, the pace is rapid. Skilled readers know how to adjust their reading rate based on the purpose for reading.

DON'T FORGET

Fluent readers adjust their rate depending upon the type of reading material and the purpose for reading.

Effective Commercial Programs

Many commercial materials are available for improving reading fluency. Some of these materials have evidence of effectiveness, whereas others do not. Lack of evidence does not mean the materials would not be effective with an individual; it just means that, as of yet, there is no research evidence to document the effectiveness. Using information from the Institute for Education Sciences (IES) What Works Clearinghouse (http://ies.ed.gov/ncee/wwc/reports/), the commercial materials showing evidence of effectiveness for improving reading fluency are

≡ Rapid Reference 9.6

Commercial Materials with Evidence of Effectiveness for Improving Reading Fluency

Title	Grade Range	Website
Corrective Reading	Grade 3 and higher	mheonline.com
Earobics	PreK–3	earobics.com
FastForword	Grades 1–12	scilearn.com
Fluency Formula	Grades 1–6	teacher.scholastic.com
Ladders to Literacy	Kindergarten	brookespublishing.com
Peer-Assisted Learning Strategies (PALS)	K–high school	kc.vanderbilt.edu/pals
Reading Mastery	Grades 1–6	mheonline.com
Reading Recovery	Grade 1	readingrecovery.org

summarized in Rapid Reference 9.6. All were found to be "Potentially Positive." An additional program found to have potentially positive effects on improving the reading fluency of students with dyslexia is the Lindamood Phoneme Sequencing (LiPS) program. The program Success for All, designed for grades PreK–8, was found to have potentially positive effects on improving the reading achievement of English language learners. Another classroom intervention with demonstrated effectiveness is Peer-Assisted Learning Strategies (PALS). PALS was originally designed for students in grades 2 through 6 and has since expanded to separate programs for kindergarten, first grade, and high school. One aspect of PALS, Partner Reading, which was described earlier in the chapter, is a fluency component that is designed to increase both reading accuracy and speed. Another program, Reading A-Z (www.readinga-z.com), addresses the five areas of reading identified by the National Reading Panel (NRP, 2000) and provides downloadable materials for each area.

Additional Commercial Programs

Several additional programs are worth noting, all of which use research-based approaches to improve reading fluency (see Rapid Reference 9.7). The Florida Center for Reading Research (www.fcrr.org) provides information about how these programs align with current research. Two programs, QuickReads and Six Minute Solution, are described briefly. The remaining four programs are

☰ Rapid Reference 9.7

Additional Commercial Programs Aligned with Research

Program	Grade Range	Website
*Great Leaps	K–12 & adult	greatleaps.com
QuickReads	2–4	quickreads.org
*RAVE-O	2–4	cambiumlearning.com
*Read Naturally	K–5	readnaturally.com
Six Minute Solution	K–9	cambiumlearning.com
*Wilson Fluency Program	K–adult	wilsonlanguage.com

*Detailed description of the program is available in the Appendix of this book.

described in-depth using information provided by the authors of those programs and are found in the Appendix of this book.

QuickReads provides short texts that are designed to be read quickly with meaning. There are 60 high-interest texts each at grades levels 2, 3, and 4. These texts are carefully structured to focus on the 1,000 most frequent words, as well as important phonic patterns. Six Minute Solution provides nonfiction passages for repeated readings by students in grades K–9. Divided into three levels, Primary (K–2), Intermediate (3–6), and Secondary (7–9), the program provides 25 reading passages at each grade level. Students are paired with another student at the same reading level. Each student reads the passage for one minute while the partner notes how many words were read correctly and provides feedback after the reading. Then the student partners switch roles and repeat the activity. This program supplements the core curriculum and the activity can be completed in six minutes.

CONCLUSION

A fluent reader has the ability to read accurately, quickly, and with appropriate expression. Fluent reading is essentially efficient and effortless. The reason fluency is so important is that it frees the reader to think about what is being read; that is to focus on comprehension. The fluent reader is not using energy to figure out words, but rather applying all energy to understanding the meaning of the text. The fluent reader can maintain or vary rate of reading to fit the content and the situation. Evaluation can pinpoint which aspects of fluency are difficult for the individual. Reading fluency is a bridge to comprehension: It is necessary to become an efficient and effective reader. A focus on increasing fluency is particularly important for individuals with dyslexia, who often have compromised reading rates and require extended time to complete all reading assignments. Although their reading rates may never be on par with classmates, systematic instruction in fluency can help close the performance gap.

🪶 TEST YOURSELF 🪶

1. The three primary elements of reading fluency are accuracy, rate, and prosody. True or False?

2. Prosody is
   a. reading with good expression.
   b. reading with proper phrasing.
   c. paying attention to the punctuation.
   d. all of the above.
   e. none of the above.

3. A distinguishing characteristic of individuals with dyslexia is difficulty with fluent reading. True or False?

4. Fluency is a bridge between word identification and
   a. speed.
   b. accuracy.
   c. comprehension.
   d. expression.

5. When assessing an individual's reading fluency, it is only necessary to establish rate using words correct per minute. True or False?

6. An effective intervention for building reading fluency is
   a. explicit modeling.
   b. repeated readings with error correction.
   c. tape-assisted reading.
   d. all of the above.

7. A reader must first be accurate before working on rate. True or False?

8. The accuracy level of an individual who reads 225 out of 250 words correctly is
   a. 55%.
   b. 75%.
   c. 90%.
   d. 95%.
   e. none of the above.

9. **An individual should be highly accurate on the text used for increasing rate. In fact, the accuracy level should be at least**

    a. 95%.

    b. 90%.

    c. 85%.

    d. 80%.

10. **Reading fluency difficulties are relatively easy to remediate. True or False?**

Answers: 1. True; 2. d; 3. True; 4. c; 5. False; 6. d; 7. True; 8. c; 9. b; 10. False

Chapter Ten

TECHNOLOGY APPLICATIONS FOR STUDENTS WITH DYSLEXIA

Kathleen Puckett and Blanche O'Bannon

Technology empowers the individual to make the world accessible according to their own needs.

—Hayden, 2011

As students with dyslexia advance through the grades, they report spending countless hours on reading and writing tasks. While they continue to struggle with the essentials of reading—phonemic awareness, phonological skills, accuracy, and fluency—their peers are moving on, using an ever-developing bank of literacy skills to increase further their vocabulary, general knowledge, and overall comprehension abilities. Even though it is important to acquire skills that remediate or fix reading difficulties, at some point in the process students must also learn compensatory skills and strategies in order to keep up with the content that reading affords. Technology tools can serve in this compensatory fashion, providing access to age-appropriate reading materials as well as the general education curriculum, allowing students with dyslexia to be equal participants in school-based learning experiences. By using technology, academic content can be read aloud, defined, translated, captured, transformed, or linked to more information. Writing tasks can be assisted with voice recognition and edited with electronic tools. Attention and organizational skills can be aided with mobile devices equipped with calendar programs. Some research suggests that technology can also serve in a remedial capacity if using these tools promotes transfer to improved skills in other areas (Edyburn, 2006; Rose & Meyer, 2002).

The Individuals with Disabilities Education Act (IDEA, 2004) provides safeguards that protect the right of students with dyslexia and other disabilities to participate in the general education curriculum. The statute and its regulations advance the use of technology as a means of achieving learning goals in this regard.

PERSONAL, INSTRUCTIONAL, AND ASSISTIVE TECHNOLOGY

The technology found in schools generally falls into three categories: technology for personal use (e.g., cell phones, iPods), technology for instructional use, and technology that assists learners with disabilities. Technology for personal use such as a cell phone, once a luxury, is now ubiquitous and multifunctional, providing access to the Internet, media, texting, and an ever-increasing array of applications and services in addition to phone calls. Heiman (2011) refers to technology used for instructional purposes as IT and identifies IT as a general category of hardware or software available to all students that is used to teach the ideas and concepts associated with schooling. Assistive technology (AT) is hardware or software that improves the functional capabilities of an individual with disabilities. AT has a legal definition that is grounded in statute (IDEA) and regulations that state that it must be considered for every student for whom an Individualized Education Program (IEP) has been developed (Zabala & Carl, 2010).

> **DON'T FORGET**
> ....
> Technology used for instruction (IT) is the technology that is readily available in classroom and used by all students. Assistive Technology (AT) improves the functioning of a student with disabilities. AT is legally defined; IT is not. As technology in general adds more and more useful features, much of the technology used for instruction can be used in an assistive manner.

As technology continues to advance, the lines between what might be considered personal use, IT, AT, and software designed or used for other purposes is blurring. Continuing advancements in readily available devices, software, and web-based tools enable students, teachers, and parents to write, read, and access information without having to purchase extra, specialized software that was designed for the disability community. These tools do not have to be categorized as assistive technology in order for them to be beneficial.

Consider, for example, the multiple functions of word processing software. For personal use, basic word processing functions on smart phones send text, read attachments, and edit documents. In school, word processing is considered an instructional application, a convenient and efficient way to advance skills in written expression. This same tool would be an assistive technology (AT) device if certain features (e.g., speech recognition, spell check, or thesaurus) were used to "improve the functional capabilities" of a student with dyslexia or other written expression difficulties.

School IEP teams and administrators are finding difficulty in differentiating the categories; what technology qualifies as AT (and may be required in the

IEP)? What technology is considered instructional and is available and accessible to all, and what tools are considered for personal use and therefore a personal responsibility? Furthermore, the rapid rate with which technology is advancing poses difficulties for teachers and parents when trying to identify useful technology tools. Edyburn (2000) referred to this dilemma as the "paradox of consideration," which questions the effectiveness of technology recommendations when the multitude of options available is generally unknown. In other words, how can teachers and parents make recommendations when they are unaware of how technology can assist with reading?

TECHNOLOGY TOOLS FOR STUDENTS WITH LITERACY BARRIERS DUE TO DYSLEXIA

Regardless of whether the technology is considered personal use, instructional, or assistive, accommodations are available to compensate for the reading and writing difficulties that accompany dyslexia. Whereas many of these accommodations are simple adjustments and/or additions to common applications that are readily available, some are more specialized, requiring additional purchases. And still others open a world of ideas to these students through collaboration and interaction.

Basics: Operating System Features and Supports

Before investing in additional software or devices that would compensate for reading and writing difficulties, it is important to be aware of features and supports that are already available. All computers have customizable options and settings included in the standard features of the operating system. On the Mac, these options are located in System Preferences, in the Universal Access window. In Windows, they are located in the control panel (*Ease of Access* or Accessibility Options folder, depending on the version of the operating system). These locations on both computer platforms house a number of customizable options that can make computing life easier, such as the contrast or color display, the speed of the keystrokes, and movements of the mouse. These options can be saved to a user's login or applied as defaults on an individual computer. Two features in particular, text to speech (TTS) and speech recognition (SR), are especially useful for students with dyslexia.

Text to speech reads the contents on the screen aloud. TTS can be used to read any digital text aloud, whether typed or obtained from a website or a file. For students with dyslexia, this single feature can represent an accessibility lifeline, enabling them to read text that is beyond their current reading levels. TTS is also useful for proofreading; the author can hear the text read back and listen for glitches in grammar or typos that have turned into words with unintended meanings. TTS will not read text that is part of a picture, nor will it read text in a PDF document unless the document was created with an optical character recognition converter, making it accessible (AFB Consulting, 2009).

CAUTION

Text to Speech typically does not read PDF files. PDF documents that were created as accessible files can be read by the Read Out Loud feature in Adobe Reader.

TTS is standard (free) in the Mac OSX operating system. As noted previously, these settings are located in the system preferences, and can be adjusted for speaking rate, voice, and choice of keystrokes used to turn it on. Once these adjustments are set, the student highlights the section of text to be read aloud and presses the predetermined key(s) to activate. Mac's TTS works with any digital text displayed on the screen. On the Windows side, accessing TTS is more complicated. While the TTS engine is present in Windows 7 operating system, this feature was removed from Microsoft Word 2007. It has been reinstated in Microsoft Word 2010, with added features for reading multiple languages. In the interim, additional TTS software (free or purchased) will be needed to activate this feature.

Both Mac and Windows operating systems have screen-reading features that read aloud the command bars, title bars, and announce keystrokes. Voice Over (Mac) and Narrator (Windows) were originally designed for the blind to access controls; however students with dyslexia may also find these features useful.

Speech recognition is used in two distinct ways, voice control of the computer and dictation. Voice control uses spoken commands to run the computer, such as opening files or switching applications. Although this feature was once considered assistive or access technology (for individuals with limited access to keyboard or mouse due to physical barriers), it is also a quick and convenient way to handle common tasks. By pairing this operating system feature with a word processor or other text entry application (e-mail, spreadsheet, etc.) speech recognition transcribes voice into text, as if dictating to a secretary. It "learns" the voice of the user through a profile that is created by the user reading a series of paragraphs aloud while interacting with commands. Occasionally, reading these paragraphs is problematic for a student with dyslexia. In such cases, teachers and parents have developed modifications by reading short phrases to the student with the mute button on, pressing play when the student repeats the phrase into the microphone. The software continuously increases the accuracy of the dictation as errors are edited and corrected.

Again, computer operating systems differ in available features. In Mac systems, voice control is available for predetermined spoken commands. Dictation functions are not available but may be added with the software program Dragon Dictate (Nuance, Inc.). In Windows, (currently System 7) voice control and dictation are available in the speech recognition feature.

Additions

While most computer systems are equipped with features to get started using TTS and SR, two additional pieces of equipment, a microphone and a scanner, will increase efficiency and convenience.

Microphone. For occasional use, or for demonstration purposes, the built-in microphone and speakers on many computers enable the use of speech recognition and text to speech. But if the student is using these features on a regular basis, a high quality microphone and earphone headset combination is essential. A microphone that can be adjusted for a consistent placement near the mouth will increase accuracy of dictated speech recognition, and earphones will protect the privacy of text to speech.

Scanners. While digitized text is becoming more readily available (online sources, e-books, etc.), materials whose only source is print-based still exist. These materials must be scanned to produce digital text. While most multi-function printers and photocopy machines have scan functions, whether or not they can be used to produce digital text depends on the appropriate software. Some scanners and photocopy machines produce documents in PDF format as an image-only scan that TTS cannot read. Scanners equipped with Optical Character Recognition (OCR) software convert the printed page to digital text that can be accessed by a TTS program. If most of the materials are from printed sources, combining a scanner with a high quality OCR scanning software program may be a more efficient use of time for teacher and student alike.

Digital Text

Digital text must be obtained or created in order to use the technology tools of access. Legislation requiring digital text be made available to students with dyslexia has been in effect since the reauthorization of IDEA (2004), requiring schools to provide textbooks and other materials in what is termed a specialized format (which includes digital) in a timely manner to students with print disabilities. The legislation references the 1996 Chaffee Amendment to the Copyright Law, enabling the distribution of copyright material, and the Library of Congress eligibility criteria (National Library Service, n.d.) to define which students qualify. Individuals with dyslexia, as currently defined, qualify as having a print disability and are eligible to obtain textbooks in these formats. Students whose disability does not interfere with the ability to learn to read, such as those with attention deficit hyperactivity disorder (ADHD) or behavioral disorders, would not qualify for access to these materials unless there are other qualifying disabilities present. These regulations established a standard file format for instructional materials source files (the National Instructional Materials Accessibility Standard, or NIMAS), and a repository for distributing these files (National Instructional Materials Access Center, or NIMAC) to state and local agencies.

Obtaining digital text. The U.S. Department of Education has partnered with Bookshare (www.bookshare.org) and Learning Ally (formerly RFB&D; www.learningally.org), two centers that provide accessible text to students with print-based disabilities and the schools that serve them. These centers are repositories for textbooks and other literature in accessible formats (NIMAS). The service is available for U.S. students, preschool through higher education, who qualify. Students and teachers must become members and provide supporting documentation certifying dyslexia. After membership is approved and activated, students (and teachers on their behalf) may download for use at home and school. Once downloaded, the texts must be opened with software that reads NIMAS files.

Membership in Bookshare is free to qualifying U.S. students and institutions that serve them. There is a nominal charge for qualifying U.S. citizens who are not students, as well as for individuals outside the United States. Bookshare provides a free web-based TTS reader (Read Outloud Bookshare Edition, Don Johnston, Inc.), or the student may open the material in any number of other literacy software tools that read NIMAS files and have TTS as a feature. Read2Go, available from iTunes, enables users to read Bookshare books on the iPad, iPhone, and iPod Touch.

Learning Ally offers individual memberships as well as memberships for schools and educators. Learning Ally provides ReadHear software to support both prerecorded audio books and text files using TTS, with human audio descriptions of charts, graphs, and images. Learning Ally Audio, available from iTunes, enables downloading these books for playback on Apple devices.

Bookshare and Learning Ally generate electronic text materials directly from a publisher's files. Digital text may also be obtained from a variety of other sources. Digital versions of out-of-copyright books, books in the public domain, and books where authors or publishers have granted copyright for single use can be obtained free from Project Gutenberg (www.gutenberg.org/).

Once text is in a digital format it can be read by TTS software. If not available as an operating system feature, a number of free and low-cost software programs are available from the web (e.g., Natural Reader and ReadPlease). Digital books can also be purchased from commercial sources (e.g., Google Books [http://books.google.com/]; iTunes [www.apple.com/itunes/]), many of which are also accessible from smart phones, iPads, and have TTS capabilities (Wissick, Heiman, & Castellani, 2011).

Creating digital text. When digital text cannot be obtained, it can be created. Electronic reading and study programs work with a scanner to convert books and other print media to digital text using optical character recognition (OCR) software. The most important feature in any such program is a highly accurate OCR that can discern text with little adjustment from the user, reducing the need to correct inaccuracies from the scan (such as "%" for "s"). Kurzweil 3000 (www.kurzweiledu.com), Read & Write GOLD (www.texthelp.com), and WYNN (www.freedomscientific.com) are representative examples of this type of software.

Product selection should be based on the needs of the individual for a specific academic task and relative cost. For example, if electronic files are generally available, high quality Optical Character Recognition software may not be needed. Other considerations are ease of use and portability of the service, such as software installed on a USB drive or accessible through web subscription. Expect to see improvements in features and operation with each upgraded version of these software programs.

An advantage of using an electronic reading and study software program is the support it provides beyond the scanning. These programs offer an array of additional literacy supports, such as dictionary, thesaurus, and translation capacities. Text highlighting and extracting key terms, split screen viewing, and text note features enable teachers to devise questions and activities, and to implement content-based reading strategies (Brozo & Puckett, 2009).

Word Processing

The word processor is perhaps the most adaptable and overlooked software for students with dyslexia (Brozo & Puckett, 2008; Phayer, 2010). Microsoft (MS) Office Word has a number of features that can be used as an instructional or assistive technology when teaching basic writing skills, assessing general curriculum standards, and providing reading support.

Writing support. Several features in MS Office Word support the writing process. Many of these features might seem obvious to students for whom writing is easy and automatic. But for students with dyslexia, directly pointing out these features and teaching how to use them can mean the difference between feelings of success and continued frustration.

Spelling, grammar checking, and thesaurus features may be turned on (the default) or off. With this feature turned on, the student can visually scan the text for notices: a red underline for a misspelled word, and a green underline for words, phrases, or punctuation that does not conform to standard grammar rules. Right-clicking either notice produces a dialog box suggesting the corrections, and, in the case of grammar notices, explains the rule and suggests options, or offers synonyms for a chosen word. Students may be encouraged to use these features in several ways, as they type or compose their work, during the editing process, and during a final revision. Turning these features off enables the teacher to use the word processor for assessments; for example, spelling tests, composing answers to essay questions, or other forms of writing in which access to spelling, grammar, or thesaurus aids would prevent the measurement of a targeted skill.

Speech recognition, whether an add-on program such as Dragon Dictate (Mac) or activated through the operating system (Windows), works with MS Office Word to transcribe dictation. With a little practice, such as reading passages into the profile so the software can learn the voice, learning to correct errors, and learning the voiced nuances between natural speech and punctuation commands (e.g., comma, period, new paragraph), the results can be surprisingly accurate. While it can ease the tedium and burden of writing for students with dyslexia, this feature is not entirely a panacea for all written expression difficulties. Students must still learn to use editing skills, correcting words that were misidentified, and sentences that ramble while the application took down everything that was said.

The *document template* is used by a number of professionals who must supply specific information within a standard format, such as legal documents, psychological reports, and medical reports. Document templates can also be created to structure writing tasks that involve communicating summaries or results. For example, a document may contain stem or starter statements with spaces or blanks for the student to add specific information. Students with dyslexia who have difficulty starting written composition or who have difficulty remembering the sequence or order of written reports may find this feature useful. An added bonus for the teachers is that a document template reopens with a different name, leaving the original document intact.

Auto correct and *auto text* are related features that make typing easier. When auto correct is turned on (the default setting), common typing and grammatical errors typically made by students with dyslexia are automatically corrected once the space bar is pressed. For example, typing the word "I" as "i" with a space after it will default to the proper form. Similarly, commonly misspelled words auto correct (e.g., "diferent" autocorrects to "different"). Auto text returns a word of choice after typing the first letter or letters and then pressing the F3 key. This abbreviated keystroke for a word feature is created by following the directions for auto text (Alt F3). Students may wish to create an auto text short-cut for words that are frequently used but most often miskeyed or misspelled. Other features in MS Office Word provide writing supports, for example, comments and forms (Lake, 2004), macros, outline view, search and replace (Phayer, 2010), highlighting, and hyperlinks (O'Bannon & Puckett, 2010).

Reading support. In addition to writing, the word processor also has features that can be used for reading support.

TTS. When text to speech is available (Mac) or added (Windows), the word processor can function as a quickly accessible text reader. The typed text can be read aloud to assist with proofreading skills. Digital text could also be copied into the word processor to be read aloud, assisting with what would otherwise be labored and dysfluent reading.

Auto Summary. Auto Summary reduces the number of words in a word processing file based on sentences with the most frequently used words. The user controls the length of the summary in terms of percent of the original and has choices of format for viewing the summary, such as showing the key points, producing an abstract, creating a new document, or showing only the summary. Auto Summary can be used to identify the main idea of the text. It works best with excerpts from structured formats, such as textbooks and reports. Results from other forms of literature, such as novels, are less impressive. Edyburn (2002) proposed the Auto Summary tool as a metacognitive strategy that students can be taught to use, evaluating their own need for the amount of information that is summarized.

Readability. Knowing the general reading level of text is important in selecting reading passages that are at or near students' reading abilities, or in assessing current reading and writing levels. MS Office Word assesses the readability of a passage using two measures. The Flesch Reading Ease Test is a 100-point scale with scores of 90–100 understandable by average 11-year-olds, 60–70 understood by 13–15 year olds, and 0–30 understood by university graduates. The Flesch Kincaid Reading Test (n.d.) takes these 100-point–scaled scores and converts them to U.S. grade-level scores. The formulae for these measures are based on word length and sentence length, with numerical constants applied to obtain index scores that are the inverse of each other; the higher the reading ease score, the lower the grade level score. Reading ease scores are used in legal contracts to assure that the reading level is not so difficult as to be confusing. For education purposes, teachers may use these scores to assess the writing level of work produced by the student, or the reading level of text that was copied into the word processing file. The formula is best applied to a document that is at least 100 words in length. This feature must first be activated by turning on the "show readability statistics" option. Its location depends on the version of MS Word. To do this in Word 2002-2003, go to Tools > Spelling and Grammar > Options > Show Readability Statistics. In Word 2007, go to the Microsoft Office Button > Word Options > Proofing > Show Readability Statistics. Readability is accessed by running a spelling and grammar check; these statistics appear in a dialog box at the conclusion of the check.

TTS Word Processors

Text to speech word processors have features that are not currently available in typical Office Suite applications, or are specially designed for use with younger children. TTS or "talking word processor" software reads the text displayed in a document. Simple programs merely read the selected text. More sophisticated text-to-speech word processors highlight text (dynamic highlighting) as it is read by chosen combination: letter-by-letter, or by word, sentence, or selection. The audio format settings can be adapted in speed, inflection, accent, and choice of voice. Most programs also have word prediction features that predict the next word based on the grammatical structure of the sentence (as opposed to auto complete features common to text messaging software, which complete a word based on its prior use).

WordTalk (www.wordtalk.org.uk/Home/) is a free text to speech plug-in for Microsoft Office Word. A number of commercial programs with this feature include Intellitalk (accessed within Classroom Suite, www.intellitools.com), Write: Outloud (accessed within SOLO Literacy Suite, www.donjohnston.com), and Read & Write GOLD (www.texthelp.com).

Rebus-based word processors allow the insertion of a picture above an individual word. Most have picture dictionaries of several thousand words and include TTS options. Digital text from a variety of sources can be copied into this word processor and converted to picture-enhanced text. Rebus reading programs are sometimes an effective learning strategy for emerging readers or for students with dyslexia, and are recommended as an adaptation to assist struggling readers to independently access classroom-based material (Edyburn, 2003). Two widely used rebus-based word processors are Picture It (www.slater software.com) and Writing with Symbols (www.mayer-johnson.com).

Concept Mapping

Although technology that supports reading is important, some students with dyslexia also have difficulty with the big ideas leading to deeper understanding of the text. Concept maps (also referred to as graphic organizers and mind maps) can assist students in organizing and synthesizing information to make the broader connections necessary for reading comprehension and writing assistance that result in improved performance in content area instruction (Brozo & Puckett, 2009; Hall & Strangman, 2002; O'Bannon & Puckett, 2010). Kidspiration, Inspiration, and Webspiration (www.inspiration.com) are popular concept mapping applications offered by Inspiration Software, Inc. and available in many schools. Kidspiration targets grades K–4, and Inspiration is designed for grades 5–adult. Webspiration is a new addition and offers an online option for grade 5–12. *ReadWriteThink* (www.readwritethink.org), a nonprofit website sponsored by technology foundations and literacy professional organizations, offers free timelines and webbing tools that are simple to use. Rapid Reference 10.1 lists a number of websites for free or low cost graphic organizers, concept mapping, and mind mapping software.

Rapid Reference 10.2 presents an exercise that provides an example of integrating some of these tools in a manner that could assist a student with dyslexia in tackling a lengthy reading assignment. In order to complete the exercise, you will need the following: a computer with access to the Internet, and a free download of TTS software, such as Natural Reader (www.naturalreaders.com).

Vocabulary support. As students progress through the grades, they increase their vocabulary knowledge through reading. For students with dyslexia, slower or difficult reading leads to reduced vocabulary knowledge. Rapid Reference 10.3 gives an annotated list of vocabulary websites, some with text and graphic organizers, others with pictures depicting the context.

Web 2.0 tools. Web 2.0 tools have made the Internet a participatory, interactive place where readers create, collaborate, and share information, bringing new and powerful opportunities to the classroom (Miers, 2004; Solomon & Schrum, 2010). Competence is no longer an independent act; it is gained from forming connections and sharing the experiences of others (Siemens, 2004). Teachers are becoming facilitators of knowledge; assisting students as they seek new information, using inquiry and working with others to solve real-world problems (Savery & Duffy, 2001; Soloman & Schrum, 2007). This new world is particularly suitable for students with dyslexia, whose oral language and reasoning abilities are often more advanced than their reading skills. In classrooms as well as in the workplace, skills and standards-based learning are essential but no

≣ *Rapid Reference 10.1*

Concept Mapping, Graphic Organizers, Mind Mapping Software

- Bubbl.us (https://bubbl.us/): Online brainstorming that exports as an image or html.
- Gliffy (www.gliffy.com): Online diagramming software, for flowcharts, floor plans, Venn diagrams, and more.
- Inspiration (www.inspiration.com): Suitable for grades 4–adult; free 30-day trial; low cost pricing. Exports outline to word processor.
- Kidspiration (www.inspiration.com): Suitable for grades 1–3; free 30-day trial; low cost pricing. Exports outline to word processor.
- Lucid Chart (www.lucidchart.com): Create collaborative flow charts and organizational charts.
- Mindmeister (www.mindmeister.com): Online collaborative concept mapping tool, free version allows 3 maps per year.
- Quicklist (www.quicklyst.com): Take notes and create outlines; accommodates mathematical formulae.
- Slatebox (www.slatebox.com/Index): Collaborative "slates" (e.g., concept mapping). In the free version, the slates are public.
- Time Line Maker (www.teach-nology.com/web_tools/materials/timelines): Make online timelines with choice of templates.
- Webspiration (www.mywebspiration.com): Suitable for grades 5–12; free 30-day trial. Online version of Inspiration.

Source: Abridged from Wissick, C. *Wissick's Web Toolboxes.* Accessed on March 28, 2011 from http://webtoolboxes.wikispaces.com/Graphic+Organizers

longer sufficient for success. The challenge for teachers of students with dyslexia and their intense focus on skill development is to continually ask larger questions, such as how can students collaborate with others to develop new and broader understandings, apply knowledge in new and different ways, and understand their own power to make and defend decisions. Web 2.0 tools aid in developing these collaborative skills. Rapid Reference 10.4 gives suggestions for getting started. Students can interface TTS and SR with most of these tools.

Google Documents. With Google Documents (www.google.com), teachers and students may access tools for word processing, spreadsheets, presentations, forms to create surveys, and drawing. Students no longer need to have compatible software on home computers or keep up with storage drives. Reports, budgets, or presentations can be started at school and finished elsewhere, and peers can be invited to add to or edit the final document. Furthermore, accessibility tools, either resident in the operating systems (e.g., speech recognition) or available as add-ons (e.g., TTS) make these tools accessible for most users.

≡ Rapid Reference 10.2

Using Multiple Tools for Reading Support

- Find a topic of interest in Wikipedia, the free web-based collaborative encyclopedia (www.wikipedia.org). Note the length and breadth of the entry. Consider the difficulty level for a student with dyslexia. Read portions of the entry aloud using TTS, such as Natural Reader.

- Change the volume of text to be read while retaining most of the meaning. Scroll down the left-hand side of the Wikipedia screen to languages, and select Simple English. Note the reduced size of the entry.

- Copy and paste this entry into MS Word. Obtain an executive summary of the main ideas by using Auto Summary. Use TTS to read this new entry. Experiment with the percent of Auto Summary to determine how much (or how little) text is needed to retain the main concepts of the entry.

- Just for fun, copy the executive summary and paste it into Wordle (www .wordle.net) to generate a word cloud picture from this text. Are words that are the largest size the same words used in the executive summary? Could this tool be used as an interest grabber in other ways?

≡ Rapid Reference 10.3

Online Tools for Vocabulary Support

Shahi (www.blachan.com/shahi/): A visual dictionary using pictures from Flickr.

Qwiki (www.qwiki.com): A search engine that provides definitions, audio support, and photos for vocabulary.

Visuwords (www.visuwords.com): Online graphic dictionary; creates a graphic organizer for a word.

WordSmyth (www.new.wordsmyth.net): Traditional look and feel to an online dictionary.

Vocabahead (www.vocabahead.com/Home/tabid/37/Default.aspx): Vocabulary videos for SAT/ACT tests.

≡ *Rapid Reference 10.4*

Web 2.0 tools
Word Processing
  Google Docs (http://docs.google.com)
Blogs
  Blogger (www.blogger.com)
  Bloglines (www.bloglines.com/)
  WordPress (http://wordpress.org)
Wikis
  PBWorks (http://pbworks.com)
  WikiSpaces (www.wikispaces.com)
  WetPaint (www.wetpaint.com)
  50 Ways to Use Wikis (www.smartteaching.org/blog/2008/08/50-ways-to-use-wikis-for-a-more-collaborative-and-interactive-classroom/)
Podcasts
  Kids Podcasts (http://kids.podcast.com)
  The Education Podcast Network (http://epnweb.org/index)
  Smithsonian Museums (http://museumpods.com/id31.html)
  Exploratorium (www.exploratorium.edu/teacher_institute/podcasts/)
Social bookmarking
  Delicious (www.delicious.com)
  Diigo (www.diigo.com)
Just for fun
  Voicethread (www.voicethread.com): An interactive, multimedia slide show tool
  Glogster (www.glogster.com): An interactive multimedia poster tool
  Prezi (www.prezi.com): An interactive alternative to PowerPoint
  Wordle (www.wordle.net): Word cloud generator, gives prominence to frequently appearing words
  Tagxedo (www.tagxedo.com) Word cloud generator with a variety of tightly produced shapes

Blogs. *Blog* is a shortened version of *weblog*, an online journal presented as a web page. Blogs can be used for reflective writing, to enhance literacy skills, or to create digital portfolios. Teachers can keep students and parents abreast of classroom and/or school happenings, and post homework and reminders of parent-teacher conferences, field trip information, and other upcoming events. While there are a number of blog tools, several (see Rapid Reference 10.4) are good choices for schools and offer free accounts to students and teachers. All of these tools typically work the same way: go to the site, set up an account, and begin to blog.

Wikis. Wikis are tools that allow individuals to create, edit, and link web pages as well as incorporate pictures, sounds, and movies into a website. They provide a means for asynchronous communication and collaboration among "members" of a wiki "community" and provide a simple method for teachers and students to work together through a web browser. Wikis allow for the sharing of original content that can be retrieved long after projects are over. The most well-known wiki is Wikipedia (http://en.wikipedia.org/wiki/Main_Page), a multilingual collaborative online encyclopedia that emerged in 2001 and has "become a clearinghouse of information based on the work of thousands of amateur researchers" (Richardson, 2006, p. 3). A variety of wiki applications are available, but the features and complexity of the tools will vary a great deal. The tools suggested in Rapid Reference 10.4 are no cost to educators, easy to use, and ad-free, making them popular choices for schools. Wikis can be configured to be private or public, making them a safe place for students to collaborate and build knowledge.

Podcasts. Podcasts are digital media files circulated through the Internet and downloaded for playback on a MP3 player or computer. Podcasts can be delivered in audio format only or in enhanced format (audio and video). The term originated as the combination of Apple's iPod and the term *broadcast* and is used to identify the content as well as the delivery form. Teacher podcasts are typically of lectures and provide a way for students to hear information on complex topics multiple times. Student-created podcasts can be on a variety of topics limited only by the imagination of the teacher. Podcasts can be created to demonstrate student understanding of a concept, to present research, or to express student point of view (Soloman & Schrum, 2010). Rapid Reference 10.4 lists a number of sites that house collections of podcasts on a variety of topics.

Social bookmarking. Social bookmarking can assist with collaborative research projects. Assignments that require students to research topics using Internet sources typically start during upper elementary school grades and continue through high school. Social bookmarking is a web service that supports the research process. Using a social bookmarking tool a student can locate, bookmark, and add tags (keywords) to identify the content found at the site. Bookmarks can be organized by tags to form lists. Individuals connect through shared tags and can subscribe to one another's lists. Classroom groups can be set up to pool findings. The advantage of social bookmarking for students with dyslexia is that they can use and contribute to a knowledge base without having to start from scratch, and their bookmarks are available anywhere with an Internet connection. Teachers who use social bookmarking can scaffold student learning by sharing bookmarks with their students. Social bookmarking tools are found in Rapid Reference 10.4.

Mobile Devices: iPod and iPad: Accessibility and Use

The price, capacity, and flexibility of handhelds have made them attractive complements to laptop and desktop computing for students with dyslexia. Students and teachers who are using smart phones or handhelds to download and listen to music and/or take and manage photos are quite accustomed to their interface, making adoption easier. The biggest concentration of handhelds used in schools reported from literature sources appears to be Apple's iPod Nano, the iPod Touch, and increasingly, the iPad (Sailers, 2010a). The interface features multitouch screens that can be operated through gestures: for example, single and double taps, two and three finger swipes, pinching, expansion, and rotations. The iPod and iPad come with built-in accessibility features similar to those of the laptop (TTS, Zoom, white on black contrast). Applications—such as calendars, word processing, spreadsheet, concept mapping, dictionary, and language translation programs—come as either standard features or low cost additions. Sailers (2010b) regularly updates lists of iTunes apps suitable for students with special needs, organized by subject area. This list offers a sampling of these selections, differentiated according to whether they are tools, used to organize, create, or access content, or teaching apps, with a fixed content. Rapid Reference 10.5 provides examples of different types of applications that students with dyslexia may find useful.

≡ Rapid Reference 10.5

Apps Suitable for Students with Dyslexia

Tool-Based Apps

App Title	Description
Organizational Apps	
Google Mobile	Search the web (using Google) with voice, access Google account.
iReward Chart	Keep up with homework, chores, and other tasks. Set up includes adding rewards and points. Great for home-school collaboration for younger children.
IEP Checklist	Check off a list of items to complete for an IEP meeting.
Reading Apps	
Kindle for the iPhone	Download and read Kindle books.

| StoryKit | Create a story with drawing, pictures, typing and voice recording. |
| Wikipanion | Access Wikipedia using a noncluttered screen and have access to an online dictionary from any word in the article. Search Wikipedia using word prediction. Set current location using GPS. |

Writing Apps

Dragon Dictation	Dictate using the built-in microphone. Tap the screen to record speech and stop recording speech. Transcription appears in a note column that can be copied to e-mail or a word processing application (Companion Dragon).
Dragon Search	Voice recognition with searching capabilities for the web.
MindMeister	Create Mind Maps (also called Concept Maps) and share on the web.

Teaching Apps

App Title	Description

Reading

iMotherGoose-Bugs	Colorful picture book of common bugs, insect names in text and spoken when the Mother Goose is touched.
See Read Say	Read and hear Dolch words organized by levels from pre-primer to third grade.
The Cat in the Hat	One of many titles of children's books in the collection, interactive with words that are highlighted as they are read.

Writing

Spel it Rite Pro	Choose the correctly spelled word from 2 choices taken from a pool of 3,000 words in this spelling game. Settings allow 10, 20, or 30 word games; choices include words such as *inherent, opportunity, conferee, hideous.*
Word Magic	Work on beginning, ending, and medial sounds with pictures and sound.
iWriteWords	Trace the formation of letters and numbers. Colors that appeal to younger children.

Music and Art

Drum Kit Pro	Play along on the drums to songs in the iTunes library.
Finger Piano	Play the piano with a small onscreen keyboard. Preloaded songs to play along with, and cues to track keys.
Doodle Kids	Draw random shapes in random colors and sizes.

Source: Adapted from Sailers, E. (2010b). iPhone, iPad, and iPod Touch Apps for (Special Education). Available from http://www.scribd.com/doc/24470331/iPhone-iPad-and-iPod-touch-Apps-for-Special-Education

Among the options available for mobile devices are commercial selections of electronic audiobooks. Teachers are discovering a multiplicity of uses for these devices with students who have dyslexia. Using standard applications, teachers and students are able to integrate the skills presented in Rapid Reference 10.6. This technology may be more readily available than expensive classroom computers, making access to technology more of a reality in schools with budgetary challenges (Banister, 2010).

Beyond the built-in applications that are standard with the purchase of a mobile device, web applications (apps) expand their use and offer customization that greatly benefits students with dyslexia. Web apps are downloadable files that can be added to devices from the Internet. Many of these apps are free or low cost. A wide range of academic support applications is available for math, social studies, science, and language (Banister, 2010). Although formal research on student outcomes with these mobile devices is not yet reported, parents and teachers have discovered a multitude of add-on apps that they report as being useful.

Rapid Reference 10.6

Classroom Uses for the iPod Touch

- Language Development: Use the voice recorder to podcast student work. After reading a book, students develop a book report that includes a brief summary of their story, and then record the report using the iPod. The teacher posts the podcast to the class website, where it can be accessed from home or classroom.
- Reading Fluency: Students record themselves reading to improve their accuracy and fluency. Students then listen to each other's recordings and follow along with the books.
- Organizational Skills: Students organize their daily classwork and homework assignments using the calendar application.
- Lesson Review: Students use the video feature to capture lesson examples in the form of short video clips. The students then review the lessons at a later date and share ideas with each other.
- Video Conferencing: Students use "Facetime," video conferencing software that works with Wi-Fi, to collaborate on homework assignments.
- Behavioral Monitoring: Teachers build a behavior check-in form using Google Forms. Students check in on this application every 15 minutes in order to self-monitor and record their own behavior.

The Intel Reader (www.intel.com/corporate/healthcare/emea/eng/reader/ index.htm) is a small, lightweight device that can be used to take a picture of a page and listen to its contents. It allows individuals with reading difficulties or with low vision to access print without being limited to prerecorded or digital content. It will also read most digital content file formats. An additional stand allows larger documents and multiple pages of content to be scanned, converted, and stored for later use.

The Mobile Reader (www.knfbreader.com/index.php) is a software program that interfaces the camera on a multifunction cell phone with OCR software and TTS. The user takes a photo of the printed material, and the software will read the contents of the document aloud, while displaying the print and highlighting each word as it is spoken on the phone's screen. This software will read and translate text between multiple languages, making it useful for the older student who is enrolled in a World Language class. The product is available in two versions, the *kReader Mobile*, designed for struggling readers and those learning a second language, and the *knfbReader Mobile*, designed for individuals who are blind.

PUTTING IT ALL TOGETHER: A FRAMEWORK FOR INSTRUCTIONAL PLANNING

Universal Design for Learning (UDL; Rose & Meyer, 2002) and Differentiated Instruction (DI; Smith & Throne, 2007; Tomlinson, 2000) are frameworks for instructional planning to ensure that students with dyslexia have access to the same curriculum and learning opportunities as their peers. The intent of both concepts is to maximize student learning by planning for flexible approaches to teaching and learning (Edyburn, 2010; Hall, Strangman, & Meyer, 2003). UDL encourages teachers to plan ahead for the widest possible range of student abilities, minimizing the need to add adaptations after the fact. DI offers suggestions on how to vary the content, process, and products of instruction based on student needs. Technology tools support both concepts in assisting teachers to plan lessons that accommodate the needs of most learners. Rapid Reference 10.7 lists the principles of UDL and DI, along with suggested technology tools.

DON'T FORGET

The UDL and DI concepts aim to increase student learning by providing flexible approaches to teaching and learning. Technology integration helps to achieve these goals.

≡ Rapid Reference 10.7

UDL, DI, and Technology Integration

UDL Framework	DI Framework Technology Integration	Potential Student Activities
Multiple Means of Representation. Present materials in many different ways, and in multiple formats, including digital media, to give students options for acquiring information and knowledge.	**Content:** Provide for variations in readiness, interests, and learning styles or preferences of the learners.	Read digital text with TTS. Use a mobile reader. Visit multimedia websites (displayed individually or with an interactive white board for the class). View a concept map on the topic. Read material from blogs. Consult a wiki. Listen to a podcast. Research through lists accessed through social bookmarks. Access online vocabulary support.
Multiple Means of Expression. Show the students examples or models of what their new learning would look like, and give them options for expressing their learning through a variety of media.	**Product:** Allow for varying forms of expression and levels of difficulty. Provide coaching, scaffolding, and guidelines.	Use word processing with SR, TTS, and other writing supports. Use word prediction. Participate in project-based learning using technology. Create a concept map. Add to a social bookmarking site. Post a blog. Create a podcast. Create a Word Cloud.
Multiple Means of Engagement. Attend to student interest, motivation, and engagement by offering choices of tools, adjusted	**Process:** Develop a variety of activities to assure the comprehension of the content, flexible groups, organizational	Use digital text with TTS. Read or Write using a rebus word processor. Use electronic literacy supports: notes, highlighting, dictionary.

UDL Framework	DI Framework Technology Integration	Potential Student Activities
levels of difficulty, and varying levels of support.	and learning strategies.	Use online tools for vocabulary support. Determine the amount of text needed in Auto Summary. Select text based on readability scores. View or create concept maps. Share a Word Cloud. Collaborate in groups with technology support: Google Docs, blogs, wiki, podcasts, social bookmarking.

CONCLUSION

This chapter provides an overview of technology tools and applications for students with dyslexia, with broad category suggestions for technology support. Teachers can choose from many different tools and vendors when integrating technology; the examples provided in this chapter are not indications of endorsement of any particular product, vendor, or tool when others with similar features are available.

Technology use cannot be a stand-alone proposition, but must be integrated into the curriculum to support grade-level academic standards in a manner that corresponds to a student's Individualized Education Program. Similarly, using technology tools for reading and writing support does not replace the need for instruction in the processes and strategies involved in comprehending what is read and in writing clearly and expressively (Brozo & Puckett, 2009).

CAUTION

Keep in mind that technology is not a substitute for good instruction.

Nevertheless, our notions of what students need to know, do, and perform are changing. As the technology advances, digital source material is beginning to evolve interactively, with multimedia and collaborative elements that have the potential to transform the reading experience with video clips, interactive graphs, GPS tags for locations mentioned in text, and social networking links all integrated into the reading experience (Dalton & Proctor, 2008; Johnson, Smith, Willis, Levine, & Haywood, 2011). Although the potential for these elements to support students with dyslexia is promising, participation still demands access to and understanding of text-based material. Technology is redefining what that means.

🖋 TEST YOURSELF 🖋

1. Text to speech software will read PDF files. True or False?
2. Printed text may be converted to digital text using OCR software. In this instance, the term OCR is an abbreviation for
   a. Office of Computer Regulations.
   b. Optimum Computer Recognition.
   c. Optical Character Recognition.
   d. Optical Compulsive Recording.
3. Materials presented in many different ways, in multiple formats, with options for obtaining information, provide
   a. multiple means of representation.
   b. differentiation of product.
   c. social networking.
   d. electronic strategy supports.
4. Differentiating Instruction by Product is most closely related to which UDL principle?
   a. Multiple Means of Representation
   b. Multiple Means of Expression
   c. Multiple Means of Engagement
   d. Multiple Means of Control
5. Some scanners and mobile devices combine a camera with software to take a picture of text. In order for this text to be read aloud, it must first be
   a. taken with the appropriate camera resolution (232 dpi or higher).
   b. converted to digital text using OCR.
   c. certified as permissible under the Chaffee Amendment to the Copyright Law.
   d. corrected for errors in translation.

6. **Auto Summary**
   a. reduces the number of words in a document by 25%.
   b. removes all difficult to pronounce words from a document.
   c. determines key points by displaying sentences that contain words used most frequently.
   d. is linked through Web 2.0 tools to encyclopedic references to determine the extent of the summary.

7. **Mary is a 14-year-old student who is in the seventh grade, having been retained twice in lower grades due to reading difficulties related to dyslexia. She is still much below grade-level standards in word recognition, vocabulary, and fluency, but comprehends grade-level text when it is read to her. The IEP team is struggling with what to recommend next. Based on the concepts in this chapter, which recommendation would give Mary the best options?**
   a. Continue with remediation programs that focus on word recognition and fluency.
   b. Focus entirely on digital texts and other compensatory strategies.
   c. Move her immediately to the ninth grade.
   d. Teach her how to use grade-level digital books, word processors, TTS, and SR, pairing these tools with strategies for word study, comprehension, and writing, while continuing remediation in word recognition and fluency.

8. **Why are instructional and assistive technology devices and services infrequently recommended for students with dyslexia?**
   a. Many teachers believe that remediation is more important than compensation.
   b. School districts are wary of the money they would have to spend if every student were given a computer.
   c. Parents and teachers are not aware of technology tools and cannot recommend what they do not know.
   d. Teachers and students are more comfortable with paper and pencil tasks.

9. **The 1996 Chaffee Amendment to the Copyright Law and the Library of Congress eligibility criteria allows for the distribution of text-based materials in alternate formats to individuals with print disabilities. Qualifying individuals include those with**
   a. emotional disturbance.
   b. attention deficit hyperactivity disorder.
   c. dyslexia.
   d. any disability covered by an IEP.

10. **Technology is changing concepts of teaching and learning**
   a. to a growing emphasis on high performance in individual skill areas.
   b. to the development of independent learning opportunities.
   c. toward the development of competence through forming connections and sharing experiences.
   d. toward reliance on clearly stated goals and objectives.

Answers: 1. False; 2. c; 3, a; 4. b; 5. b; 6. c; 7. d; 8, c; 9. c; 10. c

Chapter Eleven

DYSLEXIA IN DIFFERENT LANGUAGES AND ENGLISH LANGUAGE LEARNERS

Martha Youman

It is necessary to understand the different learning patterns of multilingual dyslexic people if teachers are to provide appropriate programmes of learning.

—Peer & Reid, 2000, p. 1

Most of what we know about dyslexia comes from research conducted in English because until recently it was believed that dyslexia was a disorder that only affected English speakers (Caravolas, 2007). In the last few decades, however, studies of reading in a number of languages have demonstrated that dyslexia occurs across languages (e.g., Davies & Cuentos, 2010; Paizi, Zoccolotti, & Burani, 2010; Su, Klingebiel, & Weekes, 2010). Because the way we read depends on the nature of the language we speak, the complexity of the language dictates which characteristics of dyslexia will be most significant. In the first section of this chapter, the language features that affect reading development and the characteristics of dyslexia in different languages are discussed. In the second section, the complex nature of reading and dyslexia in English Language Learners (ELLs) is analyzed, and information that may help distinguish second language–related reading difficulties from those associated with dyslexia is presented.

ORTHOGRAPHY IN DIFFERENT LANGUAGES

Orthography, or how a language is represented in writing, impacts both reading and spelling development and can present varying difficulties to individuals with dyslexia. The most common

DON'T FORGET

Dyslexia is a neurological disorder that occurs across languages. However, dyslexia affects individuals differently depending on the characteristics of the language they speak and read.

orthographies today can be classified into alphabetic, syllabic, and logographic writing systems. Figure 11.1 provides examples of writing in languages that use each of these orthographic systems. It is important to understand the features of different orthographies because even though it is known that dyslexia results from neurological impairments, the characteristics of each orthography affect how dyslexia is manifested in reading. Simply put, although brains are similar across cultures and languages, orthographies are not, and this changes how dyslexia affects individuals who come from different language backgrounds.

Alphabetic		Logographic		Syllabic	
Spanish		Chinese		Japanese Kana	
Letter	**Sound**	**Symbol**	**Meaning**	**Symbol**	**Syllable**
a	/a/	人	human	さ	sa
b	/b/	山	mountain	の	no
c	/c/ /s/	火	fire	へ	he
ch	/ch/	船	boat	す	su
d	/d/	讀	to read	て	te

Figure 11.1   Types of Orthographies
This figure illustrates the three different types of orthographies: alphabetic, logographic, and syllabic. In alphabetic orthographies, each symbol or combination of symbols represents a sound. In logographic orthographies, symbols or combinations of symbols represent whole words. In syllabic orthographies, each symbol represents a syllable. Spanish, Chinese, and Japanese Kana offer examples of each of these writing systems.

Alphabetic Orthographies

Alphabetic orthographies use symbols or letters to represent different sounds of speech in writing. In the simplest alphabetic systems, such as Turkish and Finnish, each symbol or grapheme is used to represent a single sound or phoneme (McDougall, Brunswick, & de Mornay Davies, 2010). This one-to-one correspondence between letters and sounds is unusual, however, with most alphabetic orthographies presenting a number of irregularities that make reading unpredictable and challenging. The term *orthographic depth* is often used to describe the degree of correspondence between the sounds in a language and the letters that represent these sounds in writing (Frost, 2007). Under the umbrella of orthographic depth, languages that map each sound to a specific letter are known as "shallow or transparent orthographies." In contrast, orthographies with multiple mappings between sounds and letters are known as "deep or opaque orthographies" (Brunswick, 2010). Figure 11.2 lists several alphabetic languages and illustrates how they can be classified according to their sound-to-print correspondences along a shallow to deep orthography continuum. A language with a shallow orthography, such as Finnish, shows a nearly perfect relationship between letters and the sounds they represent. Emergent readers learning to read in Finnish and other shallow orthographies can successfully sound out and pronounce all the words they read once they learn the sound that each letter represents. On the other hand, emergent readers of languages with deep orthographies, such as English and French, must learn a number of irregular patterns and are less able to rely on the sounds that each letter represents. Rapid Reference 11.1 provides several examples in English to demonstrate the complexity of learning to read a deep orthography.

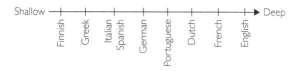

Figure 11.2   Examples of Shallow and Deep Alphabetic Orthographies
This figure represents the classification of alphabetic orthographies along an orthographic depth continuum. In shallow orthographies, such as Finnish and Greek, there is nearly a one-to-one correspondence between letters and sounds (i.e., grapheme-phoneme). Grapheme-phoneme correspondence decreases in deep orthographies, such as English and French. In these orthographies, multiple combinations of letters can represent the same speech sounds.

In some languages with a deep orthography, irregular phoneme-grapheme correspondence is complicated further by complex syllable structures. In particular, unlike most Romance languages such as Italian and Spanish that are often comprised of simple syllables (e.g., one consonant and one vowel, as in *casa*), Germanic languages like English and German tend to show complex syllable patterns (e.g., several consonants within the same syllable as in *crunch*). Research has shown that readers of languages with deep orthographies and/or complex syllable structures learn to read at different rates (Goswami, 2008; Seymour, Aro, & Erskine, 2003). Specifically, phonological awareness, a key early prerequisite for reading is developed more easily in languages with shallow orthographies and/or simple syllable structures. (See Chapter 5 for a discussion of phonological awareness.)

≡ Rapid Reference 11.1

Examples in English that Demonstrate Common Irregularities in Deep Orthographies

- Several letters (graphemes) can represent one single sound or phoneme (e.g., *fight*, *might*, *night* where the grapheme *ght* represents the sound /t/).
- Different spelling possibilities can represent words that sound the same but have different meanings (i.e., homophones; e.g., *to*, *two*, *too* and *there*, *their*, *they're*).
- Identical words can change meaning depending on the context in which they appear (e.g., "She cannot *bear* to see her father in pain." and "The *bear* attacked the campers.").
- Single letters can represent multiple sounds (e.g., *cone* and *pot* where the letter *o* represents both the sound /ō/ and /ŏ/; *cup* and *pencil* where the letter *c* represents both the sound /k/ and /s/.
- The same morpheme can be pronounced differently (e.g., *-ed* suffix indicates past tense and is pronounced as *painted* /ed/, *played* /d/, and *liked* /t/).
- Phonemes or sounds can be spelled in several different ways (e.g., the sound /f/ can be spelled with *f* as in *fog*, *ph* as in *phone*, *ff* as in *stuff*, *gh* as in *cough*, and *lf* as in *calf*).

Logographic Orthographies

Languages, such as Chinese, that use pictures to represent writing are referred to as logographic orthographies. In this type of writing system, a specific symbol is used to represent individual words or parts of words. Thus, native speakers of languages that use logographic systems must memorize thousands of characters to become literate. Few languages today, however, are purely logographic, and they often include phonetic and semantic features to support reading. For example, in Chinese Mandarin about 80 to 90 percent of words are compound characters that include a semantic element that provides meaning called a "radical" and a phonetic element that provides information about its pronunciation (McDougall et al., 2010). Figure 11.3 illustrates examples of Chinese compound characters. The word *volcano* 火山, which

> ## CAUTION
>
> Few languages today are purely logographic, or simply based on pictures to represent words. Instead, modern logographic languages often include phonetic and semantic components to support reading.

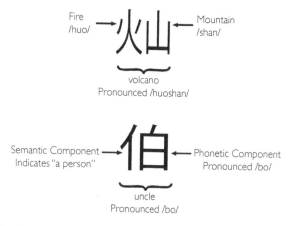

Figure 11.3   Example of Chinese (Logographic) Writing

This figure provides examples of logographic writing in Chinese. (top) The symbols for *fire* and *mountain* are logographic characters that together form the word *volcano*. The logographic symbol for *uncle* is made of a radical, semantic component on the left and a phonetic component on the right. The semantic radical indicates "a person," and the phonetic component indicates how the word is pronounced "bo."

is made of the symbols for *fire* 火 and *mountain* 山, provides an example of a purely logographic Chinese character. By contrast, the word *uncle* 伯 illustrates a compound Chinese character that has a radical component 亻 "a person," which indicates meaning, and a phonetic component 白 "bo," which indicates how the word is pronounced. Because of the complexity and the extensive number of characters that must be learned, learning to read logographic orthographies is much more difficult than learning to read alphabetic orthographies. For example, a review of reading instruction in China reported that children must learn to read 2,570 different characters by the end of the sixth year of reading instruction (Shu, Chen, Anderson, Wu, & Xuan, 2003).

Syllabic Orthographies

Syllabic orthographies, including Japanese Kana and Cherokee, use symbols to represent combinations of consonant-vowel sounds in writing. Emergent readers of syllabic orthographies learn symbols to represent syllables in their language and use these symbols to decode words. For example, in Japanese Kana, a component of Japanese language used to translate foreign words and names of places, each symbol represents a syllable. As illustrated in Figure 11.4, each syllable in the word *America* is represented by a symbol for the syllables *a-me-ri-ka*. In syllabic orthographies, emergent readers learn the sounds that each syllabic symbol represents and can decode words in a similar manner as those learning alphabetic orthographies. Studies of reading in syllabic orthographies are uncommon because most languages that use syllabic writing today use this orthography in conjunction with logographic or alphabetic orthographies. However, studying specific features of syllabic orthographies can help us understand the role of phonological awareness, word recognition, and fluency in other languages. For example, Perea and Perez (2009) conducted research that explored transposition effects in reading (e.g., reading *casual* for *causal*) using Japanese Kana. The results of the study revealed that even in syllabic orthographies, poor readers tend to transpose symbols when reading similar words, even if the smallest unit represents an entire syllable rather than a single sound.

> ## DON'T FORGET
>
> Research suggests that poor reading skills, such as transposing letters within words (e.g., *causal* for *casual*), occur across different types of orthographies.

Symbol → アメリカ

Syllable → a   me   ri   ka

Figure 11.4   Example of Japanese Kana (Syllabic) Writing
This figure illustrates the word *America* written in Japanese Kana, a syllabic language used for foreign names and translations. Each symbol on the top represents the syllable at the bottom.

DYSLEXIA ACROSS DIFFERENT ORTHOGRAPHIES

The difficulties that readers with dyslexia experience correspond to the complexity of the language they speak (Caravolas, 2007). A few key deficiencies related to language and reading, however, have been found in readers with dyslexia across languages. Rapid Reference 11.2 summarizes universal characteristics found in individuals with dyslexia. The information presented is derived from various studies of dyslexia in different languages including Chinese (Ho & Bryant, 1997; McBride-Chang et al., 2011), Dutch (Bekebrede, van der Leij,

≡ Rapid Reference 11.2

Universal Characteristics of Dyslexia Across Languages
- Slower than average reading speed.
- Slower performance on measures of Rapid Automatized Naming (RAN; Best predictor of reading fluency skills; see Chapter 5 for more information on RAN).
- Deficiencies in phonemic awareness prior to reading instruction (best predictor of later spelling skills).
- Less accurate detection and production of rhymes.
- Initial difficulty with phonological processing (often measured through reading of nonwords or pseudowords, e.g., *flib, cotch*). Because of the regularity of the language, the importance of nonword reading, however, tends to fade in transparent orthographies after the first few years.
- Inaccurate spelling.
- Poor verbal memory.

Plakas, Share, & Morfidi, 2010), Greek (Porpodas, 1999), Finnish (Leppänen, Niemi, Aunola, & Nurmi, 2006), Italian (Paizi et al., 2010), Japanese (Koeda, Seki, Uchiyama, & Sadato, 2011; Seki, Kassai, Uchiyama, & Koeda, 2007), Malay (Lee & Wheldall, 2011), Spanish (Jimenez & Ramirez, 2002), and Turkish (Babayiğit & Stainthorp, 2011).

Dyslexia in Languages with Deep Orthographies

The complexity of the writing system in deep orthographies causes readers with dyslexia problems in accurate and fluent reading and spelling. In fact, reading accuracy is often the key feature that distinguishes dyslexia in deep orthographies (Caravolas, 2007). In a deep orthography like English, about 1,100 possible letters or letter combinations represent the 44 sounds of the spoken language. In contrast, in a shallow orthography like Spanish, 34 letters or letter combinations represent the 41 possible sounds. Thus, an individual with dyslexia will have much more difficulty reading and writing in English than an individual with dyslexia reading and writing in Spanish. Simply stated, for individuals with dyslexia, languages with deep orthographies are more challenging than languages with shallow orthographies.

Another characteristic that distinguishes individuals with dyslexia in deep orthographies is the persistence of poor phonemic awareness, even after years

> ## DON'T FORGET
>
> In languages with deep orthographies, the key features that distinguish individuals with dyslexia from other readers include inaccurate and slow word reading, poor spelling, and the persistence of poor phonological skills.

of reading instruction (Brunswick, 2010). For a discussion of phonological awareness and other features of dyslexia in English, see Chapters 1 and 5. Similar findings to those discussed in these chapters have been found in other languages with deep orthographies including French (Martin et al., 2010) and Danish (Olofsson, & Niedersøe, 1999).

Dyslexia in Languages with Shallow Orthographies

Dyslexia in shallow orthographies is typically characterized by slow, but not necessarily inaccurate, reading (Davies & Cuentos, 2010). Once readers with dyslexia master the letters and corresponding sounds of the alphabet, the one-to-one correspondence between sounds and letters facilitates their reading and spelling. Although they may not have difficulty with accuracy, their reading speed and fluency may never reach the level of their peers, and they may consequently experience problems with reading comprehension (Zoccolotti, DeLuca, DiPace, Judica, & Orlandi, 1999). In addition, emergent readers who have dyslexia may show initial deficiencies in phonological processing but then appear to "overcome" their phonological impairments after a few months of reading because the transparent orthography helps them "assemble" phonemes while they read (Caravolas, 2007; Porpodas, 1999). Researchers are still debating over the role of phonological deficits in individuals with dyslexia in shallow alphabetic orthographies. It is possible that phonological deficits manifest differently in readers of languages with shallow orthographies. For example, a study of Finnish-speaking adults with dyslexia showed accurate, but delayed recognition and manipulation of sounds in words (Lindgren & Laine, 2011). Thus, while a reader of English (deep orthography) will have more errors in recognizing the sounds, a reader of Finnish (shallow orthography) will take longer to recognize the sounds but will be more accurate. For this reason, with the exception of the beginning stages of reading, it is not advisable to rely on reading accuracy measures (including nonword reading measures) described in Chapter 6 for the diagnosis of dyslexia in languages with shallow orthographies. Instead, the most reliable assessment methods include Rapid Automatized Naming (RAN) and reading fluency measures (Paizi et al., 2010).

Some findings in studies of dyslexia in shallow orthographies have also revealed reading errors associated with word "stress" (Paizi, Burani, & Zoccolotti, 2011). Most words in English are "stressed" or pronounced with emphasis on the first syllable. In languages such as Spanish and Italian, however, words tend to have stress in varying parts of the word. Readers with dyslexia in shallow orthographies tend to produce stress errors in the words they read, particularly if the words are unfamiliar. Thus a Spanish reader with dyslexia will likely be able to decode the word *cuchara* (spoon) accurately because of the transparency of the language. She may, however, place stress on the wrong syllable by reading /*cuchará*/ instead of placing the correct stress on the second syllable /*cuchára*/.

> **CAUTION**
>
> After a few years of reading, accuracy tests, such as nonword reading, and tests of phonological awareness, provide little information for the diagnosis of dyslexia in languages with shallow orthographies.

> **DON'T FORGET**
>
> A slow reading rate, rather than accuracy of word reading, distinguishes readers with dyslexia from their peers in languages with shallow orthographies.

Dyslexia in Nonalphabetic Languages

Although research in nonalphabetic orthographies is still in its early stages, the characteristics of dyslexia in nonalphabetic languages are as complex as the characteristics that make up their orthographies. For example, individuals with dyslexia learning to read in Chinese often show signs and symptoms similar to those observed in English. Like their peers who are learning to read deep alphabetic orthographies, their reading tends to be both slow and inaccurate. In writing, however, they often show poor character formation, greater character size, irregularity in their strokes, and inaccurate placement of radical and phonetic components within each character (Lam, Au, Leung, & Li-Tsang, 2011; Leong, Cheng, & Lam, 2000). Children with dyslexia learning to read in Chinese have also shown deficiencies in recognizing the tones of spoken language (Goswami, Wang, Cruz, Forker, Mead, & Huss, 2011). This trait specific to Chinese, a tonal language, is strikingly similar to deficits in phonological awareness in deep alphabetic orthographies, such as English and French, and deficits in word stress recognition in shallow alphabetic orthographies, such as Spanish and Italian.

In contrast to logographic orthographies, which tend to present challenges similar to deep orthographies, syllabic orthographies, such as Cherokee and Japanese Kana, may offer readers with dyslexia an opportunity to decode the sounds to read accurately. Still, because dyslexia occurs across languages, readers of syllabic orthographies will experience challenges similar to those seen in shallow alphabetic orthographies, mainly in slow reading speed that then affects comprehension (Seki et al., 2007). Future research will probably define more clearly how dyslexia is manifested in nonalphabetic orthographies. For now, it appears that dyslexia can affect reading in nonalphabetic orthographies, even if the writing systems rely more on memorization than phonetic decoding (Caravolas, 2007).

DYSLEXIA OR SECOND LANGUAGE LEARNING?

Other chapters in this book have highlighted the complex nature of dyslexia, which makes identification quite a challenging process. This becomes even more difficult when attempting to identify individuals who are learning English as a second language. One aspect to keep in mind, however, is that individuals who are reading in a language different from their native language will, at least for some period of second language learning, show evidence of poor reading skills (Everatt et al., 2010). The following section provides information that can help teachers and evaluators differentiate between readers with dyslexia and inexperienced second language learners.

CAUTION

Many early reading and spelling behaviors of English Language Learners (ELLs) resemble those of readers with dyslexia. It may take several years for these similarities to fade, even after intensive English as a Second Language (ESL) instruction.

Both vocabulary knowledge and phonological awareness tend to be highly correlated with success in reading. In younger readers who enter school with limited or nonexistent literacy skills in their native language (i.e., Language 1 or L1) and with low vocabulary in English (i.e., Language 2 or L2), the lack of these prerequisites becomes an obstacle that hinders reading development. These unique environmental conditions should not, however, be confused with the reading difficulties of dyslexia. Young ELL readers in monolingual settings are often learning to read a language that they do not speak and cannot form mappings between the words they read and their meanings. Even in bilingual settings, these young learners have to cope with the demands of two languages simultaneously and often fall behind their monolingual peers (Wilkinson, Ortiz, Robertson, & Kushner, 2006). While learning to read in English, ELL students often struggle with basic phonemic awareness and may experience reading difficulties because they lack L2 vocabulary (Brice & Brice, 2009). Thus, unlike interventions that focus mainly on the development of phonological and phonic skills for monolingual English readers with dyslexia (see Chapters 7 and 8), a key intervention for struggling ELL readers must include vocabulary development and literacy skills in L1 and L2 (Atwill, Blanchard, Christie, Gorin, & Garcia, 2010). More importantly, prior to the identification of dyslexia in young ELL readers, screening procedures must rule out language disadvantages that have resulted in low reading performance (IDEA, 2004).

A different picture emerges with older ELL readers, who are often literate in L1 prior to receiving reading instruction in L2. For these readers, vocabulary development in L1 may positively influence cross-language transfer of reading skills (e.g., phonological awareness), thus helping reading fluency in L2 (Atwill et al., 2010). On the other hand, a negative transfer of first-language knowledge may affect reading development in English. A few specific examples of this negative transfer of L1 into L2 are highlighted in Rapid Reference 11.3. These native language specific characteristics, adapted from an extensive review of error analysis studies by Figueredo (2006), are often seen in children and adults who learned to speak English after becoming literate in their native language. Although similar to characteristics often found in monolingual English readers with dyslexia, these characteristics occur as a result of L1 interference and should not be used to diagnose ELL struggling readers with dyslexia.

Assessment of Dyslexia in English Language Learners (ELLs)

Although most reading difficulties in ELLs are the result of limited language skills, evidence from cross-linguistic studies of dyslexia suggests that some do in fact struggle with reading because they also have dyslexia. How can language deficiencies be ruled out when screening ELLs for dyslexia? This basic question has puzzled parents, teachers, administrators, and researchers in both academic and clinical settings. Unfortunately, there is no established procedure for evaluating ELLs who are suspected of having dyslexia. Instead, a number of options are available to evaluators who must ultimately use clinical judgment to determine the cause of reading failure in English language learners. The following common evaluation practices are adapted from Ortiz (2011) to provide readers with an idea of the advantages and disadvantages of each method.

☰ *Rapid Reference 11.3*

Examples of Common Reading and Spelling Mistakes in English Language Learners (ELLs)

- If Spanish is L1:
  - Pronunciation errors due to Spanish phonological influence (e.g., reads *drogstore* for *drugstore*)
  - Spelling errors due to Spanish phonological influence (e.g., writes *rack* for *rock, mekin* for *making, clin* for *clean; chi lismi* for *she lets me*)
  - Limited knowledge of double consonants (e.g., writes *botle* for *bottle*)
  - Errors due to pronunciation of sounds nonexistent in Spanish (e.g., *v* for *b* or vice versa, writes *cavul* for *cable; j* for *s*, writes *mejure* for *measure; ch* for *sh*, writes *chow* for *show; y* for *j*, writes *yaw* for *jaw; es* for *s*, writes *estop* for *stop*)
- If Arabic is L1:
  - Lack of /p/ sound in Arabic results in confusion of /b/ and /p/ (e.g., reads or writes *bicture* for *picture*)
- If Chinese is L1:
  - Poor performance in nonword spelling and reading (i.e., pseudowords), but not in real word spelling
  - Reading and spelling errors in words with *th* and *sh* (e.g., *sink* for *think; sort* for *short*)
- If Japanese is L1:
  - Confusion of *l* with *r* in reading, speaking, and spelling (e.g., *sarary* for *salary*)

Modified or adapted tests. A common practice when assessing ELL children who are suspected of having a learning disability, such as dyslexia, often involves changing standardized procedures to meet the needs of linguistically and culturally diverse learners. Some evaluators may choose to eliminate test items that are considered culturally biased, repeat directions, accept responses in L1 or L2, administer only portions of standardized tests that do not rely on oral comprehension, and extend or eliminate time constraints. These practices are aimed at allowing learners from diverse backgrounds to perform at their full potential. Unfortunately, when any of these practices takes place during evaluation of ELLs, the norms of each test can no longer be considered valid. Because the test was not administered using the standardized procedures, the results do not provide information on how the examinee compares to his peers in the norm group. In addition, each evaluator may modify testing differently, therefore removing the objectivity of the test. In other words, because of the modifications chosen by an evaluator, a child may be diagnosed with dyslexia; however, a different evaluator, who chose different modifications, may not reach the same conclusion.

Another modification may include using an interpreter or translator to make sure the examinee understands the questions being asked and the items being administered. This practice is problematic because it assumes that if ELLs understand the directions of the test, they will be able to perform equally to their monolingual peers. However, even after understanding what is being asked, an ELL may not have the necessary language to respond, or may be confused by the test content.

CAUTION

Standardized tests that are changed to meet the needs of ELLs are no longer objective. The validity of the results depends on adhering to the test's standardized administration procedures.

Nonverbal testing. In the past, some evaluators have chosen to use nonverbal tests to assess ELLs. The directions and answers in these types of tests are given visually or via gestures, thereby eliminating the need for oral language. Unfortunately, these types of assessment procedures have little use for the diagnosis of dyslexia. From nonverbal assessments, an evaluator may be able pinpoint memory or processing deficiencies, but these may have little to do with reading. Simply put, it is difficult to assess a reading disorder without taking objective linguistic measures of reading-related abilities or reading. At a minimum, the assessment should include measures of phonemic awareness, RAN, and vocabulary.

Native-language testing. A number of assessment batteries have been translated into various languages and are often used in school and clinical setting to evaluate ELLs. Native-language testing, however, may not provide an accurate description of skills in ELLs. In particular, these tests may provide useful information about monolingual individuals in the language of the test, but may provide inaccurate information about an individual who is learning a second language. The individuals included in the norming of these tests are usually monolingual, learning to read in their native language, and growing up with monolingual parents. For example, most Spanish translations of tests used in U.S. schools were normed on individuals in Mexico or other Spanish-speaking countries. While these tests may be appropriate to diagnose dyslexia in monolingual Spanish speakers, they may not be appropriate for diagnosing dyslexia in Spanish-speaking children who are learning to speak, read, and write in English.

English language testing. In the majority of settings, ELLs are evaluated for dyslexia and other learning disabilities exclusively in English. Compared to previously discussed methods, this type of assessment is likely to yield the most biased results. Research reveals that, on average, ELLs tested in English perform significantly below their monolingual English-speaking peers (Wilkinson et al., 2006). This is likely due to the deficiencies in vocabulary and phonemic awareness frequently experienced by young ELLs in both L1 and L2. On the other hand, older ELLs who learned to read in their native language before learning to read in English are likely to transfer phonemic awareness and other phonological skills, but may still show vocabulary deficiencies in English. Furthermore, they may experience language interference of L1 when learning L2, so reading difficulties may be the result of language learning rather than dyslexia.

> **DON'T FORGET**
> ....
> Evaluation of ELLs exclusively in English is likely to produce the most biased results.

Suggested best practice. Currently, researchers are exploring best practices for the accurate diagnosis of dyslexia and other disabilities in ELLs. Although there is no one definite agreed-upon best practice, it is clear that a one-time assessment may not provide the most accurate picture of the individual. As with monolingual individuals, early identification is important so that appropriate reading interventions can be provided. If, however, the source of reading difficulties is a lack of exposure to English, ELLs should not be prematurely labeled with dyslexia. Thus, when an ELL student experiences reading difficulties, whether due to second language learning or dyslexia, the evaluation should begin with early reading intervention and periodic measures of progress in reading and oral language (Wilkinson et al., 2006). If reading continues to lag behind oral language for an extended period of time, formal assessment procedures should be employed to determine the existence of dyslexia. In addition to standardized tests, however, the evaluation should include interviews with family members and teachers, measures of reading performance in both languages, and accurate measures of English language proficiency. After careful assessment, the multidisciplinary team should make the final determination; this team should ideally include a member fluent in the native language of the individual being evaluated and/or a member familiar with evaluating individuals from diverse backgrounds.

CONCLUSION

Dyslexia is a neurological, brain-based disorder that affects individuals of all ages across different languages. This chapter provided a summary of how dyslexia is manifested in different written language systems. Individuals with dyslexia learning to read in deep alphabetic orthographies, such as English and French, demonstrate poor reading accuracy, fluency, and weak phonological skills tend to persist. On the other hand, individuals with dyslexia learning to read in shallow orthographies, such as Spanish and Italian, often experience early reading deficiencies in phonological skills and reading accuracy, but tend to "overcome" these deficiencies after a few years of reading instruction. Their reading, however, remains slow and laborious, therefore affecting reading fluency and comprehension. For individuals with dyslexia learning to read logographic and syllabic orthographies, the difficulties they experience depend on the complexity of the written language system.

For ELLs and other bilingual readers, identification of dyslexia becomes a challenging process that should take into account multiple factors and the unique characteristics of each case. In general, for young ELL readers who are learning to read and write primarily in English, reading lags behind because of limited vocabulary in L1 and L2. These young learners should receive language instruction, preferably in the native language and second language, along with an evidence-based reading intervention prior to considering a diagnosis of dyslexia. In older readers, who often have solid reading skills in their native language, reading skills tend to transfer to English reading. A lack of vocabulary knowledge and the effects of native language transfer, however, may result in confusion between the symptoms of second language learning and dyslexia. In these experienced readers, interventions should focus on second language development and diagnosis should include measures of reading in both the native language and English.

Ultimately, regardless of the demands of each language and the complexity of the orthography, the result is still the same: readers with dyslexia struggle in reading and spelling. People read to obtain meaning from text, and readers with dyslexia often fail to achieve this goal because they read inaccurately or slowly or both. Early identification and intervention are important so that these individuals have a chance to develop their reading skills. Parents, teachers, evaluators, and researchers must take special precautions when identifying dyslexia in ELLs. Rather than speculating on the causes of reading failure and waiting to see if poor reading performance is because of dyslexia, interventions should be provided early, and each individual's reading progress should be monitored carefully.

🖋 TEST YOURSELF 🖋

1. Dyslexia affects individuals differently depending on the complexity of the language they speak and read. True or False?

2. English is considered a deep orthography because
   a. it is usually learned as a second language.
   b. it has irregular letter-sound (i.e., grapheme-phoneme) correspondence.
   c. it has a larger number of symbols represented in the alphabet.
   d. all of the above.
   e. none of the above.

3. Logographic writing systems often include semantic and phonetic components that together provide information about meaning and pronunciation. True or False?

4. Readers with dyslexia in shallow orthographies tend to "overcome" initial deficiencies in phonological skills and reading accuracy because
   a. they receive intensive reading instruction during the first years of schooling.
   b. they recognize the alphabet more easily.
   c. the transparency of their language helps them assemble phonemes while they read.
   d. all of the above.

5. The universal characteristics of dyslexia include
   a. slower than average reading speed, slow RAN performance, and initial difficulties in phonological skills.
   b. persistent lack of phonemic awareness, invented spelling, and problems in simple math facts.
   c. reversals of numbers and letters, poor memory, and lower cognitive performance.
   d. limited prereading vocabulary, slow processing speed, and oral language articulation problems.

6. Reading accuracy tests, such as nonword reading and tests of phonological awareness, are useful during all stages of reading development in all languages to diagnose dyslexia. True or False?

7. The two key features that help identify dyslexia in deep orthographies are
   a. slow reading and letter reversals.
   b. memory deficiencies and slow processing.

   c. RAN tasks and letter transposing (e.g., *casual* for *causal*).

   d. inaccurate reading and spelling and the persistence of poor phonological skills.

8. **The reading difficulties of readers with dyslexia in nonalphabetic
orthographies**

   a. are identical to those experienced by English readers of dyslexia.

   b. depend on the complexity of the language.

   c. result from decreased memory abilities.

   d. all of the above.

9. **ELLs whose LI is a language with a shallow orthography are not likely
to have dyslexia. True or False?**

10. **The best assessment procedure for ELLs who are suspected of having
dyslexia is**

   a. native language testing.

   b. nonverbal testing.

   c. English language testing.

   d. modified testing.

   e. none of the above.

11. **Common reading and spelling difficulties in ELLs from Spanish speaking backgrounds include**

   a. pronunciation and spelling errors due to Spanish phonological
influence.

   b. limited knowledge of double consonants.

   c. errors in pronunciation and spelling of sounds nonexistent in
Spanish.

   d. all of the above.

12. **Limited vocabulary and literacy skills in the native language can affect
an ELL's reading development in English. True or False?**

13. **In a school setting, for an ELL who is struggling with reading, the first
step should be**

   a. formal assessment of cognitive skills and achievement in the
native language.

   b. an appropriate intervention with careful data collection to assess
progress.

   c. testing of cognitive and achievement skills using an interpreter.

   d. diagnosis of dyslexia by a certified physician.

14. **Complex syllable structures (e.g. CCCVVCCC as in *straight*) present challenges for emergent readers, as well as those with dyslexia. True or False?**

15. **Older ELLs, who are fluent readers in their native language, often**
    a. transfer their basic reading skills to English.
    b. show the same deficiencies as younger, nonliterate ELLs.
    c. read faster than they can speak.
    d. none of the above.

Answers: 1. True; 2. b; 3. True; 4. c; 5. a; 6. False; 7. d; 8. b; 9. False; 10. e; 11. d; 12. True; 13. b; 14. True; 15. a

Chapter Twelve

DYSLEXIA IN THE SCHOOLS

To teach in a manner that respects and cares for the souls of our students is essential if we are to provide the necessary conditions where learning can most deeply and intimately begin.

—hooks, 1994, p. 13

Oftentimes dyslexia is first noticed after a child enters school. Because the early grades focus on teaching children how to read, problems with matching sounds and symbols, decoding, or spelling words are often noted during the first year of schooling. For some children, however, the problems are not apparent until third grade. These children may have strong verbal skills and good memory for words so they simply memorize words in the early grades. By third grade, the amount of reading increases, so that memorization of words is no longer feasible and problems with decoding or encoding emerge.

Reading is a gateway skill. In other words, the ability to read is fundamental to and facilitates all academic learning. When a child's reading development lags behind classmates, she is at a disadvantage not only in reading, but also in writing, math, and other content areas. It is often said that children learn to read from K–3 and then read to learn after that. If a child hasn't developed proficiency as a reader by the end of third grade, regardless of how intelligent that child may be, she will fall further and further behind classmates who are proficient readers. Reading is the focus of educational reforms and legislation precisely because it is so important to academic performance.

LEGISLATION IMPACTING SCHOOLS AND STUDENTS WITH DYSLEXIA

General education at both the elementary and secondary levels is governed by the Elementary and Secondary Education Act (ESEA) known currently as the No Child Left Behind Act of 2001 (NCLB). NCLB supports standards-based education reform. The purpose of Title 1 of this act is to ensure that all children have a fair, equal, and significant opportunity to obtain high-quality education, and to reach, at a minimum, proficiency on state achievement standards and state academic assessments. NCLB specifies accountability measures, teacher training, instructional materials that align with state standards, and so on. A number of reading initiatives are specified in NCLB, including Reading First, Early Reading First, Even Start, and Improving Literacy Through Libraries. For more information about NCLB, see www.ed.gov/nclb. NCLB set the tone for revisions that occurred in special education laws, such as the Individuals with Disabilities Education Improvement Act of 2004 (IDEA, 2004). Rapid Reference 12.1 summarizes the federal mandates governing general and special education.

School-age children with disabilities have rights and protections under the Individuals with Disabilities Education Improvement Act of 2004 (P.L. 108-446, IDEA, 2004). For example, a local education agency (LEA) must make available a free appropriate public education (FAPE) to children with disabilities who are at least 3 years old but not yet 21 years old and who have not graduated from high school. FAPE is special education and related services that are free and comply with laws and is provided through an individualized education program (IEP). This applies to school-age children identified with dyslexia who are found eligible for special education services. For more information about IDEA 2004, see http://idea.ed.gov/.

Two antidiscrimination laws, the Americans with Disabilities Act and Section 504 of the Rehabilitation Act, provide legal protections to individuals with disabilities but unlike IDEA 2004, do not provide funding for programs. The Office for Civil Rights (OCR), a component of the U.S. Department of Education, enforces these laws. Under Section 504, a student with a disability may have a 504 Plan that guarantees equal access to education and allows for certain accommodations or modifications. Unlike IDEA 2004, Section 504 has no requirement for an IEP and has fewer procedural safeguards.

Some states have statewide dyslexia laws (e.g., Texas, Mississippi, Louisiana, California, Colorado, Washington, New Jersey, Hawaii, New Mexico); others are attempting to pass legislation. These laws require public schools to screen children for dyslexia during kindergarten, first, or second grade. A few of the states require teacher training colleges to offer

DON'T FORGET

A number of states currently have specific laws mandating screening for dyslexia during the first years of school.

≡ *Rapid Reference 12.1*

Federal Mandates Governing Education

General Education

No Child Left Behind Act of 2001 (NCLB, 2001) also known as the Elementary and Secondary Education Act
Governs elementary and secondary education in public schools and implements standards-based education reform.

Special Education

Section 504 of the Rehabilitation Act (Section 504)
This is a civil rights statute designed to eliminate discrimination on the basis of disability in any program or activity that receives federal financial assistance from the U.S. Department of Education.
Individuals with Disabilities Education Improvement Act of 2004, P.L. 108-446 (IDEA, 2004)
This act provides educational rights, protections, and funding for services for individuals between the ages of 3 and 21 identified with disabilities who are eligible for special education

courses on dyslexia and for teachers to have in-service training. Some states, such as Florida, provide handbooks with guidance for educators, parents, and legislators (e.g., http://www.dys-add.com/FCRRReptonDysl.pdf) Thus, it is important to check what types of legislation regarding dyslexia exist in your state.

THE ROLE OF THE PUBLIC SCHOOL IN DIAGNOSING DYSLEXIA AND PROVIDING SERVICES

As can be seen from the brief review of federal legislation, public schools play an important role in identifying and serving children who may have dyslexia or other learning disabilities. The laws do not, however, mandate diagnosing a particular disability; they simply mandate that schools determine the presence of a disability and that the student is eligible for special education services. So testing in the schools may focus more on eligibility for services

CAUTION

An evaluation conducted by school personnel may tend to focus more on determining eligibility than diagnosing a child's learning problem.

than diagnosis for dyslexia. Depending on what the criteria are for determining eligibility, a student with dyslexia may or may not qualify for special education services. Dyslexia is considered to be the most common type of learning disability. To determine eligibility under the learning disabilities category, current federal law allows eligibility determinations to be made in several ways or through use of a combination of methods: a discrepancy between the individual's ability (usually based on an IQ score) and his achievement (usually based on scores from an individually administered, norm-referenced test of achievement); a pattern of strengths and weaknesses (among an individual's cognitive and achievement scores) that suggests the presence of a specific learning disability; or failure to respond to instruction (in schools using a response-to-intervention model). Each state has specific rules and regulations that govern the implementation of the federal mandates so it is important to check the website of the appropriate State Department of Education.

Before a student is referred for a comprehensive evaluation, most schools try to intervene with additional support for the student. When concerns first arise about a child's reading performance, the teacher attempts to address the issue within the classroom. If concerns continue, the teacher may turn to a student support team for help. These teams have many different names, such as pupil services team, teacher assistance teams, or instructional support teams. The teams are composed of other educators in the school and may include the principal and relevant specialists. Recommendations are made and implemented based on the team's review of the student's performance and instructional history. If the student continues to struggle, then a comprehensive evaluation may be conducted to determine if the child has a disability and is eligible for special education services. Once identified as a child with a disability, the school is responsible for planning and providing appropriate instruction as well as monitoring the individual student's progress.

DON'T FORGET

Once a child is found eligible for special education services, the school is responsible for planning and providing appropriate instruction.

Currently, many schools are implementing an instructional model known as response-to-intervention (RTI). While there is not one standard way to implement RTI, typically three or four tiers are provided with increasing levels of intervention. Figure 12.1 illustrates a three-tier RTI model. The first tier includes all students and is the core curriculum delivered in the general education classroom. Within the RTI model, all students receive high-quality instruction in the core curriculum, and achievement is universally checked at three points throughout the school year. Students who are struggling in the core curriculum begin to receive additional, supplemental instruction, which is tier 2 and is usually delivered in small group settings. Progress is monitored more frequently at tier 2 to determine if the student needs to continue with the supplemental instruction, needs a change in instruction, or requires more intensive intervention. If the student fails to make adequate progress at tier 2, instruction is intensified (tier 3) and may include one-to-one instruction. In some RTI environments, tier 3 includes a comprehensive evaluation to determine the need for special education. In other RTI environments, an evaluation would occur at tier 4. The beauty of RTI is that it is designed to provide high-quality instruction to all students and to provide immediate additional instruction to students who are lagging behind classmates. There is no need to wait for a diagnosis of a disability to help a struggling student.

RTI models provide early interventions that may help students overcome academic difficulties before they fail. Using it exclusively, however, could bring negative consequences to struggling learners. Low reading performance alone is insufficient for the identification of dyslexia because this condition may be present in individuals for a variety of reasons (Berninger, 2011).

In particular, when a student is failing academically, RTI does not help us understand why. RTI does not diagnose a disability; it only documents a lack of adequate progress. RTI addresses the needs of the group of students, and individual differences may be ignored and each struggling student treated as if he struggles for the exact same reason and requires the exact same intervention. Clearly, this is not true. Individual differences do matter, and students with dyslexia do require the educational rights and protections guaranteed by federal law.

Another area of concern regarding the exclusive use of RTI relates to its focus on all students rather than on those who need special education services to be successful. For this reason, some fear that RTI may delay the process of diagnosis and appropriate service delivery for children with dyslexia. This is not the intent of an RTI process. On January 21, 2011, the Office of Special Education Programs (OSEP) issued a memorandum to State Directors of Special Education

> **CAUTION**
> ....
> RTI is an instructional model, not a diagnostic model. RTI does not tell us the reasons why a student is failing to make adequate reading progress.

regarding the use of an RTI process to delay or deny an evaluation for eligibility under IDEA, writing: "It has come to the attention of the Office of Special

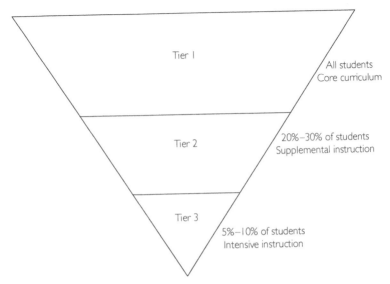

Figure 12.1   Typical Three-Tier Response-to-Intervention (RTI) Model

Education Programs (OSEP) that, in some instances, Local Education Agencies (LEAs) may be using Response to Intervention strategies to delay or deny a timely initial evaluation for children suspected of having a disability. States and LEAs have an obligation to ensure that evaluations of children suspected of having a disability are not delayed or denied because of an RTI strategy." The memo is available at OSEP's website: http://www2.ed.gov/policy/speced/guid/idea/memosdcltrs/index.html

DOES THE STUDENT HAVE CHARACTERISTICS OF A STUDENT WITH DYSLEXIA?

With a few exceptions, the term *dyslexia* is not widely used in schools. Instead, schools use terms like a specific learning disability in the area of reading or LD in reading. IDEA 2004 identifies eight areas of eligibility for students identified with a specific learning disability: basic reading skills, reading fluency, reading comprehension, math calculation skills, math problem-solving, written expression, oral expression, and listening comprehension. The most likely areas of eligibility for a student with dyslexia are basic reading skills and reading

CAUTION

....

The term *dyslexia* is not widely used in many public schools.

fluency with secondary problems possible in reading comprehension and written expression. Numerous reasons exist for why a student may struggle with reading, and not all of them are because of a disability. A student's reading can be impaired due to an inadequate oral language base, or perhaps the student has generally low performance across all areas, or maybe the student has not received appropriate instruction. The results from a comprehensive evaluation should pinpoint the reasons for the student's reading and spelling difficulties.

Although schools do not commonly use the term *dyslexia*, it is important for school personnel to be familiar with the characteristics of dyslexia and to evaluate all appropriate areas. Initially, close monitoring of the child's reading performance in relation to classmates is needed. The earliest warning signs may be noticed in the child's oral language performance, such as difficulty with speech, or trouble learning to rhyme words. The child may not want to look at print when a caregiver is reading a book. Once letters are introduced, the child may exhibit little interest in learning the letters and may demonstrate poor letter-sound knowledge. When the student is expected to read and spell, difficulties with both tasks may be noted. As time goes on, the student will lack speed when reading and writing, demonstrating limited fluency. A comprehensive evaluation is needed to determine if the student displays a pattern of performance that suggests the presence of a specific learning disability, such as dyslexia. To be identified with dyslexia, the student should have a cognitive deficit (or deficits) related to the academic deficit (or deficits) in reading and/or spelling. In addition, the student should demonstrate areas of strength, such as a relative strength in general intelligence, oral language, reasoning, and/or mathematics. Evaluators must also be alert to secondary issues, such as problems with reading comprehension due to poor decoding, or problems in written expression due primarily to spelling difficulties. Rapid Reference 12.2 lists important areas to consider and evaluate when identifying whether a child has dyslexia. Dyslexia is a complex condition with multiple and variable symptoms. Careful consideration of each individual student's symptoms is essential for diagnosing dyslexia. Special considerations are also needed when evaluating gifted students for dyslexia or students who are English language learners (ELLs).

Gifted students with dyslexia. Gifted students who also have dyslexia are often described as being twice-exceptional learners. Unfortunately, when a

DON'T FORGET

Be alert to possible secondary symptoms such as reading comprehension difficulties resulting from poor decoding skills.

≡ *Rapid Reference 12.2*

Relevant Areas to Evaluate When Determining the Presence of Dyslexia

Relevant Cognitive Deficit(s)
a. Phonological Awareness
b. Phonological Memory
c. Orthographic Awareness
d. Rapid Naming
e. Processing Speed
f. Working Memory

Relevant Academic Deficit(s)
a. Letter/Sound Knowledge
b. Word Decoding (real word and nonword reading)
c. Reading Fluency
d. Spelling

Relative Cognitive and Academic Ability Strengths
a. General Intelligence
b. Oral Language (oral expression and/or listening comprehension)
c. Reasoning
d. Mathematics (calculation and/or mathematic problem solving)

student is gifted and also has dyslexia, it is possible to miss either the dyslexia or the giftedness. A gifted student with dyslexia may still excel in some subject areas. Even reading comprehension may appear intact because the student can use language and good reasoning skills to think around the problems in decoding. These bright individuals with dyslexia use their strengths in oral language and knowledge to compensate for their weak decoding skills (Uhry & Clark, 2005). These students may even skip numerous words when reading, but are smart enough to get the gist of the passage. These types of gifted students may be identified as gifted, but their dyslexia is missed. Any difficulties noted in their decoding or spelling are often attributed to carelessness, inattention, or limited motivation. This masking of ability and disability warrants concern if RTI is used as the only protocol for the identification of dyslexia (Crepeau-Hobson & Bianco, 2011).

On the other hand, some gifted individuals have severe problems in decoding and spelling. These individuals may be identified with dyslexia, but their giftedness is overlooked. Further, depending on the criteria established for determining eligibility, the reading performance of the gifted student may not be low enough to meet eligibility criteria. For example, a score falling below the normal range (standard score less than 85) may be required in some situations. For untimed tests in particular, a gifted student with dyslexia may have performance falling in the average range, particularly if the student has had tutoring in reading. It is important then to consider the effect of prior interventions, as well as to also assess accuracy, reading rate, and oral reading when diagnosing gifted students with dyslexia. In addition, to identify individuals who are gifted with dyslexia, a measure of cognitive abilities must also be administered. Within an RTI-only framework, these students will be overlooked (Ofiesh, 2006). This information will provide teachers and parents with an understanding of the variations among the student's cognitive, linguistic, and academic abilities. To meet the needs of these twice exceptional learners, it is necessary to create a balance between attention to strengths and weaknesses within an authentic, challenging curricula (Crepeau-Hobson & Bianco, 2011).

Students with dyslexia who are also English language learners. English Language Learners (ELLs) present and face unique challenges when learning to read in English. (See Chapter 11 of this book for detailed information about ELLs and dyslexia.) At times their struggles with learning to read are attributed to lack of English language proficiency. In this situation, valuable time may be lost before appropriate interventions are employed. Research indicates that ELLs are identified as having a learning disability 2–3 years later than most English-only students (McCardle, Melee-McCarthy, Cutting, Leos, & D'Emilio, 2005). It is important to consider the student's proficiency and instructional history in her first language (L1) to more clearly understand what is happening in the second language (L2). For example, if the individual manifests problems in L1, then a learning disability may exist. Conversely, if the individual has strong linguistic skills in L1, then those skills should transfer to L2. Just as for English-only students, early identification and intervention are critical for ELL students with dyslexia.

ACCOMMODATIONS AND MODIFICATIONS

Students with dyslexia will often require accommodations and modifications in their schoolwork and school assignments, and these are often written on their IEPs or 504 plans. The difference between accommodations and modifications is that accommodations do not alter the essential elements of the task, whereas modifications alter the task demands in some way. For example, an accommodation would be if a student with dyslexia listens to a book rather than reads the book. A modification would be that the student is assigned an easier book to read, or only a portion of the book to read. When adjustments in schoolwork are written on these plans, students are provided with legal protections; that is, the accommodations are non-negotiable. For example, a teacher cannot refuse to provide a student with an oral examination if this accommodation is part of the IEP or the 504 plan.

DON'T FORGET

Accommodations and modifications that are written on IEPs and 504 plans must be provided.

When considering the unique characteristics of each student, the first goal is to identify specific strengths and how these abilities can be used to enhance performance; the second is to identify the weaker areas and abilities so that appropriate accommodations and modifications can be developed and implemented. In order to be successful, many students with dyslexia will need both accommodations and modifications in both school and homework assignments throughout their school careers. Rapid Reference 12.3 provides examples of appropriate accommodations and modifications.

CAUTION

Accommodations and modifications are designed to "level the playing field" and provide equal opportunity to students with dyslexia, not to provide an unfair advantage. Students with dyslexia are provided with extra time because they need this extra time to demonstrate their knowledge.

EMOTIONAL IMPACT OF DYSLEXIA

Dyslexia is not an emotional disorder, but it can create social and emotional difficulties for the individual. In fact, Fernald (1943) believed that the emotional impact of a reading disorder was as problematic as the disorder itself. Imagine a bright, verbal child who seems to have typical-to-advanced development prior to entering school. Then, when reading instruction begins, the child struggles for possibly the first time in his short life. A child may think, "I've always been able to understand things; why can't I get this? I thought I was smart, but maybe I'm not, maybe I'm dumb." And so it begins. Parents and teachers who view the child as bright make the assumption that the child is just not trying. The child fails to meet

≡ *Rapid Reference 12.3*

Examples of Accommodations and Modifications

Accommodations
 Books on CD or partner reading
 Use of a word processor
 Use of a scribe for recording answers
 Extended time
 Oral examinations

Modifications
 Shortened assignments
 Books selected for the instructional reading level
 Spelling words based on ability
 Alternate assignments (e.g., build a model, rather than write a report)
 Course substitutions (e.g., computer class to replace a foreign language class)

the expectations of these important adults leading to emotional pain and frustration. Further complicating things, the child will at times and on certain tasks, do well, exceeding expectations. This high performance co-existing with unexpected and unexplained low performance on reading and spelling tasks is puzzling and frustrating for the child as well as for the parents and teachers. An individual with dyslexia may experience anxiety, anger, depression, or suffer from lack of self-esteem. These emotional difficulties can also lead to peer-related problems, such as bullying and teasing, and may create problems in the home.

Children with dyslexia experience a wide range of responses at school including feelings of difference, inferiority, loneliness, and isolation (Morgan & Klein, 2000). As the individual with dyslexia continues through school, feelings of shame and embarrassment emerge over the difficulties with reading and spelling. The individual tries to hide the reading problem and may end up acting out or withdrawing. These serious short- and long-term effects of dyslexia are documented by a growing body of evidence (Rose, 2009). The following quotes from people with dyslexia provide insight into the emotional impact dyslexia has on a person's life.

"A teacher sent the following note home with a six-year-old boy: 'He is too stupid to learn.' That boy was Thomas A. Edison."

—Thomas Edison, inventor

"My childhood was extremely lonely. I was dyslexic and lots of kids made fun of me. That experience made me tough inside, because you learn to quietly accept ridicule."

—Tom Cruise, actor

"If I wasn't dyslexic, I probably wouldn't have won the Games. If I had been a better reader, then that would have come easily, sports would have come easily . . . and I never would have realized that the way you get ahead in life is hard work."

—Bruce Jenner, Olympic athlete

"I couldn't read. I just scraped by. My solution back then was to read classic comic books because I could figure them out from the context of the pictures. Now I listen to books on tape."

—Charles Schwab, entrepreneur

"When I had dyslexia, they didn't diagnose it as that. It was frustrating and embarrassing. I could tell you a lot of horror stories about what you feel like on the inside."

—Nolan Ryan, major league baseball pitcher

"Kids made fun of me because I was dark skinned, had a wide nose, and was dyslexic. Even as an actor, it took me a long time to realize why words and letters got jumbled in my mind and came out differently."

—Danny Glover, actor

"At the age of 12, I was considered uneducable mentally retarded. At the age of 38 I could score 169 on the IQ test but I couldn't read a menu in a restaurant. What the average person could read in 5 minutes would take me an hour."

—Ronald Davis, author

"I was in Special Ed classes from the time I flunked the second grade. It didn't help my self-esteem growing up with the stigma of being 'Learning Handicapped.' Even though deep inside I knew I was smart, I just couldn't prove it through the 'normal' channels of testing the way other kids could."

—Stacey Poulos, author

"When I was in the fourth grade, my self-esteem was down around my ankles. And I couldn't read. It's still difficult for me to spell, to do math, so I always thought it was important to help young people understand that they were great just the way they were. Self-esteem is the beginning and the end of living."

—Henry Winkler, actor

Early identification of dyslexia is critical so that the individual not only learns to read, but also understands why reading is hard so that these social and emotional difficulties can be mitigated. If the student understands what dyslexia is and how it affects reading and spelling development, she can learn to be a self-advocate. Parental support is another key factor that helps children develop a healthy perspective of self; parents or guardians can advocate for their children in school and provide emotional support (Wiener, 2003).

> **DON'T FORGET**
> ....
> Dyslexia can lead to serious short- and long-term social and emotional problems.

THE IMPORTANCE OF TEACHER TRAINING

Most people have heard the saying, "If you can read this, thank a teacher." Unfortunately, the truth is that most teachers are not adequately prepared to teach reading. Not only are teacher preparation courses lacking, but so are professional growth opportunities available to teachers once they graduate and are employed in the schools. Consider the following quotation from Governor James B. Hunt, Jr., of North Carolina: "Professional learning in its current state is poorly conceived and deeply flawed. Teachers lack time and opportunities to view each other's classrooms, learn from mentors, and work collaboratively. The support and training they receive is episodic, myopic, and often meaningless" (Darling-Hammond, Wei, Andree, Richardson, & Orphanos, 2009, p. 2). Rapid Reference 12.4 lists several key findings from *Professional Learning in the Learning Profession: A Status Report on Teacher Development in the United States and Abroad* published by the National Staff Development Council and the School Redesign Network at Stanford University (Darling-Hammond et al., 2009). The complete report may be viewed online (www.nsdc.org/news/NSDCstudy2009.pdf).

For children with dyslexia, Moats (1999) observed: "Teaching reading IS rocket science." Reading is not a natural act like speaking. Over 160 years ago, Carlyle said that it was the business of schools to teach children to read (Stanger &

≡ *Rapid Reference 12.4*

Select Key Findings About Professional Development for Teachers
- While teachers typically need substantial professional development in a given area (close to 50 hours) to improve their skills and their students' learning, most professional development opportunities in the United States are much shorter.
- American teachers say that much of the professional development available to them is not useful.
- U.S. teachers, unlike many of their colleagues around the world, bear much of the cost of their professional development.
- Sustained and intensive professional development for teachers is related to student achievement gains.

Donahue, 1937), and our teachers must be reading experts to accomplish this daunting task. Unfortunately, even today, many teachers lack the necessary knowledge of language structure and the components of effective reading instruction, and they do not know how to analyze the meaning of errors in student work samples (e.g., Moats, 1994, 2009; Spencer, Schuele, Guillot, & Lee, 2008). In a recent study, elementary school teachers displayed implicit skills related to certain basic language concepts (i.e., syllable counting), but failed to demonstrate explicit knowledge of others (i.e., phonics principles). In addition, teachers did not understand that poor phonological awareness was a major contributing factor to dyslexia (Washburn, Joshi, & Bins-Cantrell, 2011).

Teachers need specific knowledge of the science of reading as well as language structure including phonology, orthography, and morphology in order to teach reading effectively. Fortunately, teachers may enroll in specific training, such as provided by Wilson Language Training, or they can take specific online courses on language structure from organizations like the Neuhaus Education Center (www.neuhaus.org).

To address the inadequacy of teacher preparation in reading, the International Dyslexia Association (IDA) has developed *Knowledge and Practice Standards for Teachers of Reading* (IDA, 2010). Rapid Reference 12.5 provides a summary of these recommended standards. The complete document is available online (www.interdys.org/standards.htm).

Children with dyslexia require intensive, systematic instruction by highly qualified teachers to make progress in learning to read (Budin, Mather, &

≡ *Rapid Reference 12.5*

Summary of Knowledge and Practice Standards for Teachers of Reading (IDA, 2010)

Content Knowledge
- Understand and explain foundation concepts about oral and written language learning, including:
  - Language processing requirements of reading and writing: phonological, orthographic, semantic, syntactic, discourse
  - Other aspects of cognition and behavior that affect reading and writing: attention, executive function, memory, processing speed, graphomotor
  - Environmental, cultural, social factors that contribute to literacy
  - Typical developmental progression of oral language, phonological skill, printed word recognition, spelling, reading fluency, reading comprehension, written expression
  - Causal relationships among relevant factors
  - How relationships change among major components of literacy development with reading development
  - Reasonable goals and expectations for learners at various stages of reading and writing development
- Knowledge of the Structure of Language
  - Phonology, orthography, morphology, semantics, syntax, discourse
- Knowledge of Dyslexia and Other Learning Disorders
  - Intrinsic differences between good and poor readers
  - Recognize tenets of definition of dyslexia (NICHD/IDA)
  - Recognize that dyslexia and other reading difficulties exist on a continuum of severity
  - Identify and distinguish characteristics of dyslexia
  - Identify how symptoms of dyslexia may change across time
  - Understand state and federal laws that pertain to learning disabilities, including dyslexia
- Interpretation and Administration of Assessments for Planning Instruction
  - Different types of assessment: screening, diagnostic, outcome, and progress-monitoring
  - Principles of test construction: reliability, validity, norm-referenced
  - Principles of progress-monitoring and use of graphs
  - Range of skills typically assessed by diagnostic surveys
  - Content and purpose of tests commonly used by psychologists and educational evaluators
  - Interpret measures of reading comprehension and written expression in relation to the individual's component profile

(continued)

- Structured Language Teaching:
  - Phonology
  - Phonics and Word Study
  - Fluent, Automatic Reading of Text
  - Vocabulary
  - Text Comprehension
  - Handwriting, Spelling, Written Expression
- Ethical Standards for the Profession

Guidelines Pertaining to Supervised Practice of Teachers of Students with Documented Reading Disabilities or Dyslexia Who Work in School, Clinical, or Private Practice Settings
- Level I expectations for teachers (practitioners with basic knowledge)
  - Demonstrate proficiency to instruct individuals identified with dyslexia or documented reading disabilities
  - Implement appropriate instructional program with fidelity
  - Formulate and implement an appropriate instructional lesson plan
- Level II expectations for specialists (practitioners with advanced knowledge)
  - May work in private practice, clinical settings, or schools
  - Demonstrate proficiency in assessment and instruction of individuals with dyslexia or documented reading disabilities
  - Implement and adapt research-based programs to meet the individual's needs

Cheesman, 2010; Moats, 1994, 2009). Rapid Reference 12.6, adapted from Uhry and Clark (2005), provides a reminder of the principles of effective instruction for students with dyslexia. Research has identified effective methods for teaching reading (see Chapters 7–9), and numerous effective commercial programs exist for teaching children with dyslexia how to read and spell (see the Appendix of this book). Much is known about reading and how to teach it effectively. The challenge for our educational systems is to ensure that teachers receive the necessary training and have the time to accomplish this critically important goal of teaching all children how to read.

CONCLUSION

Schools and teachers play an essential role in identifying children with reading difficulties, including dyslexia, and are responsible for teaching them to read. As noted by the National Assessment of Educational Progress (NAEP, 2009),

≡ *Rapid Reference 12.6*

Principles of Effective Instruction for Students with Dyslexia
Reading and spelling skills are taught directly.
Demonstration, guided practice, feedback, and independent practice are provided.
Instruction is sequential with careful planning and pacing.
Instruction is built around small steps that connect old learning to new learning.
Systematic review is provided to ensure mastery of previously learned material.
Multisensory instruction is provided when needed.
Progress is monitored and evaluated frequently.

success with this important goal has been limited. As one example, NAEP has consistently found that approximately 36% of all fourth graders read at a "below basic" level. Many students struggle with reading, and these struggles impact all academic areas. In addition, many short- and long-term emotional and social issues arise when students struggle with reading, especially when they lack a clear understanding of *why* reading is so difficult.

While federal and state laws mandate certain rights and protections for individuals with disabilities, including dyslexia, schools have focused more on eligibility determination than on diagnosis and treatment. Times are beginning to change. Research is informing instruction. Educators are implementing effective methods and programs. High quality instruction can prevent some reading problems and reduce the impact of more severe reading difficulties. The challenge is to ensure that teachers really know the science of reading and the elements of effective instruction so that they can teach children with dyslexia how to read.

To meet the needs of students with dyslexia, it is necessary to (a) identify their difficulties at a young age; (b) implement targeted intensive, systematic instruction that represents evidence-based best practices; (c) monitor progress frequently and adjust instruction as needed; (d) ensure that teachers have the requisite skills and knowledge to deliver high quality instruction; and (e) provide a language-rich, safe, motivating environment for learning to read (Mather & Urso, 2008). Children who are behind in reading contend daily with the tyranny of time as the pedagogical clock continues to tick mercilessly (Kame'enui, 1993). These children require reading instruction that is more explicit, more comprehensive, and more intensive and delivered by trained teachers (Foorman & Torgesen, 2001).

With the proper help, many individuals with dyslexia have successful careers. Hallowell (2003), a well-known psychiatrist, recalled how he struggled to learn to read in first grade. As he tried to pronounce the words, his teacher, Mrs. Eldredge, put her arm around him protectively and took away his fear of learning to read. He still recalls the power of her arm and the effect it had on his development: "None of this would have happened had it not been for Mrs. Eldredge's arm. That arm has stayed around me ever since first grade. Even though Mrs. Eldredge resides now in heaven, perhaps reclining on an actual cloud as I write these words, she continues to help me, her arm to protect me, and I continue to thank her for it, almost every day" (p. 7).

🖎 TEST YOURSELF 🖎

1. Dyslexia is often first noticed after a child enters school. True or False?

2. Regardless of intelligence, a child who hasn't developed proficiency as a reader by the end of third grade will fall behind in all academic areas because

    a. children have difficulty learning to read after they reach the third grade.

    b. reading weaknesses may not be evident after third grade.

    c. the ability to read is fundamental to and facilitates all academic learning.

    d. reading is not explicitly taught after third grade.

3. Public schools do not have a legal obligation to identify and serve children with learning disabilities such as dyslexia. True or False?

4. Which is not a method being used to determine eligibility for services under the learning disabilities category in schools?

    a. A discrepancy between ability (IQ) and achievement

    b. A pattern of strengths and weaknesses among cognitive or achievement scores

    c. Informal measures of phonemic awareness, basic reading skills, and spelling

    d. Evidence of failure to respond to a targeted intervention (under RTI models)

5. **Which of the following statements about Response-to-Intervention (RTI) is not accurate?**
   a. RTI is an instructional model that helps prevent learning failures.
   b. RTI provides high-quality instruction to all students.
   c. RTI usually consists of several tiers of intervention.
   d. An RTI process can accurately diagnose dyslexia.

6. **The term dyslexia is not widely used in public schools. True or False?**

7. **A student's reading development can be affected by**
   a. an inadequate language base.
   b. the lack of appropriate instruction.
   c. low overall cognitive skills that affect all academic areas.
   d. all of the above.

8. **An Individualized Education Program (IEP) is required for students**
   a. identified as having a disability under Section 504.
   b. failing to respond to instruction in districts implementing RTI.
   c. found eligible for special education services under IDEA 2004.
   d. who have dyslexia but are not eligible for special education.

9. **A student who has dyslexia and is gifted**
   a. may be eligible for special education services.
   b. may only be perceived as having dyslexia, with her giftedness being overlooked.
   c. may only be perceived as gifted, with his or her dyslexia being overlooked.
   d. all of the above.

10. **As a result of having dyslexia, an individual may experience short- and long-term social and emotional difficulties. True or False?**

11. **The earliest warning signs of dyslexia may be noticed in the child's**
    a. low motivation.
    b. oral language performance, such as difficulty with speech or trouble learning to rhyme.
    c. refusal to complete academic work related to reading and writing.
    d. inability to write in full sentences.

12. **Students who are suspected of having dyslexia should demonstrate areas of strength, such as a relative strength in general intelligence, oral language, reasoning, and/or mathematics. True or False?**

13. Which of the following is true about teaching reading?

    a. Most teachers are not trained to teach reading to children with dyslexia.

    b. It is important to understand the science of reading in order to teach it.

    c. Knowledge of language structure is important for teaching children with dyslexia.

    d. All of the above.

    e. Both b and c.

14. A teacher expert in teaching reading has knowledge and understanding of

    a. phonology.

    b. orthography.

    c. semantics.

    d. syntax.

    e. all of the above.

    f. only a and b.

15. Children with dyslexia require intensive instruction from highly qualified teachers. True or False?

Answers: 1. True; 2. c; 3. False; 4. c; 5. d; 6. True; 7. d; 8. c; 9. d; 10. True; 11. b; 12. True; 13, d; 14. e; 15. True

Appendix

DESCRIPTIONS OF EVIDENCE-BASED PROGRAMS

This Appendix provides examples of several systematic programs for phonics, structural analysis, fluency, and spelling instruction. This list is not intended to be exhaustive but only to provide descriptions of programs that have helped students with dyslexia improve their reading and spelling skills. In most cases, the information presented here was provided by one of the authors of the program. Some of these programs require extensive, supervised teacher training (e.g., Wilson Reading System), whereas others do not (e.g., Phonic Reading Lessons). Some are targeted to parents and paraprofessionals (e.g., Barton System, Reading Reflex). Some are designed for beginning readers (e.g., Fundations, Road to the Code, Road to Reading), whereas others focus on word parts and structural analysis (e.g., REWARDS, WORDS) or increasing reading fluency (e.g., Great Leaps, Read Naturally). Some involve instruction in word reading, as well as vocabulary (e.g., RAVE-O). All of these programs follow a systematic sequence of instruction with built-in practice and review that is designed to be delivered individually or in small groups, the central characteristics of evidence-based instruction.

Product Title (listed in alphabetical order)	Age/Grade Range	Primary Instructional Area*	Description (Located on pages indicated below.)
Barton Reading & Spelling System	A: 5–adult	PA, P, F, V, C, S	263–264
Great Leaps Reading	A: 5–adult G: K–12	PA, P, F	264–266
Herman Method	G: 3–6	PA, P, F, V, C	266–268
Language!	G: 3–12	PA, P, F, V, C, W	269–271
Lindamood Phoneme Sequencing (LiPS) Program for Reading, Spelling, and Speech, 4th ed.	A: PreK–adult	PA, P, S, W	271–273

(continued)

Product Title (listed in alphabetical order)	Age/Grade Range	Primary Instructional Area*	Description (Located on pages indicated below.)
One Minute Reader	Reading at G: 1–5	F	273–275
PAL Reading & Writing Lessons	G: 1–6	P, F, C, HW, W	275–279
Patterns for Success in Reading and Spelling, 2nd Ed.	G: 1–12	P, V, S	279–280
Phonic Reading Lessons: Skills and Practice (PRL)	A: 5–adult	P	280–282
Phoneme-Grapheme Mapping	G: K–6	PA, P, S	282–285
Phono-Graphix	G: K–12	PA, P	285–287
RAVE-O	G: 2–4	PA, P, F, V, C	287–291
Read, Write, & Type!	A: 5–7	PA, P, S, W	291–293
REWARDS	G: 4–6	P, F, V, C	293–296
Road to the Code	G: K–1	PA, P	296–298
Road to Reading	G: 1–3	P, F, S	298–301
Sonday System	A: PreK–adult	PA, P, F, V, C, S	301–302
Spelling by Pattern	G: 1–3	PA, P	302–304
Spellography	G: 3–7	P, V, S	304–307
S.P.I.R.E.	G: PreK–8	PA, P, F, V, C, S, HW	307–309
Wilson Fluency/ Basic	G: 1–12	F	309–311
Wilson Fundations	G: K–3	PA, P, F, V, C, S, HW	311–314
Wilson Just Words	G: 4–12	P, S	314–315
Wilson Reading System	G: 2–12	PA, P, V, F, C	315–319
WORDS, 2nd Ed.	A: 10–15	P, S	319–320
Wordy Qwerty	A: 7–10	P, S	320–321

*Phonemic Awareness—PA, Phonics—P, Fluency—F, Vocabulary—V, Comprehension—C, Spelling—S, Handwriting—HW, Writing—W.

Program: Barton Reading & Spelling System
Author: Susan Barton
Information Provided By: Karen Austen, former Executive Director of the Dyslexia Project's Reading Solutions in Madison, OH, and Susan Barton
Appropriate for Ages/Grades: Ages 5–adult
Description: Created by Susan Barton, the *Barton System* is a one-to-one tutoring system designed to enable parents to teach their children with dyslexia how to read and spell. Also, the design of the program allows volunteer tutors with no teaching background to be effective tutors. Before ordering any materials, the potential tutor must take and pass a 5-minute phonemic awareness screening. In addition, before using the program with a student, the student must take and pass a 10-minute screening to determine if the student's auditory processing issues are too severe to benefit from this approach. This Orton-Gillingham-influenced system takes students to the mid-ninth grade level in reading and spelling. The system is divided into 10 levels. Tutors learn just one level at a time by watching their Tutor Training DVDs, and then immediately start using what they have learned. To teach the lessons, a tutor uses the detailed prepared lesson plans that contain a choice of full scripting or summary scripting. When the student nears the end of that level, the tutor or trainer orders the next level that contains two more DVDs that build on what the tutor already knows and prepares the tutor for the next set of lessons.

Each level in the *Barton Reading & Spelling System* contains two tutor-training DVDs (about 6 hours of training), a scripted lesson plan manual, color-coded letters tiles, and a packet of blackline masters of the pages the students use to write or read. There are no workbooks or consumables, and all student materials can be copied.

The 10 levels are taught in the following sequence:

Level 1: Phonemic Awareness
Level 2: Consonants, Short Vowels, & Digraphs
Level 3: Closed Syllables and Units
Level 4: Syllable Division and Vowel Teams
Level 5: Prefixes & Suffixes
Level 6: Six Reasons for Silent-E
Level 7: Vowel-R Syllables
Level 8: Advanced Vowel Teams
Level 9: Influence of Foreign Languages
Level 10: Latin Roots and Greek Words

Starting with Level 3, each level has from 10 to 14 lessons. If a student with moderate dyslexia is tutored twice a week for an hour per session, it would take about 3 years to complete all 10 levels.

Evidence of Effectiveness: Fourteen independent studies are posted on the *Barton Reading & Spelling System* website (www.BartonReading.com, click on Research, then click on Barton System) that provide evidence of the effectiveness of the program, along with an in-depth review by the Florida Center for Reading Research. The *Barton System* meets all of the requirements of No Child Left Behind, and the principles implemented are consistent with current findings on the characteristics of effective interventions. It has been approved by the California Department of Education, and is used as a Tier 3 intervention by many programs implementing a Response-to-Intervention model.

Teacher Training: Training is provided through a self-study approach using a series of DVDs. Free unlimited tutor support is available by phone, fax, e-mail, or on the tutor support website. For those who prefer to learn the *Barton System* in person, Susan Barton offers a week-long course once a year that is entitled *Tutoring People with Dyslexia.*

Contact and Ordering Information:
Barton Reading & Spelling System
2059 Camden Avenue, Suite 186
San Jose, CA 95124
Phone: 408-559-3652
Fax: 408-377-0503
e-mail: Info@BartonReading.com
Website: www.BartonReading.com

Program: Great Leaps Reading
Author: Kenneth U. Campbell
Information Provided By: Kenneth U. Campbell
Appropriate for Ages/Grades: Ages 5–adult; Grades K–12 and adult
Description: *Great Leaps Reading* is a one-on-one tutoring system designed to provide efficient and effective remediation for most children with significant reading problems. *Great Leaps* has been called the bridge from word reading to fluent reading. It has been designed so that communities can use the resources at their disposal to teach their children to read. A trained volunteer or parent can achieve virtually the same results with *Great Leaps* as professional staff.

Great Leaps uses basic phonics, high frequency word phrases, and one-minute story readings to achieve reading fluency gains as fast as present technology allows; the average across the country from two major studies is approximately two years reading growth for every year involved in the program. *Great Leaps* takes students to approximately the 4.5 grade reading level so that they can easily engage in independent reading. The level of the program that is selected is based on the age and social functioning of the student, not the reading level. Thus, a 12-year-old reading at first grade level would work out of the middle school book, not the K–2 book. The stories and interventions are developmentally appropriate and thus more reinforcing. The following levels of the program are available:

- Great Leaps K–2 (with Cecil D. Mercer)
- Great Leaps Grades 3–5
- Great Leaps Grades 6–8
- Great Leaps Grades 9–12
- Great Leaps Adult Reading

Great Leaps includes components related to comprehension and of even more importance for comprehension, expressive language. To ensure the program is used with fidelity, a fidelity checklist is available online at greatleaps.com. Students beginning the K–2 Program should be able to recognize the alphabet, have adequate sight for reading, and be able to focus for at least two minutes at a time. Students beginning the other *Great Leaps Reading Programs* should know their alphabet, most of their basic sounds in isolation, and have at least low average intelligence. For students with more severe intellectual impairments, professional expertise is needed to modify the program per the specific needs of the student.

The instructions within each teacher's edition provide enough direction for many to implement the program with fidelity. Instructors who implement the program with high fidelity generally achieve significantly higher results. *Great Leaps* should be used at least three times a week for significant results that generalize; thus, students should be scheduled at least three times a week to get one-to-one tutoring. Tutoring sessions usually last less than 10 minutes per student. The major teaching interventions of *Great Leaps* are immediate corrections during each 1-minute exercise and modeling at the end of each session. A minute or two for the expressive language activities are encouraged for students with language limitations.

A Spanish-language version of *Great Leaps* is available to meet the fluency needs of Spanish-speaking individuals. This program is not a simple translation of the English materials, but was developed specifically in Spanish for Spanish-speakers. *Great Leaps Spanish* is authored by Luz Font and Kenneth Campbell.

Evidence of Effectiveness: *Great Leaps* has been used in a large variety of settings successfully for over 15 years. A number of small studies support its efficacy as do two larger studies; one from North Florida (Mercer, Campbell, Miller, Mercer, & Lane, 2000) and another from Southern California (Spencer & Manis, 2010). The Florida Center for Reading Research approves *Great Leaps* as having appropriately researched materials. Throughout the country, *Great Leaps* has been approved by district after district as a Tier Two or Tier Three intervention for Response-to-Intervention models.

Teacher Training: Training is provided through the simplicity of the intervention program and the instructions that come with the program. Free telephone and e-mail support are available, and additional resources can be found (greatleaps.com). The author presents at many major conferences throughout the country and is willing to provide personal assistance to those who seek advice. For those who prefer in-depth training, a highly-qualified *Great Leaps* team offers inservice opportunities to school districts and groups. A train-the-trainer model is the preferred approach to training. Inservices to held during the fall or spring should be scheduled at least 9 months in advance.

Contact and Ordering Information:
Great Leaps (Diarmuid, Inc.)
P.O. Box 357580
Gainesville, FL 32635
Phone: 877-475-3277
Fax: 352-384-3883
e-mail: info@greatleaps.com
Website: www.greatleaps.com

REFERENCES

Mercer, C. D., Campbell, K. U., Miller, M. D., Mercer, K. D., & Lane, H. B. (2000). Effects of a reading fluency intervention for middle schoolers with specific learning disabilities. *Learning Disabilities Research & Practice, 15,* 179–189.

Spencer, S. A., & Manis, F. R. (2010). The effects of a reading fluency intervention program on the fluency and comprehension outcomes of middle-school students with severe reading deficits. *Learning Disabilities Research & Practice, 25,* 76–86.

Program: The New Herman Method (TNHM)
Author: Pat Sekel, Ph.D.
Information Provided By: Pat Sekel
Appropriate for Ages/Grades: Grades 3–6

Description: For more than 35 years, *The Herman Method* has been a successful small-group reading intervention. Newly revised, the program now incorporates the latest reading research into its Orton-Gillingham-based, multisensory approach to help students overcome difficulties associated with moderate-to-severe dyslexia. *The New Herman Method* (TNHM) has been streamlined and redesigned making it easier for teachers to use efficiently. It is intended for use with small groups of students (three to five) between third and sixth grades in need of remedial instruction (Tiers 2 and 3). New reading skills are introduced and reviewed with an auditory to visual discovery, chalkboard explanation, many different materials and techniques, and always reinforced through handwriting and spelling practice. Composition instruction is added at a later time in the curriculum. The sequence of instruction progresses from the most regularly used sounds, rules, and orthographic patterns of the English language to the least regularly used. *The Herman Method* sequentially and systemically teaches students reading, spelling, handwriting, and composition skills by incorporating visual, auditory, kinesthetic, and tactile modalities.

Students are grouped for instruction according to their reading abilities as indicated on the Assessment of Basic Phonetic Skills. Group size should not exceed five students. All students start remedial instruction with Level 1 of TNHM and move through the curriculum at an individualized pace as they demonstrate mastery of the sounds and letters in reading and spelling.

The instruction period is 50 minutes every school day: 25 minutes to teach Reading and Oral Spelling Skills and 25 minutes to teach the Handwriting and Written Spelling Skills. Instruction should be delivered by a teacher who has experience in working with students with dyslexia and is familiar with Orton-Gillingham teaching principles. During the teaching period, students are provided with a rapid rotation of activities that use at least two modalities (auditory, visual, kinesthetic, or tactile) simultaneously. Individual student success is designed for a minimum of 95% per lesson.

Materials: Two sets of materials are required for TNHM, Set A (Levels 1–10) and Set B (Levels 11–20). Each set contains materials for five students and takes approximately two to three semesters to complete. The *Teacher's Guide* is wire-bound and divided into two major sections: Reading Instruction, and Handwriting & Spelling Instruction. References, a glossary, suggested additional/optional materials, and activities are listed within the *Teacher's Guide.* Consumable Student Books are perforated so students can take the pages home after in-class instruction for additional practice and review. Other materials include Language Maker Book, Progress Charts Pack, Phonics Assessment

Pack, Blackline Masters, one set each of Sight Word Cards, Word Cards, Letter Cards, letter tiles for phonics and spelling, a class set of magnetic letter tiles, five small mirrors, and a metronome with battery.

Evidence of Effectiveness: *The New Herman Method* is scientifically rooted in best practices, while retaining features unique to the original *Herman Method*. TNHM incorporates the four-part processor model of reading (Seidenberg & McClelland, 1989) that makes reading possible: orthographic, phonological, meaning, and contextual. Components critical to reading instruction (National Reading Panel, 2000) are included as are elements considered essential in a multisensory structured language education (MSLE) curriculum: phonemic awareness, sound-symbol relationships, phonics, syllable types, structural analysis, spelling, fluency, vocabulary, comprehension, composition, and handwriting (Birsh, 2005 p. 196). Evidence-based research indicates that systematic phonics is effective in teaching older (Grades 2–6) lower-achieving, students with reading disabilities (McCardle, Chhabra, & Kapinus, 2008, pp. 110–111). Explicit, teacher-guided strategy instruction is a hallmark of TNHM (Mayer, 2004).

Teacher Training: Two-day training by a national trainer is available. Onsite follow-up provided as desired by district.

Contact and Ordering Information:

Sopris West
4093 Specialty Place
Longmont, CO 80504
Phone: 800-547-6747
Website: www.sopriswest.com

REFERENCES

Birsh, J. R. (Ed.). (2005). *Multisensory teaching of basic language skills* (2nd ed.). Baltimore, MD: Paul H. Brookes Publishing Company.

Mayer, R. (2004). Should there be a three-strike rule against pure discovery learning? *American Psychologist, 59,* 14–19.

McCardle, P., Chhabra, V., & Kapinus, B. (2008). *Reading research in action: A teacher's guide for student success.* Baltimore, MD: Paul H. Brookes Publishing Company.

National Institute of Child Health and Human Development. (2000). *Report of the National Reading Panel. Teaching children to read: An evidence-based assessment of the scientific research literature on reading and its implications for reading instruction* (NIH Publication No. 00-4769). Washington, DC: U.S. Government Printing Office.

Seidenberg, M. S., & McClelland, J. L. (1989). A distributed, developmental model of word recognition and naming. *Psychological Review, 96,* 523–568.

Program: LANGUAGE! The Comprehensive Literacy Curriculum (4th ed.), LANGUAGE! Focus on English Learning, LANGUAGE! 2nd Edition Clinical Version

Authors: Jane Fell Greene, Ed.D. (all); Jennifer Wells Greene, Ph.D. (coauthor of English Learning version)

Information Provided By: Jane Fell Greene

Appropriate for Ages/Grades: Grades 3–12

Description: Students who experience delays in reading invariably experience simultaneous delays in spelling, vocabulary, composition, and grammar. For many years, teachers tried to piece together a curriculum that filled all of these needs. These piecemeal programs were not, however, sequential; they were not systematic; they were not explicit; they were not integrated; they were neither linguistically sound nor educationally logical. *LANGUAGE!* is the result of 15 years of development and refinement. It provides 360 sequential, systematic, integrated lesson plans. Each lesson integrates six steps:

1. Phonemic Awareness and Phonics
2. Word Recognition and Spelling
3. Vocabulary and Morphology
4. Grammar and Usage
5. Reading and Listening Comprehension
6. Writing and Speaking

The fourth edition of *LANGUAGE!* is available in two different versions, one for native English speakers and one for English Language Learners. Each version is designed for use in grades 3–12. Materials include:

- Comprehensive Teacher Editions: TWO volumes each for books A, B, C, D, E, and F
- 360 complete lesson plans to support a detailed scope and sequence
- Descriptions of daily multisensory and interactive instructional activities
- Focus on academic language and content area reading, to support other classes
- Advanced, interactive technology tools and eReaders
- Performance monitoring, differentiation of instruction, and homework options
- Comprehensive assessment at each stage of a lesson, unit, and book
- Reading materials for independent, instructional, and challenge reading
- Explicit instruction in composition for various purposes

- All supplements needed to teach the curriculum
- Leveled reading materials whose readabilities range from grade 1 to grade 12

LANGUAGE! The Comprehensive Literacy Curriculum was created for native English speakers who are delayed in the acquisition of reading, writing, vocabulary, and spelling. While some of these students may be served in special education, the majority of them are placed in general education classes. Many may not meet criteria for special education, yet score below the 40th percentile in reading and have difficulty functioning at grade level.

The curriculum consists of six sequential and cumulative levels (A–F), each of which contains six units (1–36). All concepts are taught in dependent order, building on knowledge and skills that have been previously mastered. The curriculum's instructional methodology is multisensory. Rather than separate visual, auditory, tactile, and kinesthetic activities, this curriculum's instructional activities simultaneously employ sight, sound, touch, and movement. Accurate placement is essential; it is critical that students not be placed at levels beyond their own mastery levels. Comprehensive assessments provide mastery tests for each unit (1–36) and for each level (A–F).

LANGUAGE! Focus on English Learning was created for English learners. The Teachers' Editions for levels A, B, and C of this version contain lessons designed for English Learners. After completion of Level C, English Learners are placed with other students for the last three levels, D, E, and F, of the *Comprehensive Literacy Curriculum.* A prelude program, *LANGUAGE! Everyday English for Newcomers to English,* is available for students who are newly arrived or have had no previous exposure to English.

LANGUAGE! Second Edition Clinical Version is paced more slowly and is appropriate for use with students who exhibit significant language processing deficits.

Evidence of Effectiveness: *LANGUAGE!* has proven effective in hundreds of implementations—large and small, urban and rural school districts, as well as in special education and clinical settings. Generally, school districts conduct their own assessments, or use annual standardized tests as measures. A summary of the research base and effectiveness data is available from Cambium Learning Group (www.cambiumlearning.com).

Teacher Training: Teacher training is required. Most often, training is conducted in school districts; however, open trainings are also offered, and are generally sponsored by professional groups or by certified national *LANGUAGE!* trainers. For those interested in becoming a Trainer of Trainers (TOT), sessions are offered twice each year for individuals who can demonstrate (a) expertise in structured language, multisensory instruction; and (b) expertise in teaching adults.

Contact and Ordering Information:
Cambium Learning
17855 Dallas Parkway, Suite 400
Dallas, TX 75287
Phone: 888-399-1995
e-mail: requests@cambiumlearning.com
Website: www.cambiumlearning.com

Program: Lindamood Phoneme Sequencing (LiPS) Program for Reading, Spelling, and Speech, Fourth Edition
Authors: Patricia and Phyllis Lindamood
Information Provided By: Elizabeth Rowan and Katherine Synatschk
Appropriate for Ages/Grades: Ages preschool–adult
Description: *The Lindamood Phoneme Sequencing (LiPS) Program for Reading, Spelling, and Speech* is an intensive, multisensory program for students in pre-school through adulthood who need explicit, direct, and systematic instruction to develop phonological awareness abilities. The *LiPS program* steps are:

- Setting the Climate for Learning
- Identifying and Classifying Consonants
- Identifying and Classifying Vowels
- Tracking Simple Syllables and Words
- Basic Spelling and Reading
- Learning Sight Words and Expectancies
- Tracking Complex Syllables and Words, Multisyllabic Words
- Reading and Writing in Context

Using an oral-motor, visual and auditory feedback system, the LiPS Program develops the student's ability to distinguish phonemes (single speech sounds) in spoken patterns. In teaching sound-symbol associations, the *LiPS* tasks progress from articulatory movements to sounds to letters. Students explore the physical movements involved in producing sounds and learn to hear, see, and feel the physical characteristics of sounds and to notice the contrasts between them. *LiPS* builds on previous knowledge to introduce new skills and frequently spirals back to review until mastery. Teachers are guided in the manual to provide corrective feedback when an error is made using the Socratic method of questioning. Students learn to identify and verify sounds independently that they produce, hear, and eventually, read. The *LiPS* program is used successfully in clinical and classroom settings.

Materials and Content: The *LiPS* program provides materials for teachers, clinicians, and students. The materials include:

- An extensive and comprehensive manual with audio, video, and reproducible resources
- Magnetic manipulatives, which include:
  - Mouth pictures depicting each of the mouth movements associated with sounds
  - Large and small colored squares for tracking sounds and syllables
  - Letter tiles
  - Syllable tiles
  - Large tri-fold magnetic write-on, wipe-off board for student work space
- Small standing mirror
- Playing cards for demonstration and reinforcement of *LiPS* concepts
- *Phonological Awareness and Sequencing* (PAS) *Stories, Second Edition,* a series of eight story books aligned with the presentation sequence of skills, for engaging, decodable reading experiences. These stories help students apply independent reading skills.
- The LiPS Stick, a flash drive containing many digital resources, facilitates the use of *LiPS* materials on interactive white boards and provides reproducible versions of the resources.

Evidence of Effectiveness: An independent review of the *Lindamood Phoneme Sequencing (LiPS) Program for Reading, Spelling, and Speech,* by the Florida Center for Reading Research (www.fcrr.org) noted that the content and instructional design of the program are aligned with current reading research. In the National Reading Panel report, research studies incorporating the *LiPS* program were cited as well-designed, high quality research that highlighted the effectiveness of direct instruction in phonemic awareness and phonics (pp. 2–36, 2–127). In addition, a review of the research is included in the publication, *Phonological Processing, Reading, and the Lindamood Phoneme Sequencing Program* (2nd ed; Synatschk, 2011). The *LiPS* program has been used successfully for more than 40 years to address the phonological awareness deficits of a wide range of individuals with functional speech-language delay and second language learning to organic and traumatic neurophysiological factors, including dyslexia, cerebral palsy, hearing loss, autism, apraxia, pervasive developmental delay, closed-head trauma, and stroke.

Teacher Training: Lindamood-Bell Learning Processes offers three-day workshops on the implementation of *LiPS*. A listing of the dates and locations of these workshops can be found in their catalog or on their website (www .lindamoodbell.com/professionaldevelopment). The workshop is not a requirement for implementation of the program. The teacher's manual is written in clear and concise language to facilitate accurate implementation with sufficient content knowledge. Lindamood-Bell Learning Processes works collaboratively with schools, school districts, state departments of education, and other literacy groups to implement the *LiPS program* with students experiencing reading difficulties.

Contact and Ordering Information:
PRO-ED, Inc.
8700 Shoal Creek Blvd
Phone: 800-897-3202
Website: www.proedinc.com

REFERENCES

National Institute of Child Health and Human Development. (2000). *Report of the National Reading Panel. Teaching children to read: An evidence-based assessment of the scientific research literature on reading and its implications for reading instruction* (NIH Publication No. 00-4769). Washington, DC: U.S. Government Printing Office.

Synatschk, K. (2011). *Phonological processing, reading, and the Lindamood Phoneme Sequencing Program* (2nd ed.). Austin, TX: PRO-ED.

Program: One Minute Reader (OMR)

Author: Candyce Ihnot

Information Provided By: Brianna McGill, Sales & Marketing Associate and Karen Hunter, Director of Curriculum

Appropriate for Ages/Grades: Students whose reading level is Early 1st–Grade 5

Description: *One Minute Reader* includes key features of the classroom-based Read Naturally program in a format that can be used at home. Students who don't read well need more practice than they can get during the school day and they can't afford to stop reading when the school year ends. *One Minute Reader* offers a way for these students to keep working on their reading skills at home. *One Minute Reader* books apply the principles of modeling, repeated reading, and progress monitoring, which have been proven to be powerful strategies for helping kids become better readers.

One Minute Reader has six levels: E, 1, 2, 3, 4, and 5. Since levels are written at reading level, OMR is appropriate for students reading between an early first-grade reading level and a fifth-grade reading level. The available Placement Guide helps determine which level is right for a reader. It includes sample stories used to evaluate the reader plus complete instructions.

Each book includes five high-interest stories written at a length that encourages readers to practice without overwhelming them. The books also include extra features like graphs for charting student's progress, crossword puzzles, stickers, glossary terms, and fun facts. *One Minute Reader* books are written at different reading levels so readers can find the level that fits their ability. More than just a book of interesting stories, the *One Minute Reader* is a system for improving reading fluency, especially for people who struggle with reading.

The *One Minute Reader* steps are easy to follow, and many readers can work through the steps on their own. Parents and tutors can also help by going through stories with the reader or by listening after the reader has practiced a story and then discussing it. Parents' interest, praise, and support are important in building students' confidence.

For the best results, students should work with *One Minute Reader* three times a week, but five times a week is even better. It is usually more effective to work for a short time—maybe 15–30 minutes—several days a week rather than to work for just one long session. Each story takes about 30 minutes to complete but, because every reader is different, there is no need for concern if a student takes more or less time to finish the steps.

One Minute Reader also has a School-to-Home Program available. This program is designed so students can check out books and audio CDs from their school. Instead of writing in the books, students write on separate record sheets.

Evidence of Effectiveness: *One Minute Reader* includes key features of the classroom-based Read Naturally program. Read Naturally has conducted a number of studies that provide evidence of its effectiveness. Please refer to *Read Naturally's Rationale & Research* booklet for complete information on these studies (www.readnaturally.com/pdf/rationaleResearch.pdf).

Teacher Training: An Instructional DVD is available for an additional cost. This Instructional DVD includes a video showing the steps of the *One Minute Reader* system, as well as answers to common questions. A free, web-based presentation is also available. This webcast presentation demonstrates how the program works and how teachers and parents can use OMR to support the continued reading development of students.

Contact and Ordering Information:
Read Naturally, Inc.
2945 Lone Oak Drive, Suite 190
Saint Paul, MN 55122
Phone: 877-732-3376
Fax: 651-452-9204
e-mail: info@oneminutereader.com
Website: www.oneminutereader.com

Program: PAL Research-Based Reading and Writing Lessons, PAL Talking Letters, PAL Handwriting Lessons, and PAL Guides for Intervention
Authors: Virginia W. Berninger, Ph.D. (all); Sylvia Abbott (co-author of *PAL Reading & Writing Lessons*)
Information Provided By: Virginia W. Berninger
Appropriate for Ages/Grades: Grades 1–6 or older students reading or writing at these levels
Description: *PAL Research-Based Reading and Writing Lessons* (Berninger & Abbott) provide instruction in writing, phonics, reading fluency, reading comprehension, and help with progress-monitoring. The program has 15 lesson sets with reproducible materials to support each lesson. All lessons teach to all levels of language (subword, word, and text) to help students overcome verbal working memory problems, which many students with dyslexia experience, in learning to read and write. Each lesson set teaches words designed to help the student transfer spelling-sound and morphological relationships to word decoding and then provides practice in applying this knowledge across contexts. In addition, students keep copies of graphic displays of self-regulated strategies designed to aid independent reading and writing. Growth graphs are used to assess response to instruction on the target skills. For students who do not respond adequately, additional instructional recommendations are available.

- Lesson Set 1 Reading (grade 1 or reading at grade 1 level)
  - Teaches explicit strategies for creating automatic associations between 1- or 2-letters and the corresponding sound, transfer to self-regulated decoding of monosyllabic words, and transfer to self-regulated oral reading and rereading and text comprehension.
- Lesson Set 2 Reading (grade 2 or reading at grade 2 level or has completed Set 1)
  - Focuses on developing automatic associations between 1- or 2-letters and corresponding sounds, phonological (syllables and phonemes) and

orthographic awareness, transfer to self-regulated decoding of polysyllabic words, and transfer to self-regulated oral reading and re-reading and text comprehension.

- Lesson Set 3 Writing (grade 1 or older students with handwriting problems)
  - Teaches explicit strategies for automatic legible letter writing, for transfer to self-regulated word copying, and for transfer to self-regulated text composing on a provided topic, which is shared with peers through oral reading by author.
- Lesson Set 4 Writing (grade 2 or students spelling at grade 2 level)
  - Teaches explicit strategies for automatic correspondences between sounds and 1- or 2-letters, for transfer to self-regulated spelling of monosyllabic words, and for transfer to self-regulated composing at the text- and word-levels.
- Lesson Set 5 Writing (grade 3 or spelling at grade 3 level or has completed Set 4)
  - Focuses on teaching explicit strategies for automatic correspondences between sounds and 1- or 2-letters, for transfer to self-regulated spelling of polysyllabic words, and for transfer to self-regulated composing at the text- and word-levels.
- Lesson Set 6 Reading (grade 2 or reading at grade 2 level or has completed Sets 1 and 2)
  - Teaches grouping alternative sounds for the same spelling; explicit strategies for transferring spelling-sound correspondences to reading content and function words; and explicit strategies for comprehension at different levels of language (word, sentence, text).
- Lesson Set 7 Writing (grade 3 or writing at grade 3 level or has completed Sets 4 & 5)
  - Focuses on automatic alphabetic principle in spelling direction; word sorts for grouping alternative spellings for the same sound; explicit strategies for transferring sound-spelling correspondences to spelling content and function words; and explicit strategies for planning, text generating, and reviewing/revising on eight topics.
- Lesson Set 8 Writing (grade 4 or writing at grade 4 level or has completed Sets 4, 5, and 7)
  - Covers automatic handwriting; orthographic spelling strategy for mind's eye, phonological spelling strategy for mind's ear, and strategy for teaching the mind's eye and mind's ear to talk to each other in learning to spell; and explicit self-regulated strategy instruction—Plan (Argument

and List graphic organizer), Write, Read/Review, and Revise in same session for a provided writing topic.

- Lesson Set 9 Reading (grade 2 or reading at grade 2 level or has completed Sets 1 and 2)
  - Organized as a club, readers' warm up—automatic alphabetic principle, readers' work—finger-pointing reading, choral reading, buddy reading with classmate, reading with parents, and reading with teacher (running records) for reading fluency, and readers' play—structure word bingo and Mommylongwords contest (to develop morphological awareness in English morphophonemic orthography).
- Lesson Set 10 Writing (grade 4 or writing at grade 4 level or has completed Sets 4, 5, 7, and 8)
  - Organized as a club, writers' warm-up—automatic alphabetic principle in the spelling direction; writers' work—composing in different genre and publishing school newspaper (*Kids Writing for Kids*); writers' play—structure word bingo and Mommylongwords contest (to develop morphological awareness in English morphophonemic orthography).
- Lesson Set 11 Reading (grade 1 or reading at grade 1 level or has completed Sets 1 and 2 or 6 and 9)
  - Focuses on phonological, orthographic, and morphological awareness games, automatic alphabetic principle, word families, and automatic word-specific learning, and explicit strategies for transferring these skills to decoding Jabberwocky words, oral reading, and rereading for fluency.
- Lesson Set 12 Reading (grade 2 and above who have completed Set 11)
  - Includes sound games and looking games, structural analysis (syllables and morphemes), automatic alphabetic principle, explicit strategies for transfer of the resulting phonological, orthographic, and morphological awareness to words of different word origins (e.g., Anglo-Saxon, Romance—French and Latin), oral reading and rereading for fluency, and reading comprehension activities (summarization and reflective discussions).
- Lesson Set 13 Writing and Reading (grade 3 and above who have completed Sets 11 and 12)
  - Focuses on automatic alphabetic principle, puns in riddles and jokes, oral reading fluency, and reading comprehension in varied subject matter (content areas of the curriculum), and reading for pleasure.
- Lesson Set 14 Writing and Reading (grade 4 and above who have completed Sets 11–13)

- Focuses on handwriting automaticity, automatic alphabetic principle in the spelling direction, spelling strategies for specific words, spelling dictation (same taught words in sentence context providing repeated practice in context), reading source material in varied content areas, planning a written report, composing the written report, and reviewing and revising the report.
- Lesson Set 15 Reading and Writing (grade 4 and above who have completed Sets 11–12)
  - Covers automatic alphabetic principle, phonological, orthographic, and morphological awareness for words of different word origin, word games for practice of taught skills, reading science content paperbacks, and conducting science experiments for high intellectual engagement in reading in a content area.

PAL Talking Letters systematically teaches the connections between spelling and sound and includes a picture-sound dictionary and step-by-step directions for instruction. The alphabetic principle for high frequency spelling-sound correspondences in high frequency words is taught as procedural knowledge. Use of an explicit teaching strategy focuses attention through pointing, looking, and naming; teaches self-regulation of switching attention by frequent, rapid switches in turn-taking; and forms automatic correspondences from paired associations close in time.

- Teaches alphabetic principle for words of Anglo-Saxon origin (high frequency in primary grade reading material) and for words of Romance and Greek origin (high frequency in fourth grade and above).
- Teaches word families that have multiletter units that are larger than the spelling unit in alphabetic principle but pronunciation of that multiletter unit is predictable.

PAL Handwriting Lessons are designed to develop handwriting automaticity. Reproducible pages include two sets of 24 lessons, each presenting all 26 letters of the alphabet. Students study numbered arrow cues in a model letter in order to formulate a letter writing plan. Then the students close their eyes and picture the letter in their mind's eye. Next, they write the letter from memory, and then self-check by comparing the letter they produced with the model letter. If they do not match, the student makes revisions. After each letter has been studied, stored in, and retrieved from memory, and revised if necessary, the strategy "What I Think I Can Say, What I Can Say, I Can Write" is used to write about a topic for 5 minutes. This process helps transfer letter writing to text generating (composing written language to express ideas). Finally, students share their written text with peers by reading it orally.

PAL Guides for Intervention: Reading and Writing includes proven strategies to help students with reading and writing difficulties. Examples of content include: Sound Games, Looking Games, Before and After Writing Games, Directed Reading and Writing Activities for Creating Functional Reading and Writing Systems, Designing Individual Educational Plans (IEPs), Instructional Resources organized by component processes of functional reading and writing systems, Handouts for Parents and Teachers Explaining Reading Disabilities and Writing Disabilities.

Evidence of Effectiveness: A number of studies have been conducted to evaluate the effectiveness of the materials in improving performance of students with dyslexia on state high stakes tests in reading and writing. See the studies in the manuals of the published materials. (See also References.)

Teacher Training: The instructional materials contain sufficient information for teachers to use them. However, for educational professionals who desire more information about the interdisciplinary research on dyslexia and assessment-intervention relationships for diagnosis, instruction, and response to instruction (RTI), information about annual schedule of available workshops is available from Dr. Kunselman of the University of Washington Educational Outreach program at mkunselman@EXTN.washington.edu.

Contact and Ordering Information:

Pearson

19500 Bulverde Rd.

San Antonio, Texas 78259

Phone: 800-627-7271

e-mail: ClinicalCustomerSupport@Pearson.com

Website: www.pearsonassessments.com

REFERENCES

Berninger, V. (2009). Highlights of programmatic, interdisciplinary research on writing. *Learning Disabilities Research & Practice, 24,* 68–79.

Berninger, V., & Richards, T. (2010). Inter-relationships among behavioral markers, genes, brain, and treatment in dyslexia and dysgraphia. *Future Neurology, 5,* 597–617.

Program: Patterns for Success in Reading and Spelling, 2nd Ed.

Authors: Marcia K. Henry, Ph.D. and Nancy C. Redding

Information Provided By: Marcia K. Henry

Appropriate for Ages/Grades: Grades 1–12, Special Education

Description: The lessons in *Patterns for Success in Reading and Spelling* range from beginning phonics to advanced vocabulary. The kit includes a Teacher Manual with approximately 150 lessons in the following three parts: Letter-Sound Correspondences; Syllable Patterns, Affixes, and Additional Phonics; and Morpheme Patterns. In addition, the kits provide six card packs (irregular sight words, basic letter-sound correspondences, prefixes, suffixes, common Latin roots, and Greek combining forms) in different colors; Student Word Lists; and Student Activities for reinforcement (four activities for each lesson).

Evidence of Effectiveness: The program was used in the Northwoods Literacy Task Force teacher training programs, several Masonic Children's Learning Center training programs, and formerly used in Albuquerque Public School training for five years. (See also References.)

Teacher Training: All necessary training is provided in the Teacher Manual.

Contact and Ordering Information:

PRO-ED, Inc.

8700 Shoal Creek Blvd.

Austin, TX 78757-6897

Phone: 800-897-3202

Website: www.proedinc.com

REFERENCES

Henry, M. K. (1988). Beyond phonics: Integrated decoding and spelling instruction based on word origin and structure. *Annals of Dyslexia, 38*, 259–275.

Henry, M. K. (1989). Children's word structure knowledge: Implications for decoding and spelling instruction. *Reading and Writing, 2*, 135–152.

Program: Phonic Reading Lessons: Skills and Practice (PRL)

Authors: Skills: Samuel A. Kirk, Winifred D. Kirk, Esther H. Minskoff, Nancy Mather, and Rhia Roberts; Practice: Rhia Roberts, Ph.D. and Nancy Mather, Ph.D.

Information Provided By: Rhia Roberts

Appropriate for Ages/Grades: Ages 5–adult; for students who have adequate verbal ability and visual acuity to learn to read but who continue to struggle despite appropriate instruction.

Description: When the original version of *Phonic Reading Lessons* was published in 1936 by education pioneers Thorlief G. Hegge, Samuel A. Kirk, and

Winifred D. Kirk, the program was groundbreaking. After direct, explicit phonics instruction using multisensory methods withstood the test of time, the work was revised in 1985 (S. A. Kirk, Kirk, & Minskoff). The program was again revised extensively in 2006 by Mather and Roberts to reflect current research in phonics instruction and to update and expand the scope and sequence.

Phonic Reading Lessons is a two-volume program with an easy-to-use, systematic method of teaching reading. One volume focuses on skills and the other volume focuses on practice. Each 10- to 15-minute lesson involves modeling, instruction, practice, and assessment: approaches endorsed by recent educational research such as the National Reading Panel (2000), and legislation such as No Child Left Behind (NCLB, 2002). The lesson begins with the teaching of skills and sight words followed by decoding practice, review, and assessment of those skills. The lessons are carefully planned to include only skills that have been introduced previously. All of the lessons are reproducible so that the program can be used in small group instruction. The scope and sequence includes the following 10 units:

1. One Letter, One Sound
2. Final -e and Consonant Digraphs (two letters, one sound)
3. Consonant Blends and More Digraphs
4. R-Controlled Vowels, Vowel Digraphs (two vowels, one sound) and Diphthongs (two vowels, two sounds)
5. Common Word Endings and Spelling Rules
6. Alternative Pronunciations and Spellings
7. Prefixes
8. Suffixes
9. Latin Roots
10. Greek Roots

Stories are presented from the first lesson and increase in complexity and interest as the lessons progress. The program has eight features that are designed to support and help struggling students:

1. One response to one symbol; students practice one phoneme (sound) per grapheme (symbol) at a time to avoid confusion. Variations are added later as skill develops.
2. Minimal change; sound-symbol associations are supported early in the program by the clustering of words into onsets and rimes.
3. Progression from easy to more challenging; careful attention has been paid to the setting up of students for success.

4. Frequent repetitions; opportunities to practice are built into each lesson and are included in the *Practice* volume and in subsequent lessons.
5. Review; students practice what they have learned.
6. Verbal responses; verbal expression promotes learning and retention.
7. Multisensory learning; the program combines reading, saying, hearing, and writing each sound and word, to help with memory.
8. Selective attention; the spacing between letters (or groups of letters) shows students the graphemes that make up the words they are learning.

Evidence of Effectiveness: *Phonic Reading Lessons* meets the requirements of NCLB (2002), as well as the recommendations of the National Reading Panel (2000) for evidence-based instruction: individualized or small group instruction, systematic sequence of phonic skills, built-in practice and review, and practice reading decodable text.

Teacher Training: One of the strengths of this program is that little training is required other than the self-study training that is provided in the Introduction; parents, support staff, and teachers can easily and effectively use the lessons.

Contact and Ordering Information:
Academic Therapy Publications
20 Commercial Boulevard
Novato, CA 94949-6191
Phone: 800-422-7249
FAX: 888-287-9975
e-mail: sales@academictherapy.com
Website: www.AcademicTherapy.com

Program: Phonics and Spelling Through Phoneme-Grapheme Mapping
Author: Kathryn E. S. Grace, Med, CAGS Language & Learning Disabilities
Information Provided By: Kathryn E. S. Grace
Appropriate for Ages/Grades: Grades K–6, special education, adult literacy
Description: *Phoneme-Grapheme Mapping* was created to help students understand that the number of sounds (phonemes) they hear in a word may differ from the number of letters used to represent those sounds. This procedure employs a variety of mapping methods to illustrate the complex, yet predictable, phoneme/grapheme relationships in our written language. Graphemes are letters and letter combinations that correspond to individual speech sounds and are used in highly predictable patterns and sequences.

Phoneme-grapheme mapping highlights the phoneme-grapheme relationships thereby helping students understand the internal details of both spoken and written words and the patterns that represent them in print. Mapping also helps them to understand the alphabetic principle in an engaging, logical, organized fashion. By **mapping sounds to print**, students acquire a metacognitive approach to both decoding and spelling.

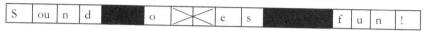

The sequential, systematic, and explicit lessons in the text *Phonics and Spelling Through Phoneme-Grapheme Mapping* are a direct outcome of the author's experience teaching young children. The program also incorporates the following best-practice principles based on empirical research:

- Knowledge of English orthography is acquired in a continuous progression.
- Awareness of phoneme-grapheme correspondences, regular and irregular, is how students hold words in memory.
- Reading and spelling development are mediated by phonological awareness. Phoneme-grapheme mapping builds a bridge between phonological awareness and phonics. It continues to strengthen phonemic awareness while simultaneously building an association of sounds to the spellings of words.
- Spelling is linked to word reading.
- Spelling is not "auditory" or "visual" but phonological, orthographic, and sensory-motor. The multisensory elements of *Phonics and Spelling Through Phoneme-Grapheme Mapping* help to bridge the brain's phonological and orthographic processors to strengthen learning and recall.
- The program supports the development of automaticity and fluency with reading and spelling for all ages in one-on-one tutoring, in small groups, and whole-group settings.
- *Phonics and Spelling Through Phoneme-Grapheme Mapping* provides the one-to-one correspondence easily grasped and familiar to young students as a math concept but not with sound to spelling relationships because of the multiple letter graphemes used to represent a single sound (e.g., "ph" or "gh" for /f/).

Phonics and Spelling Through Phoneme-Grapheme Mapping provides lessons for a wide range of reading and spelling skill levels. It is organized by syllable type, and most lessons begin with a teacher tutorial that explains the sound/symbol concept and its unique mapping procedure. Many lessons include a TEACH box that provides a student-friendly script and guidelines for teaching students the target concept. Each lesson also illustrates the phoneme-grapheme mapping of the target concept and provides comprehensive word lists that give teachers many word options for creating either single or multisyllable word lists for their students. Any lesson can be adapted for children from a very young age to adults since the words range from simple to complex within each pattern of study. The program can be used by general or special educators, paraprofessionals, remedial teachers, or parents.

Materials:
- Text: The lessons in this book are organized by phoneme-grapheme concept. The teacher tutorials (TEACH) sections offer teaching tips and lists of concept words that accompany the lessons. Explicit mapping procedures are provided for each newly introduced phoneme-grapheme pair.
- Six to 10 square tiles in two colors are included for each student to manipulate. One color represents the vowel sound, whereas the other color represents the consonant sounds. The number of tiles needed for each lesson depends on the number of phonemes in the concept words because each tile stands for just one sound. Using two colors helps children see where the vowel sound occurs in each word, which is especially important in differentiating between open and closed syllables as well as depicting where you hear a long vowel sound in a word since that offers a clue to its spelling.
- Phoneme-grapheme mapping paper.
- Plain and colored pencils.
- Colored tiles for use with an overhead projector or Smart Board.
- Several auxiliary products for white boards and the Smart Board are currently under development. For more information, please contact the author.

Evidence of Effectiveness: Classroom tested. Growth shown in both decoding and spelling when used weekly to introduce new concepts.

Teacher Training: Professional Development is available directly from the author.

Phonics and Spelling Through Phoneme-Grapheme Mapping has also been added to several LETRS modules published by Sopris West and is demonstrated in *Mapping the Alphabetic Principle (MAP)* published by Brookes Publishing.

Contact and Ordering Information:
Sopris (a division of Cambium Learning)
4185 Salazar Way

Frederick, CO 80504
Phone: 800-547-6747
Fax: 888-819-7767
e-mail: customerservice@cambiumlearning.com
Website: www.soprislearning.com
Author Contact Information:
144 South Main St.
Waterbury, VT 05676
Phone: 802-244-6419
e-mail: kgrace@etsd.org

Program: Phono-Graphix, Reading Reflex

Authors: Carmen McGuinness, B.A. and Geoffrey McGuinness, B.A.

Information Provided By: Carmen McGuinness

Appropriate for Ages/Grades: K–12 (remedial) Phono-Graphix; K–6 (home use) Reading Reflex

Description: *Phono-Graphix* is a structured, systematic, multisensory reading and spelling program. *Reading Reflex: The Foolproof Phono-Graphix Method* is a parent book containing thorough instructions and materials for teaching kindergarteners and elementary students at home. The theoretical underpinnings of *Phono-Graphix* are remarkably straightforward and sensible. It is based simply on the nature of the English code, the three skills needed to access that code, and teaching these in keeping with the way children learn. The following describes this in greater detail.

THE NATURE OF THE ENGLISH CODE

Letters are pictures of sounds.
- So these are pictures of sounds "b oa t"
- Can children understand this? Children can understand this perfectly well. Children have a remarkable ability to assess visual figures.

Sound pictures can be one or more letters.
- In "boat" the pictures can be made of one letter (b or t) or more letters (oa). So boat has three sounds /b/-/ō/-/t/, and three sound pictures b—oa—t
- Children can manage this because they reuse figures in the world around them every day.

There is variation in the code; most of the sounds can be shown with more than one picture. Variation refers to the fact that some sound pictures can represent more than one sound. For example, the sound o can be represented as oa in boat, ow in slow, o in most, oe in toe, o-e in note, and ough in though.

There is overlap in the code; some of the pictures are used for more than one sound. Overlap refers to the fact that some sound pictures can represent more than one sound. For example, "ow" as in sh<u>ow</u> and "ow" as in fr<u>ow</u>n.

The Three Skills Needed to Access the Code
- Segmenting: To use a sound picture code, one must be able to access independent sounds within words.
- Blending: To use a sound picture code, children must be able to push sounds together into words.
- Phoneme Manipulation: To use a code that contains overlap, children must be able to slide sounds in and out of words that contain overlap spellings described above.

Children Learn Best in Context and Through Active Discovery
Developmental psychologist Jean Piaget said, *"The child only deeply understands that which he has created."* Through directed discovery the *Phono-Graphix* lessons help the child to create a schema for the code that is based on its true nature and the way children learn.

Evidence of Effectiveness: A number of studies (see References) document the effectiveness of *Phono-Graphix*. In addition, a report by the Florida Center for Reading Research (www.fcrr.org) indicates the content and design of *Phono-Graphix* is based on research and includes the critical elements of beginning reading instruction.

Teacher Training: Professionals can receive training on *Phono-Graphix* online or at a four-day training available at various locations. The Read America website (www.readamerica.net) provides information regarding training. *Reading Reflex* is suitable for parent use.

Contact and Ordering Information:
Read America
P.O. Box 1246
Mount Dora, FL 32756
Phone: 800-732-3868
e-mail: contact@readamerica.net
Website: www.readamerica.net

REFERENCES

Dias, K., & Juniper, L. (2002). Phono-Graphix—who needs additional literacy support? An outline of research in Bristol schools. *Support for Learning 17*, 34–38.

Endress, S. A. (2007). Examining the effects of Phono-Graphix on the remediation of reading skills of students with disabilities: A program evaluation. *Education & Treatment of Children, 30*, 1–20.

McGuinness, C., McGuinness, D., & McGuinness, G. (1996). Phono-Graphix: A new method for remediating reading difficulties. *Annals of Dyslexia, 46*, 73–96.

McGuinness, C., & McGuinness, G. (1999). *Reading reflex: The foolproof Phono-Graphix method*. New York, Simon and Schuster.

Palmer, S. (2000). Assessing the benefits of phonics intervention on hearing-impaired children's word reading. *Deafness and Education International, 2*(3), 12–19.

Simos, P. G., Fletcher, J. M., Bergman, E., Breier, J. I., Foorman, B. R., Castillo, E. M., & Papanicolau, A. C. (2002). Dyslexia-specific brain activation profile becomes normal following successful remedial training. *Neurology, 58*, 1203–1212.

Wright, M., & Mullan, F. (2006). Dyslexia and the Phono-Graphix reading programme. *Support for Learning, 21*(2), 77–84.

Program: RAVE-O

Author: Maryanne Wolf, Ed.D.

Information Provided By: Maryanne Wolf and Yvonne Gill

Appropriate for Age/Grades: Grades 2–4 (new versions in the near future for Grades 1 and 5)

Description: *RAVE-O* (Reading Automaticity through Vocabulary, Engagement with Language, and Orthography) combines our best knowledge about the multiple components used in the reading brain's circuit with the systematic application of exemplary teaching practices and whimsical, engaging strategies for learning. Explicit emphases are placed on three large areas: (1) phonological, orthographic, semantic, syntactic, and morphological processes; (2) accuracy and fluency at the phoneme, letter pattern, word, and connected text levels; and (3) deep reading comprehension strategies that elicit the child's critical analysis, inferential reasoning, and novel thought capacities.

RAVE-O is an extensively researched and evaluated reading intervention that targets the multiple components in reading fluency and comprehension for children with serious reading challenges. Its unique, multicomponent approach targets the varied dimensions of linguistic knowledge about a word, as words are encountered (Wolf, Gottwald, & Orkin, 2009; Wolf, Miller, & Donnelly, 2000). Thus a child learns the meanings, phonemes, orthographic patterns, syntactic functions, and morpheme options of a word at the moment of learning, not at separate moments in time. In this way the approach simulates what the expert reading brain does when it reads words. In addition, the program provides engaging metacognitive strategies for learning each of these linguistic dimensions and key comprehension strategies for approaching text. A new emphasis on the child's own novel thought about the text is incorporated along with motivating methods to accelerate fluency, comprehension, and deep reading skills.

The *RAVE-O* program works systematically and simultaneously to assure accuracy and fluency at three levels: phoneme and orthographic pattern, word, and connected text. Toward these ends, *RAVE-O* employs a disarmingly simple method. Instructors teach a small corpus of carefully selected core words every week that embody what the child's brain needs to learn to activate when reading all words. Each of the four to five core words learned every week serves as a pivot for learning multiple aspects of linguistic knowledge. Thus each word incorporates the most common English orthographic patterns, multiple meanings, multiple syntactic functions, and many morpheme options. For example, the word *jam* represents at least seven common meanings, three syntactic functions, and many options for exemplifying how morphemes work in English (e.g., jams, jammed, unjammed). This is based on psycholinguistic research that is the basis for the *RAVE-O* premise—the more the child knows about a word, the faster and better the word is read and understood.

Based on the most common, major impediments to reading development across all languages (i.e., phoneme processing and fluency-related deficits) and a multicomponent conceptualization of reading fluency (see Wolf & Katzir-Cohen, 2001), *RAVE-O* attempts to address in systematic, explicit instructional activities both the major components in reading fluency and also the major known impediments to reading development at the letter, word, and connected text levels. Furthermore, every effort is made to make each activity memorable, creative, and often whimsical to facilitate memory storage and foster mutually engaged teachers and learners. The program actively seeks to elicit and harness what children already know about oral language to help teach them what they don't know yet about written language. In the process the program promotes an approach in which children view themselves anew as successful learners, poised to learn to read through their own efforts, rather than as failed readers.

The goal of *RAVE-O* is that students not only understand what they read, but interact with words and bring their own novel thoughts to the text. *RAVE-O* students become word detectives who uncover the treasures inside words and what they can mean in varied contexts. Students learn metacognitive tips through RAVE-O Town characters who are introduced each week to teach students strategies that will enhance their linguistic understanding and recall of information (e.g., the colorful spider, Ms. MIM, teaches how words have Many Interesting Meanings, which, in turn, teaches children the broader linguistic concept of polysemy and prepares them for the fact that half of the child's early words have different meanings). Every other day the child reads Minute Stories that embody all of the meanings, syntactic functions, and morpheme options of the core words that week (e.g., Sam tracked the tracks by the tracks.). Students build their own thoughts, opinions, and acquire new knowledge in response to what they read in the Minute Story Anthologies—collections of progressively difficult stories with wonderfully imaginative illustrations that actively engage new ways of thinking about text. The ultimate goals of the *RAVE-O* program are thoughtful, engaged readers who read with a level of accuracy and fluency that allows them to think their own thoughts about the text and begin their own reading life.

Program Materials: The *RAVE-O* materials are contained within the *RAVE-O* toolkit.

- Teacher Guides Volume 1 & 2 contain instruction for units 1–16. The program is fully scripted to enable teachers to implement the program with fidelity until they are confident; then the Activity Summary can be used. The lesson plans are given with objectives and the aspects of language on which each activity focuses.
- The Teacher's Resource Guide provides a program overview, Assessment Guidelines, types of word introductions, additional resource materials, and research articles.
- Online Resources, including unit assessments, additional blackline masters (master sheets for activities and wordlists), and home-school connections (parent letters and materials)
- Student Minute Story Anthologies (two volumes)
- Student WordWork Books (two volumes)
- Additional Materials
  1. Large format RAVE-O Town Poster
  2. Large Format Word Web
  3. Sixteen Posters used to introduce metacognitive tips and characters
  4. Card sets—Core words, Spelling pattern cards, Image cards, Word Wall cards, and Eye-spy word cards
  5. Dice
  6. Sound sliders
  7. Magnifying glasses
  8. Sand timers

Evidence of Effectiveness: Extensive efficacy databases for the *RAVE-O* program are based on several large, three-city (Boston, Atlanta, and Toronto), five-year, National Institute for Child Health and Human Development (NICHD) randomized treatment control studies of multiple interventions, conducted by Robin Morris, Maryanne Wolf, and Maureen Lovett. Their goals were to investigate the efficacy of single component and multicomponent state-of-the-art reading intervention packages with discrete subtypes of children with reading disabilities. Children who received the *RAVE-O* program or the other multicomponent program (PHAST or EMPOWER by Lovett and her group) showed significantly more gains in all reading and oral language measures, except rapid name retrieval, than children who received the more unidimensional programs (phonology only) or the control treatment (see Morris et al., in press). Students who received the *RAVE-O* program showed more significant gains on measures of reading fluency and fluent comprehension and expressive vocabulary on polysemy tasks for trained and untrained words than all other programs, a finding maintained a year later. *RAVE-O* was also evaluated by Tufts University's Center for Reading and Language Research in two other contexts: afterschool settings in Phoenix, Arizona, and Lowell, Massachusetts, through grants from private foundations and the Institute for Educational Science; and summer school in Malden, Massachusetts. Students who completed the *RAVE-O* curriculum showed significant gains in both specific and global reading skills across all studies, with most gains seen in the school hour context.

Teacher Training: Training is provided by members of the Center for Reading and Language Research at Tufts University, Medford, MA 02155. The 12-hour professional development program, distributed over 2 full days, prepares professionals to implement the curriculum immediately.

Attendees will learn:

1. An overview of recent reading and brain research
2. Methods and materials of the *RAVE-O* curriculum
3. Instructional strategies for putting the *RAVE-O* curriculum into practice in classrooms and tutorial settings
4. Considerations for the integration of *RAVE-O* with other phonological-based programs.

The Center for Reading and Language Research at Tufts University (CRLR) partners with hundreds of schools and districts in many states to address professional development needs. For more information about workshops or scheduling a workshop, visit the Center's website (ase.tufts.edu/crlr/).

Contact and Ordering Information:

Cambium Learning Group—Sopris West
4093 Specialty Place
Longmont, CO 80504
Phone: 800-547-6747 or 303-651-2829
e-mail: customerservice@cambiumlearning.com
Website: www.soprislearning.com

REFERENCES

Morris, R. D., Lovett, M. W., Wolf, M., Sevcik, R. A., Steinbach, K. A., Frijters, J. C., & Shapiro, M. B. (in press). Multiple-component remediation for developmental reading disabilities: IQ, socioeconomic status, and race as factors in remedial outcome. *Journal of Learning Disabilities*. doi:10.1177/0022219409355472

Wolf, M., Gottwald, S., & Orkin, M. (2009). Serious word play: How multiple linguistic emphases in RAVE-O instruction improve multiple reading skills. *Perspectives on Language and Literacy, 35,* 21–24.

Wolf M., & Katzir-Cohen, T. (2001). Reading fluency and its intervention. *Scientific Studies of Reading (Special Issue on Reading Fluency), 5,* 211–238.

Wolf, M., Miller, L., & Donnelly, K. (2000). The retrieval, automaticity, vocabulary elaboration, orthography (RAVE-O): A comprehensive fluency-based reading intervention program. *Journal of Learning Disabilities, 33,* 375–386.

Program: Read, Write & Type!

Author: Jeannine Herron, Ph.D.

Information Provided By: Talking Fingers, Inc.

Appropriate for Ages/Grades: Ages 5–7, or older children struggling with reading or learning English.

Description: *Read, Write & Type! (RWT!)* is a 40-lesson sequential software program providing instruction and games for enriching any early reading curriculum. It teaches phoneme awareness, phonics, reading, writing, spelling, and touch-typing. The unique premise of this program is that spelling out words develops fluent phonics skills and is a powerful route to reading. Children are introduced to the 40 speech sounds in English and learn to associate each phoneme with a letter or combination of letters and also a finger stroke on the keyboard. Using eyes, ears, speech, and muscle memory, they sound out and spell hundreds of words, phrases, and engaging stories. Immersed in the meaning of the words, they read without effort as they write.

The Talking Fingers approach is based on a simple idea: *text is speech made visible!* We use our mouths to talk, to make the sounds of words. We use our fingers (with a pencil or keyboard) to represent those sounds on paper. When children learn to link speech sounds with letters, they can use the alphabet code to write any word they can say. Their fingers are talking.

In the *RWT!* storyline, two houses represent the two sides of the keyboard, (one for each hand). The houses are inhabited by storytellers who want to get to the Story Tree to write their stories. A mischievous alien called Vexor tries to steal the letters and prevent the storytellers from writing down their stories. Two Helping Hands, Lefty and Rightway, help children foil Vexor through 40 exciting lessons, building hundreds of animated sentences and stories as they go.

Children are rewarded with certificates of advancement after every four letters. Each lesson includes at least four games: (1) identifying beginning, middle, and ending sounds; (2) blending sounds together to type a word or phrase across the screen; (3) sounding-out and spelling a pictured word; and (4) writing a four-sentence rhyming story to dictation. There is also a simulated e-mail game where children use word processing to write a message, then "send" it and "receive" a prestored message from a six-year-old somewhere else in the world. *RWT!* is accompanied by the *Spaceship Challenge* CD that provides periodic assessment in Phonics, Reading Comprehension, and Spelling. The player's first response is recorded (and can be displayed or printed), but cues are still given so that the child can complete each task correctly.

RWT! and *Spaceship*, both funded in part by the National Institute of Child Health and Human Development (NICHD), are widely used for early reading instruction, intervention for children struggling with reading, and for children learning English as a second language. Voice-over help is available in English, Spanish, Malaysian, Tagalog, Mandarin, Japanese, Arabic, and Farsi. (Other languages are coming soon.). The programs are available as hybrid CDs for any operating system, or online play by subscription. Currently, a single five-year subscription for online-play at home is $35. Subscription pricing for schools or districts is described on the TFI website.

Materials for Teachers: An Activity Book provides tips and lesson plans to accompany each of the 40 lessons. A sturdy paper "keyboard" picturing the two houses enables children to warm up before going to the computer. The Talking Fingers website (www.talkingfingers.com) provides printable materials such as 18 level-appropriate decodable stories, or clip art of the storytellers to paste into original stories children write.

Evidence of Effectiveness: Research with at-risk first graders comparing *Read, Write & Type!* with *The Lindamood Phoneme Sequencing Program for Reading, Spelling, and Speech (LIPS)* was carried out by Torgesen et al. (2010). At the end of first grade, there were no differences in student reading performance between students assigned to the different intervention conditions, but the combined-intervention students performed significantly better than control students who had been exposed to their school's normal reading program. Significant differences were obtained for phonemic awareness, phonemic decoding, reading accuracy, rapid automatic naming, and reading comprehension. A follow-up test at the end of second grade showed a similar pattern of differences, although only differences in phonemic awareness, phonemic decoding, and rapid naming remained statistically reliable.

Teacher Training: There are numerous videos (www.youtube.com) that can be used to introduce the program or train teachers (search for Read, Write, & Type). Training webinars for preparing teachers to get maximum benefit from the programs can be set up by contacting Talking Fingers.

Contact and Ordering Information:
Talking Fingers, Inc.
830 Rincon Way
San Rafael, CA 94903
Phone: 415-472-3103 or 415-342-3080
e-mail: herron@talkingfingers.com
Website: www.talkingfingers.com

REFERENCE

Torgesen, J. K., Wagner, R. K., Rashotte, C. A., Herron, J., & Lindamood, P. (2010). Computer assisted instruction to prevent early reading difficulties in students at risk for dyslexia: Outcomes from two instructional approaches. *Annals of Dyslexia, 60*(1), 40–56.

Program: REWARDS Intermediate, REWARDS Secondary, REWARDS Plus
Authors: Anita L. Archer, Ph.D., Mary Gleason, Ph.D., and Vicky Vachon, Ph.D.

Information Provided By: Anita L. Archer

Appropriate for Grades: Grades 4–6 (REWARDS Intermediate); Grade 6–12 (REWARDS Secondary and Reward Plus)

Description: *REWARDS Secondary* and *REWARDS Intermediate* are intense, short-term intervention programs for older students who have mastered the basic reading skills associated with first and second grade but experience difficulty reading multisyllabic words and/or who read slowly (i.e., 60–120 correct words per minute). *REWARDS* is an acronym for Reading Excellence: Word Attack and Rate Development Strategies. *REWARDS Secondary* and *REWARDS Intermediate* are parallel programs designed to teach flexible strategies for fluently reading long words consisting of two to eight syllables that appear in content area texts. A further expectation is an increase in vocabulary and fluency. *REWARDS Intermediate* is for students in grades 4–6 and consists of 25 lessons, while *REWARDS Secondary* is for students in grades 6–12 and consists of 20 lessons. Lessons from both programs are approximately 50 minutes in length and can be done in two shorter sessions if necessary. The programs may be taught by teachers or paraprofessionals in small group, whole group, or one-on-one as part of general education classes, remedial reading classes, or intensive summer school or after school classes. *REWARDS Intermediate* differs from *REWARDS Secondary* in the following ways: (a) additional lessons are provided; (b) sentences and passages are matched to fourth-to-sixth-grade levels; (c) all lessons include additional explicit instruction in vocabulary; (d) vowels and affixes are introduced at a slower rate; and (e) sentence reading is introduced before passage reading.

Both *REWARDS* programs consist of a series of preskill lessons followed by strategy lessons that lead students in a step-by-step fashion from carefully scaffolded practice to independent decoding of multisyllabic words in sentences and content passages. Preskill lesson activities focus on learning the component skills necessary for applying the flexible decoding strategy, including blending word parts to form a word; accurately pronouncing single vowels, vowel combinations, and prefixes and suffixes; correcting mispronounced words; and learning the meanings of prefixes and suffixes. During the strategy lessons, students learn, practice, and apply the flexible decoding strategy (circle the prefixes and suffixes, underline the vowels, say the parts, say the word.), which is the essence of the *REWARDS* program. Students also receive vocabulary instruction, practice in reading word families (e.g., reform, reformation), spelling dictation, and repeated reading practice to build fluency.

The Teacher's Guide for both programs includes three parts: (a) a detailed introduction containing information for successful implementation; (b) preskill and strategy lessons based on explicit instruction and the use of instructional routines; and (c) an appendix containing blackline masters, student reference charts, pretest, post-test and generalization tests, fluency graphs, and an incentive program for either motivational purposes or for determining student grades. The consumable student workbook contains all the student materials necessary for the program.

REWARDS Plus is a supplemental reading program designed for middle and high school struggling readers who have completed *REWARDS Secondary* and would benefit from continued decoding and fluency practice with additional focus on vocabulary, comprehension, and writing. Two versions of the program are offered, one with social studies articles and the other with science articles. The instructional activities are organized into *before* reading (introducing the pronunciation of words, the meaning of words, and word families), *during* reading (silent and oral reading of passage segments, answering oral questions), and *after* reading (repeated readings, answering multiple choice and short answer questions, writing passage summaries).

Evidence of Effectiveness: All the *REWARDS* programs were designed to reflect current research on decoding, fluency, vocabulary, and comprehension as well as the research on explicit instruction (Archer & Hughes, 2011). *REWARDS* programs have been used successfully in a variety of settings across the country for many years, including large implementation projects in Washington (a summer school project), Michigan (a state initiative addressing reading and behavior), New York State (a Striving Readers Grant focused on struggling readers in seventh grade), and California (a Response to Instruction and Intervention state project). The effectiveness of *REWARDS* has been validated in a number of small intervention studies (Archer, 1981; Archer, Gleason, Vachon, & Hollenbeck, 2010; Shippen, Houchins, Steventon, & Sartor, 2005; Vachon, 1998). A review of related research is found at the back of each Teacher's Guide. The *REWARDS* programs were positively reviewed by the Florida Reading Center (www.fcrr.org/FCRRReports/PDF/rewards_report.pdf) with no weaknesses indicated.

Teacher Training: Training on implementation of the *REWARDS* programs is addressed in a number of ways. First, each lesson provides a general description of instructional procedures followed by a detailed lesson, including wording that can be used during lesson delivery. In other words, the teacher's manual provides lesson-by-lesson teacher training. Second, on-line training is provided through the publisher (www.soprislearning.com), which includes information on each segment of the program, demonstrations and practice led by Anita Archer, and classroom video clips to illustrate the instructional procedures. Finally, inservice training can be arranged with certified *REWARDS* trainers across the country. These trainers work as independent contractors and are listed on the *REWARDS* website (www.rewardsreading.com). In addition, the authors facilitate a Training of Trainers (TOT) each summer for local staff development professionals.

Contact and Ordering Information:
Sopris (Cambium Learning Group)
Cambium Learning
4185 Salazar Way
Frederick, CO 80504
Phone: 800-547-6747
Website: www.soprislearning.com

REFERENCES

Archer, A. L., & Hughes, C. A. (2011). *Explicit instruction: Effective and efficient teaching.* New York: NY: Guilford Publishing.

Archer, A. L. (1981). *Decoding of multisyllabic words by skill deficient fourth and fifth grade students* (Doctoral dissertation, University of Washington, 1981).

Archer, A. L., Gleason, M. M., Vachon, V., & Hollenbeck, K. (2010). *Instructional strategies for teaching struggling fourth- and fifth-grade students to read long words.* Manuscript in preparation.

Shippen, M. E., Houchins, D. E., Steventon, C., & Sartor, D. (2005). A comparison of two direct instruction reading programs for urban middle school students. *Remedial and Special Education, 26*, 175–182.

Vachon, V. L. (1998). *Effects of mastery of multisyllabic word reading component skills and of varying practice contexts on word and text reading skills of middle school students with reading deficiencies* (Doctoral dissertation, University of Oregon, Eugene).

Program: Road to the Code: A Phonological Awareness Program for Young Children

Authors: Benita A. Blachman, Ph.D., Eileen Wynne Ball, Ph.D., Rochella Black, M.S., and Darlene M. Tangel, Ph.D.

Information Provided By: Maria S. Murray

Appropriate for Ages/Grades: Grades K–1

Description: *Road to the Code* is an evidence-based phonological awareness intervention that targets phoneme awareness and letter-sound correspondences so that children can develop the awareness that spoken words can be segmented into phonemes and that these segmented units can be represented by the letters of the alphabet. This program is ideally suited for small group instruction or for use with individual students, making it especially applicable in settings using a Response-to-Intervention (RTI) model. Forty-four developmentally sequenced lessons (approximately four 15–20 minute lessons over an 11-week period) are provided that primarily focus on the explicit and systematic research-based strategy of segmenting and blending phonemes. Each lesson is comprised of three parts:

1. *Say-It-And-Move-It* (a segmenting and blending activity based on the work of Elkonin, 1973): students move a disk for every phoneme heard in a spoken word.
2. *Letter Name and Sound Instruction*: students learn the names and sounds of the letters with illustrated alphabet cards and a variety of games.
3. *Phonological Awareness Practice*: students are given additional opportunities to practice phoneme awareness, also using a variety of games and activities (e.g., sound Bingo, puppets).

Each lesson has a script, as well as suggestions for differentiating instruction to meet individual needs. Teachers are encouraged to be flexible and use their judgment in introducing concepts more slowly or moving lessons along more quickly based on the skill levels of the students.

Evidence of Effectiveness: Evidence of effectiveness for *Road to the Code* strategies has been evaluated in numerous studies (Ball & Blachman, 1988, 1991; Blachman, Ball, Black, & Tangel, 1994; Blachman, Tangel, Ball, Black, & McGraw, 1999; Tangel & Blachman, 1992, 1995) that have appeared in peer-reviewed journals. Several of these studies were selected for inclusion in the methodologically rigorous meta-analyses that appeared in the National Reading Panel Report (NRP, 2000). The strategies used in *Road to the Code* were proven to be effective in improving phonological awareness and beginning reading and spelling abilities in kindergarten and first grade children. For example, in one study, the program was evaluated for use by kindergarten teachers and their teaching assistants (Blachman et al., 1994). Results showed that after the 11-week intervention, treatment children significantly outperformed control children on measures of phoneme segmentation, letter name and letter sound knowledge, reading measures, and a measure of invented spelling. Furthermore, these students also received a reading program in grade 1 emphasizing the alphabetic code (see *Road to Reading*). It was found that the students who participated in these programs were better readers at the end of grades 1 and 2 than similar students who did not participate in these programs (Blachman et al., 1999). More recently, a study of over 300 kindergarten children found that children who used *Road to the Code* in small groups had significantly more sophisticated invented spelling at the end of kindergarten than children who did not use the program (Murray, 2009).

Teacher Training: *Road to the Code* can be effectively used by educators who have read the manual and prepared materials. Teacher notes accompany the lessons, and all necessary materials are easily reproducible from the manual. More in-depth professional development and training can be arranged by contacting Brookes on Location (www.brookespublishing.com/onlocation/).

Contact and Ordering Information:
Paul H. Brookes Publishing Company
P.O. Box 10624
Baltimore, MD 21285-0624
Phone: 800-638-3775
Fax: 410-337-8539
Website: www.brookespublishing.com

REFERENCES

Ball, E., & Blachman, B. (1988). Phoneme segmentation training: Effect on reading readiness. *Annals of Dyslexia, 38,* 208–225.

Ball, E. W., & Blachman, B. A. (1991). Does phoneme awareness training in kindergarten make a difference in early word recognition and developmental spelling? *Reading Research Quarterly, 26,* 49–66.

Blachman, B., Ball, E., Black, S., & Tangel, D. (1994). Kindergarten teachers develop phoneme awareness in low-income, inner-city classrooms: Does it make a difference? *Reading and Writing: An Interdisciplinary Journal, 6,* 1–17.

Blachman, B. A., Tangel, D. M., Ball, E. W., Black, R. S., & McGraw, C. (1999). Developing phonological awareness and word recognition skills: A two-year intervention with low-income, inner-city children. *Reading and Writing: An Interdisciplinary Journal, 11,* 239–273.

Elkonin, D. B. (1973). U.S.S.R. In J. Downing (Ed.), *Comparative reading* (pp. 551–579). New York: Macmillan.

Murray, M. (2009). *Identifying predictors of end-of-year kindergarten invented spelling* (Doctoral dissertation). Retrieved from Dissertation Abstracts International. (UMI No. AAT 3410018).

National Institute of Child Health and Human Development. (2000). *Report of the National Reading Panel. Teaching children to read: An evidence-based assessment of the scientific research literature on reading and its implications for reading instruction* (NIH Publication No. 00-4769). Washington, DC: U.S. Government Printing Office.

Tangel, D., & Blachman, B. (1992). Effect of phoneme awareness instruction on kindergarten children's invented spelling. *Journal of Reading Behavior, 24,* 233–261.

Tangel, D. M., & Blachman, B. A. (1995). Effect of phoneme awareness instruction on the invented spelling of first grade children: A one year follow-up. *Journal of Reading Behavior, 27,* 153–185.

Program: Road to Reading: A Program for the Prevention and Remediation of Reading Difficulties

Authors: Benita A. Blachman, Ph.D. and Darlene M. Tangel, Ph.D.

Information Provided By: Kristen Munger and Maria S. Murray

Appropriate for Ages/Grades: Grades 1–3, can be adapted for use with older struggling readers

Description: *Road to Reading* is an evidence-based, systematic, and explicit program to help all children develop accurate and fluent word identification. Appropriate for use with students who can demonstrate beginning levels of phonemic awareness and who know some letter names, *Road to Reading* focuses on understanding the alphabetic principle, accurate and fluent decoding, oral reading, and spelling. It is ideal for settings using a Response-to-Intervention (RTI) model because lessons can be adapted in terms of both group size (from flexible classroom groups, to small intervention groups, to individual instruction) and intensity (lesson length and number of lessons taught) to meet the needs of students at varying levels of skill acquisition.

The program has six levels, which increase in complexity as the students progress. The levels are based on the six syllable patterns of the English language, and the level at which a student begins is determined by letter-sound and decoding assessments that are included on a CD-ROM that comes with the manual. The Road to Reading program is unscripted so that teachers have the flexibility to custom-design lessons in terms of content, time requirements (30 minutes or longer), or age (first grade or higher). To help teachers prepare lessons, the manual includes lists of words for each step, book suggestions for oral reading, and lists of words and sentences for dictation, as well as over 200 pages of materials that can be printed from the CD-ROM. Each lesson consists of five steps:

1. Review sound-symbol correspondences—students develop accuracy and automaticity with sound-symbol correspondences.
2. Teach or review new decoding skill—students practice making words with new phonetic patterns, reinforcing both phoneme awareness and phonics skills.
3. Review phonetically regular words (PRWs) and high frequency words (HFWs)—students develop fluency in reading previously introduced phonetically regular words and high frequency words and extend vocabulary.
4. Read orally in context—students read orally to develop fluency and comprehension.
5. Dictation—students spell dictated words and write sentences to reinforce skills taught earlier in the lesson.

Evidence of Effectiveness: *Road to Reading* has been shown to be effective in a variety of settings, including general education classrooms (either as a supplement to the core reading program or as the primary reading program in classes with many students at-risk for reading difficulties), remedial reading programs, resource rooms, and one-to-one tutoring. In addition, effectiveness has been documented by empirical research studies conducted since the 1980s, when Blachman (1987) developed an instructional model that could be used by primary grade teachers in general education classrooms with children who had difficulty learning to read. Additional research using this model (Blachman, Tangel, Ball, Black, & McGraw, 1999; Tangel & Blachman, 1995) found that children who participated in the 5-step program described in *Road to Reading* (and also participated in a phonological awareness program in kindergarten; see *Road to the Code*) were better readers at the end of grades 1 and 2 than children who did not participate in these programs. Results from several early studies were selected for inclusion in the meta-analyses that appeared in the influential National Reading Panel Report (2000) providing extensive evidence regarding the value of phoneme awareness and phonics for teaching children to read. In 2004, Blachman and her colleagues (Schatschneider, Fletcher, Francis, Clonan, B. Shaywitz, & S. Shaywitz) expanded the 30- to 40-minute lessons in *Road to Reading* to 50-minute lessons used in one-to-one instruction with second and third grade struggling readers. After eight months of instruction and when assessed again at a one-year follow-up, children who were randomly assigned to participate in the program significantly outperformed children who did not participate on multiple measures of reading and spelling.

Teacher Training: *Road to Reading* can be effectively used by educators who have read the manual and prepared the materials (e.g., sound cards, sound boards, word cards). A CD-ROM that is included with the manual features lesson plan forms to use as a template for preparing lessons, assessment forms, syllable reference sheets, and most of the materials needed for the lessons (e.g., all letter and word cards needed for the first three steps of the lesson can be printed from the CD-ROM). Teacher notes are distributed widely throughout the program manual in order to provide suggestions regarding topics such as pacing, how to implement the lessons, and how to find appropriate reading materials. Sample lesson plans are also included. More in-depth professional development and training can be arranged by contacting Brookes on Location (www.brookespublishing.com/onlocation/).

Contact and Ordering Information:
Paul H. Brookes Publishing Company
P.O. Box 10624
Baltimore, MD 21285-0624
Phone: 800-638-3775
Fax: 410-337-8539
Website: www.brookespublishing.com

REFERENCES

Blachman, B. (1987). An alternative classroom reading program for learning disabled and other low-achieving children. In R. Bowler (Ed.), *Intimacy with language: A forgotten basic in teacher education* (pp. 49–55). Baltimore, MD: Orton Dyslexia Society.

Blachman, B. A., Schatschneider, C., Fletcher, J. M., Francis, D. J., Clonan, S. M., Shaywitz, B. A., & Shaywitz, S. E. (2004). Effects of intensive reading remediation for second and third graders and a 1 year follow-up. *Journal of Educational Psychology, 96,* 444–461.

Blachman, B. A., Tangel, D. M., Ball, E. W., Black, R. S., & McGraw, C. (1999). Developing phonological awareness and word recognition skills: A two-year intervention with low-income, inner-city children. *Reading and Writing: An Interdisciplinary Journal, 11*, 239–273.

National Institute of Child Health and Human Development. (2000). *Report of the National Reading Panel. Teaching children to read: An evidence-based assessment of the scientific research literature on reading and its implications for reading instruction* (NIH Publication No. 00-4769). Washington, DC: U.S. Government Printing Office.

Tangel, D. M., & Blachman, B. A. (1995). Effect of phoneme awareness instruction on the invented spelling of first grade children: A one year follow-up. *Journal of Reading Behavior, 27*, 153–185.

Program: Sonday System

Author: Arlene Sonday

Information Provided By: Winsor Learning, Inc.

Appropriate for Ages/Grades: PreK-Adult

Description: The *Sonday System* instructional materials and methods have been compiled to help teachers effectively use proven literacy instructional strategies. The *Sonday System* is based on Orton-Gillingham instructional principles that have been well documented over time. The Orton-Gillingham approach has been the subject of five major reading research studies over the last 70 years, in 1940, 1956, 1969, 1979, and 1984. Citing these, The National Reading Panel identified Orton-Gillingham as one of the effective methodologies that address the needs of struggling students (National Reading Panel, 2000).

The *Sonday System* materials have been carefully crafted to incorporate the essential components of reading (phonemic awareness, phonological awareness, fluency, vocabulary, comprehension) identified by the National Reading Panel and to integrate the critical systematic spelling component. When reading and spelling are taught together, progress is faster, learning is more secure, and the learner becomes a writer as well as a reader. Spelling offers an opportunity for kinesthetic/tactile practice through tracing and writing, and provides immediate diagnostic information regarding sounds, rules, and concepts that have (or have not) been learned. This intentional integration allows students to become more proficient at reading and spelling as well as writing. Teachers can expand the spelling activities to extended writing assignments and include comprehension strategies to help children become independent readers. Reading and writing skills must be developed sequentially and cumulatively.

The *Sonday System* is offered in kits for various settings:

- Let's Play Learn (Early Childhood—PreK and K)

- Sonday System 1 (Beginning Reading and Interventions)
- Sonday System 2 (Intermediate Reading and Interventions)

Evidence of Effectiveness: Thirteen years of data collected from school districts using the *Sonday System* demonstrate a high degree of effectiveness. Educational experts in industry-leading organizations such as the National Center for Learning Disabilities (NCLD), the International Dyslexia Association (IDA), and Reading First offices in several states have independently evaluated the *Sonday System* and found that the program contained the required elements for successful reading identified by the National Reading Panel (2000). Additional information, including *Sonday System* effectiveness reports and how to access the analysis reports from NCLD and IDA, is available (www.winsor learning.com).

Teacher Training: Winsor Learning provides extensive training, coaching, and consulting services to support the use of the *Sonday System*. With ongoing, sustained professional development that includes initial training and follow-up coaching, teachers learn through explanation, demonstration, and role-playing. The strategies are consistent with those recommended by the National Reading Panel (2000).

Contact and Ordering Information:
Winsor Learning, Inc.
1620 7th Street West
St. Paul, MN 55102
Phone: 800-321-7585
Website: www.winsorlearning.com

REFERENCE

National Institute of Child Health and Human Development. (2000). *Report of the National Reading Panel. Teaching children to read: An evidence-based assessment of the scientific research literature on reading and its implications for reading instruction* (NIH Publication No. 00-4769). Washington, DC: U.S. Government Printing Office.

Program: Spelling by Pattern, Levels 1, 2, and 3
Authors: Ellen Javernick, Betty Hooper, and Louisa Moats, Ed.D.
Information Provided By: Louisa Moats
Appropriate for Ages/Grades: Grades 1–3 or remedial
Description: *Spelling by Pattern,* Levels 1–3 is a classroom instructional program that teaches students about sounds, syllable patterns, and sense in the English writing system. The program's content includes:

- Awareness of vowel and consonant phonemes
- Knowledge of productive phoneme-grapheme correspondences
- Common irregular words from the 300 most often used words in English
- Syllable spelling patterns and combinations
- Prefix, root, and suffix constructions (morphology)
- Word usage within sentence contexts
- How a word's grammatical role affects spelling
- Idioms, figures of speech, and more

Spelling by Pattern, Level 1 (Javernick & Moats) contains 30 cumulative lessons involving games, drills, songs, dictations, word sorts, reviews, and use of words in cloze exercises and simple writing tasks. A circus theme unifies and adds meaning to the lessons. The program covers all consonants, including digraphs and blends; short vowel patterns; open single syllable words; consonant-vowel-e (silent e) patterns; and the most predictable vowel teams. The first 100 most common words in writing are learned through mnemonic devices and multisensory practice routines.

Spelling by Pattern, Level 2 (Hooper & Moats) contains 28 lessons, including reviews. Organized around a safari theme, each lesson includes introduction of a concept; exploration of a 15- to 20-word list; study of "heart" words from the most commonly used word list; use of words in context; and word sorts. The content emphasizes vowel spellings, especially vowel teams and vowel-r patterns, and conditional consonant spellings (-ch/tch; -k, -ck). Each lesson ends with a safari story that includes all the lesson's words in an entertaining context. Blackline masters for each story allow students to write the words in the story context. Word lists introduce the most common suffixes (-ed, -s, -es, -ing, -y, -ly), as students are introduced to ending rules such as "drop silent e."

The theme for Level 3 of *Spelling by Pattern* (Hooper & Moats) is exploration. The patterns taught in the 28 weekly lessons include words with closed, open, VCe, vowel team, vowel-r, and c-le syllables; all common patterns for long vowel spellings; homophones; "heart" (irregular) words; and words with common prefixes and suffixes. The suffix-ending rules are re-introduced and practiced frequently with multisyllable words. Each lesson includes a crossword puzzle and a story with the lesson words embedded.

Evidence of Effectiveness: The first author of each level of *Spelling by Pattern* is a classroom teacher with more than 10 years of experience teaching the lessons and teaching other teachers to use the lessons. In each school where the program has been used, students have far exceeded average spelling levels for their grade. No large-scale or randomized, controlled studies have been conducted with the spelling program. The content and methods, however, are based on multiple studies showing that systematic, cumulative, explicit instruction focused on the structure of language is more effective than rote, visually based, whole word memorization approaches (Joshi, Treiman, Carreker, & Moats, 2008–2009; Moats, 2005).

Teacher Training: Teacher manuals explain the concepts presented in each lesson, provide scripts for each concept's introduction, and provide answer keys for exercises. Teachers should have some background in language structure, such as that provided by *Language Essentials for Teachers of Reading and Spelling* (LETRS; Cambium Learning Sopris); *Speech to Print* (2nd ed.; Paul H. Brookes Publishing); or *Multisensory Teaching of Basic Language Skills* (2nd ed.; Paul H. Brookes Publishing).

Contact and Ordering Information:
Cambium Learning Sopris
Customer Service Department, Sopris Learning
4093 Specialty Place
Longmont, CO
Phone: 303-651-2829
Website: www.soprislearning.com

REFERENCES

Joshi, R. M., Treiman, R., Carreker, S., & Moats, L. C. (Winter, 2008–2009). How words cast their spell: Spelling is an integral part of learning the language, not a matter of memorization. *American Educator, 32*(4), 6–16, 42–43.

Moats, L. C. (Winter, 2005–2006). How spelling supports reading and why it is more regular and predictable than you may think. *American Educator, 29*(4), 12–22, 42–43.

Program: Spellography: A Student Roadmap to Better Spelling
Author: Louisa Moats, Ed.D. and Bruce Rosow, Ed.D.
Information Provided By: Bruce Rosow
Appropriate for Ages/Grades: Grades 3–7, Remedial Grades 5–11
Description: *Spellography* is a word study program, not just a spelling program. Word study includes learning all one can about a word including speech sounds, spelling patterns and syllable study, morphology, semantics, syntax, and etymology. The more one knows about a word, the more accessible that word is for writing, reading, and thinking. The *Spellography* word study program supports spelling, decoding, and vocabulary development. It is designed to circle back to review concepts and be fun and engaging for students.

Spellography has two levels; beginning and advanced. The beginning or basic program includes Books A–C, and the advanced level includes Books A and B. These books include an emphasis on phonemic awareness, single syllable/within-word spelling patterns to teach consonant spelling by position as well as syllable types, and inflectional morphology (ed, ing, s and es, etc.). The Basic level is suitable for general education students in the intermediate grades (3–5) or for older students who need to circle back (grades 5–9). The Advanced level is suitable for general education students in grades 6–7 or for older students in grades 8–11 who require additional instruction.

Basic level Book A reviews closed syllable and vowel-r syllable patterns allowing for a study of complex consonant spellings (k, ck, ks, cks, x, ch, tch, ge, dge, qu, hard/soft c and g). Basic level Book B begins with the vowel circle and continues with a study of the other syllable types to learn how to spell long vowels. Basic level Book C begins with an introduction to -cle syllables and syllable review, and continues with the study of difficult vowel spellings including /aw/, /oy/, /ū/, and /yū/.

Advanced Book A parallels the content of the basic level Book A in that the focus is on closed syllables and complex consonant spellings. The difference is that the study continues at a more complex level with a greater emphasis on multisyllable words and morphological study (especially Anglo-Saxon morphology). There are no phonemic awareness exercises at this level. However, there is a sustained focus on accent shift, the schwa, and other speech sound changes that can occur in different word forms, as well as all phonological aspects of advanced word study. A qualitative spelling inventory is included to assess students' knowledge of the content in Advanced Book A.

Advanced Book B also includes a qualitative spelling inventory. Advanced Book B parallels Beginner Book B in that it includes a review of syllable types. However, the study is at a much higher level of complexity and includes a great deal of Greek and especially Latin morphology. There are separate folders for the students' lessons (without the answers), and the teacher's version (with answers and some annotation as well). There are also files that include the big ideas and lesson plans for each lesson to help the teacher see the forest through the trees.

Evidence of Effectiveness: *Spellography* was developed after Dr. Rosow studied with Dr. Louisa Moats and gained an understanding of language structure as applied to teaching reading and spelling. *Spellography* lessons were written and revised over several years, with the assistance of Dr. Moats, for public school students in Southern Vermont. The students demonstrated what worked and what didn't. For example, their performance indicated that it was important to consistently review concepts and to build on what was previously learned. It was important to have routines such as repeated readings and repeated word sorts. It was important to work on specific phonological areas, such as nasalized vowels and liquid confusions that have been shown by researchers to be more problematic than others; teach and review syllable types; and explicitly teach morphology. *Spellography* is used in language tutorials at the Greenwood School in Vermont, a *prepreparatory* boarding and day school for boys, ages 9 to 14, identified with language-based learning differences.

Although the research base for teaching spelling is far less substantial than the research base for teaching reading, the content and methods employed by this program are fully aligned with research on spelling development, disability, and instruction. (See References.)

Teacher Training: Although the manual provides all of the necessary instructions to implement the program correctly, additional training can be requested through Sopris West. Teachers with knowledge of language structure and structured, explicit code-based instruction will have the most success using *Spellography*. The Teacher Answer Book that accompanies each book at both levels provides detailed annotation to help teach teachers who are less knowledgeable learn as their students learn. In addition, The Teacher's Resource Guide provides instructions on managing all of the routines for the program as well as resources to support instruction.

Contact and Ordering Information:

All three Basic books and Advanced Book A are available through Sopris West. Advanced Book B is available from the author until such time as this material is published.

Sopris West Educational Services
4185 Salazar Way
Frederick, CO 80504
Phone: 800-547-6747
e-mail: customerservice@cambiumlearning.com
Website: www.sopriswest.com

Author Contact:
Box 66
Williamsville, VT 05362
e-mail: rosow@sover.net

REFERENCES

Bourassa, D. C., & Treiman, R. (2001). Spelling development and disabilities: The importance of linguistic factors. *Language, Speech, and Hearing Services in Schools, 32*, 172–181.

Cassar, M., Treiman, R., Moats, L., Pollo, T., & Kessler, B. (2005). How do the spellings of students with dyslexia compare with those of nondyslexic students? *Reading & Writing, 18*(1), 27–49.

Graham, S., Harris, K. R., & Chorzempa, B. F. (2002). Contribution of spelling instruction to the spelling, writing, and reading of poor spellers. *Journal of Educational Psychology, 94*, 669–686.

Joshi, R. M., Treiman, R., Carreker, S., & Moats, L. C. (Winter, 2008–2009). How words cast their spell: Spelling is an integral part of learning the language, not a matter of memorization. *American Educator, 6*–16, 42.

Moats, L. C. (1995). *Spelling: Development, disability, and instruction*. Austin, TX: Pro-Ed.

Moats, L. C. (2005). How spelling supports reading and why it is more regular and predictable than you may think. *American Educator, 12*–22, 42–43.

Roberts, T. A., & Meiring, A. (2006). Teaching phonics in the context of students' literature or spelling: Influences on first-grade reading, spelling, and writing and fifth-grade comprehension. *Journal of Educational Psychology, 98*, 690–713.

Santoro, L. E., Coyne, M. D., & Simmons, D. C. (2006). The reading-spelling connection: Developing and evaluating a beginning spelling intervention for students at risk of reading disability. *Learning Disabilities Research & Practice, 21*, 122–133.

Treiman, R. (1998). Why spelling? The benefits of incorporating spelling into beginning reading instruction. In J. L. Metsala & L. C. Ehri (Eds.), *Word recognition in beginning literacy* (pp. 289–313). Mahwah, NJ: Erlbaum.

Uhry, J. K., & Shepherd, M. J. (1993). Segmentation and spelling instruction as part of a first-grade reading program: Effects on several measures of reading. *Reading Research Quarterly, 28*, 219–233.

Wise, J., Sevcik, R., Morris, R., Lovett, M., & Wolf, M. (2007). The growth of phonological awareness by students with reading disabilities: A result of semantic knowledge or knowledge of grapheme-phoneme correspondences? *Scientific Studies of Reading, 11*, 151–164.

Program: S.P.I.R.E.

Author: Sheila Clark-Edmands, M.S.Ed.

Information Provided By: EPS/School Specialty Literacy and Intervention

Appropriate for Ages/Grades: Grades PreK–8+

Description: *S.P.I.R.E.* is a comprehensive, multisensory reading intervention program that integrates phonological awareness, phonics, handwriting, fluency, vocabulary, spelling, and comprehension in lesson plans that are specifically designed for the way struggling readers learn. Based on the Orton-Gillingham approach, *S.P.I.R.E.* incorporates the most recent research regarding best practices in reading and language arts instruction. The research around best practices for reading instruction concludes that reading lessons should be explicitly taught, systematically planned and organized, and sequenced in a way that moves from simple to complex. The 8 levels of *S.P.I.R.E.* are systematically structured to meet these criteria and follow a 10-step lesson plan that ensures students experience continuous and visible success. The 10-step lesson plan may be viewed in action (eps.schoolspecialty.com/SPIRE).

After a placement assessment, students start in the level that corresponds to concepts that they need to master. For each concept, such as short *a*, there is an introductory lesson and up to five reinforcing lessons to ensure students master each concept before they move on to the next concept. All text in *S.P.I.R.E.* is decodable. Students receive direct and explicit instruction in each concept before they apply this knowledge to controlled, decodable text. Following is the scope and sequence of the program.

- *Pre-Level 1: Sounds Sensible:* Phonological awareness and beginning phonics, consonants, short a, and beginning handwriting
- *Level 1:* Short vowels (*a, e, i, o, u*), consonant digraphs (*sh, ch, th, wh*), and welded sounds (*ang, ing, ong, ung, ank, ink, onk, unk*)
- *Level 2:* Double consonants (*ff, ll, ss*), *al* as in ball, *wa* as in wasp, *qu, ck*, trigraph *tch*, (*a-e, i-e, o-e, u-e, e-e*), and *V-se*
- *Level 3:* Open syllables (*so, he, fly*), (*ild, old, ind, ost, oll*), *-ay*, three sounds of *-ed*, suffixes without base changes (*-s, -es, -ing, -er, -est, -en, -ish, -ly, -y, -ful, -ness, -less*), twin-consonant syllable division, non twin-consonant syllable division, *ou*, and prefix *a-*
- *Level 4: ea* (eat, bread, steak), consonant *-le, oa, ai, ee, oo, igh*, and *ie* (pie, chief)
- *Level 5:* Soft c and g, (*er, ur, ir, ear, wor*), *dge*, *s* = /z/, *ow* (snow, plow), *kn, oe*, and (*or, ar*)
- *Level 6:* (Prefix *a-*, ending *-a*, suffix *-able*), *ph*, (*ought, aught*), (*ue, ew, tu*), (*oi, oy*), (*aw, au*), *ey* (donkey, prey), (*kn, wr, mb, gh, gu*), suffix *-age*, and open syllables (*a/CV, i/CV, o/CV, u/CV, e/CV*)
- *Level 7:* V/V syllables, *ct*, (*ei, eigh*), open syllables *i* (alligator, radio), (suffixes *-tion, -sion, -ci, -ti*), (suffixes *-tu, -ture, -sure*), suffix *-ous*, (suffixes *-ence, -ent, -ance, -ant, -cy, -ency, -ancy*), (*ui, eu*), and suffixes *-er, -or, -ar, -ard*
- *Level 8:* (*arV, arrV, irV, erV, errV, urV*), (prefixes *dis-, mis-, pre-, pro-, re-, de-, ex-*), (suffixes *-al, -en, -on, -an, -ain, -et, -ite, -ate, -ic*), (suffixes *-ive, -ary*), (prefixes *in-, im-, il-, ir-, un-, under-, sub-, con-, com-, cor-, col-*), (prefixes *para-, ab-, ad-, per-*) and (i = /y/, ch = /k/ and /sh/, and qu = /k/)

Materials: Teacher materials needed for implementation include Initial Placement Assessment, Teachers Guide, Blackline Masters, Word Cards, Phoneme

Segmentation Chart, and Phonogram Cards. Materials needed for each student include Student Reader, Student Workbook, Sound Circles and Rectangles, Magnet Board and Letters, and Illustrated Decodable Readers.

Evidence of Effectiveness: *S.P.I.R.E.* has been used throughout the country with great success by thousands of students who need a direct, systematic, and sequential approach to reading. The Florida Center for Reading Research reviewed *S.P.I.R.E.* and found: "It aligns with the findings of the National Reading Panel (2000) and Reading First. It is explicit and systematic in the areas of phonemic awareness, phonics and fluency. *S.P.I.R.E.* incorporates vocabulary and comprehension components at various points during instruction, typically after oral reading activities with teacher direction and additional practice in the student workbook. Each lesson includes five additional lesson plans reinforcing and practicing the same skill to provide multiple opportunities for students to learn to mastery." The entire report is available (eps.schoolspecialty.com/FCRR). Additional information on effectiveness of the program can also be found (eps.schoolspecialty.com/SPIRE).

Teacher Training: Professional development is available but not required. Nationally scheduled workshops are available or arrangements can be made to bring a *S.P.I.R.E.* trainer to a school or district. The trainers show how to implement *S.P.I.R.E.* and model effective teaching strategies for Tier 2 and 3 students. Educators who attend *S.P.I.R.E.* training learn how to place at-risk students in the appropriate instructional level, deliver explicit instruction designed to meet the needs of at-risk students, monitor student progress, and use student assessment data to make informed instructional decisions. Additional information on professional development is available (eps.schoolspecialty.com/PD).

Contact and Ordering Information:
EPS/School Specialty Literacy and Intervention
Customer Service
P.O. Box 9031
Cambridge, MA 02139-9031
Phone: 800-225-5750
e-mail: customerservice.eps@schoolspecialty.com

Program: Wilson Fluency/Basic
Author: Wilson Language Training
Information Provided By: Wilson Language Training
Appropriate for Ages/Grades: Grades 1–12 and adult
Description: *Wilson Fluency/Basic* is a supplemental fluency program appropriate for younger students with beginning reading skills or for older students

who are not reading fluently due to poor decoding. It provides extended reading passages to give students the focused practice at their instructional reading levels to help increase fluency and comprehension. It can be used with any reading curriculum that directly teaches closed syllable word structure (e.g., one vowel followed by a consonant; the vowel is short, such as in "mug"); it specifically supplements Steps 1–3 of the *Wilson Reading System*. (See description of *Wilson Reading System* in this Appendix.)

The program has the following highlights:

- Provides phonetic and high frequency word practice to improve accuracy and automaticity
- Presents controlled short phrases with taught word patterns and high frequency/sight words to practice with connected text
- Uses longer phrases, presented in meaningful chunks to develop prosody, contains both taught and untaught elements
- Develops phrasing and expression further by having students practice a phrased version of a story and then read the unphrased passage
- Includes comprehension instruction from the beginning, as students are asked to retell the story to monitor their comprehension
- Provides practice with enriched and decodable passages, enhances listening and reading comprehension and vocabulary
- Uses noncontrolled decodable passages in the Basic Reader to help students begin to transfer their emerging decoding skills to reading authentic text with support and with success
- Assessment tools to measure student rate, accuracy, and prosody are provided for each text
- Has detailed instructions for measuring student fluency levels in words correct per minute (WCPM) and prosody using the four-level scoring rubric developed by the National Assessment of Educational Progress (NAEP)
- Makes it easy to monitor student progress by including laminated Tally Sheets and Student Recording Forms
- Allows students to graph their progress in their own Student Fluency Reader
- Can be used with *Wilson Reading System, Wilson Just Words, Wilson Fundations*, and other programs focusing on instruction in closed syllables

There are four Fluency Readers: Readers 1–3 and the Basic Reader. Fluency Readers 1–3 correspond to WRS Steps 1–3; the Basic Reader includes additional decodable stories paired to enriched text passages. Each Fluency Reader contains five stories with reading passages of 200–250 words and corresponding wordlists, phrases, and phrased and unphrased passages. The *Wilson Fluency/Basic* kit provides materials for teachers and students. The teacher materials include the Instructor Guidebook, Student Record Books to monitor student progress, High Frequency Sight Word Cards, Laminated Blank Word Cards, Laminated Tally Sheets corresponding to each Student Fluency Reader, and Enriched Text Passages. Student materials include four Student Fluency Readers (six per level included in the kit). Students graph their own progress in their Fluency Readers. *Wilson Fluency/Basic* lessons are designed to be used in small group or one-on-one settings. Each lesson is approximately 10–20 minutes and should occur one to three times per week, depending on the lesson format of the program it is supplementing.

Evidence of Effectiveness: An independent review by the Florida Center for Reading Research (www.fcrr.org) noted the following: "Wilson Fluency was designed based on the research findings identified in the Report of the National Reading Panel (2000). The important relationship between fluency and reading comprehension has been well established in the research (National Reading Panel, 2000; Snow, Burns, & Griffin, 1998). Students who are able to read smoothly, effortlessly and with proper expression are more likely to understand what they are reading. This program clearly addresses these aspects of fluency. Providing multiple practice opportunities via repeated reading is a key focus of this program as students are asked to read words and phrases up to four times (Dowhower, 1987)."

Teacher Training: To implement *Wilson Fluency*, Wilson recommends the *Wilson Fluency/Basic* Workshop. This full-day workshop examines key aspects of explicit fluency instruction and reading practice necessary to develop students' skills in reading with ease and expression to understand connected text. It provides hands-on practice with each program component, and measures student fluency levels in words correct per minute (WCPM) and prosody using the four-level scoring rubric.

Contact and Ordering Information:
Wilson Language Training
47 Old Webster Road
Oxford, MA 01540
Phone: 800-899-8454
e-mail: info@wilsonlanguage.com
Website: www.wilsonlanguage.com

Program: Wilson Fundations
Author: Wilson Language Training

Information Provided By: Wilson Language Training

Appropriate for Ages/Grades: Grades K–3

Description: *Wilson Fundations* provides teachers in K–3 classrooms with a multisensory, systematic phonics, spelling, and handwriting program that benefits all students. *Fundations* activities address all five areas of reading instruction identified by the National Reading Panel (2000; phonemic awareness, phonics and word study, fluency, vocabulary, comprehension) in an integrated approach. The power of the program is that it overlaps skills and does not address these in isolation. Handwriting and spelling skills are directly taught and reinforced so that students have a strong foundation for writing.

Fundations is based on the *Wilson Reading System* principles, with its research-based, multisensory, structured, systematic, cumulative, and explicit approach. As a prevention program, *Fundations* is included in the word study block of the core language arts program for *all* students. It is also appropriate as an early intervention program for students at risk. The goal is to provide the necessary critical skills in a multisensory approach to resolve learning difficulties before they become severe. Moreover, because progress monitoring is built into the program, students who require a more intensive program such as *Wilson Reading System* can be identified early—before undergoing years of struggle with reading and spelling. *Fundations* provides a multitiered system of support:

- Prevention Model (Tier 1)—The Standard Lesson is provided to all students in the general education classroom for 30 minutes daily.
- Strategic Intervention (Tier 2)—For at-risk students in need of strategic intervention *Fundations* is conducted in a small-group setting. If *Fundations* is *already* provided in a Tier 1, whole-class setting, this strategic intervention consists of double dose lessons for an additional 30 minutes 3–5 times per week. If *Fundations* is *not* provided in a Tier 1, whole-class setting, the strategic intervention must also include the daily standard lesson plus the double dose lesson, totaling 60-minute lessons 3–5 times per week.

Fundations can be part of a multitiered literacy solution, including a literature-based language arts program in grades K–3; *Just Words*, an intervention program for grades 4–12 and adults; and *Wilson Reading System*, an intensive intervention program for grades 2–12 and adults.

Materials and Content: *Fundations* provides K–3 materials for teachers and students. Teacher materials, available for each level along with a multilevel option, include an explicit manual plus a CD with lesson demonstrations. To aid classroom instruction, teachers use sound/syllable/word cards, sentence and syllable frames, reference posters, and Echo the owl puppet, an effective tool to prompt student responses. Extensive additional resources are available online via membership in the Prevention/Early Intervention Learning Community. Student materials and manipulatives, including a magnetic letter board and letter tiles, a dry erase writing tablet, and various notebooks are used in multisensory, interactive activities. In addition, Home Support Packs for each level encourage parental involvement.

Evidence of Effectiveness: *Fundations* was developed based on the evidence of effectiveness of the *Wilson Reading System* (WRS). Ten years of data collected from school districts experiencing success using WRS led to the creation of *Fundations*, a research-based program designed to bring explicit, cumulative, systematic, and multisensory reading instruction to K–3 general education classrooms. An independent review of *Fundations* by the Florida Center for Reading Research (www.fcrr.org) noted that the content and instructional design of the program are aligned with current reading research. The report noted that *Fundations* aligns with Reading First and its research requirements. Additional information regarding the effectiveness of the program is also provided (wilsonlanguage.com).

Teacher Training: The goal is to work collaboratively with districts to improve student outcomes by fully implementing the Wilson programs with increasing fidelity. To implement *Fundations*, Wilson recommends:

For Tier 1: *Fundations* workshops for Levels K, 1, 2, and 3, and at least two Coaching Visits throughout the year.

For Tier 2 settings: *Fundations* workshops for Levels K, 1, 2, and 3, and at least two Coaching Visits for the intervention setting throughout the year. In addition, the Fundations Intervention and Progress Monitoring Workshop focuses on the Double Dose lesson and the use of the *Fundations* curriculum-based measurement tool to monitor progress. Finally, the *Wilson Fluency/Basic* Workshop instructs teachers in how to help students who are not reading fluently due to decoding deficits.

To help districts move toward fidelity and sustainability, additional coaching visits and courses are recommended, as well as the development of site-based *Fundations* Facilitators and a District Presenter. Furthermore, extensive *Fundations* support is available online via the Prevention Learning Community of Wilson Academy.

Contact and Ordering Information:
Wilson Language Training
47 Old Webster Road

Oxford, MA 01540
Phone: 800-899-8454
e-mail: info@wilsonlanguage.com
Website: www.wilsonlanguage.com

Program: Wilson Just Words
Author: Wilson Language Training
Information Provided By: Wilson Language Training
Appropriate for Ages/Grades: Grades 4–12 and adults
Description: *Wilson Just Words* is a word-level intervention program. A highly explicit, multisensory decoding and spelling program, it is "just the word study" part of *Wilson Reading System* at an accelerated pace. The program is appropriate for students in grades 4–12 and adults with mild-to-moderate gaps in decoding and spelling. *Just Words* progresses through the six English syllable types and the most common Latin roots. It features sound-symbol correspondence as related to syllable patterns; study of phonetically regular and high frequency irregular words; orthographic (spelling) rules; and morphology patterns of prefixes, roots, and suffixes.

Just Words can be part of a multitiered literacy solution that includes *Fundations*, a phonics and spelling program for grades K–3 (a component of a literature-based language arts program); *Just Words*, an intervention program for grades 4–12; and *Wilson Reading System*, an intensive intervention program for grades 2–12. *Just Words* is also very appropriate for use in adult literacy settings.

Materials and Content: *Just Words* provides materials for teachers and students. Teacher materials include an instructor manual with detailed instruction and controlled text resources for each of the 14 units and 2 bonus units. Each unit takes an average of 2 weeks. Instruction is designed to be implemented 5 days per week, 45 minutes per session, in a year-long curriculum in a class of up to 15 students. The curriculum can also be presented three days per week but will then be completed over a year and a half.

To aid classroom instruction, teachers use sound/syllable/word cards, syllable and suffix frames, a reference chart, additional resources and planning materials via the online Intervention Learning Community, and *Just Words* InterActivities, an optional interactive whiteboard application. Student materials and manipulatives, including a magnetic journal and letter tiles, a dry erase writing tablet, and workbooks, are used in a multisensory, interactive way.

Evidence of Effectiveness: *Just Words* was developed based on the evidence of effectiveness of the *Wilson Reading System* (WRS). Almost two decades of data collected from school districts experiencing success using WRS led to the creation of *Just Words*, a research-based program designed to bring word-level intervention to students in grades 4–12. Specific evidence of effectiveness is also provided (wilsonlanguage.com).

Teacher Training: To implement *Just Words*, Wilson recommends the Just Words Introductory workshop and at least two Coaching Visits throughout the year. Teachers also have extensive *Just Words* support via the online Intervention Learning Community of Wilson Academy that includes lesson planning, animated demonstrations, printable teaching aids, and monthly expert tips and a discussion board monitored by literacy specialists. To help districts move toward fidelity and sustainability, additional coaching visits and courses are recommended, as well as the development of site-based *Just Words* Facilitators and a District Presenter. The goal is to work collaboratively with districts to improve student outcomes by fully implementing the Wilson programs with increasing fidelity.

Contact and Ordering Information:
Wilson Language Training
47 Old Webster Road
Oxford, MA 01540
Phone: 800-899-8454
e-mail: info@wilsonlanguage.com
Website: www.wilsonlanguage.com

Program: Wilson Reading System
Author: Wilson Language Training
Information Provided By: Cara O'Connor and Ellen Feldman
Appropriate for Ages/Grades: Grades 2–12 and adult
Description: The *Wilson Reading System (WRS)* is an intensive program for students in grades 2–12 and adults who are making insufficient progress in intervention or who may require intensive multisensory language instruction due to dyslexia or other language-based learning disabilities. The *WRS* is based on Orton-Gillingham multisensory philosophy and principles and reading research. It is a highly structured remedial program that directly teaches the structure of the language, focusing first on basic word skills, and then on more complex language structure, including morphological principles. *WRS* provides extensive instruction in phonemic awareness, phonics, fluency, vocabulary, and comprehension.

- Offers a research-based program with 20 years of data collected and analyzed from school districts implementing the program.

- Follows a 10-part lesson plan that addresses decoding, encoding, high frequency or sight word instruction, oral reading fluency, vocabulary, and comprehension in a sensible and logical fashion.
- Provides a systematic and cumulative approach to teach total word structure for decoding and encoding.
- Aids teachers by making all instruction multisensory and interactive.
- Uses a unique "sound tapping" system early in the program to help students segment and blend sounds.
- Has one of the most extensive collections of controlled and decodable text (word lists, sentences, stories) for students beyond the primary grades.
- Provides two levels of vocabulary, one appropriate for elementary students, ELL students, and those with limited vocabulary; the other for older students and adults with advanced vocabularies.
- Uses criterion-based assessments built into the program to measure student progress and success.
- Is a comprehensive program that can follow students from grade to grade.

WRS can be part of a multitiered literacy solution that includes: *Fundations,* a phonics and spelling program for grades K–3 (a component of a literature-based language arts program); *Just Words,* a word-level intervention program for grades 4–12; and *WRS,* an intensive intervention program for grades 2–12. *WRS* is very appropriate for adult literacy settings.

Materials and Content: *WRS* provides materials for teachers and students. Teacher materials include an instructor manual, with program implementation guidelines and lesson procedures for all 12 steps of the program; the *Wilson Assessment of Decoding and Encoding (WADE),* a criterion-referenced tool used for pretesting and post testing; a Rules Notebook of basic English language rules; and Dictation Books with extensive word lists and sentences.

The WRS directly teaches the structure of English words with an organized and sequential system of 12 steps. All 12 steps address word study, fluency, vocabulary, and comprehension. The instruction becomes increasingly demanding in each of these areas as the program progresses. Mastery of each component of a step is required to advance to the next step.

Steps 1–2: The student learns to blend and segment sounds. At the end of Step 2, the student is able to fluently blend and segment up to six sounds in a closed syllable.

Step 3: The focus is on multisyllabic words. The student continues to study the six different syllable types in the English language that are taught systematically through the next six steps.

Steps 4–6: The vowel-consonant-e syllable, open syllable, consonant-le syllable, and suffix endings are taught.

Steps 7–12: The r-controlled syllable, vowel teams, and complex word structures, as well as spelling options, spelling rules, and more advanced morphology are taught.

Throughout the 12 steps, the student engages in instruction in:

• Word Study: Word Study instruction is provided, and the student is given extensive practice with controlled text for decoding and spelling application. In addition to working with phonetically regular words, the student learns to read and spell high frequency words.

• Fluency: Fluency instruction is provided using a scooping technique, introduced in Step 1, which provides a graphical representation of phrasing. Guided oral reading is done with progressively more challenging text.

• Vocabulary and Comprehension: Vocabulary and comprehension instruction are included to develop vocabulary, background knowledge, and comprehension. Instruction shifts from listening to reading comprehension as students progress through the steps. Students maintain a notebook of targeted vocabulary words selected for their high utility. Comprehension Instruction is provided using the Comprehension S.O.S. process (for **S**top, **O**rient, **S**caffold/**S**upport). This strategy was developed by Wilson to help students learn how to visualize and understand both narrative and expository text.

Each 10-part lesson is divided into 3 blocks: parts 1–5 emphasize word study, parts 6–8 emphasize spelling, and parts 9–10 emphasize fluency and comprehension. *WRS* classes are taught by (or under the direct guidance of) a *WRS*-certified instructor. Instruction is delivered 3–5 times per week for 60–90 minutes in a tutorial or a small group setting of up to 6 students. Depending on the frequency and intensity of delivery, the entire 12-step curriculum can take up to 2–3 years to complete.

To aid classroom instruction, teachers use sound/syllable/word cards, sentence and syllable frames, reference posters, and online materials. Student materials and manipulatives include a student reader with controlled word lists, sentences, and stories for each WRS step, a magnetic journal with color-coded letter tiles for word-part manipulation, workbooks, and story books for older students.

Evidence of Effectiveness: An independent review of *Wilson Reading System* by the Florida Center for Reading Research (www.fcrr.org) noted that the content and instructional design of the program are aligned with current reading research. The report states, "The Wilson Reading System provides extensive instruction in phonemic awareness, phonics, fluency, vocabulary, and comprehension." In summation, it states, "Our conclusion from reviewing current research on the Wilson Reading System is that it is consistent with the idea that the program can be used effectively to help 'close the gap' in reading skills for struggling readers." In the *closing the reading gap study*, a modified version of WRS was implemented that focused only on the word-level components (Torgesen et al., 2006). The investigators reported statistically significant effects in the area of alphabetics. The statistical significance of these findings was confirmed by the What Works Clearinghouse (WWC) and considered substantively important according to WWC criteria. A study, conducted at the Center for Cognitive Brain Imaging at Carnegie Mellon University, used fMRI to gauge the impact of intensive remedial instruction on the brain (Meyler, Keller, Cherkassy, Gabrieli, & Just, 2008). The *Wilson Reading System* was one of the programs selected to be used for instruction. The results of the study indicated that with intensive remedial instruction, the brain of a poor reader can be permanently rewired to function similarly to the brain of a good reader. Additional evidence of program effectiveness is also provided at wilsonlanguage.com.

Teacher Training: Wilson has focused on teacher support and professional development since 1992, and works collaboratively with school districts and literacy organizations to improve student outcomes by fully implementing the Wilson programs with increasing fidelity. Comprehensive support and professional development include *WRS* Level I and Level II certification programs (requiring introductory workshops, comprehensive online coursework, student practicum, and teacher observations). Wilson teachers have online access to robust course content, additional resources (such as animated demonstrations, printable teaching aids, and weekly paired decodable/enriched text passages), and a discussion board and chat via the Intensive Learning Community of Wilson Academy. To help school districts and literacy organizations move toward sustainability, the comprehensive *WRS* Trainer Development Program is recommended. Wilson is recognized by the National Staff Development Council as one of the programs for inclusion in their research-based initiative, "*What Works in K–12 Literacy Staff Development.*"

Contact and Ordering Information:
Wilson Language Training
47 Old Webster Road
Oxford, MA 01540
Phone: 800-899-8454
e-mail: info@wilsonlanguage.com
Website: www.wilsonlanguage.com

REFERENCES

Meyler, A., Keller, T. A., Cherkassy, V. L, Gabrieli, J. D. E., & Just, M. A. (2008). Modifying the brain activation of poor readers during sentence comprehension with extended remedial instruction: A longitudinal study of neuroplasticity. *Neuropsychologia, 46,* 2580–2592.

Torgesen, J. K., Myers, D., Schirm, A., Stuart, E., Vartivarian, S., Mansfield, W., . . . & Haan, C. (2006). Closing the reading gap: First year findings from a randomized trial of four reading interventions for striving readers. *Volume II: National Assessment of Title I: Interim Report to Congress.* Washington, DC: Institute of Education Sciences.

Program: WORDS, 2nd Edition

Author: Marcia K. Henry, Ph.D.

Information Provided By: Marcia K. Henry

Appropriate for Ages/Grades: Ages 10–15; Grades 3–9, general education; Grades 4–12, special education.

Description: This program provides integrated decoding and spelling instruction based on word origin and word structure. *WORDS* includes five units of instruction: Letter-Sound Correspondences; Syllable Patterns; Anglo-Saxon, Latin, and Greek Layers of Language; Morphemes (prefixes, suffixes, Latin roots, Greek combining forms); and Strategies for Decoding and Spelling Long, Unfamiliar Words. The program also contains pretests, post-tests, and unit quizzes as well as reproducible materials for reinforcement on CD-ROM. The *WORDS* program evolved from the author's doctoral dissertation and served as the basis for the intervention study.

Evidence of Effectiveness: The program is used in several Masonic Children's Learning Center training programs. (See also References.)

Teacher Training: All necessary training is provided in the manual.

Contact and Ordering Information:

PRO-ED, Inc.

8700 Shoal Creek Blvd.

Austin, TX 78757-6897

Phone: 800-897-3202

Website: www.proedinc.com

REFERENCES

Berninger, V., Nagy, W., Carlisle, J., Thomson, J., Hoffer, D., Abbott, S., et al. (2003). Effective treatment for dyslexics in grades 4–6: Behavioral and brain evidence. In B. Foorman (Ed.), *Preventing and remediating reading difficulties: Bringing science to scale* (pp. 275–308). Timonium, MD: York Press.

Henry, M. K. (1988a). Beyond phonics: Integrated decoding and spelling instruction based on word origin and structure. *Annals of Dyslexia, 38*, 259–275.

Henry, M. K. (1988b). Understanding English orthography: Assessment and instruction for decoding and spelling. *Dissertation Abstracts International, 48*, 2841-A. (University Microfilms No. 88-00,951).

Henry, M. K. (1989). Children's word structure knowledge: Implications for decoding and spelling instruction. *Reading and Writing, 2*, 135–152.

Program: Wordy Qwerty: Foundations for Reading & Writing Fluency

Author: Jeannine Herron, Ph.D.

Information Provided By: Talking Fingers, Inc.

Appropriate for Ages/Grades: Ages 7–10

Description: *Wordy Qwerty,* funded by the National Institute of Child Health and Human Development, demystifies spelling and makes it fun to learn to spell new words. This software is designed for 7–10 year olds who have learned the basics of word encoding and decoding and are poised to master more complex spelling skills. *Wordy Qwerty* uses games, songs, rhymes, and storytelling to teach children 20 spelling rules, introduce them to word families, and challenge them with "outlaw words." Familiarity with spelling conventions and the structure of words, and how parts of words are combined and recombined, is critical for comprehension and fluency. Children confidently tackle new words because they have learned the strategies and rules that will help them succeed.

In each of 20 lessons, children do 6 activities: (1) learn to recognize spelling patterns in words and use them to spell new words, (2) learn a karaoke song that represents an important spelling rule, (3) learn to recognize and spell homonyms, (4) learn to recognize and spell "outlaw" words by popping the correct word balloons, (5) write dictated four-line stories (improving their typing skills), and (6) read stories and fill in missing words, developing comprehension and fluency. The stories include words that use the spelling rule or "outlaw words" learned in that lesson.

The storyline for *Wordy Qwerty* involves two engaging characters: Midi the musician and Qwerty the word coach. They enlist children to help them accumulate "spheres" that are needed to play Midi's amazing music machine. As a reward, players get to see the amazing music machine being built, and after every four lessons they get to see a part of the music machine play (animated machines are by Animusic).

Wordy Qwerty is available as a hybrid CD (upgraded for any operating system) or it can be played online by purchasing yearly subscriptions.

Evidence of Effectiveness: Research on the effectiveness of *Wordy Qwerty* is still in progress. However, there are many testimonials at www.talkingfingers .com to attest to its effectiveness in practical classroom situations, and with individual students who are struggling with reading and spelling. *Wordy Qwerty* includes a periodic spelling assessment that is scored and can be displayed or printed out for individual or class records.

Teacher Training: Downloadable materials and videos can be found at www.talkingfingers.com for introducing teachers and parents to *Wordy Qwerty*. Training webinars can be arranged by contacting Talking Fingers.

Contact and Ordering Information:

Talking Fingers

830 Rincon Way

San Rafael, CA 94903

Phone: 415-472-3103 or 415-342-3080

e-mail: herron@talkingfingers.com

Website: www.talkingfingers.com

GLOSSARY

A

accuracy *See* **reading accuracy.**

ADHD Abbreviation for attention deficit hyperactivity disorder.

affix An element added to a base word to form a new word (e.g., prefixes and suffixes).

alexia A reading problem that results from a brain injury, sometimes referred to as *acquired alexia.*

alphabetic mapping Phonological decoding, or the ability to translate a printed word into its corresponding phonemes.

alphabetic orthography A writing system that uses symbols to represent the sounds existent in a given language, e.g., English.

alphabetic principle The basic understanding that spoken language is made up of speech sounds (phonemes) that can be represented by a letter or letter string (grapheme).

ability-achievement discrepancy *See* **discrepancy formula.**

analogy phonics approach An instructional approach that teaches new words by analogy to known words. For example, if the person knows the word *think,* then the rime *-ink* can be used to learn unfamiliar words such as *brink, sink,* or *blink.* Word families are often used in this approach.

analytic phonics approach An instructional phonics approach which teaches analysis of whole words to detect phonetic and orthographic patterns then splits them into smaller parts. Assumes some level of phonemic awareness is present.

anterior Situated at the front, such as the front portion of the brain (as used here).

aphasia An acquired language disorder resulting from brain damage in which one or several language modalities are affected.

apps Short form of applications commonly used for files that can be downloaded from the web that are designed for specific purposes.

assistive technology (AT) Hardware or software that improves the functional capabilities of individuals with disabilities.

attention deficit hyperactivity disorder (ADHD) A condition characterized by inattention, impulsivity, and hyperactivity.

automaticity The ability to read a word immediately without conscious use of effort or attention.

axon An appendage, or tail, of a neuron that sends electrical signals to other neurons.

B

blending The ability to combine individual sounds together to create spoken words.

brainstem The lower portion of the brain that connects with the spinal cord and controls reflexes, e.g., breathing.

Broca's area An anterior system in the inferior frontal gyrus of the brain that is associated with articulation and also serves an important function in word analysis.

C

cerebellum A part of the brain that coordinates voluntary movements.

cerebral cortex The neural tissue that covers the cerebrum and is folded in on itself, giving the brain its characteristic appearance of ridges and furrows.

cerebrum Largest part of the brain, divided into two hemispheres.

closed syllable A syllable consisting of a short vowel followed by one or more consonants.

co-articulation When saying a word aloud, the phonemes, or sounds, overlap and are not heard individually.

cognate A word that has a similar look and meaning in two different languages (e.g., *telephone* and *teléfono*).

cognitive Of, or pertaining to, cognition (mental processes).

comorbidity Two different disorders that are present within an individual, but do not cause each other.

complex syllable A syllable containing one or more consonant clusters.

concept map Also known as *graphic organizers* or *mind maps*, helps students organize and synthesize information.

consolidated alphabetic reading A reading stage characterized by accurate and automatic reading; the reader uses both orthographic and morphological knowledge.

consolidated alphabetic writing A writing stage characterized by awareness of many conventions of English orthography.

conventional spelling The final spelling stage where the writer incorporates knowledge of phonology, orthography, and morphology into spelling attempts.

correlate An underlying ability that is associated with performance, (e.g., phonemic awareness and dyslexia).

D

decodable text Reading materials that are used to practice common phonic elements; includes words with regular sound-symbol correspondences (e.g., *hat, cat, rat*).

decoding Applying knowledge of sound-symbol correspondences to correctly pronounce a written word; word recognition.

deep dyslexia A type of dyslexia that is characterized by semantic errors and severely impaired nonword reading. Often defined as an acquired reading disorder following a stroke or head injury.

deep orthography A written language that does not have a one-to-one correspondence between the phonemes (speech sounds) and graphemes (written letters). Words are not always spelled the way they sound and are influenced by orthography, morphology, and various syllable structures.

dendrites The branching process of a neuron that receives electrical impulses from other neurons.

developmental dyslexia *See* **dyslexia.**

differentiated instruction (DI) A framework for instructional planning that maximizes student learning through flexible approaches; suggests how to vary the content, process, or product to meet individual student needs.

diffusion tensor imaging (DTI) A variation of an MRI that allows study of the connections between different parts of the brain by revealing the directionality and magnitude of water diffusion in the brain.

digraph Two adjacent consonant or vowel letters that make one new sound (e.g., *ph, oa*).

diphthong Two adjacent vowel sounds that slide together when pronounced (e.g., *ou, ow, oi*, and *oy*) and make a new sound.

discrepancy formula A formula that predicts a person's potential for reading, based on the difference, or discrepancy, between measured intelligence and the achievement area.

double-deficit theory of dyslexia Having a deficit in both phonemic awareness and rapid automatized naming.

dysfluent Lacking automaticity of decoding or encoding.

dyslexia A neurobiological disorder that causes a marked impairment in the development of basic reading and spelling skills.

E

Elkonin method A method for teaching phoneme-grapheme relations by using boxes or tiles to represent each sound in a word.

ELL English language learner; someone whose first language is not English.

embedded phonics An implicit approach that embeds phonics instruction within text reading. Often used in conjunction with a whole language approach.

encoding Spelling, translating speech sounds into graphemes.

explicit instruction An approach that involves direct instruction; the teacher demonstrates the task, provides guided practice with immediate corrective feedback, before the student attempts the task independently.

F

fissures Large sulci (grooves) in the cerebral cortex of the brain.

fluency The ability to read a text accurately, quickly, and with appropriate expression.

frontal lobe The front part of both brain hemispheres; plays a critical role in higher mental functioning, e.g., executive functioning.

full alphabetic A reading phase characterized by accurate connections between sounds and letters.

functional magnetic resonance imaging (fMRI) A technique that measures brain activity by detecting changes in blood oxygenation and flow that occur while performing a specific task.

G

genes Hereditary units located on chromosomes that instruct cells what to do.

genome Contains all the biological information needed to build a human and consists of 20,000–25,000 genes, based on current estimates.

genotype The inherited characteristics; the genetic makeup of an organism.

grapheme The fundamental print unit in a written language; graphemes are used to represent phonemes, but also include both numbers and punctuation marks.

gyrus (plural: gyri) The raised, smooth areas, sometimes referred to as *ridges*, in the cerebral cortex of the brain.

I

IEP Individualized Education Program; a written plan required by law for all students who are eligible for special education services under IDEA, 2004.

IT Instructional technology readily available in classrooms for use by all students.

L

lexical access   The process of retrieving and producing the target sound, syllable, or word from memory.

linguistic   Of or belonging to language.

logographic orthography   A writing system that uses visual symbols to represent whole words or word parts, rather than individual sounds (phonemes).

M

memory span   The ability to listen to information and then repeat it verbatim within a short period of time.

morpheme   Smallest unit of meaning in a language (e.g., -*s* signals plural).

morphology   The identification, analysis, and description of the structure of morphemes and other units of meaning in a language.

multisensory teaching methods   Instructional methods that involve multiple senses (e.g., seeing, saying, tracing) to teach a skill, such as print-sound awareness and reading.

myelinated   Wrapped with myelin, a fatty, white neurological matter, which serves as an electrical insulator and speeds electrical impulses between neurons.

N

neural signature for dyslexia   Disruption of posterior reading systems during reading real words and pseudowords that is observed in readers with dyslexia during fMRI studies.

neurobiological   Having to do with the anatomy and physiology of the nervous system.

neurodevelopmental   Having to do with the development of the nervous system.

neuron   A specialized cell that is the main functional unit of the nervous system.

nonsense words   *See* **pseudowords.**

O

occipital lobe   The part of the brain involved in visuospatial processing; located in the back of the brain; referred to as the *visual cortex.*

OCR   Optical character recognition; software that converts printed text to digital text.

onset   The initial consonant or consonants in a syllable that precede the vowel.

orthography   The writing system of a language, including the spelling, punctuation, and capitalization rules.

orthographic awareness   The ability to perceive and manipulate aspects of a writing system and the visual aspects of reading and spelling, such as the letters, letter patterns, and words.

Orton-Gillingham   A multisensory instructional method for teaching reading and spelling.

P

paired-associate learning   The learning of items in pairs, e.g., sounds and symbols.

parietal lobe   The part of the brain that perceives and interprets sensations and contains the primary sensory-motor cortex.

partial alphabetic   An emergent reading skill characterized by some connection between sounds and letters, particularly consonants and long vowel sounds.

perceptual processing   The ability to make sense of information taken in through the senses (i.e., vision, hearing, touch).

phenotype   The observable characteristics that result from the interaction of genetics and environment.

phoneme-grapheme connections   The relationships between the speech sounds (phonemes) and the spellings (graphemes).

phonemes   The individual speech sounds of spoken language.

phonemic awareness   The ability to recognize that words are composed of discrete segments of speech sounds.

phonetic spelling   Spellings that demonstrate phoneme-grapheme correspondence; the words are spelled the way they sound even though the correct letter combinations are not used.

phonics   An instructional reading method for teaching the relationships between sounds and letters and how to represent those sounds in writing.

phonics through spelling   An instructional approach that teaches the student to segment a word into its phonemes and then select the letters that represent each phoneme to spell the word. This approach teaches the student to spell phonetically.

phonological awareness   The ability to perceive and manipulate the sounds, word parts, or words of a language.

phonological dyslexia   A type of dyslexia characterized by difficulty with speech sounds such as connecting sounds to letters and sounding out words. Sometimes referred to as *auditory,* or *dysphonetic, dyslexia.*

phonology   The study of the speech sounds of a language.

planum temporale   An area of the brain involved in processing speech.

podcast   A digital media file on the Internet that can be downloaded and played on a computer or MP3 player; can be audio only or video and audio.

posterior   Situated toward the back of the brain.

prealphabetic reading   An early stage in reading in which words are recognized based on the environmental cues (e.g., saying "Stop" when looking at a stop sign).

prephonetic spelling   An early stage of writing characterized by using random letters to spell a word or to communicate a message.

processing speed   The ability to quickly and accurately perform simple cognitive tasks.

prosody   The rhythms and intonations of a language (i.e., expression).

pseudowords   Nonsense words or nonwords that conform to English spelling rules and patterns.

R

rapid automatized naming (RAN)   The ability to name quickly familiar objects or symbols.

reading accuracy   The ability to recognize or decode words correctly.

reading rate   Speed of reading at the single word level or at the connected text level.

rime   The ending part of the English syllable that begins with a vowel (e.g., *-ay*).

S

schwa   Neutral vowel sound that may represent vowels with nondistinct or neutral pronunciation; usually in unaccented syllables.

segmentation   The ability to break apart spoken words into syllables or phonemes.

semiphonetic spelling   An emergent writing stage characterized by the use of a few correct letters to represent the main sounds in a word.

shallow orthography   *See* **transparent orthography.**

SLD   Specific learning disability.

SLI   Specific language impairment.

social bookmarking   A web service that promotes the research process.

Specific Learning Disability   A broad category that includes several types of learning disorders, including dyslexia.

SR   Speech recognition software that converts the spoken word to printed text.

SSD   Speech sound disorder.

strephosymbolia A term coined by Orton to describe reversal errors in reading and writing that literally means "twisted symbols."

sulcus (plural: sulci) The grooves or furrows in the cerebral cortex of the brain.

supramarginal gyri Located in the back of the left hemisphere of the brain; thought to be critical for reading.

surface dyslexia A type of dyslexia characterized by difficulty with whole word recognition and spelling especially when the words have irregular spelling-sound correspondences. Individuals with this type of dyslexia are sometimes referred to as having *visual*, or *dyseidetic, dyslexia.*

syllabic orthography A writing system that uses a symbol to represent every syllable in the spoken language in writing.

syllable A unit of speech containing one vowel sound, with or without surrounding consonants.

synthetic phonics approach An instructional phonics approach that begins with explicit teaching of single sounds and how to represent those sounds with graphemes and then blend the sounds to pronounce words.

T

tactile-kinesthetic A learning approach that involves touching, experiencing, moving, and doing.

temporal lobe Located on the sides of the brain; associated with sound perception and interpretation.

temporal processing The rate at which auditory information is processed by the brain.

text to speech (TTS) Software or operating system option that allows text on the screen to be read aloud.

transparent orthography A writing system that has nearly one-to-one correspondence between sounds and the written symbols that represent them; also referred to as *shallow orthography.*

U

unexpected underachievement When an aspect of one's academic performance is below her other abilities (e.g., oral language, reasoning, general intelligence).

universal design for learning (UDL) A framework for instructional planning that addresses the needs of a wide range of students and minimizes the need for adaptations.

V

visual crowding The visual stimuli surrounding the target word interfere with perception; words or letters in the periphery compete for attention thus requiring many more fixations to identify the target word.

VWFA (visual word form area) An area of the brain thought to be instrumental in the rapid recognition of words.

W

Wernicke's area An area in the temporal lobe that is associated with verbal memory and the understanding of language.

word blindness An early term used to define a type of dyslexia where an individual had trouble memorizing and recalling the visual images of words.

working memory The capacity to hold information in immediate awareness while manipulating or transforming that information in some way.

REFERENCES

Aaron, P. G., Joshi, R. M., & Quatroche, D. (2008). *Becoming a professional reading teacher*. Baltimore, MD: Paul H. Brookes.

Abu-Hamour, B. (2010). The relationships among cognitive ability measures and irregular word, non-word, and word reading. *Thalamus, 26*(1), 41–50.

Adams, M. J. (1990). *Beginning to read: Thinking and learning about print*. Cambridge, MA: MIT Press.

Adams, M. J., & Bruck, M. (1995). Resolving the "Great Debate." *American Educator, 19*, 7–20.

AFB Consulting. (2009). *Accessing PDF documents with assistive technology: A screen readers user's guide*. Accessed from www.adobe.com/accessibility/pdfs/accessing-pdf-sr.pdf

Alexander, A. W., & Slinger-Constant, A. (2004). Current status of treatments for dyslexia: Critical review. *Journal of Child Neurology, 19*, 744–758. PMid:15559890

Allport, S. (1986). *Explorers of the black box: The search for the cellular basis of memory*. New York, NY: W. W. Norton.

American Psychiatric Association. (2000). *Diagnostic and statistical manual of mental disorders* (4th ed., text rev.). Washington, DC: Author.

Anderson, P. L., & Meier-Hedde, R. (2001). Early case reports of dyslexia in the United States and Europe. *Journal of Learning Disabilities, 34*, 9–21. doi:10.1177/002221940103400102

Anthony, J. L., & Francis, D. J. (2005). Development of phonological awareness. *Current Directions in Psychological Science, 14*, 255–259. doi:10.1111/j.0963-7214.2005.00376.x

Arena, J. (1978). An interview with Samuel Kirk. *Academic Therapy, 13*, 617–620.

Armbruster, B. B., Lehr, F., & Osborn, J. (2001). *Put reading first: The research building blocks for teaching children to read*. Jessup, MD: National Institute for Literacy.

Atwill, K., Blanchard, J., Christie, J., Gorin, J., & García, H. (2010). English-language learners: Implications of limited vocabulary for cross-language transfer of phonemic awareness with kindergartners. *Journal of Hispanic Higher Education, 9*, 104–129. doi:10.1177/1538192708330431

Babayiğit, S., & Stainthorp, R. (2011). Modeling the relationships between cognitive-linguistic skills and literacy skills: New insights from a transparent orthography. *Journal of Educational Psychology, 14*, 169–189. doi:10.1037/a0021671

Baddeley, A. (2003). Working memory: Looking back and looking forward. *Nature Reviews, Neuroscience, 4*, 828–839. doi:10.1038/nrn1201

Baddeley, A. D., & Hitch, G. (1974). Working memory. In G. A. Bower (Ed.), *The psychology of learning and motivation* (pp. 47–90). London: Academic Press.

Baird, G., Slonims, V., Simonoff, E., & Dworzynski, K. (2011, May). Impairment in non-word repetition: A marker for language impairment or reading impairment? *Developmental Medicine & Child Neurology,* doi:10.1111/j.1469-8749.2011.03936.x. [Epub ahead of print]

Bakwin, H. (1973). Reading disability in twins. *Developmental Medicine and Child Neurology, 5*, 184–187. doi:10.1111/j.1469-8749.1973.tb15158.x

Banister, S. (2010). Integrating the iPod Touch in K–12 education: Visions and vices. *Computers in the Schools, 27*(2), 121–131. doi:10.1080/07380561003801590

Bear, D., Invernizzi, M., Templeton, S., & Johnston, F. (2007). *Words their way: Word study for phonics, vocabulary, and spelling instruction* (4th ed.). Columbus, OH: Allyn & Bacon.

Begeny, J. C., Daly, E. J., & Vallely, R. J. (2006). Improving oral reading fluency through response opportunities: A comparison of phase drill error correction with repeated readings. *Journal of Behavioral Education, 15*, 229–235. doi:10.1007/s10864-006-9028-4

Bekebrede, J., van der Leji, A., Plakas, A., Share, D., & Morfidi, E. (2010). Dutch dyslexia in adulthood: Core features and variety. *Scientific Studies of Reading, 14*, 183–210. doi:10.1080/10888430903117500

Benjamini, Y. (2008). Comment: Microarrays, empirical Bayes and the two-groups model. *Epidemiology, 23*(1), 23–28. doi:10.1214/07-STS236B

Berkhan, O. (February 1885). Über die Störung der Schriftsprache bei Halbidioten und ihre Ähnlichkeit mit dem Stammeln [About the disorder of written language of half-idiots and their similarity with dislalia]. *Archiv für Psychiatrie und Nervenkrankenheiten, 16*(1), 78–86. doi:10.1007/BF02227300

Berlin, R. (1884). Über Dyslexie [About dyslexia]. *Archiv fur Psychiatrie, 15*, 276–278.

Berninger, V. (1990). Multiple orthographic codes: Key to instructional interventions for developing orthographic-phonological connections underlying word identification. *School Psychology Review, 19*, 518–533.

Berninger, V. W. (2011). Evidence-based differential diagnosis and treatment of reading disabilities with and without comorbidities in oral language, writing, and math. In D. P. Flanagan & V. C. Alfonso (Eds.). *Essentials of specific learning disability identification* (pp. 203–232). Hoboken, NJ: John Wiley & Sons.

Berninger, V., & Fayol, M. (2008). Why spelling is important and how to teach it effectively. *Encyclopedia of Language and Literacy Development* (pp. 1–13). London, ON: Canadian Language and Literacy Research Network. www.literacyencyclopedia.ca/pdfs/topic.php?topId=234

Berninger, V. W., & May, M. O. (2011). Evidence-based diagnosis and treatment for specific learning disabilities involving impairments in written and/or oral language. *Journal of Learning Disabilities, 44,* 167–183. doi:10.1177/0022219410391189

Berninger, V. W., Nielsen, K. H., Abbott, R. D., Wijsman, E., & Raskind, W. (2008). Gender differences in severity of writing and reading disabilities. *Journal of School Psychology, 46,* 151–172. doi.org/10.1016/j.jsp.2007.02.007

Berninger, V., & Richards, T. (2010). Inter-relationships among behavioral markers, genes, brain and treatment in dyslexia and dysgraphia. *Future Neurology, 5,* 597–617. doi:10.2217/fnl.10.22

Berninger, V. W., & Wolf, B. J. (2009). *Teaching students with dyslexia and dysgraphia: Lessons from teaching and science.* Baltimore, MD: Paul H. Brookes.

Betts, E. A. (1936). *The prevention and correction of reading difficulties.* Evanston, IL: Row, Peterson and Company.

Betts, E. A. (1946). *Foundations of reading instruction.* New York, NY: American Book Company.

Bishop, D. V. M. (2009). Genes, cognition, and communication: Insights from neurodevelopmental disorders. *Annals of the New York Academy of Sciences, 1156,* 1–18. doi: 10.1111/j.1749-6632.2009.04419.x

Bishop, D. V. M., Adams, C. V., & Norbury, C. F. (2004). Using nonword repetition to distinguish genetic and environmental influences on early literacy development: A study of 6-year-old twins. *American Journal of Medical Genetics: Neuropsychiatric Genetics, 129,* 94–96. doi:10.1002/ajmg.b.30065

Bishop, D. V. M., & Snowling, M. J. (2004). Developmental dyslexia and specific language impairment: Same or different? *Psychological Bulletin, 130,* 858–888. doi:10.1037/0033-2909.130.6.858

Blevins, W. (2001). *Building fluency: Lessons and strategies for reading success.* New York, NY: Scholastic Professional Books.

Boada, R., Willcutt, E. G., Tunick, R. A., Chhabildas, N. A., Olson, R. K., DeFries, J. C., & Pennington, B. F. (2002). A twin study of the etiology of high reading ability. *Reading and Writing: An Interdisciplinary Journal, 15,* 683–707. doi:10.1023/A:1020965331768

Boder, E. (1971). Developmental dyslexia: Prevailing diagnostic concepts and a new diagnostic approach. In H. R. Myklebust (Ed.), *Progress in learning disabilities, 2* (pp. 293–321). New York, NY: Grune & Stratton.

Bowers, P. G. (1993). Text reading and rereading: Determinants of fluency beyond word recognition. *Journal of Reading Behavior, 25*(2), 133–153. doi:10.1080/10862969309547807

Bowers, P. G., & Swanson, L. B. (1991). Naming speed deficits in reading disability: Multiple measures of a singular process. *Journal of Experimental Child Psychology, 51,* 195–219. doi:10.1016/0022-0965(91)90032-N

Brady, S. A. (2011). Efficacy of phonics teaching for reading outcomes: Indications from post-NRP research. In S. A. Brady, D. Braze, & C. A. Fowler (Eds.),

Individual differences in reading: Theory and evidence (pp. 69–96). New York, NY: Psychology Press.

Brambati, S., Termine, C., Ruffino, M., Danna, M., Lanzi, G., Stella, G., . . . Perani, D. (2006). Neuropsychological deficits and neural dysfunction in familial dyslexia. *Brain Research, 1113*(1), 174–185. doi:10.1016/j.brainres.2006.06.099

Breznitz, Z. (2006). Fluency in reading: Synchronization of processes. Mahwah, NJ: Erlbaum.

Brice, R., & Brice, A. (2009). Investigation of phonemic awareness and phonic skills in Spanish-English bilingual and English-speaking kindergarten students. *Communication Disorders Quarterly, 30*, 208–225. doi:10.1177/1525740108327448

Brizzolara, D., Chilosi, A., Cipriani, P., Di Filippo, G., Gasperini, F., Mazzotti, S., . . . Zoccolotti, P. (2006). Do phonologic and rapid automatized naming deficits differentially affect dyslexic children with and without a history of language delay? A study of Italian dyslexic children. *Cognitive and Behavioral Neurology, 19*(3), 141–149. doi:10.1097/01.wnn.0000213902.59827.19

Broadbent, W. H. (1872). Cerebral mechanisms of speech and thought. *Transactions of the Royal Medical and Chirurgical Society, 55*, 145–194.

Brozo, W., & Puckett, K. (2009). *Supporting content area literacy with technology.* Boston, MA: Allyn & Bacon.

Bruck, M. (1992). Persistence of dyslexics' phonological awareness deficits. *Developmental Psychology, 28*, 874–886. doi:10.1037/0012-1649.28.5.874

Bruck, M. (1998). Outcomes of adults with childhood histories of dyslexia. In C. Hulme & R. Joshi (Eds.), *Cognitive and linguistic bases of reading, writing, and spelling* (pp. 179–200). Mahwah, NJ: Erlbaum.

Brunswick, N. (2010). Unimpaired reading development and dyslexia across different languages. In N. Brunswick, S. McDougall, & P. de Mornay Davies (Eds.), *Reading and dyslexia in different orthographies* (pp. 131–154). Hove, East Sussex: Psychology Press.

Bryant, D. P., Smith, D. D., & Bryant, B. (2008). *Teaching students with special needs in inclusive classrooms.* Boston, MA: Allyn & Bacon.

Budin, S. G., Mather, N., & Cheesman, E. (2010). Examining promising practices to improve linguistic knowledge and inform practice in teacher education. *Perspectives on Language and Literacy, 36*(4), 13–17.

Calhoon, M. B., Greenberg, D., & Hunter, C. V. (2010). A comparison of standardized spelling assessments: Do they measure similar orthographic qualities? *Learning Disability Quarterly, 33*, 159–170.

Caravolas, M. (2007). The nature and causes of dyslexia in different languages. In M. Snowling & C. Hulme (Eds.), *The science of reading: A handbook* (pp. 336–355). Malden, MA: Blackwell.

Carlisle, J. (2004). Morphological processes that influence learning to read. In A. Stone, E. Silliman, B. Ehren, & K. Apel (Eds.), *Handbook of language and literacy: Development and disorders* (pp. 318–339). New York, NY: Guilford Press.

Caron, C., & Rutter, M. (1991). Comorbidity in child psychopathology: Concepts, issues, and research strategies. *Journal of Child Psychology and Psychiatry, 32,* 1063–1080. doi:10.1111/j.1469-7610.1991.tb00350.x

Carreker, S. (2005a). Teaching reading: Accurate decoding and fluency. In J. R. Birsh (Ed.), *Multisensory teaching of basic language skills* (2nd ed., pp. 141–182). Baltimore, MD: Paul H. Brookes.

Carreker, S. (2005b). Teaching spelling. In J. R. Birsh (Ed.), *Multisensory teaching of basic language skills* (2nd ed., pp. 257–295). Baltimore, MD: Paul H. Brookes.

Carver, R. P. (1990). *Reading rate: A review of research and theory.* San Diego, CA: Academic Press.

Castles, A., & Coltheart, M. (1993). Varieties of developmental dyslexia. *Cognition, 47,* 149–180. doi:10.1023/A:1020965331768

Castles, A., & Coltheart, M. (2004). Is there a causal link from phonological awareness to success in learning to read? *Cognition, 91,* 77–111. doi:10.1016/S0010-0277(03)00164-1

Catts, H. W., & Adlof, S. (2011). Phonological and other language deficits associated with dyslexia. In S. A. Brady, D. Braze, & C. A. Fowler (Eds.). *Individual differences in reading: Theory and evidence* (pp. 137–151). New York, NY: Psychology Press.

Catts, H. W., Adlof, S. M., Hogan, T. P., & Ellis-Weismer, S. E. (2005). Are specific language impairment and dyslexia distinct disorders? *Journal of Speech, Language, and Hearing Research, 48,* 1378–1396. doi:10.1044/1092-4388(2005/096)

Chall, J. S. (1996). Stages of reading development (2nd ed.). Fort Worth, TX: Harcourt-Brace.

Chard, D. J., & Dickson, S. V. (1999). Phonological awareness: Instructional and assessment guidelines. *Intervention in School and Clinic, 34,* 261–270. doi:10.1177/105345129903400502

Chard, D. J., Vaughn, S., & Tyler, B. (2002). A synthesis of research on effective interventions for building reading fluency with elementary students with learning disabilities. *Journal of Learning Disabilities, 35,* 386–406. doi:10.1177/00222194020 350050101

Christo, C., Davis, J., & Brock, S. E. (2009). *Identifying, assessing, and treating dyslexia at school.* New York, NY: Springer. doi: 10.1007/978-0-387-88600-8

Clarke, P., Hulme, C., & Snowling, M. (2005). Individual differences in RAN and reading: A response timing analysis. *Journal of Research in Reading, 28*(2), 73–86. doi:10.1111/j.1467-9817.2005.00255.x

Cohen, L., & Dehaene, S. (2004). Specialization within the ventral stream: The case for the visual word form area. *Neuroimage, 22*(1), 466–476. doi:10.1016/j.neuroimage.2003.12.049

Cohen, L., Dehaene, S., Naccache, L., Lehéricy, S., Dehaene-Lambertz, G., Hénaff, M. A., & Michel, F. (2000). The visual word form area: Spatial and temporal characterization of an initial stage of reading in normal subjects and posterior split-brain patients. *Brain, 123,* 291–307. doi:10.1093/brain/123.2.291

Cohen, L., Jobert, A., LeBihan, D., & Dehaene, S. (2004). Distinct unimodal and multimodal regions for word processing in the left temporal cortex. *Neuroimage, 23*, 1256–1270. doi:10.1016/j.neuroimage.2004.07.052

Coltheart, M. (1978). Lexical access in simple reading tasks. In G. Underwood (Ed.), *Strategies of information processing* (pp. 151–216). London: Academic Press.

Coltheart, M. (1980). Reading phonological recording and deep dyslexia. In M. Coltheart, K. Patterson, & J. C. Marshall (Eds.), *Deep dyslexia* (pp. 197–226). London: Routledge & Kegan Paul.

Coltheart, M. (2007). Modeling reading: The dual-route approach. In M. J. Snowling & C. Hulme (Eds.), *The science of reading: A handbook* (pp. 6–23). Malden, MA: Blackwell.

Coltheart, M., Patterson, K., & Marshall, J. C. (1980). *Deep dyslexia.* London, UK: Routledge & Kegan Paul.

Crepeau-Hobson, F., & Bianco, M. (2011). Identification of gifted students with learning disabilities in a response-to-intervention era. *Psychology in the Schools, 48*, 102–109. doi:10.1002/pits.20528

Crisp, J., Howard, D., & Lambon Ralph, M. A. (2011). More evidence for a continuum between phonological and deep dyslexia: Novel data from three measures of direct orthography-to-phonology translation. *Aphasiology, 25*, 615–641. doi:10.1080/02687038.2010.541470

Crisp, J., & Lambon Ralph, M. A. (2006). Unlocking the nature of the phonological-deep dyslexia continuum: The keys to reading aloud are in phonology and semantics. *Journal of Cognitive Neuroscience, 18*, 348–362. doi:10.1162/jocn.2006.18.3.348

Critchley, M. (1964). *Developmental dyslexia.* Westport, CT: William Heinemann.

Dalton, B., & Proctor, C. P. (2008). The changing landscape of text and comprehension in the age of new literacies. In J. Coiro, M. Knobel, C. Lankshear, & D. Leu (Eds.), *Handbook of research on new literacies* (pp. 297–324). Mahwah, NJ: Erlbaum.

Darling-Hammond, L., Chung Wei, R., Andree, A., Richardson, N., & Orphanos, S. (2009). *Professional learning in the learning profession: A status report on teacher development in the United States and abroad.* Oxford, OH: National Staff Development Council.

Davies, R., & Cuentos, F. (2010). Reading acquisition and dyslexia in Spanish. In N. Brunswick, S. McDougall, & P. de Mornay Davies (Eds.), *Reading and dyslexia in different orthographies* (pp. 155–180). Hove, East Sussex: Psychology Press.

DeFries, J. C., Singer, S. M., Foch, T. T., & Lewitter, F. I. (1978). Familial nature of reading disability. *British Journal of Psychiatry, 132*, 361–367. doi:10.1192/bjp.132.4.361

Dehaene, S., Cohen, L., Sigman, M., & Vinckier, F. (2005). The neural code for written words: A proposal. *Trends in Cognitive Sciences, 9*, 335–341. doi:10.1016/j.tics.2005.05.004

Dejerine, J. (1891). Sur un cas de cécité verbale avec agraphie, suivi d'autopsie. *C. R. Société du Biologie, 43*, 197–201.

Dejerine, J. (1892). Contribution àl'étude anatomo-pathologique et clinique des différentes variétés de cécitéverbale. *Mémoires de la Sociétéde Biologie, 4*, 61–90. doi:10.1093/neucas/6.4.275

De Jong, P. F., & Van der Leij, A. (2003). Developmental changes in the manifestation of a phonological deficit in dyslexic children learning to read a regular orthography. *Journal of Educational Psychology, 95*(1), 22–40. doi:10.1037/0022-0663.95.1.22

Demb, J. B., Boynton, G. M., & Heeger, D. J. (1998). Functional magnetic resonance imaging of early visual pathways in dyslexia. *Journal of Neuroscience, 18*, 6939–6951.

Denckla. M. B., & Cutting, L. E. (1999). History and significance of rapid automatized naming. *Annals of Dyslexia, 49*, 29–42. doi:10.1007/s11881-999-0018-9

Denckla, M. B., & Rudel, R. G. (1976). Rapid automatised naming (R.A.N.): Dyslexia differentiated from other learning disabilities. *Neuropsychologia, 14*, 471–479. doi:10.1016/0028-3932(76)90075-0

Deno, S. L. (2003). Developments in curriculum-based measurement. *Remedial and Special Education, 37*, 184–192. doi:10.1177/00224669030370030801

Denton, C. A., & Al Otaiba, S. (2011). Teaching word identification to students with reading difficulties and disabilities. *Focus on Exceptional Children, 43*(7), 2–16.

deQuiros, J. B., & Schrager, O. L. (1978). *Neuropsychological fundamentals in learning disabilities.* Novato, CA: Academic Therapy Publications.

Duff, F. J., & Clarke, P. J. (2010). Practitioner review: Reading disorders: What are the effective interventions and how should they be implemented and evaluated? *Journal of Child Psychology and Psychiatry, 52*(1), 3–12. doi:10.1111/j.1469-7610.2010.012310.x

Ebejer, J. L., Coventry, W. L., Byrne, B., Willcutt, E. G., Olson, R. K., Corley, R., & Samuelsson, S. (2010). Genetic and environmental influences on inattention, hyperactivity-impulsivity, and reading: Kindergarten to Grade 2. *Scientific Studies of Reading, 14,* 293–316. doi:10.1080/10888430903150642

Eckert, M. A., Leonard, C. M., Richards, T. L., Aylward, E. H., Thomson, J., & Berninger, V. W. (2003). Anatomical correlates of dyslexia: Frontal and cerebellar findings. *Brain, 126*, 482–494. doi:10.1093/brain/awg026

Eden, G. F., & Vaidya, C. J. (2008). ADHD and developmental dyslexia: Two pathways leading to impaired learning. *Annals of the New York Academy of Sciences, 1145,* 316–327. doi:10.1196/annals.1416.022

Edyburn, D. L. (2000). Assistive technology and mild disabilities. *Focus on Exceptional Children, 32*(9), 1–24.

Edyburn, D. L. (2002, April/May). Cognitive rescaling strategies: Interventions that alter the cognitive accessibility of text. *Closing the Gap, 21*(1), 1, 10–11, 21.

Edyburn, D. L. (2003). Reading difficulties in the general education classroom: A taxonomy of text modification strategies. *Closing the Gap, 21*(6), 1, 10–13, 31.

Edyburn, D. L. (2006). Failure is not an option: Collecting, reviewing, and acting on evidence for using technology to enhance academic performance. *Learning and Leading With Technology, 34*(1), 20–23.

Edyburn, D. L. (2010). Would you recognize universal design for learning if you saw it? Ten propositions for new directions for the second decade of UDL. *Learning Disability Quarterly, 33*(1), 33–41.

Efron, B. (2008). Microarrays, empirical Bayes and the two-groups model. *Statistical Science, 23*(1), 1–22. doi:10.1214/08-STS236REJ

Ehri, L. C. (1997). Learning to read and learning to spell are one and the same, almost. In C. A. Perfetti, L. Rieben, & M. Fayol (Eds.), *Learning to spell: Research, theory, and practice across languages* (pp. 237–270). Mahwah, NJ: Erlbaum.

Ehri, L. C. (1998). Grapheme-phoneme knowledge is essential for learning to read words in English. In J. L. Metsala & L. C. Ehri (Eds.), *Word recognition in beginning literacy* (pp. 3–40). Mahwah, NJ: Erlbaum.

Ehri, L. C. (2000). Learning to read and learning to spell: Two sides of a coin. *Topics in Language Disorders, 20*(3), 19–36. doi:10.1097/00011363-200020030-00005

Ehri, L. C. (2002). Phases of acquisition in learning to read words and implications for teaching. *British Journal of Educational Psychology*: Monograph Series I, 7–28.

Ehri, L. C. (2005). Learning to read words: Theory, findings, and issues. *Scientific Studies of Reading, 9,* 167–188. doi:10.1207/s1532799xssr0902_4

Ehri, L. C. (2006). Alphabetics instruction helps students learn to read. In R. M. Joshi & P. G. Aaron (Eds.), *Handbook of orthography and literacy* (pp. 649–677). Mahwah, NJ: Erlbaum.

Ehri, L. C. (2007). Development of sight word reading: Phases and findings. In M. J. Snowling & C. Hulme (Eds.), *The science of reading: A handbook* (pp. 135–154). Malden, MA: Blackwell.

El-Baz, A., Casanova, M., Gimel'farb, G., Mott, M., & Switala, A. (2008). An MRI-based diagnostic framework for early diagnosis of dyslexia. *International Journal of Computer Assisted Radiology and Surgery, 3,* 3–4. doi:10.1007/s11548-008-0210-0

Eliez, S., Rumsey, J. M., Giedd, J. N., Schmitt, J. E., Patwardhan, A. J., & Reiss, A. L. (2000). Morphological alteration of temporal lobe gray matter in dyslexia: An MRI study. *Journal of Child Psychology and Psychiatry, and Allied Disciplines, 41,* 637–644. doi:10.1111/1469-7610.00650

Everatt, J., Ovampo, D., Veii, K., Nenopoulou S., Smythe I., al Mannai, H., & Elbeheri G. (2010). Dyslexia in biscriptal readers. In N. Brunswick, S. McDougall, & P. de Mornay Davies (Eds.), *Reading and dyslexia in different orthographies* (pp. 221–245). Hove, East Sussex: Psychology Press.

Fawcett, A. J. (2007). Dyslexia, learning, and pedagogical neuroscience. *Developmental Medicine & Child Neurology, 49,* 306–311. doi:10.1111/j.1469-8749.2007.00306.x

Feifer, S. (2011). How SLD manifests in reading. In D. P. Flanagan & V. C. Alfonso (Eds.), *Essentials of specific learning disability identification* (pp. 21–41). Hoboken, NJ: John Wiley & Sons.

Fernald, G. M. (1943). *Remedial techniques in basic school subjects.* New York, NY: McGraw-Hill.

Fernald, G. M., & Keller, H. (1921). The effect of kinaesthetic factors in the development of word recognition in the case of non-readers. *Journal of Educational Research, 4*, 355–377.

Ferrer, E., Shaywitz, B. A., Holahan, J. M., Marchione, K., & Shaywitz, S. E. (2010). Uncoupling of reading and IQ over time: Empirical evidence for a definition of dyslexia. *Psychological Science, 21*(1), 93–101. doi:10.1177/0956797609354084

Fiez, J. A., & Peterson, S. E. (1998). Neuroimaging studies of word reading. *Proceedings of the National Academy of Sciences, 95*, 914–921. doi:10.1073/pnas.95.3.914

Figueredo, L. (2006). Using the known to chart the unknown: A review of first-language influence on the development of English-as-a-second-language spelling skill. *Reading and Writing, 19*, 873–905. doi:10.1007/s11145-006-9014-1

Flesch-Kincaid Readability Test. (n.d.) Retrieved from Wikipedia http://en.wikipedia.org/wiki/Flesch%E2%80%93Kincaid_readability_test

Fletcher, J. M., Lyon, G. R., Fuchs, L. S., & Barnes, M. A. (2007). *Learning disabilities: From identification to intervention.* New York, NY: Guilford Press.

Foorman, B. R., Schatschneider, C., Eakin, M. N., Fletcher, J. M., Moats, L. C., & Francis, D. J. (2006). The impact of instructional practices in grades 1 and 2 on reading and spelling achievement in high poverty schools. *Contemporary Educational Psychology, 31*, 1–29. doi:10.1016/j.cedpsych.2004.11.003

Foorman, B. R., & Torgesen, J. K. (2001). Critical elements of classroom and small-group instruction promote reading success in all children. *Learning Disability Research & Practice, 16*, 203–212. doi:10.1111/0938-8982.00020

Frackowiak, R., Friston, K., Frith, C., Dolan, R., Price, C., Zeki, S., . . . Penny, W. D. (2004). *Human brain function* (2nd ed.). San Diego, CA: Academic Press, Elsevier Science.

Fraser, J., Goswami, U., & Conti-Ramsden, G. (2010). Dyslexia and specific language impairment: The role of phonology and auditory processing. *Scientific Studies of Reading, 14*, 8–29. doi:10.1080/10888430903242068

Friedman, R. B. (1996). Recovery from deep alexia to phonological alexia: Points on a continuum. *Brain and Language, 52*, 114–128. doi:10.1006/brln.1996.0006

Frith, U. (1999). Paradoxes in the definition of dyslexia. *Dyslexia, 5,* 192–214. doi:10.1002/(SICI)1099-0909(199912)5:4<192::AID-DYS144>3.3.CO;2-E

Frost, R. (2007). Orthographic systems and skilled word recognition processes in reading. In M. Snowling & C. Hulme (Eds.), *The science of reading: A handbook* (pp. 336–355). Malden, MA: Blackwell.

Fuchs, D., Fuchs, L., & Burish, P. (2000). Peer-Assisted Learning Strategies: An evidence-based practice to promote reading achievement. *Learning Disabilities Research & Practice, 15*, 85–91. doi:10.1207/SLDRP1502_4

Fuchs, L. S., Fuchs, D., Hamlett, C. L., Walz, L., & Germann, G. (1993). Formative evaluation of academic progress: How much growth can we expect? *School Psychology Review, 22*(1), 27–48.

Fuchs, L. S., Fuchs, D., Hosp, M. K., & Jenkins, J. R. (2001). Text fluency as an indicator of reading competence: A theoretical, empirical, and historical analysis. *Scientific Studies of Reading, 5,* 239–256. doi:10.1207/S1532799XSSR0503_3

Galaburda, A. M. (1989). Ordinary and extraordinary brain development: Anatomical variation in developmental dyslexia. *Annals of Dyslexia, 39,* 67–80. doi:10.1007/BF02656901

Galaburda, A. M., LoTurco, J., Ramus, F., Fitch, R. H., & Rosen, G. D. (2006). From genes to behavior in developmental dyslexia. *Nature Neuroscience, 9,* 1213–1217. doi:10.1038/nn1772

Gathercole, S. E., Willi, C. S., Baddeley, A. D., & Emslie, H. (1994). The children's test of nonword repetition: A test of phonological working memory. *Memory, 2,* 103–127. doi:10.1080/09658219408258940

Geiger, G., & Lettvin J. Y. (1987). Peripheral vision in persons with dyslexia. *New England Journal of Medicine, 316,* 1238–1243. doi:10.1056/NEJM198705143162003

Genovese, C., Lazar, N., & Nichols, T. (2002). Thresholding of statistical maps in functional neuroimaging using the false discovery rate. *NeuroImage, 15,* 870–878. doi:10.1056/NEJM198705143162003

Gentry, J. R. (1984). Developmental aspects of learning to spell. *Academic Therapy, 20,* 11–19. doi:10.1177/105345128402000102

Georgetown University Medical Center. (2003, May). Was Orton right? New study examines how the brain works in reading: Offers key to better understanding dyslexia. *Science Daily.* Retrieved December 9, 2010, from http://www.science daily.com/releases/2003/05/030519083450.htm

Georgiou, G. K., Parrila, R., & Kirby, J. (2006). Rapid naming speed components and early reading acquisition. *Scientific Studies of Reading, 10,* 199–220. doi:10.1207/s1532799xssr1002_4

Geschwind, N., & Levitsky, W. (1968). Human brain: Left-right asymmetries in temporal speech region. *Science, 161,* 186–187. doi:10.1126/science.161.3837.186

Gillingham, A., & Stillman, B. W. (1973). *Remedial training for children with specific disability in reading, spelling, and penmanship.* Cambridge, MA: Educators Publishing Service.

Glass, G. G. (1973). *Teaching decoding as separate from reading.* Garden City, NY: Easier to Learn. New York, NY: Adelphi University.

Glass, G. G. (1976). *Glass-Analysis for decoding only teacher guide.* Garden City, NY: Easier to Learn. New York, NY: Adelphi University.

Goldstein, S., & Brooks, R. (2007). *Understanding and managing children's classroom behavior: Creating sustainable, resilient schools* (2nd ed.). Hoboken, NJ: John Wiley & Sons.

Good, R. H., Simmons, D. C., & Kame'enui, E. J. (2001). The importance of decision-making utility of a continuum of fluency-based indicators of foundational reading skills for third-grade high stakes outcomes. *Scientific Studies of Reading, 5,* 257–288. doi:10.1207/S1532799XSSR0503_4

Goswami, U. (2006, March). Reading and its development: Insights from brain science. *Literacy Today, 28–29.*

Goswami, U. (2008). The development of reading across languages. *Annals of the New York Academy of Sciences, 1145*(1), 1–12. doi:10.1196/annals.1416.018

Goswami, U. (2010). Phonology, reading and reading difficulty. In K. Hall, U. Goswami, C. Harrison, S. Ellis, & J. Soler (Eds.), *Interdisciplinary perspectives on learning to read: Culture, cognition and pedagogy* (pp. 103–116). London: Routledge.

Goswami, U., Wang, H. L. S., Cruz, A., Fosker, T., Mead, N., & Huss, M. (2011). Language-universal sensory deficits in developmental dyslexia: English, Spanish, and Chinese. *Journal of Cognitive Neuroscience, 23*, 325–337. doi:10.1162/jocn.2010.21453

Gough, P. B., & Tunmer, W. E. (1986). Decoding, reading and reading disability. *Remedial and Special Education, 7,* 6–10. doi:10.1177/074193258600700104

Grigorenko, E. L. (2004). Genetic bases of developmental dyslexia: A capsule review of heritability estimates. *Enfance, 56*, 273–288. doi:10.3917/enf.563.0273

Grigorenko, E. L. (2005). A conservative meta-analysis of linkage and linkage-association studies of developmental dyslexia. *Scientific Studies of Reading, 9*, 285–316. doi:10.1207/s1532799xssr0903_6

Grigorenko, E. L. (2009). At the height of fashion: What genetics can teach us about neurodevelopmental disabilities. *Current Opinion in Neurology, 22,* 126–130. doi:10.1097/WCO.0b013e3283292414

Hall, T., & Strangman, N. (2002). *Graphic organizers.* Wakefield, MA: National Center on Accessing the General Curriculum. Retrieved from www.cast.org/publications/ncac/ncac_go.html

Hall, T., Strangman, N., & Meyer, A. (2003). *Differentiated instruction and implications for UDL implementation.* Wakefield, MA: National Center on Accessing the General Curriculum. Retrieved from http://aim.cast.org/learn/historyarchive/backgroundpapers/differentiated_instruction_udl

Hallahan, D. P., & Mercer, C. D. (2002). Learning disabilities: Historical perspectives. In R. Bradley, L. Danielson, & D. P. Hallahan (Eds.). *Identification of learning disabilities: Research to practice* (pp. 1–67). Mahwah, NJ: Erlbaum.

Hallgren, B. (1950). Specific dyslexia (congenital word-blindness): A clinical andgenetic study. *Acta Psychiatrica et Neurologica Supplement, 65,* 1–287.

Hallowell, E. M. (2003). Life and death and reading words. *Perspectives, 29*(3), 6–7.

Hammill, D. (1993). A brief look at the learning disabilities movement in the United States. *Journal of Learning Disabilities, 26,* 295–310. doi:10.1177/002221949302600502.

Hart, S. A., & Petrill, S. A. (2009). The genetics and environments of reading: A behavioral genetic perspective. In Y. K. Kim (Ed.), *Handbook of behavior genetics* (pp. 113–123). New York, NY: Springer. doi:10.1007/978-0-387-76727-7_8

Hasbrouck, J. (2006, Summer). Drop everything and read—but how? *American Educator, 30*, 22–31.

Hawelka, S., & Wimmer, H. (2005). Impaired visual processing of multielement arrays is associated with increased number of eye movements in dyslexic reading. *Vision Research, 45,* 855–863. doi:10.1016/j.visres.2004.10.007

Hawelka, S., & Wimmer, H. (2008). Visual target detection is not impaired in dyslexic readers. *Vision Research, 48,* 850–852. doi:10.1016/j.visres.2007.11.003

Hawke, J. L., Olson, R. K., Willcutt, E. G., Wadsworth, S. J., & DeFries, J. C. (2009). Gender ratios for reading difficulties. *Dyslexia, 15,* 239–242. doi: 10.1002/dys.389

Hawke, J. L., Wadsworth, S. J., & DeFries, J. C. (2006). Genetic influences on reading difficulties in boys and girls: The Colorado twin study. *Dyslexia, 12*(1), 21–29. doi:10.1002/dys.301

Hayden, D. (2011, April 11). Quoted in Arizona State University students win top U.S. spot at Imagine Cup, the "world championships of technology," with assistive note-taking solution. Retrieved from http://www.freshnews.com/news/478833/arizona-state-university-students-win-top-u-s-spot-imagine-cup-world-championships-tech

Heckelman, R. G. (1969). A neurological-impress method of remedial-reading instruction. *Academic Therapy, 4,* 277–282.

Heckelman, R. G. (1986). N.I.M. revisited. *Academic Therapy, 21,* 411–420.

Hegge, T. G., Kirk, S. A., & Kirk, W. D. (1936). *Remedial reading drills.* Ann Arbor, MI: Wahr.

Heiman, B. (2011). Instructional technology for special education administrators. In J. Castellani & B. Heimann (Eds.) *Instructional technology: Helping students access curriculum content* (pp. 3–7). Reston, VA: Technology and Media Division of the Council for Exceptional Children.

Helenius, P., Tarkiainen, A., Cornelissen, P., Hansen, P. C., & Salmelin, R. (1999). Dissociation of normal feature analysis and deficient processing of letter-strings in dyslexic adults. *Cerebral Cortex, 4,* 476–483. doi:10.1093/cercor/9.5.476

Henderson, E. H. (1990). *Teaching spelling* (2nd ed.). Boston, MA: Houghton Mifflin.

Henderson, E. H., & Beers, J. (Eds.). (1980). *Developmental and cognitive aspects of learning to spell: A reflection of word knowledge.* Newark, DE: International Reading Association.

Henderson, E. H., & Templeton, S. (1986). A developmental perspective of formal spelling instruction through alphabet, pattern, and meaning. *Elementary School Journal, 86,* 304–316. doi:10.1086/461451

Henry, C., Gaillard, R., Volle, E., Chiras, J., Ferrieux, S., Dehaene, S., & Cohen, L. (2005). Brain activations during letter-by-letter reading: A follow-up study. *Neuropsychologia, 43,* 1983–1989. doi:10.1016/j.neuropsychologia.2005.04.007

Henry, M. K. (2010). *Unlocking literacy: Effective decoding & spelling instruction* (2nd ed.). Baltimore, MD: Paul H. Brookes.

Herron, J. (2011). *Making speech visible.* San Rafael, CA: Talking Fingers Publications.

Hinshelwood, J. (1902). *Congenital word-blindness with reports of two cases.* London: John Bale, Sons & Danielsson, Ltd.

Hinshelwood, J. (1917). *Congenital word-blindness*. London: Lewis.

Hintze, J. M., & Silberglitt, B. (2005). A longitudinal examination of the diagnostic accuracy and predictive validity of R-CBM and high-stakes testing. *School Psychology Review, 34,* 372–386.

Ho, C. S. H., & Bryant, P. (1997). Development of phonological awareness of Chinese children in Hong Kong. *Journal of Psycholinguistic Research, 26,* 109. Retrieved from http://www.springer.com/psychology/journal/10936

hooks, b. (1994). *Teaching to transgress. Education as the practice of freedom.* London: Routledge.

Hudson, R. F., High, L., & Al Otaiba, S. (2007). Dyslexia and the brain: What does current research tell us. *Reading Teacher, 60,* 506–515. doi:10.1598/RT.60.6.1

Hudson, R. F., Lane, H. B., & Pullen, P. C. (2005). Reading fluency assessment and instruction: What, why, and how? *Reading Teacher, 58,* 702–714. doi:10.1598/RT.58.8.1

Huey, E. B. (1908). *The psychology and pedagogy of reading.* Cambridge, MA: Massachusetts Institute of Technology Press.

Hulme, C., Goetz, K., Gooch, D., Adams, J., & Snowling, M. J. (2007). Paired-associate learning, phoneme awareness and learning to read. *Journal of Experimental Child Psychology, 96,* 150–166. doi:10.1016/j.jecp.2006.09.002

Hulme, C., & Snowling, M. J. (2009). *Developmental disorders of language learning and cognition.* West Sussex, United Kingdom: Wiley-Blackwell.

Individuals with Disabilities Education Improvement Act of 2004, 20 U.S.C. § 1400 *et seq.* (2004) (reauthorization of the Individuals with Disabilities Education Act of 1990).

International Dyslexia Association. (2010). *Knowledge and practice standards for teachers of reading.* Washington, DC: Author.

Jenkins, J. R., Fuchs, L. S., van den Broek, P., Epsin, C., & Deno, S. L. (2003). Accuracy and fluency in list and context reading of skilled and RD groups: Absolute and relative performance levels. *Learning Disabilities Research & Practice, 18,* 237–245. doi:10.1111/1540-5826.00078

Jiménez, G. J. E., & Ramírez, S. G. (2002). Identifying subtypes of reading disability in the Spanish language. *The Spanish Journal of Psychology, 5,* 3–19. Retrieved from http://www.ucm.es/info/psi/docs/journal/

Johnson, D. J., & Myklebust, H. R. (1967). *Learning disabilities: Educational principles and practices.* New York, NY: Grune & Stratton.

Johnson, L., Smith, R., Willis, H., Levine, A., & Haywood, K. (2011). *The 2011 Horizon Report.* Austin, TX: The New Media Consortium.

Johnson, R., & Rayner, K. (2007). Top-down and bottom-up effects in pure alexia: Evidence from eye movements. *Neuropsychologia, 45,* 2246–2257. doi:10.1016/j.neuropsychologia.2007.02.026

Joseph, J., Noble, K., & Eden, G. (2001). The neurobiological basis of reading. *Journal of Learning Disabilities, 34,* 566–579. doi:10.1177/00222194010340060

Kail, R. (1991). Development of processing speed in childhood and adolescence. *Advances in Child Development and Behavior, 23,* 151–184. doi:10.1016/S0065-2407(08)60025-7

Kail, R., & Hall, L. K. (1994). Processing speed, naming speed, and reading. *Developmental Psychology, 30,* 949–954. doi:10.1037/0012-1649.30.6.949

Kail, R., & Hall, L. K. (1999). Processing speed, exposure to print, and naming speed. *Applied Psycholinguistics, 20,* 303–314. doi:10.1037/0012-1649.30.6.949

Kail, R., Hall, L. K., & Caskey, B. J. (1999). Processing speed, exposure to print, and naming speed. *Applied Psycholinguistics, 20,* 303–314. doi:10.1017/S0142716499002076

Kame'enui, E. J. (1993). Diverse learners and the tyranny of time: Don't fix blame; fix the leaky roof. *Reading Teacher, 46,* 376–383.

Katzir, T., & Pare-Blagoev, J. (2006). Applying cognitive neuroscience research to education: The case of literacy. *Educational Psychologist, 41,* 53–74. doi:10.1207/s15326985ep4101_6

Kirk, S. A. (1963). Behavioral diagnosis and remediation of learning disabilities. In Anonymous, *Proceedings of the conference on exploration into problems of the perceptually handicapped child.* Chicago, IL: Perceptually Handicapped Children.

Kirk, S. A. (1974, May 19). Correlates of reading disability. Speech delivered at II Congreso Hispano americano de dificultades en el aprendizaje de la lectura y escritura. Mexico City, Mexico.

Kirk, S. A., & Johnson, G. O. (1951). *Educating the retarded child.* Cambridge, MA: Houghton Mifflin.

Kirk, S. A., Kirk, W. D., Minskoff, E., Mather, N., & Roberts, R. (2007). *Phonic Reading Lessons: Skills.* Novato, CA: Academic Therapy.

Kirk, S. A., McCarthy, J. J., & Kirk, W. D. (1968). *Illinois Test of Psycholinguistic Abilities* (Rev. ed.). Urbana, IL: University of Illinois Press.

Klingberg, T., Hedehus, M., Temple, E., Salz, T., Gabrieli, J. D. E., Moseley, M. E., & Poldrack, R. A. (2000). Microstructure of temporo-parietal white matter as a basis for reading ability: Evidence from diffusion tensor magnetic resonance imaging. *Neuron, 25,* 493–500. doi:10.1016/S0896-6273(00)80911-3

Koeda, T., Seki, A., Uchiyama, H., & Sadato, N. (2011). Dyslexia: Advances in clinical and imaging studies. *Brain and Development, 33,* 268–275. doi:10.1016/j.braindev.2010.11.006

Korhonen, T. (1995). The persistence of rapid naming problems in children with reading disabilities: A nine year follow-up. *Journal of Learning Disabilities, 28,* 232–239. doi:10.1177/002221949502800405

Kronbichler, M., Hutzler, F., Staffen, W., Mair, A., Ladurner, G., & Wimmer, H. (2006). Evidence for a dysfunction of left posterior reading areas in German dyslexic readers. *Neuropsychologia, 44,* 1822–1832. doi:10.1016/j.neuropsychologia.2006.03.010

Kuo, L. J., & Anderson, R. C. (2006). Morphological awareness and learning to read: A cross-language perspective. *Educational Psychologist, 41,* 161–180. doi:10.1207/s15326985ep4103_3

Kussmaul, A. (1877a). Disturbances of speech. In H. von Ziemssen (Ed.) & J. A. McCreery (Trans.), *Cyclopedia of the practice of medicine* (p. 595). New York, NY: William Wood.

Kussmaul, A. (1877b). Die Störungen der Sprache. Ziemssen's Handbuch d. Speciellen. *Pathologie u. therapie, 12,* 1–300.

Kussmaul, A. (1877c). Word deafness and word blindness. In H. von Ziemssen (Ed.) & J. A. T. McCreery (Trans.), *Cyclopedia of the practice of medicine* (pp. 770–778). New York, NY: William Wood.

LaBerge, D., & Samuels, S. (1974). Toward a theory of automatic information processing in reading. *Cognitive Psychology, 6,* 293–323. doi:10.1016/0010-0285(74)90015-2

Lake, D. (2004). *Using Microsoft Word like a pro, part 1.* Retrieved from http://www.techlearning.com/article/2270

Lam, S. S. T., Au, R. K. C., Leung, H. W. H., & Li-Tsang, C. W. P. (2011). Chinese handwriting performance of primary school children with dyslexia. *Research in Developmental Disabilities, 32,* 1745–1756. doi:10.1016/j.ridd.2011.03.001

Landerl, K., & Wimmer, H. (2008). Development of word reading fluency and orthographic spelling in a consistent orthography: An 8-year follow-up. *Journal of Educational Psychology, 100,* 150–161. doi:10.1037/0022-0663.100.1.150

Lazar, N. (2009). Discussion of "Puzzlingly high correlations in fMRI studies of emotion, personality and social cognition" by Vul et al. (2009). *Perspectives on Psychological Science, 4,* 308–309. doi:10.1111/j.1745-6924.2009.01129.x

Lebel, C., Shaywitz, B., Holahan, J., Shaywitz, S., Marchione, K., & Beaulieu, C. (2010, June). *Diffusion tensor imaging of reading ability in dysfluent and non-impaired readers.* Organization for Human Brain Mapping, 16th Annual Meeting, Barcelona, Spain.

Lee, L. W., & Wheldall, K. (2011). Acquisition of Malay word recognition skills: Lessons from low-progress early readers. *Dyslexia, 17,* 19–37. doi: 10.1002/dys.421

Lefly, D. L., & Pennington, B. F. (1991). Spelling errors and reading fluency in compensated adult dyslexics. *Annals of Dyslexia, 41,* 143–162. doi:10.1007/BF02648083

Leonard, C., & Eckert, M. (2008). Asymmetry and dyslexia. *Developmental Neuropsychology, 33,* 663–681. doi:10.1080/87565640802418597

Leong, C. K., Cheng, P. W., & Lam, C. C. (2000). Exploring reading-spelling connection as locus of dyslexia in Chinese. *Annals of Dyslexia, 50*(1), 239–259. doi:10.1007/s11881-000-0024-4

Leppanen, U., Nieme, P., Aunola, K., & Nurmi, J. E. (2006). Development of reading and spelling Finnish from preschool to grade 1 and grade 2. *Scientific Studies of Reading, 10,* 3–30. doi:10.1207/s1532799xssr1001_2

Lerväg, A., & Hulme, C. (2010). Predicting the growth of early spelling skills: Are there heterogeneous developmental trajectories? *Scientific Studies of Reading, 14,* 485–513. doi: 10.1080/10888431003623488

Levi, D. M., Song, S., & Pelli, D. G. (2007). Amblyopic reading is crowded. *Journal of Vision, 7*(2), 1–17. doi:10.1167/7.2.21

Levy, B. A., Abello, B., & Lysynchuk, L. (1997). Transfer from word training to reading in context: Gains in reading fluency and comprehension. *Learning Disabilities Quarterly, 20,* 173–188. doi:10.2307/1511307

Liberman, I. Y., & Shankweiler, D. (1991). Phonology and beginning reading: A tutorial. In L. Rieben & C. A. Perfetti (Eds.), *Learning to read: Basic research and its implications* (pp. 3–17). Hillsdale, NJ: Erlbaum.

Lindamood, C. H., & Lindamood, P. C. (1998). *Lindamood phoneme sequencing program (LiPS) for reading, spelling, and speech.* Austin, TX: PRO-ED.

Lindamood, P. C., & Lindamood, P. D. (2011). *Lindamood phoneme sequencing program for reading spelling and speech* (4th ed.). Austin, TX: PRO-ED.

Lindgren, S.-A., & Laine, M. (2011). Cognitive-linguistic performances of multilingual university students suspected of dyslexia. *Dyslexia, 17,* 184–200. doi: 10.1002/dys.422

Lindstedt, K., & Zaccariello, M. J. (2008). A tale of two assessments: Reading fluency. In J. N. Apps, R. F. Newby, & L. W. Roberts (Eds.), *Pediatric neuropsychology case studies: From the exceptional to the commonplace* (pp. 191–199). New York, NY: Springer.

Lorusso, M. L., Facoetti, A., Pesenti, S., Cattaneo, C., Molteni, M., & Geiger, G. (2004). Wider recognition in peripheral vision common to different subtypes of dyslexia. *Vision Research, 44,* 2413–2424. doi:10.1016/j.visres.2004.05.001

Lyon, G. R., Shaywitz, S. E., & Shaywitz, B. A. (2003). A definition of dyslexia. *Annals of Dyslexia, 53,* 1–14. doi:10.1007/s11881-003-0001-9

Maisog, J. M., Einbinder, E. R., Flowers, D. L., Turkeltaub, P. E., & Eden, G. F. (2008). A meta-analysis of functional neuroimaging studies of dyslexia. *Annals of the New York Academy of Sciences, 1145,* 237–259. doi:10.1196/annals.1416.024

Manis, F., Doi, L. M., & Badha, B. (2000). Naming speed, phonological awareness, and orthographic knowledge in second graders. *Journal of Learning Disabilities, 33,* 325–333. doi:10.1177/002221940003300405

Manis, F. R., Seidenberg, M. S., & Doi, L. M. (1999). "See Dick RAN." Rapid naming and the longitudinal prediction of reading subskills in first and second graders. *Scientific Studies of Reading, 3,* 129–157. doi:10.1207/s1532799xssr0302_3

Martelli, M., Di Filippo, G., Spinelli, D., & Zoccolotti, P. (2009). Crowding, reading, and developmental dyslexia. *Journal of Vision, 9*(4), 1–18. doi:10.1167/9.4.14

Martin, J., Cole, P., Leuwers, C., Casalis, S., Zorman, M., & Sprenger-Charolles, L. (2010). Reading in French-speaking adults with dyslexia. *Annals of Dyslexia, 60,* 238–264. doi:10.1007/s11881-010-0043-8

Mather, N., Bos, C., Podhajski, B., Babur, N., & Rhein, D. (2000). *Screening of early reading processes.* Unpublished manuscript, University of Arizona–Tucson.

Mather, N., & Goldstein, S. (2008). *Learning disabilities and challenging behaviors: A guide to intervention and classroom management* (2nd ed.). Baltimore, MD: Paul H. Brookes.

Mather, N., & Urso, A. M. (2008). Younger readers with reading difficulties. In R. Morris & N. Mather (Eds.), *Evidence-based practices for students with learning and behavioral challenges* (pp. 163–192). Mahwah, NJ: Erlbaum.

McBride-Chang, C., & Manis, F. (1996). Structural invariance in the associations of naming speed, phonological awareness, and verbal reasoning in good and poor readers: A test of the double deficit hypothesis. *Reading and Writing, 8,* 323–339. doi:10.1007/BF00395112

McBride-Chang, C., Wong, T. T. Y., Lam, F., Lam, C., Chan, B., Fong, C. Y. C., & Wong, S. W. L. (2011). Early predictors of dyslexia in Chinese children: Familial history of dyslexia, language delay, and cognitive profiles. *Journal of Child Psychology and Psychiatry and Allied Disciplines, 52,* 204–211. doi:10.1111/j.1469-7610.2010.02299.x

McCardle, P., Mele-McCarthy, J., Cutting, L., Leos, K., & D'Emilio, T. (2005). Learning disabilities in English language learners: Identifying the issues. *Learning Disabilities: Research & Practice, 20,* 1–5. doi:10.1111/j.1540-5826.2005.00114.x

McCardle, P., Scarborough, H. S., & Catts, H. W. (2001). Predicting, explaining, and preventing children's reading difficulties. *Learning Disabilities Research & Practice, 16,* 230–239. doi:10.1111/0938-8982.00023

McCoy, K. M., & Prehm, H. J. (1987). *Teaching mainstreamed students: Methods and techniques.* Denver, CO: Love Publishing.

McDougall, S., Brunswick, N., & de Mornay Davis, P. (2010). Reading and dyslexia in different orthographies: An introduction and overview. In N. Brunswick, S. McDougall, & P. de Mornay Davies (Ed.), *Reading and dyslexia in different orthographies* (pp. 3–21). Hove, East Sussex: Psychology Press.

McGrath, L. M., Pennington, B. F., Shanahan, M. A., Santerre-Lemmon, L. E., Barnard, H. D., Willcutt, E. G., . . . & Olson, R. K. (2011). A multiple deficit model of reading disability and attention-deficit/hyperactivity disorder: Searching for shared cognitive deficits. *Journal of Child Psychology and Psychiatry, 52,* 547–557. doi:10.1111/j.1469-7610.2010.02346.x

Meaburn, E., Harlaar, N., Craig, I. W., Schalkwyk, L. C., & Plomin, R. (2008). Quantitative trait locus association scan of early reading disability and ability using pooled DNA and 100K SNP microarrays in a sample of 5760 children. *Molecular Psychiatry, 13,* 729–740. doi:10.1038/sj.mp.4002063

Meisinger, E. B., Bloom, J. S., & Hynd, G. W. (2010). Reading fluency: Implications for the assessment of children with reading disabilities. *Annals of Dyslexia, 60,* 1–17. doi:10.1007/s11881-009-0031-z

Menghini, D., Finzi, A., Benassi, M., Bolzani, R., Facoetti, A., Giovagnoli, S., . . . Vicari, S. (2010). Different underlying neurocognitive deficits in developmental dyslexia: A comparative study. *Neuropsycholgogia, 48,* 863–872. doi:10.1016/j.neuropsychologia.2009.11.003

Meyer, M. S., & Felton, R. H. (1999). Repeated reading to enhance fluency: Old approaches and new directions. *Annals of Dyslexia, 49,* 283–306. doi:10.1007/s11881-999-0027-8

Miers, J. (2004). Belts or braces? Is BELTS, (Basic e-Learning Tool Set) developed by the Learning Federation to enable schools to gain access to its digital learning objects, able to support a constructivist e-learning environment for students or is a different solution required? (Grant Report 9). Retrieved from http://www.teachers.ash.org.au/jmresources/research.htm

Miller, C. J., Sanchez, J., & Hynd, G. W. (2003). Neurological correlates of reading disabilities. In H. L. Swanson, K. R. Harris, & S. Graham (Eds.), *Handbook of learning disabilities* (pp. 242–255). New York, NY: Guilford Press.

Moats, L. C. (1991). Spelling disability in adolescents and adults. In A. M. Bain, L. L. Bailet, & L. C. Moats (Eds.), *Written language disorders: Theory into practice* (pp. 23–42). Austin, TX: PRO-ED.

Moats, L. C. (1994). The missing foundation in teacher education: Knowledge of the structure of spoken and written language. *Annals of Dyslexia, 44,* 81–102. doi:10.1007/BF02648156

Moats, L. C. (1999). *Teaching reading is rocket science.* Washington, DC: American Federation of Teachers.

Moats, L. C. (2005). *Language essentials for teachers of reading and spelling: Module 2: The speech sounds of English: Phonetics, phonology, and phoneme awareness.* Longmont, CO: Sopris West Educational Services.

Moats, L. C. (2009). Knowledge foundations for teaching reading and spelling. *Reading and Writing: An Interdisciplinary Journal, 22,* 379–399. doi:10.1007/s11145-009-9162-1

Moats, L. C. (2010). *Speech to print: Language essentials for teachers* (2nd ed.). Baltimore, MD: Paul H. Brookes.

Moats, L. C., Carreker, S., Davis, R., Meisel, P., Spear-Swerling, L., & Wilson, B. (2010). *Knowledge and practice standards for teachers of reading.* International Dyslexia Association, Professional Standards and Practices Committee.

Moats, L. C., & Foorman, B. R. (2003). Measuring teachers' content knowledge of language and reading. *Annals of Dyslexia, 53,* 23–45. doi:10.1007/s11881-003-0003-7

Molfese, V. J., Molfese, D. L., & Modglin, A. (2001). Newborn and preschool predictors of second grade reading scores: An evaluation of categorical and continuous scores. *Journal of Learning Disabilities, 34,* 545–554. doi:10.1177/002221940103400607

Monroe, M. (1932). *Children who cannot read.* Chicago. IL: University of Chicago Press.

Monroe, M. (1935). Diagnosis of reading disabilities. In G. M. Whipple (Ed.), *The thirty-fourth yearbook of the National Society for the Study of Education: Educational diagnosis* (pp. 201–228). Bloomington, IL: Public School Publishing.

Monroe, M., & Backus, B. (1937). *Remedial reading: A monograph in character education.* Boston, MA: Houghton Mifflin.

Morgan, E., & Klein, C. (2000). *The dyslexic adult in a non-dyslexic world.* London: Whurr.

Morgan, W. P. (1896, November 7). Word blindness. *British Medical Journal, 1378,* 98.

Morris, D., & Slavin, R. E. (2002). *Every child reading.* Boston, MA: Allyn & Bacon.

Muter, V., & Snowling, M. J. (2009). Children at familial risk of dyslexia: Practical implications from an at-risk study. *Child and Adolescent Mental Health, 14,* 37–41. doi: 10.1111/j.1475-3588.2007.00480.x

Myklebust, H. (1954). *Auditory disorders in children: A manual for differential diagnosis.* New York, NY: Grune & Stratton.

Myklebust, H., & Johnson, D. (1962). Dyslexia in school children. *Exceptional Children, 29,* 14–25.

Nakamura, K., Dehaene, S., Jobert, A., Le Bihan, D., & Kouider, S. (2005). Subliminal convergence of Kanji and Kana words: Further evidence for functional parcellation of the posterior temporal cortex in visual word perception. *Journal of Cognitive Neuroscience, 17,* 954–968. doi:10.1162/0898929054021166

Nakamura, K., Hara, N., Kouider, S., Takayama, Y., Hanajima, R., Sakai, K., & Ugawa, Y. (2006). Task-guided selection of the dual neural pathways for reading. *Neuron, 52,* 557–564. doi:10.1016/j.neuron.2006.09.030

National Assessment of Educational Progress. (1995). *Listening to children read out loud: Oral fluency, 1*(1). NCES 95–762. Available from: http://www.EDPubs.gov/

National Assessment of Educational Progress. (2009). *NAEP 2009 reading report card for the nation and the states.* Princeton, NJ: Educational Testing Service.

National Joint Committee on Learning Disabilities. (2005). Responsiveness to intervention and learning disabilities. *Learning Disability Quarterly, 28,* 249–260. doi:10.2307/4126964

National Library Service. (n.d.) NLS: Governing Legislation. Title 36 Code of Federal Regulations. Retrieved from http://www.loc.gov/nls/sec701.html

National Reading Panel. (2000). *Teaching children to read: An evidence-based assessment of the scientific research literature on reading and its implications for reading instruction* (National Institute of Health Pub. No. 00-4769). Washington, DC: National Institute of Child Health and Human Development.

Nelson, J. S., Alber, S. R., & Gordy, A. (2004). The effects of error correction and repeated readings on the reading achievement of students with learning disabilities. *Education and Treatment of Children, 27,* 186–198.

Nettelbeck, T. (1994). Speediness. In R. J. Sternberg (Ed.), *Encyclopedia of human intelligence* (pp. 1014–1019). New York, NY: Macmillan.

Neuhaus, G. F., & Swank, P. R. (2002). Understanding the relations between RAN letter subtest components and word reading in first-grade students. *Journal of Learning Disabilities, 35,* 158–174. doi: 10.1177/002221940203500206

Nichols, T., & Hayasaka, S. (2003). Controlling the familywise error rate in functional neuroimaging: A comparative review. *Statistical Methods in Medical Research, 12,* 419–446. doi:10.1191/0962280203sm341ra

Nicolson, R. I., Fawcett, A. J., & Dean, P. (2001). Developmental dyslexia: The cerebellar deficit hypothesis. *Trends in Neurosciences, 24,* 508–511. doi:10.1016/S0166-2236(00)01896-8

Oakhill, J. V., Cain, K., & Bryant, P. E. (2003). The dissociation of word reading and text comprehension: Evidence from component skills. *Language and Cognitive Processes, 18,* 443–468. doi:10.1080/01690960344000008

O'Bannon, B., & Puckett, K. (2010). *Preparing to use technology: A practical guide to curriculum integration* (2nd ed.). Boston, MA: Allyn & Bacon.

Ofiesh, N. (2006). Response to intervention and the identification of specific learning disabilities: Why we need comprehensive evaluations of the process. *Psychology in the Schools, 43,* 883–888. doi:10.1002/pits.20195

Oliver, B. R., & Plomin, R. (2007). Twins' Early Development Study (TEDS): A multivariate, longitudinal genetic investigation of language, cognition and behavior problems from childhood through adolescence. *Twin Research and Human Genetics, 10,* 96–105. doi:10.1375/twin.10.1.96

Olofsson, A., & Niedersøe, J. (1999). Early language development and kindergarten phonological awareness as predictors of reading problems: from 3 to 11 years of age. *Journal of Learning Disabilities, 32,* 464–472. doi:10.1177/002221949903200512

Olson, R. (2011). Genetic and environmental influence on phonological abilities and reading achievement. In S. A. Brady, D. Braze, & C. A. Fowler (Eds.). *Individual differences in reading: Theory and evidence* (pp. 197–216). New York, NY: Psychology Press.

Olson, R. K. (2006). Genetic and environmental influences on the development of reading and related cognitive skills. In R. M. Joshi & P. G. Aaron (Eds.), *Handbook of orthography and literacy* (pp. 679–707). Mahwah, NJ: Erlbaum.

O'Malley, K. J., Francis, D. J., Foorman, B. R., Fletcher, J. M., & Swank, P. R. (2002). Growth in precursor and reading-related skills: Do low-achieving and IQ-discrepant readers develop differently? *Learning Disabilities Research & Practice, 17,* 19–34. doi:10.1111/1540-5826.00029

Ortiz, S. O. (2011). Separating cultural and linguistic differences (CLD) from specific learning disability (SLD) in the evaluation of diverse students: Difference or disorder? In D. P. Flanagan & V. C. Alfonso (Eds.), *Essentials of specific learning disability identification* (pp. 299–324). Hoboken, NJ: John Wiley & Sons.

Orton, J. (1966). The Orton-Gillingham approach. In J. Money (Ed.), *The disabled reader: Education of the dyslexic child* (pp. 119–145). Baltimore, MD: Johns Hopkins University Press.

Orton, S. T. (1925). Word-blindness in school children. *Archives of Neurology and Psychiatry, 14,* 581–615.

Orton, S. T. (1937). *Reading, writing, and speech problems in children.* New York, NY: W. W. Norton.

Paizi, D., Burani, C., & Zoccolotti, P. (2011). Lexical stress assignment in Italian developmental dyslexia. *Reading and Writing, 24,* 443–461. doi 10.1007/s11145-010-9236-0

Paizi, D., Zoccolotti P., & Burani, C. (2010). Lexical reading in Italian developmental dyslexic readers. In N. Brunswick, S. McDougall, & P. de Mornay Davies (Eds.), *Reading and dyslexia in different orthographies* (pp. 181–198). Hove, East Sussex: Psychology Press.

Parilla, R., Kirby, J. R., & McQuarrie, L. (2004). Articulation rate, naming speed, verbal short-term memory, and phonological awareness: Longitudinal predictors of early reading development? *Scientific Studies of Reading, 8*, 3–26. doi:10.1207/s1532799xssr0801_2

Paulesu, E., Demonet, J. F., Fazio, F., McCrory, E., Chanoine, V., Brunswick, N., . . . Frith, U. (2001). Dyslexia-cultural diversity and biological unity. *Science, 291*, 2165–2167. doi:10.1016/S1053-8119(01)91927-5

Peer, L., & Reid, G. (2000). *Multilingualism, literacy and dyslexia: A challenge for educators.* London: David Fulton.

Pennington, B. F. (2009). *Diagnosing learning disorders: A neuropsychological framework* (2nd ed.). New York, NY: Guilford Press.

Pennington, B. F., & Lefly, D. I. (2001). Early reading development in children at family risk for dyslexia. *Child Development, 72,* 816–833. doi:10.1111/1467-8624.00317

Pennington, B. F., & Olson, R. K. (2007). Genetics of dyslexia. In M. J. Snowling & C. Hulme (Eds.), *The science of reading: A handbook* (pp. 453–472). Malden, MA: Blackwell.

Pennington, B. F., Peterson, R. L., & McGrath, L. M. (2009). Dyslexia. In B. F. Pennington, *Diagnosing learning disorders* (2nd ed.; pp. 45–82). New York, NY: Guilford Press.

Perea, M., & Perez, E. (2009). Beyond alphabetic orthographies: The role of form and phonology in transposition effects in Katakana. *Language and Cognitive Processes, 24*, 67–88. doi:10.1080/01690960802053924

Perfetti, C. (2011). Phonology is critical in reading: But a phonological deficit is not the only source of low reading skill. In S. A. Brady, D. Braze, & C. A. Fowler (Eds.). *Individual differences in reading: Theory and evidence* (pp. 153–171). New York, NY: Psychology Press.

Pernet, C., Valdois, S., Celsis, P., & Démonet, J. F. (2006). Lateral masking, levels of processing and stimulus category: A comparative study between normal and dyslexic readers. *Neuropsychologia, 44,* 2374–2385. doi: 10.1016/j.neuropsychologia.2006.05.003

Phayer, J. (2010). Using Microsoft Word with students with dyslexia. *Closing the Gap, 29*(3), 26–31.

Pickle, J. M. (1998). Historical trends in biological and medical investigations of reading disabilities: 1850–1915. *Journal of Learning Disabilities, 31,* 625–635. doi:10.1177/002221949803100614

Pikulski, J. J., & Chard, D. J. (2005). Fluency: Bridge between decoding and reading comprehension. *Reading Teacher, 58,* 510–519. doi:10.1598/RT.58.6.2

Pinnell, G. S., Pikulski, J. J., Wixson, K. K., Campbell, J. R., Gough, P. B., & Beatty, A. S. (1995). *Listening to children read aloud.* Washington, DC: U.S. Department of Education, National Center for Education Statistics.

Porpodas, C. D. (1999). Patterns of phonological and memory processing in beginning readers and spellers of Greek. *Journal of Learning Disabilities, 32,* 406–416. doi:10.1177/002221949903200506

Powell, D., Stainthorp, R., Stuart, M., Garwood, H., & Quinlan, P. (2007). An experimental comparison between rival theories of rapid automatized naming performance and its relationship to reading. *Journal of Experimental Child Psychology, 98,* 46–68. doi:10.1016/j.jecp.2007.04.003

Price, C., & Mechelli, A. (2005). Reading and reading disturbance. *Current Opinion in Neurobiology 15,* 231–238. doi:10.1016/j.conb.2005.03.003

Puolakanaho, A., Ahonen, T., Aro, M., Eklund, K., Leppänen, P. H. T., Poikkeus, A. M., . . . Lyytinen, H. (2007). Very early phonological and language skills: Estimating individual risk of reading disability. *Journal of Child Psychology and Psychiatry, 48,* 923–931. doi:10.1111/j.1469-7610.2007.01763.x

Rack, J. P., Snowling, M. J., & Olson, R. K. (1992). The nonword reading deficit in developmental dyslexia: A review. *Reading Research Quarterly, 27,* 28–53. doi:10.2307/747832

Ramus, F., & Szenkovits, G. (2008). What phonological deficit? *Quarterly Journal of Experimental Psychology, 61*(1), 129–141. doi:10.1080/17470210701508822

Rasinski, T. V. (2001). Speed does matter in reading. *Reading Teacher, 54,* 146–156.

Rasinski, T. V. (2004). *Assessing reading fluency.* Pacific Resources for Education and Learning: Honolulu, Hawaii.

Rasinski, T. (2006). Reading fluency instruction: Moving beyond accuracy, automaticity, and prosody. *Reading Teacher, 59,* 704–706. doi:10.1598/RT.59.7.10

Rasinski, T. V., Padak, N. D., McKeon, C. A., Wilfong, L. G., Friedauer, J. A., & Heim, P. (2005). Is reading fluency a key for successful high school reading? *Journal of Adolescent and Adult Literacy, 49,* 22–27. doi:10.1598/JAAL.49.1.3

Raskind, W. H. (2001). Current understanding of the genetic basis of reading and spelling disability. *Learning Disability Quarterly, 24,* 141–157. doi:10.2307/1511240

Rastle, K., Tyler, L. K., & Marslen-Wilson, W. (2006). New evidence for morphological errors in deep dyslexia. *Brain and Language, 97,* 189–199. doi:10.1016/j.bandl.2005.10.003

Rice, M. L., Smith, S. D., & Gayan, J. (2009). Convergent genetic linkage and associations to language, speech and reading measures in families of probands with specific language impairment. *Journal of Neurodevelopmental Disorders, 1,* 264–282. doi 10.1007/s11689-009-9031-x

Richardson, S. O. (1992). Historical perspectives on dyslexia. *Journal of Learning Disabilities, 25,* 40–47. doi:10.1177/002221949202500107

Richardson, W. (2006). *Blogs, wikis, podcasts, and other powerful web tools for classrooms.* Thousand Oaks, CA: Corwin Press.

Richlan, F., Kronbichler, M., & Wimmer, H. (2009). Functional abnormalities in the dyslexic brain: A quantitative meta-analysis of neuroimaging studies. *Human Brain Mapping, 30,* 3299–3308. doi:10.1002/hbm.20752

Roberts, R., & Mather, N. (2007). *Phonic Reading Lessons: Practice*. Novato, CA: Academic Therapy.

Rodrigo, M., & Jiménez, J. E. (1999). An analysis of the word naming errors of normal readers and reading disabled children in Spanish. *Journal of Research in Reading, 22*, 180–197. doi:10.1111/1467-9817.00081

Roivanien, E. (2011). Gender differences in processing speed: A review of recent research. *Learning and Individual Differences, 21*, 145–149. doi:10.1016/j.lindif.2010.11.021

Romani, C., Olson, A., & Di Betta, A. M. (2007). Spelling disorders. In M. J. Snowling & C. Hulme (Eds.), *The science of reading: A handbook* (pp. 431–447). Malden, MA: Blackwell.

Rooney, K. J. (1995). Dyslexia revisited: History, educational philosophy, and clinical assessment applications. *Intervention in School and Clinic, 31*, 6–15. doi:10.1177/105345129503100102

Rose, D., & Meyer, A. (2002). *Teaching every student in the digital age: Universal design for learning*. Alexandria, VA: Association for Supervision and Curriculum Development. Retrieved from: www.cast.org/teachingeverystudent

Rose, J. (2009, June). *Identifying and teaching children and young people with dyslexia and literacy difficulties*. An independent report from Sir Jim Rose to the Secretary of State for Children, Schools and Families. Nottingham, England: DCFS Publications. Retrieved from: http://www.education.gov.uk/publications/

Rumsey, J. M., Nace, K., Donohue, B., Wise, D., Maisog, J. M., & Andreason, P. (1997). A positron emission tomographic study of impaired word recognition and phonological processing in dyslexic men. *Archives of Neurology, 54*, 562–573.

Sailers, E. (2010a). How schools can successfully implement iPod touch and iPad for children with special needs. *Closing the Gap, 29*(4), 8–10.

Sailers, E. (2010b). iPhone, iPad, and iPod touch Apps for (Special Education). Available from http://www.scribd.com/doc/24470331/iPhone-iPad-and-iPod-touch-Apps-for-Special-Education

Samuelsson, S., Byrne, B., Olson, R. K., Hulslander, J., Wadsworth, S., Corley, R., . . . DeFries, J. C. (2008). Response to early literacy instruction in the United States, Australia, and Scandinavia: A behavioral-genetic analysis. *Learning and Individual Differences, 18*, 289–295. doi.org/10.1016/j.lindif.2008.03.004

Savage, R., Lavers, N., & Pillay, V. (2007). Working memory and reading difficulties: What we know and what we don't know about the relationship. *Educational Psychology Review, 19*, 185–221. doi:10.1007/s10648-006-9024-1

Savage, R., Pillay, V., & Melidona, S. (2007). Deconstructing rapid automatized naming: Component processes and the prediction of reading difficulties. *Learning and Individual Differences, 17*, 129–146. doi:10.1016/j.lindif.2007.04.001

Savery, J. R., & Duffy, T. M. (2001). *Problem-based learning: An instructional model and its constructivist framework* (CRLT Technical Report No. 16-01). Bloomington, IN: Center for Research on Learning and Technology.

Sawyer, D. J. (1987). *Test of Awareness of Language Segments*. Austin, TX: PRO-ED.

Scerri, T. S., & Schulte-Körne, G. (2010). Genetics of developmental dyslexia. *European Child Adolescent Psychiatry, 19,* 179–197. doi 10.1007/s00787-009-0081-0

Schatschneider, C., Carlson, C. D., Francis, D. J., Foorman, B. R., & Fletcher, J. M. (2002). Relationship of rapid automatized naming and phonological awareness in early reading development: Implications for the double-deficit hypothesis. *Journal of Learning Disabilities, 35,* 245–256. doi:10.1177/002221940203500306

Schulte-Körne, G., Deimel, W., Bartling, J., & Remschmidt, H. (2004). Neurophysiological correlates of word recognition in dyslexia. *Journal of Neural Transmission, 111,* 971–984. doi 10.1007/s00702-004-0141-z

Seki, A., Kassai, K., Uchiyama, H., & Koeda, T. (2008). Reading ability and phonological awareness in Japanese children with dyslexia. *Brain and Development International Edition, 30,* 179–188. doi:10.1016/j.braindev.2007.07.006

Semrud-Clikeman, M., Biederman, J., Sprich-Buckminster, S., Lehman, B. K., Faraone, S. V., & Norman, D. (1992). Comorbidity between ADDH and learning disability: A review and report in a clinically referred sample. *Journal of the American Academy of Child and Adolescent Psychiatry, 31,* 439–448. doi:10.1097/00004583-199205000-00009

Seymour, P. H. K., Aro, M., & Erskine, J. M. (2003). Foundation literacy acquisition in European orthographies. *British Journal of Psychology, 94,* 143–174. doi:10.1348/000712603321661859

Shanahan, M. A., Pennington, B. F., Yerys, B. E., Scott, A., Boada, R., Willcutt, E. G., . . . DeFries, J. C. (2006). Processing speed deficits in attention deficit/hyperactivity disorder and reading disability. *Journal of Abnormal Child Psychology, 34,* 585–602. doi:10.1007/s10802-006-9037-8

Shastry, B. S. (2007). Developmental dyslexia: An update. *Journal of Human Genetics, 52,* 104–109. doi:10.1007/s10038-006-0088-z

Shaywitz, B., Shaywitz, S., Pugh, K., Mencl, W., Fulbright, R., Skudlarski, P., . . . Gore, J. C. (2002). Disruption of posterior brain systems for reading in children with developmental dyslexia. *Biological Psychiatry, 52*(2), 101–110. doi:10.1007/s10038-006-0088-z

Shaywitz, B. A., Skudlarski, P., Holahan, J. M., Marchione, K. E., Constable, R. T., Fulbright, R. K., . . . Shaywitz, S. E. (2007). Age-related changes in reading systems of dyslexic children. *Annals of Neurology, 61,* 363–370. doi:10.1002/ana.21093

Shaywitz, S. E. (2003). *Overcoming dyslexia: A new and complete science-based program for reading problems at any level.* New York, NY: Knopf.

Shaywitz, S. E., Fletcher, J. M., Holahan, J. M., Shneider, A. E., Marchione, K. E., Stuebing, K. K., . . . Shaywitz, B. A. (1999). Persistence of dyslexia: The Connecticut Longitudinal Study at adolescence. *Pediatrics, 104,* 1351–1359. doi:10.1542/peds.104.6.1351

Shaywitz, S. E., & Shaywitz, B. A. (2001, August). The neurobiology of reading and dyslexia. *Focus on Basics: Connecting research and practice, 5*(A), 11–15. Retrieved from: http://www.ncsall.net/fileadmin/resources/fob/2001/fob_5a.pdf

Shaywitz, S. E., & Shaywitz, B. A. (2003). Neurobiological indices of dyslexia. In H. L. Swanson, K. R. Harris, & S. Graham (Eds.), *Handbook of learning disabilities* (pp. 514–531). New York, NY: Guilford Press.

Shaywitz, S. E., & Shaywitz, B. A. (2005). Dyslexia (Specific Reading Disability). *Biological Psychiatry, 57*, 1301–1309. doi:10.1542/pir.24-5-147

Shaywitz, S. E., & Shaywitz, B. A. (2008). Paying attention to reading: The neurobiology of reading and dyslexia. *Development and Psychopathology, 20*, 1329–1349. doi:10.1017/S0954579408000631

Shaywitz, S. E., & Shaywitz, B. A. (in press). Dyslexia. In K. F. Swaiman, S. Ashwal, D. M. Ferriero, & N. F. Schor (Eds.), *Pediatric neurology: Principles & practice* (5th ed.). Philadelphia, PA: Elsevier.

Shaywitz, S. E., Shaywitz, B., Fulbright, R., Skudlarski, P., Mencl, W., Constable, R., . . . Gore, J. C. (2003). Neural systems for compensation and persistence: Young adult outcome of childhood reading disability. *Biological Psychiatry, 54*(1), 25–33. doi:10.1016/S0006-3223(02)01836-X

Shaywitz, S. E., Shaywitz, B. A., Pugh, K. R., Fulbright, R. K., Constable, R. T., Mencl, W. E., . . . Gore, J. C. (1998). Functional disruption in the organization of the brain for reading in dyslexia. *Proceedings of the National Academy of Science USA, 95*, 2636–2641. doi:10.1073/pnas.95.5.2636

Shu, H., Chen, X., Anderson, R. C., Wu, N., & Xuan, Y. (2003). Properties of school Chinese: Implications for learning to read. *Child Development, 74*, 27–47. doi:10.1111/1467-8624.00519

Siemens, G. (2004). Connectivism: A learning theory for the digital age. Retrieved from http://www.elearnspace.org/Articles/connectivism.htm

Simmons, D. C., & Kame'enui, E. J. (Eds.). (1998). *What reading research tells us about children with diverse learning needs: Bases and basics.* Mahwah, NJ: Erlbaum.

Sireteanu, R., Goertz, R., Bachert, I., & Wandert, T. (2005). Children with developmental dyslexia show a left visual "minineglect." *Vision Research, 45*, 3075–3082. doi:10.1016/j.visres.2005.07.030

Slingerland, B. H. (1981). *A multisensory approach to language arts for specific language disability children: A guide for primary teachers* (Book 3). Cambridge, MA: Educators Publishing Service.

Smartt, S. M., & Glaser, D. R. (2010). *Next STEPS in literacy instruction: Connecting assessments to effective interventions.* Baltimore, MD: Paul H. Brookes.

Smith, C. R. (1997, February). *A hierarchy for assessing and remediating phonemic segmentation difficulties.* Paper presented at the Learning Disabilities Association International Conference, Chicago, IL.

Smith, G., & Throne, S. (2007). *Differentiating instruction with technology in K–5 classrooms.* Eugene OR: International Society for Technology in Education.

Snowling, M. J. (2000). *Dyslexia* (2nd ed.). Oxford, England: Blackwell.

Snowling, M. J. (2005). Literacy outcomes for children with oral language impairments: Developmental interactions between language skills and learning to read.

In H. W. Catts & A. G. Kamhi (Eds.), *The connections between language and reading disabilities* (pp. 55–76). Mawhah, NJ: Erlbaum.

Snowling, M. J. (2011). Beyond phonological deficits: Sources of individual differences in reading ability. In S. A. Brady, D. Braze, & C. A. Fowler (Eds.). *Individual differences in reading: Theory and evidence* (pp. 121–136). New York, NY: Psychology Press.

Snowling, M. J., & Hulme, C. (2011). Evidence-based interventions for reading and language difficulties: Creating a virtuous circle. *British Journal of Educational Psychology, 81,* 1–23. doi:10.1111/j.2044-8279.2010.02014.x

Snowling, M. J., Muter, V., & Carroll, J. (2007). Children at family risk of dyslexia: A follow-up in early adolescence. *Journal of Child Psychology and Psychiatry 48,* 609–618. doi:10.1111/j.1469-7610.2006.01725.x

Sofie, C. A., & Riccio, C. A. (2002). A comparison of multiple methods for the identification of children with reading disabilities. *Journal of Learning Disabilities, 35,* 234–244. doi:10.1177/002221940203500305

Soifer, L. H. (2005). Development of oral language and its relationship to literacy. In J. R. Birsh (Ed.), *Multisensory teaching of basic language skills* (2nd ed., pp. 43–81). Baltimore, MD: Paul H. Brookes.

Soloman, G., & Schrum, L. (2007). *Web 2.0: New tools, new schools.* Eugene, OR: International Society for Technology in Education.

Soloman, G., & Schrum, L. (2010). *Web 2.0 How-to for educators.* Eugene, OR: International Society for Technology in Education.

Sousa, D. A. (2005). *How the brain learns to read.* Thousand Oaks, CA: Corwin Press.

Spencer, E. J., Schuele, C. M., Guillot, K. M., & Lee, M. W. (2008). Phonemic awareness skill of speech-language pathologists and other educators. *Language, Speech, and Hearing Services in Schools, 39,* 512–520. doi:10.1044/0161-1461(2008/07-0080)

Stage, S. A., & Jacobsen, M. D. (2001). Predicting student success on state-mandated performance-based assessment using oral reading fluency. *School Psychology Review, 30,* 407–419.

Stahl, S. A., & Kuhn, M. R. (2002). Making it sound like language: Developing fluency. *Reading Teacher, 55,* 582–584.

Stanger, M. A., & Donohue, E. K. (1937). *Prediction and prevention of reading difficulties.* New York, NY: Oxford University Press.

Stanovich, K. E. (1980). Toward an interactive-compensatory model of individual differences in the development of reading fluency. *Reading Research Quarterly, 16,* 32–71. doi:10.2307/747348

Stanovich, K. E. (1991). Discrepancy definitions of reading disabilities: Has intelligence led us astray? *Reading Research Quarterly, 26,* 7–29. doi:10.2307/747729

Stein, J., & Walsh, V. (1997). To see but not to read: The magnocellular theory of dyslexia. *Trends in Neurosciences, 20*(4), 147–152. doi:10.1007/s10802-006-9037-8

Strauss, A., & Lehtinen, L. (1947). *Psychopathology and education of the brain injured child.* New York, NY: Grune & Stratton.

Su, I., Klingebiel, K., & Weekes, B. (2010). Dyslexia in Chinese: Implications for connectionist models of reading. In N. Brunswick, S. McDougall, & P. de Mornay Davies (Ed.), *Reading and dyslexia in different orthographies* (pp. 199–219). Hove, East Sussex: Psychology Press.

Sun, Y. F., Lee, J. S., & Kirby, R. (2010). Brain imaging findings in dyslexia. *Pediatrics and Neonatology, 51,* 89–96. doi:10.1016/S1875-9572(10)60017-4

Swanson, H. L., & Sachse-Lee, C. (2001). A subgroup analysis of working memory in children with reading disabilities: Domain-general or domain-specific deficiency? *Journal of Learning Disabilities, 34,* 249–263. doi:10.1177/002221940103400305

Tallal, P., Miller, S., Bedi, G., Byma, G., Wang, X., Nagara-jan, S., . . . Merzenich, M. (1996). Language comprehension in language-learning impaired children improved with acoustically modified speech. *Science, 27,* 81–84. doi:10.1126/science.271.5245.81

Temple, E., Poldrack, R. A., Salidis, J., Deutsch, G. K., Tallal, P., Merzenich, M. M., & Gabrieli, J. D. et al. (2001). Disrupted neural responses to phonological and orthographic processing in dyslexic children: An fMRI study. *NeuroReport, 12,* 299–307. doi:10.1097/00001756-200102120-00024

Therrien, W. J., & Kubina, R. M. (2006). Developing reading fluency with repeated reading. *Intervention in School and Clinic, 41,* 156–160. doi:10.1177/1053451206041 0030501

Thomson, J. B., & Raskind, W. H. (2003). Genetic influencs on reading and writing. In H. L. Swanson, K. R. Harris, & S. Graham (Eds.), *Handbook of learning disabilities* (pp. 256–270). New York, NY: Guilford Press.

Tomlinson, C. (2000). *Differentiation of instruction in the elementary grades.* (ERIC Document Reproduction Service No. ED443572).

Tønnessen, F. E. (1997). How can we best define "dyslexia"? *Dyslexia, 3,* 78–92.

Torgesen, J. K. (2007). Recent discoveries from research on remedial interventions for children with dyslexia. In M. Snowling & C. Hulme (Eds.), *The science of reading: A handbook* (pp. 521–537). Malden, MA: Blackwell.

Torgesen, J. K., Alexander, A. W., Wagner, R. K., Rashotte, C. A., Voeller, K., Conway, T., & Rose, E. (2001). Intensive remedial instruction for children with severe reading disabilities: Immediate and long-term outcomes from two instructional approaches. *Journal of Learning Disabilities, 34,* 33–58. doi:10.1177/002221940103400104

Torgesen, J. K., & Hudson, R. (2006). Reading fluency: Critical issues for struggling readers. In S. J. Samuels & A. Farstrup (Eds.). *Reading fluency: The forgotten dimension of reading success.* Newark, DE: International Reading Association.

Torgesen, J. K., & Mathes, P. M. (2000). *A basic guide to understanding, assessing, and teaching phonological awareness.* Austin, TX: PRO-ED.

Torgesen, J. K., Rashotte, C. A., & Alexander, A. W. (2001). Principles of fluency instruction in reading; Relationships with established empirical outcomes. In M. Wolf (Ed.), *Dyslexia, fluency, and the brain* (pp. 333–355). Timonium, MD: York Press.

Torgesen, J. K., Wagner, R. K., Rashotte, C. A., Burgess, S. R., & Hecht, S. A. (1997). The contributions of phonological awareness and rapid automatic naming ability to the growth of word reading skills in second to fifth grade children. *Scientific Studies of Reading, 1,* 161–185. doi:10.1207/s1532799xssr0102_4

Tosun, D., Jolley, J., Kan, E., Shaywitz, B. A., Toga, A. W., & Sowell, E. (2009). Morphological cerebral alterations in developmental dyslexia. *Neuroimage, 47,* S175. doi:10.1016/S1053-8119(09)71898-1

Treiman, R. (1998). Why spelling? The benefits of incorporating spelling into beginning reading instruction. In J. L. Metsala & L. C. Ehri (Eds.), *Word recognition in beginning literacy* (pp. 289–313). Mahwah, NJ: Erlbaum.

Treiman, R., & Bourassa, D. C. (2000). The development of spelling skill. *Topics in Language Disorders, 20*(3), 1–18. doi:10.1097/00011363-200020030-00004

Tressoldi, P. E., Stella, G., & Faggella, M. (2001). The development of reading speed in Italians with dyslexia: A longitudinal study. *Journal of Learning Disabilities, 34,* 67–78. doi:10.1177/002221940103400503

Tunmer, W., & Greaney, K. (2010). Defining dyslexia. *Journal of Learning Disabilities, 43,* 229–243. doi:10.1177/0022219409345009

Uhry, J. K. (2005). Phonemic awareness and reading: Research, activities, and instructional materials. In J. R. Birsh (Ed.), *Multisensory teaching of basic language skills* (pp. 83–111). Baltimore, MD: Paul H. Brookes.

Uhry, J. K., & Clark, D. B. (2005). *Dyslexia: Theory & practice of instruction* (3rd ed.). Austin, TX: PRO-ED.

Valencia, S., Smith, A., Reece, A., Li, M., Wixson, K., & Newman, H. (2010). Oral reading fluency assessment: Issues of construct, criterion, and consequential validity. *Reading Research Quarterly, 45,* 270–291. doi:10.1598/RRQ.45.3.1

Van Bergen, E., de Jong, P. F., Regtvoort, A., Oort, F., van Otterloo, S., & van der Leij, A. (2011). Dutch children at family risk of dyslexia: Precursors, reading development, and parental effects. *Dyslexia, 17,* 2–18. doi:10.1111/j.1469-7610.2011.02418.x

Vellutino, F. R., & Fletcher, J. M. (2007). Developmental dyslexia. In M. J. Snowling & C. Hulme (Eds.), *The science of reading: A handbook* (pp. 362–378). Malden, MA: Blackwell.

Vernon, P. A. (1983). Speed of information processing and general intelligence. *Intelligence, 7*(1), 53–70. doi:10.1016/0160-2896(83)90006-5

Vinckier, F., Dehaene, S., Jobert, A., Dubus, J., Sigman, M., & Cohen, L. (2007). Hierarchical coding of letter strings in the ventral stream: Dissecting the inner organization of the visual word-form system. *Neuron, 55*(1), 143–156. doi:10.1016/j.neuron.2007.05.031

Voeller, K. K. S. (2004). Dyslexia. *Journal of Child Neurology, 19,* 740–744. doi: 10.1177/08830738040190100301

Vukovic, R. K., Wilson, A. M., & Nash, K. K. (2004). Naming speed deficits in adults with reading disabilities: A test of the double-deficit hypothesis. *Journal of Learning Disabilities, 37,* 440–450. doi:10.1177/00222194040370050601

Vul, E., Harris, C., Winkielman, P., & Pashler, H. (2009). Puzzlingly high correlations in fMRI studies of emotion, personality and social cognition. *Perspectives on Psychological Science, 4*, 274–290. doi:10.1111/j.1745-6924.2009.01125.x

Wadsworth, S. J., DeFries, J. C., Olson, R. K., & Willcutt, E. G. (2007). Colorado longitudinal twin study of reading disability. *Annals of Dyslexia, 57*, 139–160. doi:10.1007/s11881-007-0009-7

Wagner, R. F. (1973). Rudolf Berlin: Originator of the term dyslexia. *Annals of Dyslexia, 1*, 57–63. doi: 10.1007/BF02653841

Wang, P. P. (2011). Nature, nurture and their interactions in child development and behavior. In R. G. Voight (Ed.), *Developmental and behavioral pediatrics* (pp. 5–22). Elk Grove Village, IL: American Academy of Pediatrics.

Washburn, E. K., Joshi, R. M., & Binks-Cantrell, E. S. (2011). Teacher knowledge of basic language concepts and dyslexia. *Dyslexia, 17*, 165–183. doi:10.1002/dys.426

Wiederholt, J. L. (1974). Historical perspectives on the education of the learning disabled. In L. Mann & D. Sabatino (Eds.), *The second review of special education* (pp. 103–152). Philadelphia, PA: JSE Press.

Wiener, J. (2003). Resilience and multiple risks: A response to Bernice Wong. *Learning Disabilities Research & Practice, 18*, 77–81. doi:10.1111/1540-5826.00061

Wilkinson, C., Ortiz, A., Robertson, P., & Kushner, M. (2006). English language learners with reading-related LD. *Journal of Learning Disabilities, 39*, 129–141. doi: 10.1177/00222194060390020201

Willcutt, E. G., Betjemann, R. S., Pennington, B. F., Olson, R. K., Defries, J. C., & Wadsworth, S. J. (2007). Longitudinal study of reading disability and Attention-Deficit/Hyperactivity Disorder: Implication for education. *Mind, Brain, and Education, 1*(4), 181–192. doi:10.1111/j.1751-228X.2007.00019.x

Willcutt, E. G., & Pennington, B. F. (2000). Comorbidity of reading disability and attention-deficit/hyperactivity disorder: Differences by gender and subtype. *Journal of Learning Disabilities, 33*, 179–191. doi:10.1177/002221940003300206

Willcutt, E. G., Pennington, B. F., Chhabildas, N. S., Olson, R. K., & Hulslander, J. L. (2005). Neuropsychological analyses of comorbidity between RD and ADHD: In search of the common deficit. *Developmental Neuropsychology, 27*, 35–78. doi:10.1207/s15326942dn2701_3

Williams, J., & O'Donovan, M. C. (2006). The genetics of developmental dyslexia. *European Journal of Human Genetics, 14*, 681–689. doi:10.1038/sj.ejhg.5201575

Wilson, B. A. (2006). *Wilson Fluency/Basic*. Oxford, MA: Wilson Language Training.

Wimmer, H., & Mayringer, H. (2002). Dysfluent reading in the absence of spelling difficulties: A specific disability in regular orthographies. *Journal of Educational Psychology, 94*, 272–277. doi:10.1037/0022-0663.94.2.272

Wimmer, H., Mayringer, H., & Landerl, K. (2000). The double-deficit hypothesis and difficulties in learning to read a regular orthography. *Journal of Educational Psychology, 92*, 668–680. doi:10.1037/0022-0663.92.4.668

Wissick, C., Heiman, B., & Castellani, J. (2011). Technology interventions for reading and written language. In J. Castellani & B. Heimann (Eds.), *Instructional technology: Helping students access curriculum content* (pp. 31–48). Reston, VA: Technology and Media Division of the Council for Exceptional Children.

Wiznitzer, M., & Scheffel, D. L. (2009). Learning disabilities. In R. B. David, J. B. Bodensteiner, D. E. Mandelbaum, & B. Olson (Eds). *Clinical pediatric neurology* (pp. 479–492). New York, NY: Demos Medical Publishing.

Wolf, M. (2007). *Proust and the squid: The story and science of the reading brain.* New York, NY: Harper Collins Publishers.

Wolf, M., & Bowers, P. (1999). The "Double-Deficit Hypothesis" for the developmental dyslexias. *Journal of Educational Psychology, 91*, 1–24. doi:10.1037//0022-0663.91.3.415

Wolf, M., & Bowers, P. (2000). The question of naming-speed deficits in developmental reading disability: An introduction to the Double-Deficit Hypothesis. *Journal of Learning Disabilities, 33*, 322–324. doi:10.1177/002221940003300404

Wolf, M., Bowers, P. G., & Biddle, K. (2000). Naming-speed processes, timing, and reading: A conceptual review. *Journal of Learning Disabilities, 33*, 387–407. doi:10.1177/002221940003300409

Wolf, M., & Obregón, M. (1992). Early naming deficit, developmental dyslexia, and a specific deficit hypothesis. *Brain and Language, 42*, 219–247. doi:10.1016/0093-934X(92)90099-Z

Xue, G., Chen, C., Jin, Z., & Dong, Q. (2006). Language experience shapes fusiform activation when processing a logographic artificial language: An fMRI training study. *Neuroimage, 31*, 1315–1326. doi:10.1016/j.neuroimage.2005.11.055

Yoshimasu, K., Barbaresi, W. J., Colligan, R. C., Killian, J. M., Voigt, R. G., Weaver, A. L., & Katusic, S. K. (2010). Gender, ADHD, and reading disability in a population-based birth cohort. *Pediatrics, 126,* e788–e795. doi: 10.1542

Young, A., & Bowers, P. G. (1995). Individual differences and text difficulty determinants of reading fluency and expressiveness. *Experimental Child Psychology, 60*, 428–454. doi:10.1006/jecp.1995.1048

Zabala, J., & Carl, D. (2010). The aiming for achievement series: What educators and families need to know about accessible instructional materials. *Closing the Gap, 29*(4), 11–14.

Zadina, J. N., Corey, D. M., Casberque, R. M., Lemen, L. C., Rouse, J. C., Knaus, T. A., & Foundas, A. L. (2006). Lobar asymmetries in subtypes of dyslexic and control subjects. *Journal of Child Neurology, 21*, 922–931. doi:10.1177/088307380602 10110201

Ziegler, J. C., & Goswami, U. (2006). Becoming literate in different languages: Similar problems, different solutions. *Developmental Science, 9*, 429–436. doi: 10.1111/j.1467-7687.2006.00509.x

Zoccolotti, P., DeLuca, M., DiPace, E., Judica, A., & Orlandi, M. (1999). Markers of developmental surface dyslexia in a language (Italian) with high grapheme-phoneme correspondence. *Applied Psycholinguistics, 20*, 191–216. doi:10.1017/S0142716499002027

ANNOTATED BIBLIOGRAPHY

Aaron, P. G., Joshi, R. M., & Quatroche, D. (2008). *Becoming a professional reading teacher.* Baltimore, MD: Paul H. Brookes Publishing Company.

This comprehensive book provides a thorough discussion of what teachers need to know to teach reading most effectively. Research-supported instructional strategies are described for addressing problems in phonemic awareness, word recognition, vocabulary knowledge, and reading comprehension. As noted on the back cover, the book addresses the *what,* the *how,* and the *why* of effective literacy instruction.

Alfonso, V. C., & Flanagan, D. P. (Eds.). (2011). *Essentials of specific learning disability identification.* Hoboken, NJ: John Wiley & Sons.

Chapters by leading researchers and scholars in the field of learning disabilities are contained in this edited book. The latest research on reading and math disability subtypes is presented. Differential diagnosis of dyslexia, dysgraphia, dyscalculia, and oral and written language learning disability is also highlighted. An RTI hybrid model and several alternative research-based models for identifying SLD are described. The overall theme of the book is that identification of SLD requires an evaluation of multiple data sources gathered via multiple methods and procedures.

Berninger, V. W., & Wolf, B. J. (2009). *Teaching students with dyslexia and dysgraphia: Lessons from teaching and science.* Baltimore, MD: Paul H. Brookes Publishing Company.

This book is designed to help teachers meet the needs of students with three types of learning disability: dyslexia, students who have impairments in word decoding and spelling; dysgraphia, students who have impairments in handwriting; and oral and written language learning disability. It addresses the needs of students who have impairments in several aspects of reading (word reading, fluency, comprehension), as well as problems in both oral and written expression. The book is filled with current research findings and extensive instructional guidelines that show educators how to teach students with learning differences in explicit but engaging ways.

Birsh, J. R. (2005). (Ed.). *Multisensory teaching of basic language skills* (2nd ed.), Baltimore, MD: Paul H. Brookes Publishing Company.

The chapters in this edited book provide in-depth descriptions of how teachers can provide students with dyslexia and other learning disabilities with multisensory instruction. The contributing authors cover topics including phonological awareness, letter knowledge, fluency, handwriting, spelling, comprehension, composition, and mathematics. The presented methods are supported by research, as well as the experience of the authors.

Christo, C., Davis, J., & Brock, S. E. (2009). *Identifying, assessing, and treating dyslexia at school.* New York, NY: Springer.

This book is designed to help school professionals understand the causes of dyslexia, the most common learning disability. Emphasis is placed on helping enable practitioners to provide early, effective assessment and intervention. The authors explain the responsibilities of school personnel and offer research-based findings on both evaluation and appropriate interventions.

Henry, M. K. (2010). *Unlocking literacy: Effective decoding & spelling instruction* (2nd ed.). Baltimore, MD: Paul H. Brookes Publishing Company.

The focus of this book is on helping teachers increase their abilities to provide effective decoding and spelling instruction so that all students can become skilled readers and writers. From reading this textbook, teachers will learn how to (a) promote phonological and print awareness, (b) improve students' spelling skills, and (c) deepen students' understanding of language structure.

Moats, L. C. (2010). *Speech to print: Language essentials for teachers* (2nd ed.). Baltimore, MD: Paul H. Brookes Publishing Company.

Developed by a renowned reading expert, this book is designed to help teachers develop a thorough and deep understanding of English language structure and how this knowledge relates to helping children learn to read and spell. The author clearly explains how this essential foundational knowledge is related to the delivery of high-quality reading and writing instruction. Educators will learn to identify, understand, and solve the problems students may encounter when learning to read and write.

Shaywitz, S. E. (2003). *Overcoming dyslexia: A new and complete science-based program for reading problems at any level.* New York, NY: Knopf.

From one of the world's leading experts on reading and dyslexia, this book provides a clear explanation for both parents and teachers who wish to further their understanding of the cause and treatment of phonologically based dyslexia. The book is filled with research findings, practical advice, and specific resources that are designed to help students with dyslexia increase their reading ability. Guidance is provided for establishing a home program for reading that includes exercises, teaching aids, and information on computer programs. The book is divided into four main sections: The Nature of Reading and Dyslexia; Diagnosing Dyslexia; Helping Your Child Become a Reader; and Overcoming Dyslexia: Turning Struggling Readers into Proficient Readers. This is a valuable resource for anyone wishing to understand and help individuals with reading difficulties.

Snowling, M. J. (2000). *Dyslexia* (2nd ed.). Oxford, England: Blackwell.

This scholarly book provides a synthesis of the research on the cognitive defects associated with dyslexia and reviews evidence concerning its biological bases. The central thesis is that dyslexia is a consequence of poor phonological representations. In addition to a theoretical explanation of dyslexia, the author addresses the impact on both social and emotional development.

Uhry, J. K., & Clark, D. B. (2005). *Dyslexia: Theory & practice of instruction* (3rd ed.). Austin, TX: PRO-ED.

This book provides a clear explanation of dyslexia, as well as in-depth descriptions of various reading programs designed for the treatment of dyslexia. It is divided into three sections: The first section describes the underlying psychological and cognitive processes related to reading, the second section presents the basic principles of instruction that are most effective with struggling readers, and the third section describes specific reading programs for students with reading difficulties.

ABOUT THE AUTHORS

Dr. Nancy Mather is a Professor of Special Education in the Department of Disability and Psychoeducational Studies at the University of Arizona in Tucson, AZ. In addition to her teaching responsibilities, she conducts numerous presentations and workshops each year for conferences both nationally and internationally. She is a widely published author of tests, a reading program, books, and articles. She is a co-author of the *Woodcock-Johnson III* and has co-authored two books on the use and interpretation of this test. Her most recent books, published by John Wiley & Sons, Inc., include: *Essentials of Evidence-Based Academic Interventions* and *Comprehensive Evaluations: Case Reports for Psychologists, Diagnosticians, and Special Educators*.

Barbara J. Wendling is an educator, author, and consultant specializing in assessment and instruction. She has taught in both general and special education settings and has an M.A. in Learning Disabilities. She conducts presentations and workshops nationwide on topics related to assessment and evidence-based instruction. With Dr. Mather, she has coauthored *Essentials of Evidence-Based Academic Interventions* and *Writing Assessment and Instruction for Students with Learning Disabilities*. In addition, she serves as the Education Director for the Woodcock-Muñoz Foundation and has co-authored a number of publications related to the Woodcock-Johnson III, most recently the *Woodcock Interpretation and Instructional Interventions Program (WIIIP)* and the *Essentials of WJ III™ Cognitive Abilities Assessment, Second Edition*.

INDEX

Ability-achievement discrepancy, 33–34, 38, 244

Accelerated Reader, 175

Accommodations or modifications:
  definition of, 250
  examples of, 251
  legal requirement for, 249–250
  requirement for extended time, 56–57

ADHD, see *Attention deficit hyperactivity disorder*

Affixes, see *Morphology*

Alexia, 44

Alphabet prosody, 192–193

Alphabetic orthographies, see *Orthography*

Alphabetic principle, 79, 105–106

Americans with Disabilities Act (ADA), 242

Aphasia, 19
  Broca's, 44
  Wernicke's, 44

Assessment:
  goal of, 77
  of decoding, 116–119
  of memory, 99–100
  of morphology, 115–116
  of orthography, 112–114
  of phonological awareness, 83–89
  of rapid automatized naming, 90–92
  of reading fluency, 121–131
  of spelling, 116–119

Assistive technology (AT), see *Technology*

Attention deficit hyperactivity disorder (ADHD), 6, 69–71

Automaticity, 14, 91, 106–108, 179

Barton Reading & Spelling System, 174, 263–264

Berkhan, Oswald, 22

Berlin, Rudolph, 22

Betts, Emmett, 8, 19

Bilingual learners, see *English language learners*

Blending, see *Phonics; Phonological Awareness*

Brain:
  abnormalities implicated in dyslexia, 24–25, 27–29, 55–56
  anatomy of, 45–47
  functions of major areas, 45–46
  historical studies of, 20–29, 43–44
  imaging of, 47–52, 55–56
  language processing area, 47
  neural signature of dyslexia, 50–51
  neural systems for reading, 47–53

Lightning Source UK Ltd.
Milton Keynes UK
UKOW06f0358230515

252131UK00007B/13/P